WHEN IN ROME

THE ROMAN EMPIRE IN 125

■ VII CLAUDIA LEGION DEPLOYED
⊙ BURDIGALA ROMAN CITY
GALATIA ROMAN PROVINCE
COLCHIS CLIENT STATE
Via Appia MAIN ROAD
Vetus
        IMPERIAL BORDER
        BORDER OF THE ROMAN CLIENT
        STATES

6000 m
2000 m
1500 m
1000 m
400 m
200 m
0 m

0   250   500   750   1000
            kilometers

N

HIBERNI   CALEDONII

OCEANUS

Oceanus
Germanicus

ANGLII   SUIONES

Mare Suebicum

FENNI

AESTII

CHAUCI   SUEBI   RUGII

GOTHONES

VENETI

SARMATAE

ALANI

EBORACUM
DEVA   VI VICTRIX
II AUGUSTA
BRITANNIA
ISCA SILURUM
XX VALERIA VICTRIX
LONDINIUM
GESORIACUM
NOVIOMAGUS
IX HISPANA
CASTRA VETERA
XXX ULPIA VICTRIX
COLONIA
BONNA
MINERVIA
GERMANI   BURGUNDIONES
VANDILII   BASTARNAE
DACI   SCYTHAE
REGNUM
BOSPORI
Macotis
Palus
TANAIS

BELGICA
AUGUSTA
TREVERORUM
GERMANIA
INFERIOR
XXII PRIMIGENIA
MARCOMANNI
QUADI

PORTUS
NAMNETUS
LUTETIA
LUGDUNENSIS
ARGENTORATE
VIII AUGUSTA
GERMANIA
SUPERIOR
AUGUSTA
VINDELICORUM
RAETIA
NORICUM
VIRUNUM
VINDOBONA
CARNUNTUM
XIV GEMINA
BRIGETIO
I ADIUTRIX
X GEMINA
PANNONIA
SUPERIOR
AQUINCUM
II ADIUTRIX
PANNONIA
INFERIOR
IAZYGES
POTAISSA
V MACEDONICA
APULUM
XIII GEMINA
DACIA
ROXOLANI
CHERSONNESOS
COLCHIS

Pontus Euxinus

AUGUSTODUNUM
BURDIGALA
LUGDUNUM
MEDIOLANUM
AQUILEIA
CLAUDIA
Via Postumia
SIRMIUM
SINGIDUNUM
IV FLAVIA
VIMINACIUM
VII CLAUDIA
DUROSTORUM
NOVAE
XI CLAUDIA
TOMIS
SINOPE
TRAPEZUS

BRIGANTIUM
CASTRA LEGIONIS
VII GEMINA
TOLOSA
NARBONENSIS
NARBO
MASSILIA
GENUA
ARIMINUM
PISAE
DALMATIA
FELIX
MOESIA
SUPERIOR
I ITALICA
MOESIA
INFERIOR
NAISSUS
SATALA
XV APOLLINARIS

CAESARAUGUSTA
TARRACONENSIS
TARRACO
ALERIA
CORSICA
ET
SARDINIA
ROMA
ITALIA
SALONA
DYRRACHIUM
THRACIA
BYZANTIUM
PERINTHUS
NICOMEDIA
BITHYNIA ET PONTUS
ANCYRA
CAPPADOCIA
ARMENIA
MELITENE
XII FULMINATA
SAMOSATA
XVI FLAVIA FIRMA

FELICITAS IULIA
LUSITANIA
AUGUSTA
EMERITA
CORDUBA
BAETICA
GADES
TOLETUM
VALENTIA
Via Augusta
NOVA CARTHAGO
CARALIS
NEAPOLIS
Mare
Tyrrhenum
BRUNDISIUM
MACEDONIA
THESSALONICA
PERGAMUM
ASIA
GALATIA
CILICIA
IV SCYTHICA
TARSUS
ANTIOCHIA
PALMYRA
SYRIA

TINGI
MAURETANIA
TINGITANA
VOLUBILIS
LIXUS
CAESAREA
SALDAE
CIRTA
MAURETANIA
CAESARIENSIS
CARTHAGO
PANORMUS
SICILIA
RHEGIUM
SYRACUSAE
Mare
Ionium
PATRAE
ACHAIA
CORINTHUS
ATHENAE
EPHESUS
ATTALIA
LYCIA ET
PAMPHILIA
CYPRUS
PAPHUS
RAPHANA
III GALLICA, VI FERRATA

MARE
HIBERICUM
MARE
LAMBAESIS
THEVESTIS
THAPSUS
III AUGUSTA
AFRICA PROCONSULARIS
TACAPE
INTERNUM
Aegaeum
CRETA
GORTYNA
ET
III CYRENAICA
BOSTRA
GERASA
JERUSALEM
X FRETENSIS
JUDAEA
ARABIA
PETRAEA
PETRA
ARABES
NABATAEI
REGNUM
PARTHICUM

MAURI   GAETULI

Desertum

LEPTIS MAGNA
Mare
Libycum
Syrtis
Major
CYRENE
CYRENAICA
ALEXANDRIA
II TRAIANA,
XXII DEIOTRAIANA
MEMPHIS
AEGYPTUS
HERACLEOPOLIS

Libycum

1. ALPES POENIAE
2. ALPES COTTIAE
3. ALPES MARITIMAE

WHEN IN ROME

SOCIAL LIFE IN ANCIENT ROME

PAUL CHRYSTAL

FONTHILL

For Derrick Holman—friend and colleague for forty years

Balnea, vina, Venus corrumpunt corpora nostra; sed vitam faciunt balnea, vina, Venus

Bathing, wine and sex ruin our bodies; but bathing, wine and sex are what life is all about.

Corpus Inscriptionum Latinarum 6, 15258

Fonthill Media Language Policy

Fonthill Media publishes in the international English language market. One language edition is published worldwide. As there are minor differences in spelling and presentation, especially with regard to American English and British English, a policy is necessary to define which form of English to use. The Fonthill Policy is to use the form of English native to the author. Paul Chrystal was born and educated in Scotland and England; therefore British English has been adopted in this publication.

Fonthill Media Limited
Fonthill Media LLC
www.fonthillmedia.com
office@fonthillmedia.com

First published in the United Kingdom and the United States of America 2017

British Library Cataloguing in Publication Data:
A catalogue record for this book is available from the British Library

Typeset in 10.5pt on 13pt MinionPro
Printed and bound in England

Acknowledgements

Plate 9. With permission from Virginia Museum of Arts, Richmond, Adolph D. and Wilkins C. Williams Fund; VA (object # 60.2).

Plates 12 and 32. By kind permission of Inga Mantle who took the photographs and Caroline Vout who published them in *Omnibus*, 65 (2013). They are now in the National Museum of the Bardo, Tunis.

Plate 13. Courtesy of York Museums Trust, YORYM 1998.695 [ID 1131].

By the same author

Women in Ancient Rome (2013)
Roman Women: The Women Who Influenced Roman History (2015)
In Bed with the Romans: Sex and Sexuality in Ancient Rome (2015)
Wars and Battles of the Roman Republic: The Bloody Road to Empire (2015)
Roman Military Disasters: Dark Days and Lost Legions (2015)
Ancient Greece in 100 Facts (2017)
In Bed with the Ancient Greeks: Sex and Sexuality in Ancient Greece (2016)
Women in Ancient Greece: Seclusion, Exclusion, or Illusion? (2017)
Women at War in the Classical World (2017)
Roman Record Keeping & Communication (2017)
Wars & Battles of Ancient Greece (2017)
How to be a Roman (2017)

For a full list, please visit www.paulchrystal.com

CONTENTS

Introduction

Si fueris Romae, Romano vivite more

These words from St Ambrose can be translated as 'If you're ever in Rome, live the way the Romans live' or more famously: 'When in Rome, do as the Romans do'.[1] The aim of this book—a collection of passages from Roman and Greek writers, epigraphs, graffiti and other primary sources spanning 1,200 years from 753 BCE to the later years of the fifth century—is to establish just what 'the Roman way' was and how the Romans went about their lives. By 'Rome' and 'Ancient Rome', I mean not just the city of Rome but also the wider Roman world, taking in the Roman experience, and Roman influence in the Mediterranean basin and parts of northern Europe. The book, then, will provide a history of Roman social life, culture, and thought in its widest sense, giving a fascinating picture of what the citizens of Rome—and the foreigners who came into contact with them—saw, heard, thought, smelled, and tasted in their daily routine.

Due to the social standing of the authors quoted, this picture is inevitably refracted largely through elite eyes, and through elite male eyes at that; however, flashes of lives lived by women and by the lower and servile classes are inextricably interwoven throughout the book from epigraphical evidence, graffiti, and from what we can still see in the visual arts. It is the life experiences of these liminal inhabitants on the margins of Roman society that give the book its necessary balance: enslavement, repression, hunger, squalor, poverty, prejudice, pain, and punishment compete with the relatively comfortable, replete, and successful world of the middle and upper classes.

The 'Roman world' was a dynamic world, evolving over a thousand and more years. Life for the first Romans was predominantly agrarian, primitive, and confined to the villages on hills around the Tiber. It expanded—largely through serial warfare, conquest and annexation—to take in the whole Italian peninsula and then the neighbouring territories around the Mediterranean, extending into northern Europe. Urbanisation, civilisation, and cultural Romanisation—making the Roman world more Roman—took hold; the Romans were said to have become more Greek than the civilised and civilising Greeks.

The Romans too were very good at absorbing and adapting; they often took the best things from their conquests or allies and made them Roman. They could be receptive, tolerant, and inclusive. Overseas expansion spread like a rash, but it was a two-way phenomenon; it came with an inexorable influx into Roman towns and cities of foreign and exotic immigrants with their foreign goods, strange, un-Roman ways, diverse languages, exotic cultures, and mysterious religions. The copious spoils of war, and not a little corruption, introduced abundant slaves, social and religious diversity, and cosmopolitanism on a huge scale. When Roman citizenship was granted to all free persons within the empire by Caracella in 212 CE, Roman citizenship was enjoyed as far afield as Britannia, Germania, Portugal, Egypt, and Syria; inhabitants across wide swathes of Europe, Africa, and the Middle East could then say *civis Romanus sum*—'I am a citizen of Rome'.[2] The Romans absorbed, manipulated, adapted, and adopted many things that they considered good and valuable in the world they were conquering; Roman culture, politics, religion, society, science, and slaves all benefited from syncretism, judicious tolerance, and selective inclusiveness.[3]

When in Rome describes this. It is built on evidence gleaned from historiography, poetry, letters, scientific, technical and agricultural treatises, medical textbooks, business and legal contracts, curse tablets, archaeological remains, graffiti, and tombstone inscriptions. We have found this evidence on papyrus, etched on tombstones, scrawled on the walls of inns and brothels, elegantly carved on arches, columns, and statuary; it comes to us on stone, marble, wax clay, and metal. It is written by professional historians, philosophers, urbane, satirical, romantic or salacious poets, educationalists, agricultural experts, war correspondents, novelists, tragic or comic dramatists and letter writers, the bereaved wife and husband, the obsessive curser, and the '(wo)man in the street' going about their business, doing their job, or enjoying a night of alcohol-fuelled sex.

Time is also a factor. The Roman world in its broadest geographical and cultural senses can be said to have existed from 753 BCE, the date of its legendary foundation, to its fall in the fifth century CE. Our span of social history here comes from or alludes to events and conditions across the whole 1,200 years, with all the differences and changes that means. All make a valid contribution to our picture whatever the time, wherever the place, and whatever the source—they all combine to form a composite picture of Roman society; that picture, though, will never be complete because our sources are nothing like complete. What has survived has survived by pure chance; what is preserved has been preserved in the most random fashion with much more lost to us than has been found and recorded.

Attitudes to the seemingly endemic greed and corruption, the hazards and disadvantages of living in a hectic Rome as opposed to the calming country or by the sea, dinner parties and their protocol, foreigners and immigrants, women, the benefits of a healthy lifestyle, suicide, moral rectitude, married life, sexual preferences, slavery, disability and deformity, domestic pets, education, superstition, religion and public entertainment are covered here, along with revealing glances at relationships with enemies of the state, allies, patrons, the emperor of the day, and fellow *literati*.

Much of what the writers and the other evidence tell us is universal and timeless; many of their themes still resonate and challenge us today some 2,000 years after they were written. Issues that troubled the Romans continue to inform our own twenty-first century views and behaviour. Many of the dynamics observable in early imperial Roman society still drive our society. As well as providing a graphic view of everyday life in Rome, the book also reminds us how successive ages and societies often disregard the lessons of history and continue to recycle the mistakes of the past. Juvenal was right: we still do many of the same things, we still crave many of the same things and we still agonise over many of the problems which exercised him and his predecessors (*Satires* 1, 147–9). There is then, in reading some of these extracts, a very real sense of déjà vu; many of the issues and problems that faced the Romans are still with us today, they are just manifested in a different way.

The book is about life, living, and people; it is social history, and for that reason the vast subjects that are political, military, diplomatic, and constitutional history only feature where they impinge directly on the lives of the Roman people.

The pieces included here can be dipped into at random, read in sequence as social history, or as self-contained, themed chapters. The selection of passages make it a convenient one-stop sourcebook for the general historian, and for students and teachers of classical civilization and classics courses. Up until the publication of *When in Rome*, with a few notable exceptions, the passages included have only been available scattered in a number of separate books. If you want a social history of the ancient Roman world based on hard evidence, then this is the book. The book features a number of passages not, or rarely, featured in the existing published sourcebooks.

One of the valuable features of *When in Rome* is its inclusion of a number of social issues not always dealt with in books about ancient Rome, even in our enlightened times. These include disability and deformity, xenophobia, superstition, female genital mutilation, household pets, and domestic and sexual violence. It is high time that these important issues were dealt with and took their rightful place in Roman social history.

Indeed, *When in Rome* is a book for anyone interested in Roman society and the Roman way of doing things—anyone who is looking for a book that comprehensively covers all facets of Roman society and does not shirk from the more unsettling aspects of life in Rome and attitudes towards it. It is, moreover, a book for anyone interested in the lessons we can, and should, learn from the Roman way of doing things—be they classicist, social historian, or general reader.

On being a Roman: *Romanitas*— What is Was and What it Meant

We have established that 'Rome', for the purposes of this book, could be the city of Rome, or it could be anywhere outside the city that fell under the sway of Rome. A 'Roman' was a citizen of Rome in its broadest sense: a citizen of the city or of the many places subdued, colonised, or annexed by Rome, either as republic or empire.

Due to the immense geographical and chronological scales involved, there was never one such identifiable entity or concept as a Roman. The Roman man and woman was forever changing and evolving, a moving target, in place and in time. The Roman in fourth century BCE Latium was very different from, and largely unrecognisable to, the Roman in fourth century CE Eboracum, York. However, we can identify certain qualities that, with historical hindsight, are commonly and consistently attributable to Romans, wherever and whenever they were. Those qualities fall conveniently under the term *Romanitas*, a word that was never used by the Romans themselves until the third century CE Roman writer, Tertullian (c. 155–c. 240 CE), an early North African Christian, who coined it in his *De Pallio*, *On the Cloak* (4, 1).[1] Even then, the concept was hardly imbued with the grandeur we might expect in a description of the quintessential nature of such a civilisation as Rome; Tertullian's use is pejorative, describing those fellow Carthaginians who aped Roman ways. Juvenal had said it in so many words two hundred years or so earlier, vilifying his fellow Romans who were slaves to the ways of Greeks and to Graecisms. Juvenal's disgust at the vogue for women speaking Greek gives a taste of the vitriol to come in this misogynist satire:

What is more sickening than this: no woman thinks herself beautiful unless she's changed from being a Tuscan to a little Greek bit, from Sabine Sulmo to unadulterated subject of Cecrops? Everything has gone Greek: however, it's even more grotesque when Romans have no Latin. In Greek they show their fear, their anger, their joys and their worries; they pour out every secret of their souls in this tongue. What else is there? Oh yes, they even have sex in Greek! You might allow this in a young girl, but will you still be Greeking it when you're pushing eighty-six? Such a way of speaking is surely not right for a little old lady.

Juvenal 6, 184–191

Martial had said much the same:

> Laelia, although you don't live in Greek Ephesus, or Rhodes, or Mitylene, but in a house
> in a posh part of town; and although your mother was a dusky Etruscan who never
> wore make-up; and although your father was a hard man from Aricia region, you, how
> shameful to say it, are a citizen of Roman Hersilia and Egeria, but keep bombarding me
> in Greek with 'My master, my sweet, my soul.' Such expressions should be reserved for
> the bed, but not for the bed you always hear about, only the sort of bed which a mistress
> has made for her lascivious lover. You'd like to learn how to speak like a chaste matron?
> But you couldn't be sexier when you move your hips like that. You might be allowed to
> learn and refer to everything about Corinth—but Laelia, you'll never be a Lais.
>
> Martial 10, 68

Aelius Aristides (120–189 CE) eulogised Rome in his panegyric, *The Roman Oration*,
particularly the period between Nerva's reign starting in 96 CE to the death of the
emperor Marcus Aurelius in 180 CE—the *Pax Romana* or Roman Peace. It was then,
under the so-called Five Good Emperors, that Rome reached the zenith of its military
expansion and wealth. Although Aristides is more interested in rhetorical fireworks
than an accurate description, he nevertheless clearly illustrates how the Romans liked
to see themselves and how they wanted to present themselves to other nations: it was
the ancient equivalent of a home page on their website—a mission statement for all the
world to see. Here is an excerpt that gives the flavour of the piece:

> But the most notable and praiseworthy feature of all, a thing unparalleled, is your
> magnanimous conception of citizenship. All of your subjects (and this implies the
> whole world) you have divided into two parts: the better endowed and more virile,
> wherever they may be, you have granted citizenship and even kinship; the rest you
> govern as obedient subjects. Neither the seas nor expanse of land bars citizenship;
> Asia and Europe are not differentiated. Careers are open to talent … Rich and poor
> find contentment and profit in your system; there is no other way of life. Your polity
> is a single and all-embracing harmony …
>
> Translation by Moses Hadas, *A History of Rome* (1956)

Tertullian defended himself against attacks made against him for no longer wearing
the Roman toga but rather the *pallium*, the cloak favoured by philosophers.[2]

> Why now, if Romanitas is the saviour of everything, are you still inclined towards
> Greek ways, even dishonourable Greek ways? Or, if that is not the case, where in
> the world do the exertions of the wrestling ring come from in the better organised
> provinces which are naturally more suited more to working the land? These are bad
> ways of growing old—futile labour—greasing up yellow and rolling in the dust: an
> arid way of getting fattened up. Why among some long-haired Numidians is there a
> barber who cuts down to the skin, even for the horses? The only thing that doesn't

get shaved is the top of the head. Why among the hirsute and hairy is there such a rapacious resin on the bum, and such thieving tweezers on the chin? It's monstrous that this goes on without the pallium but this is what happens in all of Asia. Libya and Europe—what are those elegant porticos to you when you don't know how to dress? In reality, is it better to be depilated in the Greek way than to be cloaked like a Greek?

Tertullian, De Pallio 4, 1–2

Nevertheless, the concept of *Romanitas* was improved over time and took on an air of respectability and nobility much more in tune with the 'grandeur that was Rome'. It has come to mean 'Roman-ness'—what it means to be a Roman and how the Romans regarded themselves; it defines a Roman and encapsulated the Roman ideal.[3]

No one epitomised that Roman ideal better than Lucius Quinctius Cincinnatus. Cincinnatus was an aristocrat who was consul in 460 BCE and dictator in 458 BCE and later in 439 BCE; he was widely regarded as a paragon of Roman *virtus* and rectitude. In 461, his son, Caeso Quinctius, was falsely accused of murder and fled to the Etruscans. His father and some friends stood bail for Ceaso but he absconded and was condemned to death *in absentia*; his father was consequently saddled with a huge debt, which he paid by selling his lands and downsizing in retirement to a small farm.

The battle of Mons Algidus (458 BCE) was a conflict with the Aequi who broke a truce made with Rome only the previous year. The Aequi made camp on Mons Algidus about fourteen miles south-east of Rome; the Roman commander, Minucius, was ineffective and paid for his dithering when the enemy walled him into his own camp. There was panic in Rome. Lucius Quinctius Cincinnatus was promptly recalled from retirement and appointed dictator with the brief to resolve the situation. Livy makes Cincinnatus an exemplum of the Roman who was not motivated by greed or wealth: he did what he did as his duty to Rome; to Livy, Cincinnatus was the ideal, the true Roman, *homo vere Romanus,* acting with bravery and dignity, exuding *pietas* to Rome.

And they were pleased that a dictator should be commissioned to get them out of their crisis: Lucius Quintius Cincinnatus was duly appointed with unanimous approval. Those who spurn anything humane in preference to riches, and those who suppose that there is no place for high honour or virtue, unless prodigious riches are involved, would do well to listen to this. Lucius Quintius, the last hope of the Roman people, worked a farm of four acres, on the other side of the Tiber… There, whether leaning on a stake while digging a ditch or ploughing—for certain, busy on some rustic work—after the formalities had been exchanged, he was requested by the envoys to put on his gown and listen to the senate, so that both he and the state were happy. He was surprised and kept asking 'whether all was safe,' he asked his wife Racilia to quickly bring his toga from his hut. As soon as he was dressed and after first wiping off the dust and sweat, he came out. The ambassadors, congratulated him and saluted him as dictator: they called him into the city to explain to him the terror now besetting the army.

Livy, Ab Urbe Condita 3.26–9

At the battle, Cincinnatus led from the front while Lucius Tarquitius, his *magister equitum*, attacked with his cavalry. Many of the Aequi were destroyed; the surviving commanders implored Cincinnatus not to slaughter them. Cincinnatus showed clemency, telling the Aequi that they could live if they submitted and brought their leader, Gracchus Cloelius, and his officers to him bound in chains. A yoke was set up, made of the traditional three spears, under which the humiliated Aequi passed, *sub iugum missi*. Warde Fowler neatly describes this as 'a kind of dramatised form of degradation'. Cincinnatus then immediately disbanded his army, resigned his office promptly, and returned to his farm some sixteen days after assuming the dictatorship. He refused any share of the spoils—perfect conduct for a dictator.

A Roman dictator of this time was quite different from later dictators in different ages, in different civilisations with their associations with tyranny and absolute, undemocratic power. Roman dictators were appointed for a period of six months as a *magistratus extraordinarius*—an extraordinary magistrate—to deal with a specific military or domestic crisis; they were obliged to resign the post once it was dealt with—in short, they were an expedience and represented a focusing of the powers of the consulship.

While the Romans were different in different parts of the Roman world and changed over time, there was always an element of conservatism and traditionalism running through the marrow of the Roman people. This evolved over time into a national character which had its roots in the early humble, agricultural days and was characterised as demonstrating hard-work, honesty, exuding *gravitas* (dignified, serious, or solemn conduct) and being diligent; moreover, the true Roman lived by and respected the *mos maiorum*, the way the ancestors went about things. They were expected to be dutiful, to exhibit *pietas,* in every sphere of life—towards family, friends, country, fellow citizens, comrades in arms and gods. *Romanitas*, *gravitas*, and *pietas* defined the Roman.

Cincinnatus had these qualities in spades, as did Horatius Cocles who almost single-handedly defended Rome against an Etruscan attack by courageously holding up the enemy while the bridge was being dismantled beneath his feet. Risking one's life for Rome was a good Roman trait which suggested *Romanitas*:

> When the enemy appeared, all the Romans left their fields for the city, which they barricaded with fortifications. Some parts seemed safe because of the walls, others because of the river Tiber. The Pons Sublicius almost gave the enemy a way in, were it not for one man, Horatius Cocles; he was the line of defence which the fortune of the City of Rome that day depended on. Horatius happened to be on guard at the bridge when the Janiculum was captured in a surprise enemy attack.
>
> Livy 2, 10

Horatius' comrades panicked: they threw down their arms and deserted; Horatius ordered them to dismantle the bridge while he held them off.

> Then he made for the head of the bridge, standing out among the fugitives who could clearly be seen turning their backs on the battle. He armed himself, ready for hand to

hand fighting, stupefying the enemy with his amazing courage…. The state was grateful for such bravery and set up a statue of Cocles in the comitium, and he was awarded as much land as he could plough in one day. Goodwill stood out too from the private citizens in the midst of his official honours; despite their great losses, everybody donated some family goods, even though in so doing they robbed himself of their own provisions.

Livy 2, 10

Xenophobia

As with many societies today, there was always a difficult line to be drawn between syncretism and xenophobia. Some conservative Romans deplored the foreign influences, believing that it diluted and compromised Romanitas. As champion of the *mos maiorum* and despiser of Greek things, Cato the Elder (234–149 BCE) spoke out sternly against what he saw as a period of moral decline and the erosion of the sturdy principles on which Rome had lain her foundations.[4] Among other things, he identified the growing independence of the women of Rome as an ominous ingredient in this.[5] The defeat of Hannibal at Zama in 202 BCE, the victory over the Macedonians at Pydna in 168, and the final extinguishing of the Carthaginian threat in 146 BCE all allowed Rome to relax more and encouraged an unprecedented influx of Greek and eastern influences and luxuries into a receptive Rome.[6]

But from the start Cato, when this zeal for discussion came pouring into the city, was not very happy, fearing lest the young men, by basing their ambition on this, should come to love a reputation based on mere words more than one achieved by warlike action … So, he mocked all Greek culture and training, out of his zealous patriotism. He says, for instance, that Socrates was a mighty prattler, who attempted, as best he could, to be his country's tyrant, by abolishing its customs, and by enticing his fellow citizens into opinions contrary to the laws … declaring, in the tone of a prophet or a seer, that Rome would lose her empire when she had become infected with Greek letters … It was not only Greek philosophers that he despised, but he was also suspicious of Greek doctors who practised medicine at Rome. He had heard, it would seem, what Hippocrates had replied when the Great King of Persia consulted him, with the promise of a fee of many talents, namely, that he would never put his skills at the disposal of barbarians who were enemies of Greece.

Plutarch, *Cato* 22–23.
Adapted from translation by Bernadotte Perrin, Loeb Classical Library (1914)

The debauched nature of the young men in Rome had reached such a height, and erupted in such extravagance, that there were many instances of men purchasing a jar of Pontic salt-fish for three hundred drachmae. In reference to which an indignant Cato once said to the people, that no better proof could be shown of the degeneracy of the state than that good-looking slaves should fetch more than a farm, and a jar of salt-fish more than a carter.

Polybius 31, 24.

Adapted from translation by Evelyn S. Shuckburgh, Loeb Classical Library (1889)

The character and attitudes of the man are reflected in his writings. He is the author of our first history of Rome written in Latin, the *Origines*; sadly, the seven books only survive in fragments but we know that he tells of the foundation of Rome and of other Italian cities. His *De Agri Cultura* (*On Farming*) is the oldest surviving complete prose work in Latin. It deals with the cultivation of vines, olives and livestock, and the origins of ancient customs and superstitions.

Cicero too was a stickler for *Romanitas*. The Latin language, or rather the ability to speak it, and the practice of Roman law were equally potent badges of Roman-ness:

> Ordinary men, born in obscurity, go to sea and they go to places which they have never seen before; places where they can neither be known to the men among whom they have arrived, nor where they can always find an advocate. However, due to this singular faith in their Roman citizenship, they think that they will be safe, not only among our own magistrates, who are constrained by fear of the law and of public opinion, nor among our fellow citizens only, who are joined with them by a common language and laws among many other things; but wherever they come they think that this will protect them.

Cicero, *in Verrem* 2, 5, 167

In *Brutus*, 37, 140, he is even more explicit, declaring that it is a matter of shame (*turpe*) not to know Latin; a capacity for Latin was a mark of the Roman citizen:

> In short, it is not such a good thing to speak our native tongue correctly, as it is disgraceful not to know how to speak it; nor is it so much the property of a good orator, as of a well-bred citizen.

We learn from Suetonius that Tiberius believed it important that soldiers in the Roman army be able to speak Latin from an incident when he refused a Greek soldier permission to reply in Greek when summonsed to give evidence. The conquering army was the prime vehicle for Romanisation: speaking Latin was a key element in Romanisation. There is good evidence that foreign troops and mercenaries in the Roman army did learn Latin.

> Though he was comfortable and fluent in Greek, he did not use it everywhere; he especially avoided it in the senate, an example being when he used the word *monopolium* (monopoly), he first asked to be excused for having to use a foreign word. And when, in a decree of the senate, the word ἔμβλημα (emblem) was read out, he proposed to have it changed, and a Latin word substituted in its place, or, if the right

one could not be found, to express it by circumlocution. He would not allow a [Greek] soldier who was being questioned as a witness in a trial to reply unless it was in Latin.

Suetonius ,*Tiberius* 71[7]

Until the reign of Severus (r. 193–211 CE), wills had to be written in Latin; tombstones for soldiers throughout the empire, whether Roman or foreign, are always in Latin, except for Roman Egypt where Greek is used. To the Romans, it seems that Latin and Greek were the only languages of any significance; it would not have occurred to them to learn a 'barbarian' tongue. Latin symbolized Roman civilisation. Greek Cleopatra VII must have seemed exceptional to them because she, unlike her Ptolemaic predecessors, learnt and spoke Egyptian when she became pharaoh. Valerius Maximus tells us how early Roman magistrates throughout the Roman world used Latin as a weapon in upholding Roman *maiestas*, greatness, when they insisted that court proceedings be in Latin and that the Greeks use interpreters to translate into Latin.[8] In 191 BCE, Cato defiantly addressed a Greek audience in Athens in Latin.[9] Speaking Latin inculcated respect for Roman power and symbolised Roman-ness. That exertion of power is evident when Apuleius describes a Roman soldier bullying a humble Greek-speaking gardener in the *Metamorphoses*; the arrogant soldier beats the gardener (who is riding on Lucius, the narrator, transformed into a donkey) for not having any Latin. Although Latin was never the official language of the Roman army, its use was significant in the spread and domination of Romanitas in the Roman world.

> We encountered a tall soldier, a legionary—his manner and appearance indicated this—who, with haughty and arrogant words asked
>   'Where are you leading this unladen donkey to?'
>   'My master, still confused by the grief and without any Latin, rode on saying nothing. The soldier, unable to restrain his characteristic insolence, and indignant at my master's silence as if it were an insult, smacked him with the vine- stick which he was holding and hurled him from my back. Then my master, the gardener, politely answered that he did not know his language and so did not understand what he was saying; so the soldier asked again, but in Greek this time, where are you leading your ass to.
>
> Apuleius, *Metamorphoses* 9, 39

Caution and suspicion regarding things Greek is also evident in Tacitus at the end of the first century BCE. In the *Agricola,* published in 98 CE, Tacitus ascribes good Roman matronly qualities to Agricola's mother, Julia Procilla: *rara castitas—a paragon of feminine virtue.* One of her important achievements as his mother was to ensure that Agricola grew up with all the right characteristics:

> As a young boy he lived in and went to school in Massilia—a place where Greek politeness and provincial thrift are well mixed ... [Julia Procilla] wisely tempered his ardent passion [for philosophy].
>
> Tacitus, *Agricola* 4, 2–4

It is Juvenal who provides us with the last word in xenophobia; his fourth satire, quoted in full in the section on lifestyle choices where he parades an abhorrence of city life, is a *tour de force*, excoriating all things Greek in a rant to end all rants.

Patrons and clients

Another enduring and characteristic facet of Roman society was the client-patron system which prevailed from the earliest days of Rome. This was a paternalistic relationship between aristocratic patricians and lower order plebeians in which the former helped out the latter with protection and a range of welfare and public service issues. In exchange, the patrons (*patres*), expected gratitude and deference, and the reciprocal provision of various services. Essentially, it was an extension of the family in which the father (*pater*) expected similar demonstrations of *pietas* from his wife and children. Clients would form part of the patron's retinue—the bigger the retinue, the more powerful a patron appeared to be. Success in the senate or at the bar enabled the patron to help more clients and expand his retinue. Cicero explains how it works:

> Men of the lower orders have one chance only by which to earn favours from men of our rank, or to pay us back for the favours we have given them: namely, attending us as a client and working hard on our political campaigns. For it is neither possible, nor something we or the equites should ask for, that they attend their patron for whole days at a time. If they all meet up at our house, if we are sometimes led to the forum, if we are privileged by their attending us for the distance of one basilica, then it looks like we have been respected and honoured diligently. Our lesser friends are not busy and they [have the time to] provide this constant attendance; no good and generous men are without these lesser men.
>
> Cicero, *Pro Murena* 34

The empire brought with it the end of popular elections and with it a reduction in the usefulness of client to patron. Clients then came to be regarded as sycophantic—servile almost—and often were no more than hangers-on, looking for a hand-out or an invitation to dinner. Seneca and Martial highlight this fawning and greed, much of which was evident at the morning reception, the *salutatio*:

> Your clients? But none of them attend you for what you are but for what they can get out of you. They used to seek friends, but now they just look for loot; if a lonely old man changes his will, the morning-caller just goes to another door.
>
> Seneca, *Letters* 19, 4

This morning, Caecilianus, I happened to greet you simply by your name, omitting to call you 'My Master.' Do you want to know how much that liberty cost me? It cost me a hundred farthings.

Martial 6, 88

Pliny abhors the meanness of a dinner host and the rudeness in grading one's guests and feeding them accordingly:

To Junius Avitus

To tell it would take too long and it doesn't matter how it happened anyway, how I came to be dining with a man I barely knew. He thought of himself as refined and sensible, but to me he was both mean and extravagant at the same time. The best dishes were served to him and to a select few others; the rest got inferior fare and less of it. He even poured the wine into little goblets divided into three different types, not so that we had the chance to choose but so that we couldn't refuse what were offered. One type for him and us, another for his lesser friends (he graded his friends) the other for his and our freedmen. The guest reclining next to me noticed this and asked if I approved. When I said that I didn't; he asked 'What do *you* do then?'

'I serve the same to everyone because I invite guests for the dinner, not to give them marks out of ten; I consider them equal in every respect and they get the same courses and couches'.

'Even the freedmen?'

'Even the freedmen because I consider them as my companions at table, not as freedmen'.

He replied: 'Isn't that expensive?'

'No'

'How's that?'

'Because the freedmen don't drink what I do but I drink what they do.'

Good god man—if you control your appetite it's no problem everyone having what you yourself have. It is this excess that you need to control, that should be reduced to the ranks, if you're cutting back on costs and you can manage to do this a lot better through self-restraint rather than by insulting anyone.

So what is the point of all this? To stop a young man like you of the best character being duped by extravagance, hiding under the guise of frugality—as you can see at the tables of certain people. Whenever I come across such a thing my affection for you makes me warn you about the things you should avoid, using this as an example. So remember that nothing is more repellent than the modern fusion of extravagance and miserliness—repulsive enough when separate and apart—even more repulsive when together.

Pliny, *Epistles* 2, 6

2

Family Life

Life expectancy in ancient Rome was, by western standards today, a meagre twenty-seven years; seriously high child mortality rates, maternal death in childbirth, death in battle, and fatal diseases all made their contribution and took their toll. The comparatively young average age of death had major consequences for the family unit and led to frequent remarriages of one or other partners to form blended families in which step-parents, stepchildren, and half siblings proliferated. There was, of course, no welfare to speak of or depend on, so families had to be strong, close-knit units and the individual members were obliged to help each other; marriages were often made in order to strengthen alliances and bonds between families, relying on dependable assistance that was on hand as and when required. For the elite families at least, love had very little do with who married whom.

The father

The glue binding all families together was the *paterfamilias* (the father), who exercised his authority (*patria potestas*) over the *familia*. His function was to ensure that family members always united to help each other, so as to ensure the survival of their family, and to cement those alliances with other *familiae* to guarantee mutual assistance when required.

He also had a responsibility to ensure the continuation of his family line through the fathering of children. Generally speaking, though, he would have greeted the birth of a daughter somewhat less enthusiastically than that of a son even if his wife, the mother, saw things differently. *Patria potestas* empowered him, by virtue of *ius patrium, ius vitae necisque*, to exercise the power of life and death, to kill or sell off unwanted or surplus members of the family. In extreme cases, baby girls were exposed, largely, it seems, for financial reasons: a girl could not always go out to work and contribute to the household income; she may also require an expensive dowry in the relatively near future.[1] A girl's father was the prime mover in the choice of her husband; he would be looking for a match that would guarantee family stability, engender powerful ties with other families, and bring in wealth. Boys also had to be careful. Dionysius of Halicarnassus describes the supreme power invested in Roman fathers:

> But [Romulus] gave almost full power to the father for his whole life over his son, whether he resolved to imprison him, to whip him, to bind him in chains and keep him labouring in the fields, or to put him to death…he even allowed the father to sell his son… to make a profit by selling his son as often as three times, thereby giving greater power to the father over his son than to the master over his slaves.
>
> Dionysius of Halicarnassus, *The Roman Antiquities* 2, 26–27
> Translation adapted from the Loeb Classical Library edition, 1937

In 63 BCE, the senator Aulus Fulvius had his son executed because he was involved in an attempted coup against the government, the Catilinarian Conspiracy.

The right to exact capital punishment may not have been exercised very often in reality. Horace gives us an insight into what is probably a more typical father-son relationship:

> If I live a life pure and innocent and am dear to my friends, my father is responsible reason for this… he was my most faithful guardian, my chaperone… more praise is due to him, and from me more gratitude. As long as I remain sane I will never be ashamed of such a father as he, and therefore make no apology [for being the son of a freedman], as many do, saying it is not their fault.
>
> Horace, *Satires* 1, 6, 65–92

Child exposure and child murder

According to the *Twelve Tables* (*Leges Duodecim Tabularum*), the basis of Roman law laid down in about 450 BCE, deformed babies of either sex should be disposed of as soon as possible after birth: 'A dreadfully deformed child shall be killed' (*Twelve Tables* 4,1). Dionysius of Halicarnassus made the following allegation about Romulus in the so-called *Law of Romulus*:

> [Romulus] obliged the inhabitants to raise all their male children and the first-born female, and forbade them to kill any children under three years of age unless they were deformed or congenitally abnormal from birth. He permitted their parents to expose these, provided they first showed them to their five nearest neighbours and they also approved. Anyone who disobeyed this law was liable to various penalties, including the confiscation of half their property.
>
> Dionysius of Halicarnassus, *The Roman Antiquities* 2, 15
> Translation adapted from the Loeb Classical Library edition, 1937

Nevertheless, legalised child murder had its opponents; Philo of Alexandria (20 BCE–50 CE) equated exposure of infants with infanticide and luridly reports cases of strangulation and drowning:

> And as for their murders and infanticides … some of them slay them with their own hands, and stifle the first breath of their children, and smother it altogether, because they are terribly cruel and insensitive; others throw them into a deep river, or a sea, after they have attached a weight to them, to make them sink to the bottom more quickly. Others, again, carry them out into a desert to expose them there, purportedly with the hope that they may be saved by some one, but in real truth to inflict on them still more painful suffering; for that is where all the beasts which devour human flesh, since there is no one to keep them off, attack them and feast on the delicate banquet of children…And carnivorous birds fly down and lick up the remainder of their bodies, if they are not themselves the first to discover them; for when they discover them themselves they do battle with the beasts of the earth for the whole carcass.
>
> Philo of Alexandria, *de Specialibus Legibus* 114–115
> translation adapted from that by Charles Duke Yonge, London, H. G. Bohn, 1854–1890

Livy tells in 207 BCE of a monstrously deformed child being cast adrift, alive in a box, to rid Rome of what was considered a repulsive portent.[2] Suetonius describes a decree in 63 BCE that all boys should be exposed; Musonius Rufus in the first century CE deplores child murder.[3] Soranus, the gynaecologist, provided a checklist for midwives to help them determine the newborn disorders which permitted exposure.[4] In Greece, Aristotle had advocated that all deformed babies be exposed (*Historia Animalium*) and Plutarch later described the Spartan practice under Lycurgus whereby the Elders examined all babies and abandoned those who were deformed at Apothetae at the foot of Mount Taygetus.

In an otherwise touching and sensitive letter, Hilarion, away from home on business in Alexandria, is quite adamant that his pregnant wife, Alis, expose their baby if it is a girl—the affection he shows to Alis makes the demand all the more chilling:

> Please, please look after the child; I'll send you money if I get paid soon. If you have the baby before I get back let it live if it's a boy; if it's a girl, expose it … how can I forget you? Please don't worry'.
>
> *P. Oxy* 744

Ovid, in the mythological story of Iphis and Ianthe, tells a similar tale—low-born Ligdus was poor but he had morals and was honourable; his pregnant wife was near her time and he wished her an easy labour and a boy:

> There are two things which I pray for: that the birth is with the least of pain, and that you give birth to a boy. Girls are a burden, and fortune denies us the means.

Therefore, and I hate to say it, if by chance you produce a girl—God forgive me— she must die.

Ovid, *Metamorphoses* 9, 675–679

Ligdus was adamant, but Iphis, their baby girl, was secretly raised as a boy and was eventually changed into a boy by the gods. Despite being mythology, its message surely reflects real-world practice; significantly, Ovid considers Ligdus to be acting morally and honourably.

Some fathers exercised their *ius vitae necisque* on moral grounds; around 642 BCE Horatia, the fiancée of one of the enemy Curiatii, mourned his death after he was slain by one of her three brothers, two of whom also died in the fight. The surviving brother, Publius, stabbed her to death, proclaiming 'any woman who mourns an enemy of Rome will die like this'. Her father sanctioned the sororicide, adding that he would have killed her himself had her brother not.

> Horatius was marching as commander, carrying his triple spoils before him. His sister, who had been engaged to one of the Curiatii, met him in front of the Capene gate. She recognised the cloak of her fiancé on her brother's shoulders, the cloak which she herself had made; in tears she let down her hair and called out the name of her dead lover. Horatius was so furious at his sister's outburst in the middle of his victory and during the public rejoicing that he unsheathed his sword and ran the girl through. 'Go,' he exclaimed, 'go to your betrothed with your untimely love, forgetting your dead brothers, the brother who is still alive and your country! So die every Roman woman who grieves for an enemy!' … Publius Horatius the father, declared that his daughter had been justly killed; if this was not the case he would have exerted his authority as a father by punishing his son.
>
> Livy 1, 26

In 449 BCE, Appius Claudius, one of the legendary authors of the *Twelve Tables*, ardently stalked a young lady called Verginia; her father stabbed her in the heart to save her from the *stuprum* (debauched or lewd behaviour) he believed a liaison with Appius Claudius would have inevitably brought.

> A passionate desire took hold of Appius Claudius to violate a young plebeian woman … Appius was going mad with desire for this young adult woman, noted as she was for her beauty; he attempted to entice her by bribes and promises but when he saw that there was no way through her modesty, he decided on cruel and arrogant violence… and there [her father], snatching up a knife from a butcher, said, 'In the one way that I can, I give you your liberty.' He then stabbed the girl in the heart.
>
> Livy 3, 44–58

It was not until 374 CE that child exposure was outlawed when infanticide became the legal equivalent of murder. There was the *Puellae Faustinianae* (the Girls of Faustina), the charity that Antoninus Pius established in memory of his wife, Faustina the Elder, after her death in 141 CE. The charity provided for the poor girls of the city as depicted on a Roman denarius. An inscription (*CIL* 8, 1641) etched onto a monument in Sicca, North Africa between 169 and 180 CE announces that Publius Licinius Papirianus was donating 1,300,000 sesterces—a good sum plus its annual interest—to feed and maintain 300 boys and 300 girls aged three to fifteen each year.[5]

In later bids to restrict the practice and deter parents from taking this last resort, Theodosius introduced a welfare assistance plan in 315 CE whereby funds were granted to poor parents who could not afford to raise their children:

> A law…to stop parents killing their children and show them better alternatives … if any parent reports that poverty prevents them from raising their child then food and clothing should be issued straightaway since the bringing up of an infant should not tolerate any delay. We offer the funds from our treasury and private finances.
>
> *The Code of Theodosius* 11, 27, 10

Soon after, Constantine offered food parcels and clothing to new parents and legalized the sale of babies, mainly into slavery, in 329 CE in a bid to prevent their exposure. However, blatant child murder was still going on some years later; the skeletons of 100 or so infants were excavated from the bottom of a drain in Ashkelon dating from the sixth century CE.[6]

Some mothers were forced to give their children away, or to sell them due to abject poverty; one papyrus tells of a widow, Aurelia Herais, who has to surrender all claim to her nine-year-old daughter. The raw emotion shines through the officialese:

> My husband died and I was left to work and suffer for our daughter just to give her the most meagre necessities. And now I simply can't feed her … she is about nine years old, please take her from me as your own daughter … I understand that from now on I have no right to reclaim her.
>
> *P. Oxy* 1895

An example of an adoption agreement from 335 CE has also been found at Oxyrhynchus in Egypt (*P. Oxy* 1206). Many girls would end up in the slave markets; others would be sold as potential prostitutes. Orphans with nowhere to go were common among the lower classes; this plangent message sent by Tare, from Apamea in Syria says it all:

> Dear aunt. My mother, your sister, has been dead some time now…she was my whole family. Since her passing I have been all on my own in a strange land with no one to help me. Remember me dear aunt and, if you find someone to help, send him.
>
> *P. Bour.* 25 6

Paternal and maternal love

Of course, most baby girls (and boys) were allowed to live, and were loved by mother and father alike. Some scholars argue that, due to the high rate of infant mortality, Roman parents were able to inure themselves to the harsh fact that their baby might well die, so as to minimise and mitigate the grief that is normal in such a tragic situation. The employment of wet nurses, and the knowledge that some Romans 'farmed out' their infants for the first two years or so of their lives, may suggest a level of parental indifference. Cicero says as much: 'no one pays much notice if he dies in the cradle.' (Cicero, *Tusc.* 1, 39, 93); although he does concede that the death of an older child demands consolation.

The writing on the tombstone of twelve-year-old Julia Pothousa from Arcadia may endorse this apparent parental indifference: her parents wish that she had died earlier, before they had grown to love her as she grew older. The parents of ten-year-old Marcus Ortorios Eleutherios, however, were overcome with grief for their 'sweetest child'; this stark epitaph speaks volumes of grief: 'Quintus Hetterius Ephebus and Julia Zosime gave this memorial for their most unlucky daughter Hatteria Superba who lived for one year, six months and twenty-five days.' (*CIL* 6, 19159)

Given the importance among elite families of engaging surrogate mothers in the form of slaves or freedwomen acting as nurses, Quintilian emphasises how important it is to employ one with the right credentials:

> Above all ensure that the child's nurse speaks correctly… without doubt the most important thing is that they should be of good character: but they should speak correctly as well. The child hears his nurse first and it is her words that he will first try to copy. We naturally retain best those things we learned as a child…do not, therefore, let the boy even in infancy get used to a way of talking he will later have to unlearn.
>
> Quintilian, *Institutio Oratoria* 1, 1, 4–5

The hired nurse played a vital role in child development. She also provided crucial support for children when they were growing up. Some grew very attached to their nurses and formed enduring attachments. Pliny, for example, bequeathed his farm to his nurse (*Letters* 6, 3).

Pedagogues were also important; they were the male slaves who played with, amused and taught basic life skills to their young charges. They chaperoned young children from an early age to the baths and theatre, and did the school run, accompanying them to and from school. In essence, they were full-time baby-sitters. Cicero acknowledges their vital role while, at the same time, recommending that, socially, an appropriate distance be kept:

> Generally speaking, we should not make decisions about friendships until we are grown up and know our own minds. Otherwise our nurses and pedagogues—on

the grounds that it is they who know us best—will lay claim to the best part of our affections. These people must not be neglected, but should be regarded differently from those friends we have made as grown-ups.

Cicero, *On Friendship* 20, 74

Martial finds that some pedagogues just will not let go in a lament which, no doubt, remains familiar today:

As far as you're concerned [Charidemus] I still haven't grown up ... you won't let me have a good time or have sex ... you tell me off, you watch me like a hawk, you complain and sigh and it takes you all your time to keep your angry hand off the birch. If I get dressed up in flash Tyrian clothes or slick back my hair you exclaim 'Your father never did that!' You ... count every glass of wine I drink. Stop! ... my girlfriend will explain that I am a man now.

Martial 11, 39

Two further epigrams by Martial that mourn the death of slave girl Erotion—his delight (*deliciae*)—just before her sixth birthday show pathos and the poet's deep grief. In the first, he hopes she will not be frightened by the horrors of Tartarus that await her, and that the turf over her body will not weigh too heavily; in the second, he asks for the anniversary of her death to be celebrated by subsequent owners of the house, where she lies buried.

May little Erotion not be horrified by the black shades nor the many mouths of the Tartarean dog [Cerberus]. She would only have completed her sixth cold winter if she'd not lived as many days too few. Now, let her frolic and play with old friends, and chatter and lisp my name. May the spongy turf cover her soft bones: earth, lie lightly on her—she was not heavy on you.

Here lies Erotion in the shade that too early descended, snatched away by criminal Fate in her sixth winter. Whoever you may be that, after me, rules over this little plot of land, bring annual devotions to her gentle shade. So, with home in perpetuity, so, with your family ever in health, may this stone be the only one that is tearful on your land.

Martial, 5, 34; 10, 61.

Cicero is also distraught at the death of his thirty-year-old daughter Tullia in childbirth in 45 BCE. His pet name for her was Tulliola; he also addresses her as *deliciolae* (darling). He pours out his grief in two letters to Atticus in which he describes his anguish, sorrowful memories, and being consumed day and night by grief; there is no solace to be found, not even in his books or his library. In the first letter, profound depression has caused him to cut himself off from all society, living in a deep, dark forest, coming out only at night, and weeping inconsolably. Despite what we saw earlier, affection between father and daughter is, to Cicero, quite natural; his letters are full of recollections of his efforts to make her happy, devoid of any criticism—even on the vexed question of her marriage to Dolabella.[7]

In this lonely place I have no one to talk to; I plunge into a dense and wild wood early in the day I don't leave it till evening. Apart from you, I have no greater friend than loneliness where my only conversation is with books. Even that is punctuated by tears, which I fight against as long as I can, but as yet I am not up to it.

You may ask if there is any consolation to be had from my books. Sadly, they just make matters worse; without them I may have been stronger—education fosters neither insensitivity nor callousness.

Cicero, Ad Atticum 12, 15; 12, 46

Quintilian is struck by grief at the death of his two sons in quick succession:

My younger son, who died the first of the two, when he was just over five took from me, as it were, one of the two lights of my life. I do not want to make a show of my misfortunes or exaggerate the reason for my tears; on the contrary, I wish that I could find a way to reduce them. But how can I bear to contemplate his beautiful face and the sweetness in his expressions? ... I would have loved such a child, even if he had been the son of a stranger. It was the will, too, of insidious fortune, to torture me all the more, that he should show more affection for me than for anyone else ...

I then laid my only hope and pleasure on my remaining son ... having entered his tenth year; I noticed in him not just a facility for learning, for which, over long experience, I have seen no child more remarkable, ... but signs that he was honourable, dutiful, compassionate, and generous ... he had greater qualities still: bravery, resolve and strength to resist pain and fear, for with what courage, with what admiration from his doctors did he endure eight months of illness!

Institutio Oratoria 6, praefatio 6–11

A teenager called Eucharis is remembered on a tombstone; she was fourteen at the time of her death, unmarried, educated, and a celebrated dancer and actress. Her grieving, proud, father has her tell us 'I had an education and was taught as if by the Muses ... the patrons of learning ... are silenced by my charred corpse and by my death.' (*CIL* 1, 1214)

A mother's grief over her daughter, Marcia Doris, celebrates the 'best and most devoted daughter', while Bitte's mother shows the cruel irony in her daughter's death when she has her poignantly say in the inscription 'Here I lie, a marble statue, instead of a woman.'[8] Epitynchanus tells us that Philete, *filia dulcissima* (the sweetest of daughters), died on her seventh birthday.[9]

Valerius Maximus records the story of the Sabine Valesius' desperate attempts, ultimately successful, to save the lives of his dying children—two boys and a girl. To Valesius, it seems, sons and daughters were equally precious.[10]

A century and a half later, in his letter to Marcellinus, Pliny the Younger deplores the premature death of the Fundanus' daughter, Minicia Marcella, soon before her thirteenth birthday. Despite her youth, she displayed considerable maturity and all the qualities befitting a grown woman—a *matrona*; she was a sweet child and modest, affectionate to her father and respectful to her nurses and teachers; she died with Stoic fortitude. Significantly, Pliny, though saddened, is equally troubled by the fact that Minicia did not live long enough to see marriage—the *sine qua non* of girls around that age—although she was engaged. Tragically, her dowry was transferred to pay towards the funeral arrangements. The passage is telling because it neatly reflects the situation of girls in middle class Roman society: girls married young, soon after puberty— marriage and child-rearing was the expectation, being a crucial goal in life. Females like Minicia went straight from being little girls to womanhood, with all the stresses and responsibility that brought.

> Fundanus' younger daughter has died. I never saw a girl so happy and amiable, worthy of a longer life or even of immortality. She was not yet fourteen, but she had the sense of a mature woman, the gravitas of a *matrona*, the sweetness of a girl and the modesty of a maiden… she has left us many deeper causes of grief and pain. What a sad and clearly bitter death…words cannot express how my mind is wounded.
>
> Pliny the Younger, *Epistles* 5, 16 1–7.

The Roman world was a very dangerous place, for children as well as for adults. Ten-year-old Julia Restuta from Salonae in Dalmatia was the victim of a fatal mugging— robbed and killed for her jewellery; eight-year-old Revocata and her four-year-old brother both drowned off Brattia on the Dalmatian coast; and fourteen-year-old Murra died when she was hit on the head with a toy weapon in Lugudunum.[11]

Love and affection for their children is clearly evident in *matronae*. In the first half of the first century CE, Seneca, in a piece that often rings true today, concludes that fathers are extremely demanding of their children, sometimes reducing them to tears; mothers, on the other hand, are more sensitive and indulgent:

> Can't you see how fathers show their love in one way, and mothers in another? The father orders his children to get out of bed so that they can get on with the day,— even on holidays he does not allow them to be lazy, and he makes them sweat and sometimes cry. But the mother sits them on her knee, sheltering them in the shade, protecting them from unhappiness, tears and distress.
>
> Seneca the Younger, *De Providentia* 2, 5

We have seen how in the *Agricola*, published in 98 CE, Tacitus ascribes matronly qualities to Agricola's mother, Julia Procilla, *rara castitas*—a paragon of feminine virtue. It was her guidance which imbued Agricola with all the right characteristics.[12]

This chimes with Tacitus' general belief:

In the good old days, every citizen's son, the children of any respectable mother were brought up, not in the room of a hired nurse but in the embrace of their mother. She was honoured to look after the home and to do right by her children.

Tacitus, *Dialogus de Oratoribus* 28

In 144 CE, Marcus Aurelius gives a rare glimpse of a warm relationship between mother and son—a very personal letter to his friend Fronto describes his mother sitting on the edge of his bed chatting to him; it shows an intimacy that is almost unique in the surviving evidence and a world apart from the sometimes arid, impersonal tombstone inscriptions:

Then I had a long talk with my mother who came in and sat at the end of my bed… while we were talking and gossiping and jesting each other over who of us two loved you three best, the gong sounded to indicate that my father had gone to take his bath.

Marcus Aurelius, *M. Cornelius Fronto: Epistulae ad M. Aurelium* 4, 6

Papyrus evidence describes an over-solicitous third century CE mother fretting over her son's minor accident at work.[13]

I went to your boss, Serapion and asked him how you were; he told me that you had injured your foot on a splinter of wood. I was concerned that you wouldn't be able to walk very fast and only then with some difficulty …don't forget to write, son, and tell me how you are. You know how a mother worries about her son.

BGU 380

For Cornelia, it is her two sons, the brothers Gracchi, who are her real jewels (*ornamenta*), not the ostentatious sparklers she wears.[14] In the third century CE, Dio Cassius tells how the intelligent and witty Julia Domna, wife of Septimius Severus (r. 193–211), championed the cause of her younger son, Geta, in his claim for Caracella's throne—although her motives may not have been entirely altruistic.[15] Evidence of a mother's love for her daughter can be found on a funerary inscription raised by Quarta Senenia, a freedwoman, for Posilla.[16]

Stop, stranger, and also read what is written here: a mother was not allowed to enjoy her only daughter. I believe that some god or other looked askance on her life since her mother was not allowed to dress her up when she was alive; her mother, nevertheless, did this after her death.

CIL 1, 1837

As with us, proud Roman parents took pleasure in announcing the birth of their children; both of these were written on walls in Pompeii:

Our daughter was born early in the evening of Saturday, 2 August

Announcing the birth of Cornelius Sabinus

CIL 4, 294; 8149

Cicero announced the birth of his son to Atticus: 'Let me tell you that I have been blessed with a little son. Terentia is doing well' (Cicero, *Ad Atticum* 1, 2, 1).

Pliny the Younger gives an example of a caring grandmother; he describes Ummidia Quadratilla as being spritely (*viridis*) and in good physical shape, until her last illness—*etiam ultra matronalem modum*—very unusual for a woman. In his letter, Pliny is most concerned about his protégé, Ummidius Quadratus, and the preservation of his good character. Pliny was anxious because the recently deceased seventy-nine-year-old grandmother had been something of a rich old raver, enthusiastically managing a troupe of pantomime dancers, playing draughts, being decadent, and generally living it up. However, despite her wealth and the evident luxury of her home, she reverently shielded Ummidius from it all—he lived *severissime*, she *obsequentissime*; he lived an austere life, she an indulgent one. Pliny is highly respectful of the old lady and the efforts she went to in bringing up her grandson with such honour, with *pietas*. In the end, she left one third of her fortune to her grandson and another third to her granddaughter:

> Ummidia Quadratilla is dead, having lived to nearly eighty. She was a spritely lady until her last sickness, with a strength and good physical shape unusual even to matrons in their prime... Ummidius Quadratus lived ascetically chez party grandmother ... I love to relive a pleasure by writing about it; I rejoice at the *pietas* shown by Quadratilla, and the honour she gave to that best of young men.
>
> Pliny, *Epistles* 7, 24

Statius manages to combine a moving description of wifely devotion, a mother's devotion to her daughter, and a stepfather's pride in his step-daughter. It comes in a poem inspired by his unpopular intention, in his autumn years, to move the family back to Naples from Rome. His wife Claudia's loyalty (*fides*) to him has been equal to that of the heroines of old Greece and Rome; her devotion to her daughter is just as great:

> Nor is your concern and devotion (*pietas*) for your daughter any the less: you love her as a mother, your daughter is never out of your mind; night and day you hold her fixed in your innermost soul.
>
> Statius, *Silvae* 3, 5

He praises his step-daughter's beauty, her good attitude, her accomplishments on the lute, and in singing. Her mother's concern is that her daughter is unmarried and that

Rome is the best place for her to find a husband; Statius argues that she will find a husband whether she is in Rome or Naples.

Daughters and sons, then, if they survived childbirth and were not exposed, were clearly cherished by loving parents.

The *matrona*: mother and wife

The essentials of Roman womanhood are enshrined in the concept of the *matrona*— the wife and mother of the household. The qualities expected of a *matrona* are all there in the inscriptional evidence. They include *pudicitia* (sexual propriety, the opposite, almost, of *stuprum*—depravity), modesty, virtuousness, loyalty, strength of character and fortitude, *pietas* towards the family, being a 'one-man' woman (*univira*), and devotion to her children. A girl took on these responsibilities the minute she arrived at her husband's house during her wedding ceremony.

Two famous inscriptions provide a detailed description of the ideal *matrona* and mother. Murdia's son tells how she was without peer when it came to *virtus, virtuousness,* diligence and intelligence, modesty, integrity, chastity, obedience, working the wool, and loyalty: all the usual qualities. This late first century BCE inscription is important because it goes some way to explain why funerary inscriptions for women often read like anonymous formulae: the range of a woman's achievements was circumscribed by their duty to the household and the family; most women, we can presume, fulfilled this adequately and so the same characteristics and virtues appear over and over again. The funerary inscriptions are often a reflection both of the restrictions on women's activities in Roman society and the dedication they were expected to show towards the *familia*.[17] Murdia, nevertheless, stands out because the inscription also shows that she was at pains to ensure the fair distribution of her property after her death.

> It is not easy for women to win praise ... because their lives are lived with a narrower range of opportunity ... my mother merited more praise than others because in modesty, integrity, chastity, obedience, working the wool, diligence and loyalty she was equal to other excellent women, peerless in virtue, hard work and wisdom.
>
> *CIL* 6, 10230

The gold standard of wifely conduct can also be seen in the second century BCE Turia inscription—the *Laudatio Turiae* erected in Rome by her husband, Quintus Lucretius Vespillo. This celebrates, at some length, the life of a dutiful and exceptional wife (*c.* 60 BCE—5 BCE) and gives another catalogue of those qualities expected of the good *matrona*: *pietas*, wool-working, looking after the household gods, modesty of dress and elegance, financial generosity, bravery and shrewdness in the face of her husband's enemy. Turia concealed Lucretius in their roof space and convincingly acted out the role of the bereft wife dressing in rags, looking disheveled and grieving over an apparently lost husband.

> Marriages as long as ours are exceptional: marriage, that is, ended by death and not broken by divorce. For we were lucky enough to see our marriage last without discord for forty years. I wish that our long union had ended through something that had happened to me instead of you … should I mention your domestic virtues: your loyalty, obedience, affability, reasonableness, hard wool-working, religion without superstition, modest dress and sober manner? Should I focus on your love for your relatives, your devotion to your family? You showed the same care toward my mother as you did to your own parents.
>
> *CIL* 6, 1527

The Cornelias

Three role models to emulate were Cornelia, mother of the Gracchi; Aurelia Cotta, Julius Caesar's mother; and the mother of Augustus, Atia Balba Caesonia. Quintilian believes that it was a mother's duty to ensure their children receive the best possible education, whatever her own academic achievement, also citing Cornelia as a fine role model.[18]

> We learn that the eloquence of the Gracchi brothers owed a lot to their mother Cornelia, whose letters still to-day attest to her style … even those who have not been lucky enough to have had a good education should not for that reason neglect their son's education but, on the other hand, should be even more careful in other matters where they help their children.
>
> Quintilian, *Institutiones Oratoriae* 1.1. 6–8, 15–17

Cornelia is described as the ideal *matrona* by Plutarch in his *Life of Gaius Gracchus*. We know little of her life, other than that Pliny the Elder records how she was born with her vagina closed up (labial adhesion), an inauspicious condition presaging the deaths of her two revolutionary sons.[19] The daughter of Scipio Africanus, she remained dignified when speaking of the exploits and tragic deaths of her two boys. Her company and conversation were much enjoyed by scholars and monarchs:

> Cornelia is reported to have borne all her misfortunes in a noble and magnanimous spirit, and to have said of the sacred places where her sons had been killed that they were tombs worthy of the dead which occupied them … but [she was] most admirable when she spoke of her sons without grief or tears, and narrated their achievements and their fate to anyone who asked as if she were speaking of men of the early days

of Rome. Some were therefore led to think that old age or the depth of her sorrows had impaired her mind and made her insensible to her misfortunes, whereas, really, such persons themselves were insensible how much help in the banishment of grief mankind derives from a noble nature and from honourable birth and rearing, as well as of the fact that while fortune often prevails over virtue when it endeavours to ward off evils, she cannot rob virtue of the power to endure those evils with calm assurance.

Plutarch, *Life of Gaius Gracchus* 19, 1–3
Translated adapted from Loeb Classical Library edition, 1921

Despite a proposal of marriage from the very eligible Ptolemy VIII (Physkon), Cornelia remained a widow and *univira*. The surviving daughter, Sempronia, married Scipio Africanus the Younger; she brought up her sons, Gaius and Tiberius, 'with such care and such ambitious hopes, that ... they were considered to owe their virtues even more to their education than to their lineage'. Cornelia provided that education.[20]

At the end of the first century BCE, Propertius describes a different Cornelia, the daughter of Scribonia and wife to Lucius Aemilius Paullus, Augustus' step-daughter.[21] She too can boast excellent credentials as a *matrona*: dutiful daughter, dutiful wife and dutiful mother, the ideal role model for her children. All the fine, matronly qualities are here—her life was faultless from beginning to end: 'Nor did the way I lived change in any way; it was blameless throughout, I lived a woman respected between marriage torch and funeral torch' (Propertius 4, 11, 45–6).

Cornelia is the perfect poster girl for Augustus' recently enacted moral legislation, the *lex Julia de maritandis ordinibus*. She is quite the opposite of Cynthia, Propertius' decadent mistress: Propertius enumerates traditional *matrona* qualities in Cornelia to highlight, by comparison, the unconventional, capricious, and outrageous behaviour of Cynthia. Cornelia, though, in the eyes of Propertius, remains a somewhat empty character who lives a proper but uninteresting life, following her own *cursus honorum* to the letter; to him she is a victim of Roman tradition suppressing the behaviour of women. Despite her obvious intelligence and obvious attractions, she lived a rather submissive and confined life.

Chastity and *virtus*

Pudicitia is clearly evident in Cornelia, Lucretia, and Verginia—the three great *matronae* of Rome. It is variously translated as chastity, sexual integrity, or sexual propriety. For Lucretia and Verginia, the preservation of *pudicitia* was so important that it cost them their lives. Women could also exhibit *virtus*, with its connotations of manliness (*vir*) and traditional male attributes of strength and bravery, as well as of virtue. According to Livy and Seneca, Cloelia exhibited *virtus*.[22] Seneca describes the 'conspicuous valour' of Cornelia and Rutilia as *conspecta virtus*. In the *Ad Marciam*, he spells out his belief that women are just as capable of displaying *virtutes* as men.[23]

> But who says that nature has been mean with the mental abilities of women when she restricted their physical strength? Believe me, they are just as strong as men intellectually, and have the same facility for honourable action. Given the right training, they are just as able to endure sorrow or graft. Good god, I say this in the very city ... in which Cloelia, for the great courage with which she was contemptuous of the enemy and the river, has come down to us almost as a man...If you want me to show you examples of women who have bravely endured the loss of their children, I will not seek further details: in one family I can quote two Cornelias, one the daughter of Scipio, and the mother of the Gracchi ...
>
> Seneca, *Ad Marciam* 16, 1

The elderly Ummidia Quadratilla shows vitality (*viridis*) and a physique unusual in an octogenarian woman.[24]

Matronly virtues, familial devotion, and *pietas* were not, of course, the preserve of the middle and upper classes. These qualities were also exhibited by women of the lower classes, as a 45 BCE inscription for Larcia Horaea clearly shows; she was a confident and faithful freedwoman, respected in her social circle, obedient to her master and mistress, and faithful to her husband—virtues which won her her freedom and status as a *matrona* in her own right.

> All good people respected me; no honourable woman disliked me. I was obedient to my aged master and mistress and was dutiful to him. For that they gave me my freedom and he married me. I looked after the house for all of twenty years from being a girl...death did not take away the glory of my life.
>
> CIL 1, 1570

Another freedwoman, Allia Potestas, can boast more than her fair share of virtues— perfect in every way, she is first up in the morning and the last to go to bed in the evening, forever weaving, faultless to the end; in fact, some scholars think that the epitaph is ironical, as this woman is depicted as being so perfect:

> No one was more precious than she in the world. No one has seen so diligent a woman ... She was brave, chaste, tenacious, honest, a faithful guardian. Smart at home, and smart when she went out, popular with the people. She, uniquely, could face up to anything. She didn't go on and on and so was never criticised. She was first to get up, and last to go to her bed after she had tidied up. Her wool never left her hands unless there was a good reason. She respectfully conceded to all; she had good habits; she was never smug, and never thought of herself as a free woman.
>
> CIL 6, 37695

Nor were matronly virtues confined to women of Roman birth. Martial describes Claudia Rufina; she is of British stock—a barbarian—but nevertheless is Latin at heart and would pass for a Roman or a Greek. Like all good *matronae*, she is fertile (*fecunda*), *univira* (a one-man woman), and looking forward to her children's marriages:

> Even though she was born among the blue painted Britons, Claudia Rufina has the heart of a Roman! How beautiful she is! The matrons of Italy would take her for a Roman; those of Attica one of their own. The gods have ordained that that she remains fertile to her revered husband, and that, while still a young woman, she can hope for sons-in-law and daughters-in-law! May heaven grant her ever to rejoice in just one husband, and to take joy in being the mother of three children.
>
> Martial 11, 53

Matronae were recognisable in the street by the *stola* (or *instita*, the shoulder straps of the *stola*) they wore—a long, ankle length dress—and their *vittae*, hair bands. These items instantly marked out the Roman *matrona* from unmarried girls, from women without Roman citizenship, adulteresses, prostitutes, and other women of dubious occupation such as dancers, actresses, and anyone else working in the entertainment or hospitality industries. The words *stola, instita*, and *vittae* themselves became metonyms for respectability and chastity: Ovid uses them when he disingenuously dissuades *matronae* from reading his racy *Ars Amatoria* despite the promise that he is writing about safe sex; Martial mentions the decency (*pudor*) of the *stola*; Valerius Maximus *verecundia stolae*, the modesty of the stola.[25]

> Stay away from here, you fine headband fillet wearing Vestal Virgins, you matronly badges of modesty with your ankle-hiding dress. I sing of safe passion, permissible intrigue, and there'll be no sin in my song.
>
> Ovid, *Ars Amatoria* 1, 1, 31–34

Sisterly and brotherly love; filial devotion and stepmothers

An example of sisterly affection for a brother was found on the side of the Cheops pyramid in the fourteenth century by a traveller; it had been carved in the second century CE by a girl called Terentia and describes him as *dulcissimus*—very dear. Sadly, the inscription was subsequently lost when the facing of the pyramid was removed.

I've seen the pyramids of Egypt without you, sweetest brother, and here grief poured out my tears. I etch this lament, a memorial of our grief. So may there remain on this lofty pyramid the name Decimus Gentianus, priest and friend.

ILS 1046a/ *CIL* 321

Cicero gives us a touching example of brotherly love in a letter to his younger brother, Quintus, sent in 58 BCE while travelling in exile in Macedonia:

When I am missing you, is it only the absence of a brother I am missing? Not really: the brother I am missing is, in the delightful companionship he brings, just like a friend; in obedience, just like a son; in wisdom, just like a father. Was I ever happy when you weren't there, or you when I was not around?

Cicero, *Letters to His Brother Quintus* 1, 3, 3

Good mothers sometimes earn the devotion of their children. However, although Roman children undoubtedly loved their mothers, expressions of love for a mother from sons and daughters are somewhat rare for a number of reasons: the children may never have known their mother if she died in childbirth, as was often the case; on divorce the father was awarded custody; so stepmothers were, therefore, the maternal figure in many families. Also, child care in middle and upper class families was often delegated to slaves.

A second century CE fragment shows filial devotion—and a lack of it—when Sempronius rebukes his elder brother, Maximus, for not looking after their mother and for causing her grief after their father's death.[26] Sempronius advises Maximus to give their other brothers a good slap if they upset her. Maximus is now the father figure, assuming *patria potestas*; he should join Sempronius in worshipping her as a goddess, as she is good and virtuous.

Agricola was, quite naturally, mortified when his mother was brutally murdered by marauders from Otho's navy.[27]

The high incidence of early death, divorce, and re-marriage in Rome resulted in many step parents and step children. Seneca, in a piece written while he was in exile for alleged adultery with Julia Livilla (the sister of Caligula) gives an account of Helvia's commendable attitude and behaviour towards her step-mother. Helvia's natural mother died in childbirth. Helvia's step-mother was happily left with no choice but to assume a birth mother's role because of the absolute obedience and loving affection Helvia had shown her. In short, their relationship was little different from a natural mother-daughter relationship.[28] Helvia displays all the characteristics of the *matrona*. Her sixteen years as wife of the governor of Egypt were entirely blameless, adopting as she did a discreet life-style which won her a reputation locally for being *unicum sanctatis exemplum*—a unique example of integrity. Filial and sibling affection is evident in a later Helvia passage where Seneca recommends Helvia seeks solace with his mother:

You grew up under the care of a stepmother, but, by your complete obedience and *pietas* which was as great as you would see in any daughter, you made her a true mother. But every child pays a high price for a good stepmother...I have not mentioned your greatest source of comfort—your sister... neither her retiring ways, nor her modesty, so provincial compared to the wanton behaviour of today's women, nor her quietness, nor her tendency to be on her own and devotion to leisure never prevented her from always wanting to help me. You will gain comfort and renewed strength from my dear mother. Be with her as much as you can and hold her in warm embrace.

Seneca the Younger, Ad Helviam 19, 1–3

Conjugal love

We have felt Cicero's inconsolable grief at the death of his daughter. Other writers describe emotion and empathy between husbands and wives—Martial gives us a widow's tragic double grief:

Nigrina brought home her dear husband's ashes, holding them close to her heart and complaining that the journey home was all too brief. When she surrendered the sacred urn to the tomb (and she was jealous of that tomb), she couldn't then help feeling that she had been widowed twice over for the husband who had been snatched from her.

Martial 9, 30, 3–6

Quintilian is distraught at his young wife's death, aged nineteen; she had given birth to two sons who also predeceased their father. She exhibited every virtue a woman could have. He adds poignantly that her girlish qualities made it seem as if he had lost a daughter:

After giving birth to a second son, while still aged nineteen, she died, but though cut off before her time, the death was a mercy. I was so upset that no amount of good fortune afterwards could make me completely happy. She exhibited every virtue a woman can. She has not only caused endless grief to her husband, but, being of the age of a girl, especially when compared with my own, her loss might could be considered the same as the loss of a daughter.

Quintilian, Institutes Oratoriae Praefatio Book 6, 3–6

There is much literary evidence for love shown to living wives. A letter from Pliny to Calpurnia reflects mutual affection:

You write that you are missing me terribly and take comfort only when you hold my books, often putting them where I should be. I'm glad that you miss me and I'm glad that you are comforted in this way. As for me, I read your letters over and over again, constantly picking them up as if they had just arrived. In doing this I burn with desire all the more.[29]

Pliny the Younger, *Epistles* 6, 7

The letter also hints at his appreciation of his wife's literacy and intelligence as confirmed for us in a separate letter to Corellia Hispulla, Calpurnia's aunt, spoiled rather by his smug appreciation of his own talents.

[Calpurnia is] very clever, very prudent, and her love for me is a mark of her chastity. You can add to these qualities her study of literature which has been developed by her devotion to me. She has all my books, reads them and even learns them by heart ... she has even set my verses to music and sings them accompanied with a lyre, taught not by a musician but by love—the best teacher.

Pliny the Younger, *Epistles* 4, 19

To Pliny, Corellia Hispulla shows many traits worthy of a *matrona*, demonstrated not least by the role she played bringing up her niece:

You are a paragon of dutiful conduct and you love the best and most devoted of brothers as much as he loves you; you love his daughter as if she was your own, and your affection for her is not so much as an aunt but more as the father she lost ... nothing else would be worthy of a woman educated in your hands, steeped in your ideas and who had seen nothing but purity and integrity in your company.

Pliny the Younger, *Epistles* 3, 3

Notably, it is to Corellia Hispulla whom Pliny writes—and not to her husband—when advising on the choice of a rhetoric teacher, a *rhetor Latinus*, for her son; it was important that he had only the best.

In his *Tristia* (1, 6, 26), composed in Black Sea exile, Ovid describes the loyal and devoted wife; she is *exemplum coniugis bonae*—the model of a good wife; she would hold first place among the sacred heroines of mythology and, somewhat disingenuously and sycophantically on Ovid's part, would be an equal to the first lady, Livia, wife of Augustus—if it is allowed to compare the great with the small.

Loyalty, bravery and suicide

The praise of the *matrona*, whether inscriptional or literary, to some degree follows a pattern; 'paragons of feminine virtue' are everywhere: the spinning of wool, the modesty and chastity, the devotion, the being seen and not really heard, and being *univira*—they are all symbols and emblems of 'the good wife'.[30] Nevertheless, we have seen ample funerary and literary evidence to show that women were appreciated more as individuals in their own right for their love and devotion to the family (sometimes to the death), their social skills, their education, and their single-mindedness.

Strength of character, loyalty, and bravery were among other hallmarks of the *matrona*. The rape of Lucretia by Sextus Tarquinius, and her subsequent suicide, firmly implicates matronly *pudicitia* and valour in the traditional foundation of Rome. Livy tells how Tarquinius blackmailed Lucretia by threatening to claim that she had been *in flagrante delicto* with a slave; he threatened to have her and the slave killed, their bodies placed alongside each other in bed, if she does not yield to him. Lucretia cannot live with the shame that such a calumny would bring and succumbs; her body is defiled but, she protests, her mind remains pure.[31] Despite the unconditional forgiveness of her father, Lucretius, and of Collatinus, her husband, Lucretia commits suicide—brave, virtuous and forever inextricably linked with Rome's proud early beginnings. Rome, like Lucretia, was compromised and violated by the Tarquins; the noble reaction of Lucretia and her avengers symbolizes Rome's honourable struggle against regal tyranny and led to the rejection of monarchy for a Republic. Livy makes her an unimpeachable exemplar of feminine virtue in a Rome—in Livy's day at least—beset by rampant adultery and failing marriages.

> On fire with passion, he waited till it seemed to him that all around was safe and everybody was fast asleep; then, drawing his sword, he came to the sleeping Lucretia. Forcing the woman down with his left hand on her breast, he said, 'Be quiet, Lucretia! I am Sextus Tarquinius. I've got my sword in my hand. Make a noise, and you're dead!' Terrified, the woman started out of her sleep: no help was in sight, but only imminent death. Then Tarquinius began to tell her of his love, to beg, to mingle threats with prayers, to twist everything around in the woman's heart. When he found her unwilling and unmoved even by fear of death, he added shame to fear, saying that when she was dead he would slay his slave and lay him naked next to her, giving the impression that she had been put to death in sordid adultery. Her steadfast modesty was overcome by this terrible prospect, by his victorious lust, as if by force; ferocious Tarquinius left, having wrecked a woman's honour …
>
> Livy 1, 58, 2

Lucretia explains the dire situation to her husband when he returns:

> What can be well with a woman when she has lost her chastity? Collatinus, the traces of a strange man are in your bed. Yet my body may have been violated; my heart is innocent, as death will testify. But pledge your right hands and your resolve that the adulterer shall not go unpunished.
>
> Livy 1, 58, 7

The rape is all the more heinous and significant because Livy prefaces it with a story emphasising Lucretia's virtue. During a drinking session, which included Tarquinius and Collatinus, at the siege of Ardea, the subject of wives, good or otherwise, came up; an alcohol-fuelled decision was then made to ride back to Rome and Collatia to establish whose wife was the most virtuous. The princes' wives were found ensconced in a sumptuous dinner party, *in convivio luxuque*. On the other hand, even though it was late at night, Lucretia was found sitting surrounded by her maids in the hall working away at the wool by lamplight. This of course left no doubt as to who had won the contest. According to Ovid, Lucretia was working on a cloak for Collatinus.[32]

Pliny the Younger gives an example of the exceptional devotion of a *matrona* to her husband in a letter to Maecilius Nepos. Arria, a shining example and comfort, does everything she possibly can to show her husband Aulus Caecina Paetus that his impending suicide, ordered by Emperor Claudius, will not be painful. 'Paetus, it doesn't hurt' (*Paete, non dolet*); this came after she has bravely shielded the news of their son's recent death from her husband to spare him additional grief:

> Whenever he asked how the boy was doing she responded: 'He's had a good rest and is ready to eat something'. Then, when she couldn't hold her tears back any longer, she left the room and burst into tears, succumbing there to her anguish. Her grief sated, she dried her eyes, composed herself and went back into the room, almost as if she had left her bereavement outside. It was a glorious thing for her when she pulled out a dagger, plunged it into her breast, pulled the dagger back out and offered it to her husband with the immortal, almost divine, words: 'Paetus, it doesn't hurt'. By doing what she did and saying what she said she was looking glory and immortality straight in the eye. On the other hand, it was an even greater thing when, without the reward of immortality and without the reward of glory, she hid her tears and concealed her grief and continued to play the mother even when she had lost her son.

Later in the letter, we learn of Arria's brave determination to end her own life:

> 'It's no use' she said: 'you can have me die a horrible death but you can't stop me dying.' As she said this she leapt from her chair, smacked her head really hard against the wall opposite and slumped to the ground. When she came round she said: 'I told you that I would find a hard way to die if you denied me the easy way out.'
>
> Pliny the Younger, Epistles 3, 16, 3–6

Martial (1, 13) too honours chaste (*casta*) Arria's bravery; he, perceptively, has her say that while her wound doesn't hurt (*non dolet*), the one that Paetus is about to inflict on himself certainly will hurt her.

Such courage ran in the family: Arria's grand-daughter, Fannia, had been married to Helvidius Priscus, an agitator against Vespasian who had him executed in 75 CE. Pliny extols the virtues of Fannia, doubting very much whether the world will see the like of her again—the perfect model of a wife with the rare qualities of charm and amiability, clever enough to appreciate the value of her husband's library, which she spirited away into safekeeping in exile despite orders to burn his books. Fannia has displayed *fortitudo, sanctitas, castitas, gravitas*, and *constantia*: bravery, purity of mind, purity of body, dignity, and self-control. She followed her husband twice into exile and was herself condemned to exile for her troubles; Tacitus sees this loyalty as an example of female *virtus*.[33] Fannia later died from tuberculosis contracted from a consumptive Vestal Virgin whom she had volunteered to nurse.[34]

Arria displayed other signs of strong character and determination, when she risked her life:

> [Paetus] was dragged back to Rome after Scribonianus had been killed. He was about to board the boat when Arria begged the soldiers to take her too: 'Surely a consul should be allowed a few slaves to serve his meals, dress him and put on his shoes—I am the only person to excel at all these things.' She didn't get her way, so she hired a small fishing boat to follow the big boat in her little one.
>
> Pliny the Younger, *Epistles* 3, 16, 7–9

Sulpicia dressed up as a slave to follow her proscribed husband, Lentulus Cruscellio, into exile in Sicily.[35] The wife of Rubellius Plautus accompanied him in exile and two of the wives of the Piso conspirators went with their husbands. Valerius gives us two further instances of loyalty and fortitude: first, as we have seen, Turia bravely and successfully concealed her proscribed husband, Quintus Lucretius Vespillo, in the rafters of their house in 42 BCE; second, Tertia Aemilia, wife of Scipio Africanus, had full knowledge of her husband's affair with a slave girl but chose to turn a blind eye and, on Scipio's death, emancipated the girl and organised her marriage to one of her freedmen.[36] Not only does this exemplify loyalty to a husband, but it also illustrates the double standard which persisted in Roman marriages where a man could philander, but a wife was forced to remain chaste, and was encouraged, expected even, on her husband's death to continue widowhood as a one man woman.

The intention behind enforcing these moral standards was to ensure that a wife could only bear her husband's children and that the husband could assume that he was the father of his wife's children. A man was only immoral if he compromised the integrity of another man's family by sleeping with that man's wife. Sleeping with slave girls, or boys, or prostitutes was quite acceptable. Tolerance of her husband's sexual infelicities was the price a Roman *matrona* had to pay for family stability.

Augustine converted to Christianity in 387 CE, he explains how his mother never argued with his father over his sexual indiscretions, nor, for that matter, his physical and psychological abuse.

> She tolerated the wrongs done in her bed and never ever showed jealousy over this to her husband… And besides, just as he was outstanding in kindness, so was he violent

in anger; but she had learned not to resist an angry husband either in deed, or even in word.

Augustine, *Confessions* 9, 9

It is of course impossible to conclude anything about the attitude of women to this; many women probably accepted the situation, seeing it as a relief from the often relentless cycle of sex, impregnation, childbirth and more sex. However, the very real possibility of a promiscuous man infecting his wife, or indeed his unborn child, with a sexually transmitted infection seems to have gone unacknowledged in the surviving literature.[37]

Appian records a number of brave and devoted acts by women following the proscriptions imposed after the assassination of Julius Caesar in 44 BCE. The wife of Acilius used her jewellery to bribe and distract the soldiers who had come to arrest him and fled with him to Sicily; Apuleius' wife threatened to turn him in if he refused to let her escape with him; Antius' wife concealed him in a blanket to affect their escape; and the wife of Rheginus hid him in a sewer and dressed him as a donkey-driving charcoal seller to make good their escape.[38] Dio Cassius describes a woman who heroically defends another woman's virtue when he records how Pythias, a slave girl under interrogation and torture stands up for Nero's wife, Octavia, in 63 CE.

When all of Octavia's other slaves except Pythias had sided with Sabina in her attack on Octavia, despising Octavia because she was in dire straits and sucking up to Sabina because she was very powerful. Pythias alone had refused, though cruelly tortured, to tell lies against her mistress, and finally, as Tigellinus continued to goad her, she spat in his face, saying: 'Tigellinus, my mistress's fanny is cleaner than your mouth.'

Dio Cassius 62, 13, 4. Translation adapted from Loeb edition (1925)

Sempronia, the Catilinarian conspirator, also showed bravery but, not surprisingly in the circumstances, it attracted condemnation and vilification. Sallust writes that she exhibited a boldness worthy of a man: she was well married with children; versed in Latin and Greek; accomplished in the lyre and a good dancer; and an excellent and convivial conversationalist—in short, her social and artistic skills and abilities were highly commendable. However, Sallust adds that marriage and motherhood apart, she displayed none of the qualities expected of the conventional *matrona*: she was impulsive, louche, passionate, a perjurer, an accessory to murder, a liar, and a spendthrift. Sempronia was a kind of anti-*matrona* to Sallust; while undoubtedly brave and gifted, she broke the mould and stepped far beyond the traditional boundaries laid down for Roman women. Her support for Catiline and the stigma involved in this, her independence of mind, and ostentatious social skills would have caused outrage and anger in some quarters.[39]

Despite its apparent frequency, female bravery was thought to be exceptional. Seneca, in the same breath as he extolls *virtus* in women, specifically in Helvia and

Marcia, qualifies his remarks when he compares them with women generally. Marcia is far removed from the *infirmitas muliebriter animi* (womanish weakness of mind), while Helvia is advised to avoid womanly weeping. All women have their *vitia*—faults.[40]

But that did not stop some of them committing suicide for or with their husbands. Pliny the Elder describes how a woman joined her husband in suicide by jumping, roped together, into Lake Como after his condition had been diagnosed, (variously thought to be a urogenital cancer, syphilis or urogenital tuberculosis) as incurable.[41] Porcia, the wife of Brutus, stabbed herself in the thigh to show her husband that she too could endure pain and was worthy of sharing his concerns.[42] When Brutus was killed in 43 BCE, she committed suicide by swallowing hot coals, an act which Valerius Maximus describes as 'her woman's spirit equal to her father's manly death'.

Tacitus recounts a number of female suicides. Paxaea commits suicide with her husband Pomponius Labeo, governor of Moesia, arraigned by Tiberius in 34 CE for maladministration.[43] Lucius Antistius Vetus was proscribed by Nero for his involvement in the Pisonian conspiracy in 65 CE: his mother-in-law, Sextia and daughter, Antistia Pollitta, joined him in opening their veins, but not before Pollitta had courageously remonstrated with Nero: 'she wailed like a woman' but she also 'screamed at him in a most unwomanly' rage.[44, 45] Aemilia Lepida took her life to avoid persecution; Sextia opts to die with her husband, Mamercus Aemilius Scaurus, who is under prosecution; so too does Paulina, the wife of Seneca, although she is confounded by Nero and lives on 'praiseworthy in the memory of her husband'.[46, 47]

Suicide by wives for their husbands is, in one way, an extension of the *univira* ideal— not only should a woman marry only one man, but she should not outlive him. Arria, whom we have just met, admonishes Vibia, wife of Scribonianus, who lived on after her husband had been murdered in her very arms; Arria urges her own daughter to commit suicide should her husband die before her.[48]

Matronae sometimes acted bravely *en masse*. The proposal in 195 BCE to repeal the *Lex Oppia* of 215 BCE evoked distaste and condemnation among men when women came out from their homes and demonstrated in the Forum to support the repeal. The law had restricted the use of luxuries by women in the wake of the Battle of Cannae some twenty years before. It limited the amount of gold women could own and required that all the assets of wards, single women, and widows be handed over to the State; the wearing of dresses with purple trim and riding in carriages within Rome or nearby towns was also prohibited, except during religious festivals. The feeling among women was that the law had by now served its purpose and had run its course. Livy records the speech given by Marcus Porcius Cato and his embarrassment and disgust at what he saw as indecorous behaviour ill-befitting Roman women. To give it some context, Cato, generally no friend of women, had famously paraphrased Themistocles when he asserted: 'All men rule their wives; we rule all men; our wives rule us'. He harps back to the days of the ancestors who permitted women no public activity or commercial dealings without a guardian, safeguarding the power of fathers and husbands. Cato is appalled by this populist action and by the very public demand that they be heard.[49]

The repeal, nevertheless, was upheld, thanks in no small part to the reasonable and balanced arguments of Lucius Valerius:

> For a long time our matrons lived by the highest standards of behaviour without any law: what is the risk when it is repealed, that they will give in to luxury? ... Are we to forbid only women to wear purple? When you, a man, can use purple on your clothes, can you not permit the mother of your family to have a purple cloak, and will you let your horse be more finely saddled than your wife is dressed?
>
> Livy 34, 2, 1—2

Around the same time, Plautus piles on the paranoia and insecurity when he has Megadorus, the misogynistic neighbour of Euclio, the old miser in *Aulularia* (*The Pot of Gold*), deliver a rant on female extravagance, with particular reference to those employed in the tailoring and clothing trades.[50]

> MEGADORUS No, I never want to hear a wife say 'I brought you more in dowry than your whole property was worth, so I have a right to expect you to give me purple and gold, mules, servants, stableman, footmen, page-boys and carriages to ride in.
>
> Plautus, *Aulularia* 498–550

The palaver had not died down some 200 years later when Valerius Maximus reminded his readers that 'men of the time had no idea of the extravagance to which women's indomitable passion for the latest in fashion would lead, or the extremes to which their brazenness would go.' (Valerius Maximus 9, 1, 3)

Cicero relies heavily on the support of his wife, Terentia, during his exile in 58 and 57 BCE.[51] His letters to her reflect his isolation, homesickness, and affection, both for her and for their daughter: Terentia is *fidissima atque optima uxor ... mea lux* (most faithful and best of wives ... light of my life).

Tullia and Terentia both interceded bravely on Cicero's behalf during his exile.[52] They also had to deal with his business affairs, the slaves, and household as well as the upbringing of their young son; Terentia remained the supportive wife even though their marriage was automatically annulled when he went into exile. The two women demonstrated ostentatiously by wearing their hair unkempt and donning black mourning clothes when visiting friends in Rome in order to canvas support for Cicero's return. When their house on the Palatine was torched by Clodius' thuggish mob, Terentia sought sanctuary in the house of the Vestal Virgins. According to Plutarch, in earlier days Terentia seems to have been influential in her husband's handling of the Catilinarian conspiracy. In the same piece, he records how Cicero himself says that Terentia was more active in his political life than she ever was in domestic affairs.

> While Cicero was in this quandary, a sign was given to the women who were sacrificing. The altar, it seems, although the fire was already thought to have gone

out, sent a bright blaze out from the ashes and burnt bark. The rest of the women were terrified at this, but the Vestal Virgins told Terentia to hurry to her husband and tell him to carry out his plans for Rome, since Vesta was giving him a beacon on this path to safety and glory. So Terentia, who was generally of no mild spirit nor without natural courage, but an ambitious woman, and, as Cicero himself tells us, more inclined to make herself a partner in his political problems than to share with him her domestic concerns, gave him this message and incited him to act against the conspirators.

Plutarch, *Cicero* 20; translation adapted from 1919 Loeb edition

Ovid's third and final wife is equally supportive and loyal to him in his exile; nine of his *Tristia* are addressed to her. He describes his first two wives as 'useless' although 'faultless' in the same poem as he expresses his gratitude to the third:

I was married briefly to a worthless and useless wife when I was barely more than a boy. She was followed by a bride who, though without fault and blameless, was never going to share my bed for long. Lastly, there is she who stayed with me till I was old, who's lived to be the bride of an exiled husband.

Ovid, *Tristia* 4, 10, 69ff

Working the wool and household management

In the earlier days of the Republic, spinning and weaving were crucial skills in all Roman households at all levels of society; they were a badge of the good mother and wife. Augustus alleged that he wore home spun clothes and enthusiastically promoted the traditional skill of weaving, boasting that all the women in his household could spin.[53] At one time, Livia's domestic staff comprised five patchers (a person who stitches patches onto clothing), two supervisors, six women in charge of clothing, one cloak maker, one tailor, and two fullers. The Statilii Tauri family had eight spinners, one supervisor of the wool, four patchers, four weavers, two dyers, and four fullers.[54] Ovid reminds us that the goddess Pallas Minerva not only teaches children reading and literature, but also how to weave and spin.[55]

By the mid-first century CE, Lucius Junius Moderatus Columella, the Spanish-born writer on agriculture and husbandry complains that homespun clothes were now unfashionable and clothing was routinely bought from shops at extortionate prices.[56] Bread-making suffered the same fate when bakeries and bakers shops replaced home-made bread in the second century BCE. Indeed, Aelius Aristides tells us that only in the poorest households did women do routine housework—slaves did most, if not all, of it.[57]

On the catering front, if Trimalchio's *Fortunata* is anything to go by, the *materfamilias* (the woman of the house) was heavily involved—in a managerial capacity—in the preparation and serving of meals. Fortunata organises the slaves throughout and her evening is only finished when she has made their supper.[58]

As important as competency in spinning and weaving was in the realm of the Roman family, the skill became redundant over time and merely symbolic as Roman society became more and more sophisticated and urbanised. Unlike her Greek counterpart, the wealthier Roman woman would spend much of her time supervising the slaves, ensuring that they performed all the mundane tasks a lower class housewife might be expected to do. This freed her up to go out: shopping, attending festivals and spectacles, visiting friends, educating their children, and going to those dinner parties Nepos tells us about:

> What Roman is ashamed to bring his wife along to a feast, or whose consort does not occupy the best room in the house, and live in with people all around her? But in Greece the case is very different: a wife is not admitted to a feast, except if it is with relations, nor does she sit anywhere in the house but in the innermost apartment of the house, which is called the gynaeconitis; nobody else goes in there except close relations.
>
> Cornelius Nepos, *De Viris Illustribus praef.* 6.
> Translation adopted from that by the Rev. John Selby Watson, 1886

Apart from bewailing the popularity of shop-bought clothing at the expense of homespun, Columella is nostalgic for the times when women reputedly did do all the housework, when they provided a sanctuary for stressed husbands returning from work to an environment of unquestioned respect and total harmony, where even the prettiest wife complemented and complimented her husband's achievements by her own enthusiastic efforts around the house. In so doing Columella makes an interesting comparison with the old and the new as it relates to the domestic role of women. In those days everything was jointly owned and the woman's domestic work was as important as the husband's public work, obviating the need for household managers. Nowadays, Columella laments, women are obsessed with luxury and laziness, the making of wool has ceased and women moan when they have to look after the farm just for a few days.

Later, he prescribes a woman's responsibilities in the rural homestead. When the weather prevents work in the fields she should busy herself with wool-work, using wool she has prepared earlier. She should check that the slaves are fully occupied; anyone who is ill—or pretending to be—should be taken for treatment as an unproductive slave is no use to anyone; she should never stand still but keep on the move: teaching wool-work, learning wool-work, doing wool-work, checking on the slaves in the kitchen, ensuring that the kitchens, cowsheds and pens are clean; she should periodically clean the sick room.[59] No rest, then, for the woman in Columella's house.

Children

In law, all children fell under the control of the father, the *paterfamilias* in the *familia*, daughters as *filiafamilias*. Women had no legal control over their children—the father had custody of his daughter's children, determined how they were educated, and whom they married; he controlled their property. In practice, the extent of this power was probably quite variable and depended on the relationship between father and daughter; we have already seen how some mothers looked after their children's education. Nevertheless, *patria potestas* prevailed and, for widows and unmarried mothers, influence over their children was further diminished by the guardian. Even after divorce, any children remained under the power of the mother's father, whatever the child's best interests.

Seneca the Younger saw himself as a model of good behaviour, as befits a Stoic upbringing: 'I was obedient to my parents; I did as they told me whether they were fair, unfair or harsh' (*On Kindness* 3, 38, 2). Elsewhere, Seneca lays down some rules to ensure good behaviour:

> We must not allow outbursts of anger in them, or blunt their individuality… a boy's boisterousness increases with too much freedom while it is depressed with repression. Praise lifts the spirits and engenders confidence; too much praise, though, causes arrogance and anger. We must steer him through a middle course, then, deploying carrot and stick. Don't treat him like a slave or degrade him; don't let him beg for anything and don't give him anything for begging. Anything he gets must be as a reward for good behaviour or the promise of good behaviour. In competition with his peers don't let him sulk or lose his temper… he can have leisure time but don't make him lazy or slothful … the boy who always gets his own way, whose anxious mother is forever drying his tears, who always gets one over his pedagogue, that boy will never cope with the real world.
>
> Seneca the Younger, *On Anger*, 2, 21, 1–6

Guardians

A further restriction for women came in the form of guardians—*tutores*. As mothers, wives, or aunts, women themselves could not be guardians; as daughters, they came under the guardianship of male *tutores*. The death of a father or husband meant the appointment of a guardian to look after the affairs of prepubescent (under fourteen) sons, and of daughters of any age—a privilege originally laid down in *Table* V, 1 of the *Twelve Tables* which women, apart from Vestal Virgins, shared with lunatics and spendthrifts (V, 7). *Tutela impuberis* ended at age twelve for girls and was immediately replaced by *tutela mulieris*. Cicero and later Ulpian writing in the early third century

CE both explain that women need guardians because women are socially and intellectually inferior, and they have no legal or commercial sense.[60]

Gaius, in his *Institutiones*, confirmed that, on reaching puberty, boys relinquished their guardians, but not girls—the reason being *propter animi levitatem*—they were considered to be what today some would disparagingly call 'airheads'. Even less flatteringly, when a woman was about to marry, a new guardian would be appointed to arrange her dowry only if the existing one was deaf or insane. Ulpian explains that a guardian's approval is necessary in the following circumstances:

> If they take legal action in accordance with statute or judgment, if they undertake an obligation, if they transact any civil business, if they permit a freedwoman of theirs to cohabit with the slave of another, if they alienate saleable property.
>
> Ulpian, *Regulae* 11, 1, 21, 27, 28

However, in something of a concession, the *Leges Iuliae* and the *Lex Papia-Poppaea* allowed freeborn women to be released from guardianship on the birth of their third child (*ius trium liberorum*), freedwomen on the birth of the fourth; one of the benefits of this independence was that women could now make their own wills. Women had some protection, in theory at least, from rape by their guardians who could face a sentence of deportation and confiscation of property if convicted.

The power of the guardian waned over time as women became more independent and business-minded: women could appeal against guardians' decisions to the magistrates; they could also apply for a guardian to be replaced. We hear much about the commercial activities of Cornelia and Terentia, Cicero's wife, but nothing about the intervention of any guardians.

Concubines

In that they lived in the household, the concubine (*paelex*) was an integral part of some Roman families. Festus records the existence of the *paelex* from around the reign of King Numa in the 8th century where they were forbidden to touch the Temple of Juno—transgressions required a loosening of the hair and the sacrifice of a lamb. Scipio Africanus kept a concubine, famously tolerated—indeed rewarded—by his wife Tertia Aemilia; conservative Cato the Censor kept one and eventually married her.[61] At the Imperial level, both Domitian and Commodus had them. In Plautus, there is, for example, Casina in *Casina*, and Pliny the Younger mentions Lutulla.

Family law

As we have noted, the *Twelve Tables* enshrined the right of fathers to punish their children—be they boys or girls—including the administration of capital punishment, eventually made illegal around 370 CE.[62] Legally speaking, men were always subject to the public justice of the state, but women were sometimes referred to their families for *in camera* trial. Examples are the suppression of the Bacchanalia in 186 BCE when women implicated in the orgiastic rites were handed over to their families for execution; the case of Publilia and Licinia, *nobiles feminae*, accused of poisoning their consular husbands and strangled by their relatives in 154 BCE, according to Livy and Valerius Maximus; and Pomponia Græcina, a distinguished lady, *insignis femina*, wife of the Plautius who returned in triumph from conquering Britannia—she was accused of some foreign superstition (*superstitio externae*), possibly Christianity, and passed over to her husband's judicial decision.[63] 'Following ancient precedent, he heard his wife's case in the presence of kinsfolk and found her innocent' (Tacitus *Annals* 13, 32). This all shows that, in the eyes of the law, women were considered to be the responsibility of the family rather than of the state, even in serious cases such as murder. Augustus's *Lex Julia* put an end to the family kangaroo courts.

Family pets

One of the great paradoxes of Roman society is the way in which the Romans showed great affection towards their family pets but, at the same, time clamoured to watch other animals butchered by gladiators or tearing one another to bits in the arena. It seems that on one day Romans might grieve over and bury their deceased pets with fondness, and the very next day would go to the games and watch scores of lions, rhinos, and other such magnificent beasts massacred before their eyes, baying for their blood.

Most of us are familiar with the image of the guard dog on the *cave canem* ('beware of the dog') mosaic from Pompeii. This, and perhaps Catullus' *passer*, sparrow (or bullfinch), poem and a number of epigraphs and other literary references to companion animals tell us that the family pet was alive and well in ancient Rome.

The mosaic, which was found at the entrance to the House of the Tragic Poet, warns us that a dangerous dog is on guard within, even though it is clearly chained up. Petronius describes a similar scene: 'There on the left as you go in ... was a huge dog with a chain round its neck. It was painted on the wall and over it, in block capitals, was written: Beware of the Dog' (Petronius, *Satyricon* 29). Some archaeologists have argued that the warning was for visitors to be careful not to tread on the small dogs within, possibly Italian greyhounds.

Elsewhere, Molossian hounds are described as baying, terrifying guard dogs in Horace's tale of the town and country mice, while Spartan hounds run amok in Trimalchio's dinner party (Petronius, *Satyricon* 40). Lucretius vividly describes Molossian guard dogs in his *De Rerum Natura* (5, 1063–72) while Petronius introduces his huge, chained guard dog Scylax to his dinner guests as guardian of home and slaves (*Satyricon* 64). The beast re-emerges when Trimalchio's guests try to escape, its barking sending two of them headlong into the fish pool. Meanwhile, Croesus, Trimalchio's boyfriend, has encouraged his obese black pet puppy, Margarita, to attack Scylax— who responds by almost ripping the puppy to shreds.

A century or so before that dog was prowling around The House of the Tragic Poet, the love poet Catullus composed his poem, with distinct erotic undertones, celebrating his mistresses's pet sparrow (*passer*):

Sparrow, my girl's delight with whom she would play, whom she would hold to her breast, for whom, seeking greedily, she would offer her fingertip to provoke sharp nibbles, whenever it pleases my shining desire to have some fun and solace for her grief, I believe, so that her heavy passion may subside. If only I could play with you like she does, and lighten the sad cares of your mind.

Catullus 2

However, the joy is short-lived because in the very next poem we find that the *passer*, her *deliciae*, is dead:

My girlfriend's sparrow is dead, the sparrow, my girl's delight, whom she loved more than her own eyes. For it was honey-sweet and it had known its mistress as well as any girl knew her mother, and it did not move from her lap but hopping around here and there would keep on chirping, only to his mistress.

Catullus 3, 1–6

Catullus' *passer* poem was influential with poets over the next hundred or so years. Ovid wrote an elegy on the death of Corinna's parrot (*psittacus*):

Parrot, the mimic, the winged one from India's East,
is dead—Go, birds, form a flock and follow him to the grave! ...

A burial mound holds his bones—a burial mound that is just the right size –
whose little stone carries a fitting epitaph for him:
'His grave holds one who gave pleasure to his mistress:
his speech to me was cleverer than the speech of other birds'.

Ovid *Amores* 2, 6, 1–2; 59–62

While Martial's epigram on Publius's pet dog Issa, actually references Catullus 2:

Issa is naughtier than Catullus's sparrow. Issa is purer than the kiss of a dove. Issa is more loving than any young girl. Issa is dearer than Indian jewels. The little dog Issa is the pet of Publius. If she complains, you would think she was speaking. She feels both her master's sorrow and the joy. She lies reclined upon his neck, and sleeps, so that not a breath is heard from her... So that her final hour may not carry her off completely, Publius has had her portrayed in a picture, in which you will see an Issa so life-like, that not even she is so like herself. In a word, place Issa and the picture side by side, and you will imagine either both real, or both painted.

Martial 1, 109

translation adapted from Martial, *Epigrams* Book 1. Bohn's Classical Library (1897)

Pet birds were especially popular, and we can add a number of other species to the *passer* and the *psittacus*: nightingales, starlings, ravens, and magpies, for example. The popularity of 'talking' nightingales was so great in the third century CE that Clement of Alexandria was forced to chastise those people who preferred to have them as pets, along with parrots and curlews, rather than discharging their responsibility to look after their fellow humans. Indeed, Seneca the Younger had been no less tolerant in the first century CE when he referred to those who 'thought nothing of raising puppies and birds and other silly pets'.[64]

Sentimentality and affection, however, were probably more typical of the average Roman's attitude to the household pet, as evidenced by Petronius when he tells of a father who kills his son's pet gold finches—his son who is 'mad on birds'—but it is, nevertheless, a silly hobby according to the father who lies that a weasel killed them.[65] Martial's menagerie of pets that his acquaintances indulges perhaps indicates their general popularity, and Martial's contempt for such people. We have a long-eared fox or lynx (*lagalopex*); a gazelle (*dorcas*); Publius's lapdog (as mentioned above); an ugly long-tailed monkey just as ugly as Comius, its owner; a mischievous Egyptian rat; a garrulous magpie, a neck-curling cold skinned serpent; and Telesilla's deceased nightingale, for which she was sufficiently bereaved to erect a burial mound.[66] To Martial, they are all just monsters (*monstra*).

By the early empire, spoiled pets were getting their own solemn funeral epithets, a practice which began with the Greeks in the Hellenistic age.[67] The popular green Indian parrot answered a desire for talking birds, and, according to Pliny the Elder, even greeted emperors; they were, he adds, particularly talkative after a sip of wine: *in vino psittacus*.[68] Pliny tells the story of the shoemaker who owned a raven which was in the habit of greeting Tiberius, Germanicus, and Drusus Caesar; whether the bird ever cheered up the notoriously saturnine emperor is not recorded, but we do know that on its death, it was buried with great ceremony and many a floral tribute. The bier was carried by two Ethiopians preceded by a flautist along the Appian Way. A neighbouring cobbler had killed the bird out of angry jealousy, claiming that its droppings had splattered his shoes; he was lynched by the even angrier mob. Pliny acidly points out that no one avenged the death of Scipio Aemilianus, even though he had destroyed Carthage and Numantia.

We have Pliny to thank for informing us that it was Marcus Laenius Strabo who introduced the aviary to the world when he established one in Brundisium full of different species. Pliny adds, just as acidly, that it was thanks to him that we started imprisoning birds in cages, birds that nature had intended for the skies. By the end of the first century BCE, avaries were all the rage according to Varro and Cicero.[69]

In the *Silvae*, Statius celebrates Melior's parrot in an echo of Ovid's poem:

> Parrot, leader of birds, your owner's eloquent pleasure, clever imitator, Parrot, of the human tongue, what sudden fate brought an end to your talking? Yesterday, sad bird, while we dined, you were near death, though we watched you sampling the banquet's bounty with pleasure, grazing from couch to couch past midnight. And you talked to us, speaking the words you'd learned.
>
> Statius, *Silvae* 2, 4, 1–7

Apuleius reveals that teaching a parrot to swear simply results in an endless repertoire of expletives; the only remedy then is to cut out its tongue or return it to the wild.[70] Pliny the Younger writes of the bonfire of family pets made by Regulus on the funeral pyre of his young son to ensure he enjoyed the pets in the afterlife:

> The boy had a few ponies, some in harness and others not broken in, dogs both big and small, nightingales, parrots and blackbirds—Regulus slew all these at his pyre.
>
> Pliny, *Epistles* 4, 2, 3

Excavations around Roman camps in Britannia have yielded up the bones of ravens—soldiers' pets, no doubt. Persius, Statius, Petronius, and Pliny all mention magpies that were commonly deployed on thresholds to greet visitors.[71]

Children and lovers were given pet names: one of Marcus Aurelius's letters to Fronto describes how he is sitting with his mother musing on what Fronto's daughter, Gratia, might be doing; she is described as a little sparrow—*passercula*.[72] In Plautus's *Asinaria*, Philenium and Leonida exchange endearments with Leonida insisting on pet names:

> PHILENIUM to LEONIDA: Apple of my eye, my rose, my life, my delight, Leonida, do give me the money, and don't sever us lovers asunder.
>
> LEONIDA to PHILENIUM: Call me, then, your little sparrow, your chick, your quail, your pet lamb: tell me that I'm your pet kid or your pet calf.
>
> Plautus, *Asinaria* 3, 3, 103

In his chapter on birds, Pliny the Elder tells us all about talking birds—parrots, parakeets, and magpies. He then goes on to inform us that Nero's mother, Agrippina, owned a talking pet thrush—unique up until then. Britannicus and Nero, as young boys, had a starling and nightingales that spoke Latin and Greek; the birds practised every day and added constantly to their vocabulary. 'Tuition' took place in a private room with a (human) teacher and nothing to disturb the intensive wrote learning ('parrot fashion') that was encouraged and motivated by tit-bits.[73]

Sometimes, parrots, some of which may have been originally kept as pets, ended up on the dinner plate, as in Apicius' recipe; the eccentric emperor Elgabalus served up parrots' brains to his guests.[74]

Other references to birds that might have been kept as pets include nightingales (Pliny *NH* 10, 81); pigeons as carrier pigeons in a military context: Fronto, in his treatise on military strategy tells how Hirtius sent messages to Brutus by pigeon post (*Srategematon* 3, 13, 8); as the prize possessions of pigeon fanciers (Pliny *NH* 10, 110); emperor-saluting parrots (again, Martial 14, 73); a saluting crow (Martial 3, 95 and 14, 74); a loquacious magpie (Martial 14, 76); as well as an ivory cage fit for a bird like Catullus' *passer* (Martial 14, 77).

Pliny rated magpies along with nightingales in terms of loquacity; indeed, their determination to learn new words was so great that they would die in despair if a word failed them or if they forgot a word (*NH* 18, 87).

Greek literature and inscriptional evidence tell how pets received burials—for example we hear of Alexander's horse, a dolphin, a gander, dogs, and a murena (lamprey) all being buried; this, as well as Telesella's nightingale and the cobbler's raven mentioned above would suggest that the practice was not uncommon in Rome. It seems inconceivable that Catullus' *passer* did not receive appropriately reverential funeral rites, as did Martial's Lydia:

> Brought up among the trainers of the amphitheatre, bred for the chase, fierce in the forest, gentle in the house, my name was Lydia, a most faithful servant to my master Dexter, who would not have preferred to me the hound of Erigone, or the dog which followed Cephalus from the land of Crete, and was translated with him to the stars of the light-bringing goddess. I died, not from long years, nor of useless old age, as was the fate of the hound of Ulysses; I was killed by the flashing tooth of a foaming boar, as huge as that of Calydon or that of Erymanthus. Nor do I complain, even though so prematurely hurried to the shades below; I could not have died a nobler death.
>
> Martial 11, 69

Martial's friend Stella, it seems, had written a poem mourning the death of a dove— *columba*—one of those words used as a pet name for a girl (1, 2, 102). Martial rates Stella's *columba* poem greater than Catullus' *passer*, and Stella a poet superior to Catullus (Martial 1, 7).

Aelian has the story of a tame eagle (taken from the Hellenistic historian Phylarchus) raised by a young boy as a younger brother. When the boy fell ill, the eagle kept vigil by his side and refused to eat when the boy did not eat. When the boy died, the eagle flung itself to its death on his funeral pyre (*De Natura Animalium* 6, 29).

Columella recommends keeping peacocks as a hobby or as pets because of their beauty (*De Re Rustica* 8, 11). He is also a devotee of geese, which make excellent guards, better even than dogs; the legend of the cackling geese that famously alerted the Romans during the 390 BCE attack by the Gauls is called to mind; the guard dogs disappointingly remained silent.

The visual arts offer two depictions of pet birds: the *stele* in New York shows a young girl holding two pigeons and kissing the beak of one of them, while in the British Museum we have a vase on which a woman is shown temptingly holding out a dove or pigeon to a not disinterested cat.

Peacocks were kept as pets in Greece and again, there is no reason to suppose that the Romans did not do likewise. The evidence comes from Old Comedy writer Strattis of Chios (fl. around 420 BCE) in his *Pausanias*, and from Anaxandrides' *Melilotus* who asks why you would want a peacock when you could buy two statues for the same money (certainly a statue would be much quieter). Anaxandrides of Athens was a prolific and successful Athenian Middle Comedy dramatist who was active around 376 BCE.

Much the same could be said about hares; they feature frequently on Greek pottery and on the sarcophagus of the Roman emperor Balbinus (r. 238 CE) where a boy is seen holding a hare. Julius Caesar tells us that we Britons did not eat hare, goose or chicken but did keep them for pleasure (*De Bello Gallico* 5, 12). Pet hares feature in wall paintings: one from Trastevere depicts the endearing scene of a woman musician being presented with a baby hare; two paintings from Rome show hares on their haunches on the knees of girls, while a tombstone now in Lincoln cathedral has the moving scene of a boy cuddling his pet hare.

Cats lived a charmed life for centuries in Egypt and were treated like royalty—the penalty for killing a cat, even by accident, was death. The jealous protection of the cat by the Egyptians may explain why their arrival in Greece and Rome came so late—exportation was banned. The first evidence of domestic cats in Italy comes from silver coins from the fifth century BCE minted in Tarentum and Rhegium on which, for example, a boy plays with a cat, teasing it with either a bird or a morsel of food, or where the cat plays with a ball. The cats depicted are so realistic that they must surely have been modelled on domesticated cats roaming around the engravers' houses. Cats also star on Apulian and Campanian vases, examples of which are in the British Museum and depict cats either playing with balls or, in one case, confronting a goose.

The most celebrated images of cats come, of course, from two mosaics found in Pompeii. One shows a cat pawing a partridge with two ducks and other potential meals in a lower section; the other shows a cat threatening two parrots and a dove perched precariously on the rim of a bowl.

Diodorus Siculus tells us how a Roman soldier serving in Egypt in the reign of Ptolemy XI Alexander II (r. 80 BCE) was attacked by an angry mob when he killed a cat by mistake (1, 71), and Herodotus reports that if a cat died in the house then the occupants shaved off their eyebrows (2, 66). The Egyptian word for a cat was 'maou'—the last word in onomatopoeia. Cicero, Ovid, Seneca, and Pliny all refer to the house cat.[75]

The cat—like the weasel, ferret, and snake—performed a role in eradicating mice and rats from the home and may have doubled up as pets, as they do today.[76] Seneca asks why mice fear cats but not dogs. Juvenal, Hyginus (*c.* 64 BCE–17 CE), and Aulus Gellius all refer to the house cat as *aelurus*.[77] Palladius (*fl.* 350 CE) is the first to use the word *cattus* in his *Opus Agriculturae* (20, 8) when he bizarrely recommends them for catching moles in artichoke beds. On a larger scale, Evagrius (*c.* 593 CE) tells us that, as a boy, St Simeon Stylites walked his tame pet panther around on a lead (*Historia Ecclesiastica* 6, 23). In two of his epigrams, Agathias (527–565 CE) records that his house-born cat ate his tame partridge when it should have been pursuing mice (*Anthologia Palatina* 7, 204; 7, 205). In the chapter on medicine below, we will see how Aetius recommended inserting the liver of a cat inside a tube fitted to the woman's left foot as a contraceptive device.

We get some interesting images of domesticated cats in Roman sculpture. There is a fine example of one on a sarcophagus from the first half of the first century CE inscribed with the occupant's name, Calpurnia Felicla—'pussy' (*CIL* 6, 14223). In the Capitoline Museum in Rome, we can see a cat being trained to dance by a woman to the strains of a lyre with a tempting brace of birds suspended above it. The Musée des Antiques in Bordeaux has on display a delightful relief showing a girl holding a kitten while a cockerel pecks at its tail. In Auxerre Museum, a fragmentary statuette has a cat wearing a collar.

There were numerous other pets enjoyed by the Romans. Paintings on vases and reliefs show goats yoked to children's carts while a Pompeian wall painting depicts a woman feeding a branch to a goat in her bedroom. Cicadas competed with songbirds to provide musical entertainment; eleven epigrams describe these pets chirruping away in their specially made reed and osier cages.[78] Pliny, Plutarch, Aulus Gellius, Appian, and Frontinus all refer to Sertorius' pet white fawn.[79] Attic vases show women playing with deer, and deer pulling children's carts; again, nothing exists from Roman times, but there is no reason to believe that the attraction ended with the Greeks. A Dresden terracotta shows a boy with a bowl and a mouse sitting on the rim.

Unsurprisingly, the Roman emperors were less than satisfied with deer and mice. Statius describes for us Domitian's pet lion, appearing at first to rub salt in the lion's wounded pride but concluding with words of sympathy:

What's the good now in quenching your rage, be tamed;
Unlearn crime and the slaughter of men;
Put up with being controlled, obey a less powerful master;
Get used to going to and from your prison cage;

And choosing to leave your captive booty;
To loosing your jaws, to releasing the hand put inside your mouth?
You are dead, trained slayer of bigger creatures.

Statius, Silvae 2, 5, 1–7

Cassius Dio tells how Caracella's lion, Acinaces, shared his dinner table with him and even slept with him (79, 7, 2–3). Aelius Lampridius, one of the six authors of the *Augustan History,* tells us that Antoninus Heliogabalus (21, 1) kept emasculated lions and leopards as pets; Ammianus Marcellinus records that Valentinian kept a pair of ferocious sows in cages near his bedroom (29, 3, 9); they went by the names Goldflake and Innocence.

Seneca, in *De Ira*, teaches how wild animals are mollified by kindness from humans:

See how bulls yield their necks to the yoke, how elephants allow boys and women to dance on their backs unhurt, how snakes glide harmlessly over our chests and in and out of our drinking-cups, how within their dens bears and lions submit to be handled with complacent mouths, and wild beasts fawn upon their master.

Seneca, De Ira 2, 31, 6
translation adapted from Bohn's Classical Library Edition; George Bell and Sons, 1900.

Evidence for pet monkeys go back to the third century BCE when Plautus refers to one in the *Miles Gloriousus*: old Periplectomonos from Ephesus commands his slaves to remove anyone found on his roof pretending to be up there to catch the monkey (160–163); in the *Mercato,* Demipho describes a dream in which he gives a nanny goat to a tame monkey to look after (229–233). A Cathaginian boy is bitten on the hand by his pet monkey in the *Poenulus* (1,073). We have just met Comius' ugly barbary ape.

Pliny describes the pride shown by tame monkeys for their young which have been born inside the house, showing them off, encouraging people to stroke them and hugging them, indeed sometimes hugging them too tightly and cuddling them to death (*NH* 8, 80). What look very much like a pair of domesticated apes feature in a marble relief from the second century CE depicting a butcher's shop in the Via del Foce in Ostia—a kind of living sales aid.

Tame and bejewelled fish seem to have been all the rage. Cicero sneers at the people who think they have died and gone to heaven when the bearded mullet they keep in their ponds feed from their hands (*Ad Atticum* 2, 1, 7); Martial delights in the myriad fish at balmy Formiae, which swim obediently towards their master in capitulation to a show of leisurely, effortless fishing (10, 30, 22–4); Pliny tells how Antonia Minor adorned her lamprey with gold and earrings and how they were passed down to Claudius and then to Agrippina, mother of Nero, after Antonia's death as an heirloom (*NH* 9, 55). The fishpond involved was located in Antonia's opulent summer house in Bauli (Bacoli today) south of the racey resort of Baiae. The people of Arethusa in Chalcis were witnessed by Athenaeus (*Deipnosophistae* 8, 331) with their tame mullets and eels adorned with silver and gold earrings being fed green cheese and scraps from sacrificial victims. Presumably, the rings were inserted in the gills in the same way as they are into the lobes of ears or other parts of the body. Aelian (d. 222 CE) records how Crassus the Censor put earrings and a necklace on his female *murena* which had been trained to respond to his voice. When it died, he mourned it as he would a daughter and buried it (*De Natura Animalium* 9, 10).

Equally bizarre was the sadistic behaviour of Publius Vedius Pollio (d. 15 BCE) whom we shall meet again in the chapter on slavery. Lampreys, trained to kill, brought out the worst in Pollio and the best in Augustus, his friend for a while. Whenever Vedius was irritated by his slaves, he had them thrown into a pool of lampreys which proceeded to tear the unfortunate victim to shreds. On one occasion, Vedius was about to despatch a slave who had broken a crystal cup, but Augustus, who was a guest at the time, was so horrified that he halted the execution attempt and had all of Pollio's drinking vessels smashed to pieces. Augustus then went on to demolish Vedius' sumptuous villa, which he had inherited after the sadist's death.

Varro tells us about his friend, Quintus Hortensius, the orator, who would never eat the contents of his pool, but bought all his fish from the market instead (*De Re Rustica* 3, 17, 5); he would rather sell a mule than a bearded mullet. Hortensius was just as solicitous when his fish were sickening as he was over an ill slave. When his *murena* died, he too wept. When Julius Caesar was celebrating his triumph and wanted Gaius Hirrius's *murenae* to show off at his banquets, Gaius Hirrius refused to sell them and would only lend them to Caesar: Varro (3, 17, 3) puts the number of fish at 2,000, Pliny at 6,000 (*NH* 9, 81).

According to Martial (4, 30, 3–7), Domitian had a fish pool at Baiae populated with fish which had been given personal names, recognised the emperor and came swimming up to lick his hand when he called their names.

Puppies found themselves involved in a whole range of activities, all of which were rather unfortunate and unsavoury. It is possible that some of them at least started off as family pets. We shall see how quack doctors used seven day old puppy brains in a cure for glaucoma; how Ovid saw puppies eviscerated in a sacrifice to Robigus, god of mildew; and how a voodoo doll was fashioned into the shape of a puppy dog and implanted with the eyes of a dead bat in a curse to make an unresponsive women sleepless so that she would sleep with the curser.

Non-poisonous snakes had a good reputation as pets in ancient Rome, in contrast to the eternal vilification and damnation they earned in Jewish and Christian culture. They were representative of beneficent spirits of the dead, they had apotropaic characteristics and were associated with deities of healing and fertility.

Pets, then, of all kinds were an essential feature of Roman households and families, at least for those who could afford extra mouths to feed. As today, they were often terribly indulged but gave great pleasure and comfort to their owners. The death of a pet sometimes evoked considerable grief and burials fit for a human.

3

Marriage, Divorce, and Adultery

Marriages were pre-arranged by the father in keeping with his position of power at the head of the family; in the absence of a father, a guardian or some other male relative would take responsibility. Girls seldom had a say in whom they married. Catullus prescribes the very business-like protocol of marriage; marriage not only makes the young girl dear to her husband but also less inimical (*invisa*) to her father:

> Young girl, do not fight against such a match. It is not right for you to struggle against the man to whom your father has handed you over—your father and your mother whom you must obey. Your virginity is not all yours, part of it is your parents': a third is your father's, a third your mother's, and only a third is yours: don't fight against these other two, who have given their rights to their son-in-law, along with the dowry.
>
> Catullus, 62, 63–70

Generally speaking, the Roman woman was essentially domestic and domesticated; her function as a wife was to bear children and keep the home in good order while her husband went about his work, advancing his career, or perfecting his trade. The very word for marriage (*matrimonium*) is rooted in *mater*, meaning mother—marriage literally spelled motherhood. In the early days of the Republic, the Roman woman married into a state of *manus*—dependence before the law, she had little chance of initiating divorce, no rights over property, and no jurisdiction over her children. If a woman's husband died when she was pregnant, the baby became the property of her late husband's family. A woman was someone else's property throughout her life: first her father's, then her husband's and finally, depending on circumstances, her sons'. She was always defined as daughter, wife, or mother. If a woman's father or husband died, she did not become independent; a guardian was appointed to look after her affairs. Even when *manus* marriage became obsolete, to be replaced by a freer form of marriage, and when divorce became more common, things changed little for the average woman. Livy (34, 7) asserts that 'a woman's enslavement lasts as long as her male relatives are still alive'.

Getting engaged

Betrothal was sealed with a kiss and the slipping on of an iron ring (*anulus pronubus*) onto the third finger of the future bride's left hand. According to Aulus Gellius, this finger was significant because it is connected by the autonomic nervous system to the heart. A party—the *sponsalia*—ensued. The termination of an engagement could be initiated by either party without penalty; it simply required the doom-laden words *condicione tua non utor* (literally, 'I don't abide by your terms'), for the man to return any part of the dowry that had been paid, and for the woman to return any gifts from her intended husband.

Statius' *epithalamium* (*Silvae* 1, 2) gives some detail about the terms of an engagement in an elite family in the first century CE. The divinely beautiful Violentilla surpasses all the *matronae* of Latium; she is urged by the goddess Venus to make the most of her beauty and renounce her chastity for Lucius Arruntius Stella, her soon-to-be husband. She is financially independent but her mind is richer still. Much of the content of the wedding song is conventional but the allusion to wealth and intelligence is an interesting indication, perhaps, of what Stella was looking for in a wife.

Plutarch has plenty advice for bride and groom in his *Moralia*, in the section entitled *Advice to Bride and Groom*:

> So you two must think those couples to be wrong who, for the sake of pleasure occupy the same bed, but sleep in separate beds when they get into some angry argument; they ought, instead, especially at these times, invoke Aphrodite, who is the best doctor for such disorders… At all times and in all places a wife should try to avoid any conflict with her husband, and a husband with his wife, but they ought to be especially careful not do this in the privacy of their bedchamber… the disagreements, recriminations, and angry passions which the bed generates are not easily settled in another place and in a different time.
>
> Plutarch, *Moralia* 138–9
> translation adapted from Loeb Classical Library edition, 1928

Child brides

Roman girls could be betrothed at twelve and married within the year.[1] An example of a thirteen-year-old wife can be found on a funerary inscription from Gaul; it remembers Blandinia Martiola:

> To the everlasting memory of Blandinia Martiola, a girl without fault, who lived eighteen years, nine months, five days. Pompeius Catussa, a Sequanian citizen and plasterer, dedicates this to his wife who was a woman beyond compare and always

kind to him; she lived with him five years, six months, eighteen days without any shadow of a fault … you, who are reading this, go and bathe in the Baths of Apollo, just as I used to do with my wife. I wish I still could.

CIL 13, 1983

Aurelia Philematium's marriage at seven years of age was precocious even by Roman standards; the first century BCE inscription in memory of this butcher and his wife unusually gives both sides of the story. Lucius Aurelius inscribes that his loving and much loved wife, Aurelia Philematium, was devoted and dutiful:

Aurelius Hermia, freedman of Lucius, butcher on the Viminal hill. This woman, who has died before me, chaste of body, loving of mind, my one and only wife, lived faithful to her equally faithful husband, ever optimistic even when times were bad, with mutual devotion.

However, we do not have to take Aurelius' word; she herself writes about herself:

[Aurelius was] chaste, modest, unsullied by the common herd, faithful to my husband, whom I am now sadly without; he was freedman to this same Lucius and both in fact and in truth more than and beyond a parent. He took me to his heart at the age of seven years. At the age of forty years I am in death's power. My husband flourished in the eyes of everyone due to my constant dutifulness.

CIL 1, 1221

They had known each other since she was seven, some thirty-three years previously.

There is plenty of evidence attesting the early age of marriage. Pliny had already been married twice before when, aged forty or so, he wed the much younger Calpurnia Fabata in 100 CE. We have seen Quintilian's grief at the death of his nineteen-year-old wife, the mother of two deceased sons even then. We have also noted noted Pliny's concern that the young Minicia died before she could be married off. Faggura, wife of Julianus, was married and a mother by the time she was fourteen years old.[2] Tullia, Cicero's daughter, got engaged when she was twelve, married at sixteen, and was widowed when she was twenty-two. Octavia, the Emperor Claudius' daughter, married at thirteen while Agrippina, mother of Nero, married when she was twelve. On the other hand, some elite women married later: Julia, Caesar's daughter, was twenty when she married Pompey; Agrippina Maior was about eighteen when she and Germanicus tied the knot in 4 CE; and Antonia Minor was twenty or so when she married Drusus.

Inscriptional evidence backs up the early age of female marriage, particularly in the middle and upper class families who were more likely to be able to afford tombstones. From the 171 inscriptions in a recent study, sixty-seven (39 per cent) showed women married before they were fifteen and 127 before age nineteen (74 per cent).[3]

Marital discord

Cicero gives us an interesting insight into an unhappy marriage:

> As to what you say in your letter about your sister, she will confirm the trouble I
> have gone to see that my brother Quintus should show her the affection which she
> deserves. Believing that he tends often to be angry with her, I wrote to him in such
> a way as I thought would not hurt his feelings as a brother, while giving him some
> good advice him being younger than me, and rebuking him for getting it wrong. I am
> happy that the outcome is, judging from the frequent letters received from him since,
> that everything is as it should be and as we should want it to be.
>
> Cicero, *Ad Atticum* 1, 5, 1

However, all was not well, as a later letter reveals:

> I never saw my brother so kind and conciliatory towards your sister as he was on
> that occasion…when we got to Arcanum Quintus said, in the kindest way possible,
> 'Pomponia, you ask the ladies to come in; I will invite the men.' I thought that nothing
> could have been more courteous, not just in what he said, but also in the look on his face.
> But she, so that we could all hear, shouted 'I am just a stranger here!' … Quintus said
> to me, 'There, that's what I have to put up with every day!' … indeed, she had annoyed
> even me: her retort had been so needlessly acrimonious, both in word and look. I hid
> my irritation and we all sat down apart from her. Quintus sent her dishes out from the
> table, which she rejected. I never saw anyone more even tempered than my brother, or
> angrier than your sister … He told me that she had refused to sleep with him.
>
> Cicero, *Ad Atticum* 5, 1, 3–4

After their divorce, Quintus thought better of remarrying, preferring instead the
sanctuary of a single bed (14, 13, 5).

Plutarch gives us a perceptive case study. Criticised for divorcing Papiria when all looked
well with the marriage from the outside, Aemilius Paullus gives his side of the story:

> It is a mistake for a woman to rely on her wealth, her breeding and her looks; she
> should think more of the qualities which affect her husband's life, of those traits of
> character which bring harmony to domestic relationships. Instead of being impassive
> or irritating all the time, she must be sympathetic, inoffensive and affectionate … it is
> a steady drip drip of small imperceptible needlings and irritations, coming day after
> day between a man and his wife, which destroys the marriage.
>
> Plutarch, *Moralia* 141A
> translation adapted from Loeb Classical Library edition, 1928;
> see also Plutarch, *Aemilius Paullus* 5,2ff.

Same-sex marriages

Celebrity sham marriages were not unknown during the early Empire: Nero 'married' a male lover, Pythagoras, in 64 CE; according to Suetonius, in between raping a Vestal Virgin and committing incest with his mother, Nero had a young boy, Sporus, castrated before marrying him. Around the same time, Sempronius Gracchus married a boy cornet player with a dowry of 400,000 sesterces. Valeria Messalina, while wife of Claudius, astonishingly married a common Roman citizen, much to the surprise and indignation of her husband, the emperor of Rome (Tacitus, *Annals* 15, 37, 8f; Suetonius, *Nero* 28,1; Juvenal 2, 117ff). Martial describes the same-sex wedding between Callistratus and Afro, complete with dowry.

Matchmaking and the dowry (*dos*)

Most marriages, we know, were arranged by the *paterfamilias*, or by another male relative, as a function of his *patria potestas*. Just how important a duty this was, and how vital it was to find the right match, is shown in a letter by Pliny to Junus Mauricus who had asked him to find a husband for his niece.[4]

> You ask me to keep an eye out for a husband for your brother's daughter: you do well to pick me me for such a task… I would have had to look long and hard had Minicius Acilianus not been to hand… there is nothing to be found in his entire family which will fail to please you, just as much as if it were your own family.
>
> Pliny, *Epistles* 1, 14

The father's consent was a legal requirement where one or both of the partners were under *patria potestas*; however, not surprisingly, some older couples took the initiative and made their own decisions. Cicero's daughter, Tullia, much to her absent-in-exile father's dismay but with her mother's complicity, proceeded with her third marriage to the infamous Publius Cornelius Dolabella.[5] Tullia's previous marriages were less controversial. She was betrothed at twelve in 67 BCE to her first husband, Gaius Calpurnius Piso Frugi and married him in 63 BCE. In 57 BCE, he died and she was betrothed to Furius Crassipes when she was twenty-three; the subsequent marriage was dissolved in 51 BCE.[6]

Arranged marriages were not necessarily the emotionally arid, restrictive, and restricting contracts they are often made out to be; as in various societies today, they probably involved more mutual consent, *concordia*, than we have actual evidence for. They were prudent arrangements designed to protect and consolidate the family politically, economically and socially. No doubt, Roman parents would have argued that the arrangement was intended to be in the daughter's best interests; indeed, few twelve or thirteen year olds would have been in a position to make an informed decision about whom to marry.

A dowry, certainly among the wealthier classes, was an expected, though not legally required, and a welcome item in the bride's baggage. By the early Empire, around one million sesterces payable in three annual instalments was the norm among the more comfortable classes. The dowry became the husband's property but was recoverable on divorce, or if the husband died after the death of his father-in-law. Valerius Maximus records that Gnaeus Cornelius Scipio Calvus, while on active service in Spain requested leave to go home to arrange his daughter's dowry; the Senate was reluctant to allow such a key commander to leave the field and voted a dowry out of the public purse worth 40,000 asses to keep him in the line—a small amount compared with later dowries, but significant enough for the time.[7]

The precedent for such public largesse was set around 280 BCE when the Senate voted a dowry for the daughter of the famously incorruptible Gaius Fabricius Luscinus Monocularis whose family was in financial straits.

Polybius tells how Scipio Africanus generously paid the dowries of his two daughters in one-off payments to their respective husbands, Tiberius Gracchus and Scipio Nasica.

> Next he had to pay the daughters of the great Scipio, the sisters of his adoptive father, half of their portion. Their father had agreed to give each of his daughters fifty talents [about £1.25 million today], and their mother had paid the half of this to their husbands on their marriage, but not the other half because she died before she could. So Scipio had to pay this debt to his father's sisters. According to Roman law, the part of the dowry still due had to be paid to the ladies within three years, the personal property being first handed over within ten months according to Roman custom. But Scipio at once ordered his banker to pay each of them the whole twenty-five talents in ten months.
>
> Polybius 31, 27
> translation adapted from Loeb Classical Library edition, 1922–1927

In 50 BCE, Cicero was unable to find the money to pay the third instalment of Tullia's dowry in her marriage to Dolabella. Cicero toyed with the idea of arranging a divorce and writing off the first two instalments that had been paid.[8]

> Concerning the dowry, I implore you, in the name of all the gods, to get on the case and protect that poor girl who has been reduced to distress through my non-payment and carelessness. Use my funds and your own if you can without any inconvenience. You say that she is penniless: do not allow this state of affairs to continue.
>
> Cicero, *Ad Atticum* 11, 2, 2

Financial embarrassment came again in 47 BCE when he divorced Terentia and had to find the money to repay the dowry; his scheme to remarry and win a new dowry failed when the marriage to Publilia, his well-off ward, ended after a few months.[9] Terentia, however, remarried and lived to the age of 103.[10]

Aemilius Paulus married off one of his daughters, Aemilia Paulla Secunda, to a member of the illustrious, though by then not so affluent, Aelia dynasty—Q. Aelius Tubero—giving two pound in silver as a dowry from the booty collected after his victory over Perseus of Macedon at the Battle of Pydna in 171 BCE.[11]

We need go no further than Pliny to realise the importance of the dowry: twice he generously contributes to the dowries of young brides. One to the daughter of Quintilianus who needed clothes and a retinue of servants appropriate to her new husband's, Nonius Celer's, social standing; the other to Calvina, a relative of his who was deep in debt:

TO CALVINA.
    However, I am now the sole creditor … When your father was alive, and just before you were to be married, I put 100,000 sesterces towards your dowry, in addition to the sum which your father assigned as your wedding portion, out of my own pocket … Moreover, I authorise you to enter as paid whatever sum your father owed to me.

Pliny, *Epistles* 2, 4

Aulus Gellius records that dowry recovery had become so complicated by the end of the Republic that Sulpicius Rufus wrote a book on it.[12] On divorce, a husband whose wife had been found guilty of adultery might retain one sixth of the dowry; as he would have custody of the children, he would also keep one sixth for each child up to a maximum of three children. Repayments were made in three instalments unless the husband had been proven adulterous in which case he repaid it in one lump sum. After Augustus' *Julian* laws, a wife found guilty of adultery was punished by exile and a fine equal to half her dowry.

The dowry was in no way a gift to the husband; its purpose was to help defray the extra costs incurred in accommodating and maintaining the wife and possibly her slaves. The dowry was usually invested in land with only the profits available to spend.

Adultery

We have seen how double standards persisted in how extra-marital sex and adultery were perceived. An adulterous husband attracted no stigma; an adulterous woman did, and much worse, as Cato the Elder tells: if a man discovers his wife's adulterous behaviour, he can kill her with impunity; when the boot is on the other foot, she can do absolutely nothing.

I have written down the words of Marcus Cato's words from the his speech entitled On the Dowry, in which it is also written that husbands could legally kill wives taken by surprise in adultery: 'When a man sues for divorce,' he says, 'he judges the woman as a censor would, and has full power if she has done any wrong or hideous act; if she has been drinking, she is punished; if she has committed adultery with another man, she is condemned to death.' Regarding the legality surrounding the execution it was written: 'If you catch your wife in adultery, you may with impunity kill her without a trial; but if you yourself should commit adultery or be an adulterer, she must not dare to lay a finger on you; it is not legal.'

Aulus Gellius, Noctes Atticae 10, 23, 5.

We should perhaps question some of the stories narrated by satirists Horace and Juvenal about cuckolded husbands subjecting their wives' lovers to castration, beatings, being urinated on by the kitchen slaves, anal rape by the husband or his slaves, or anal penetration with a red mullet.

Under the *Lex Julia* (18 BCE), women convicted of adultery joined that group of fallen and stigmatised women which included prostitutes, actresses, dancing girls, women with criminal records—collectively, the shameful (*probrosae*) and were forbidden to marry freeborn citizens of Rome. They could not testify in a court of law, nor could they, while unmarried, inherit. Prostitution was sometimes the only escape.

Here are some excerpts from the Julian laws and other, similar moral legislation:

From now on, no one will commit rape or adultery knowingly or with malice aforethought. The law applies both to him who abets and he who commits the crime.

The Julian Law to control adultery punishes not only those who damage the marriages of others but also who commit debauchery by seducing or raping, with or without force, a virgin or respectable widow.

A husband who profits from the adultery is to be flogged.

A husband is allowed to kill an adulterer who is a pimp, actor, slave, criminal or freedman caught in the act with his wife in his own home but not in the home of his father-in-law.

Acta Divi Augusti, Rome 1945: 99, 113–116, 123, 126

Adultery legislation in the *Lex Julia* states:

Public prosecutions are as follows....the *Lex Julia* for the suppression of adultery punishes with death not only those who dishonour the marriage bed of another but also those who indulge in unspeakable lust with males. The same *Lex Julia* also punishes the offence of seduction, when a person, without the use of force, deflowers a virgin or seduces a respectable widow. The penalty imposed by the statute on such offenders is the confiscation of half their estate if they are of respectable standing, corporal punishment and banishment in the case of people of the lower orders.

Institutes of Justinian 4, 18, 2–3

But as regards the provisions of the *Lex Julia*....a man who confesses that he has committed the offence [i.e. adultery] has no right to ask for a remission of the penalty on the ground that he was under age; nor, as I have said, will any remission be allowed if he commits any of those offences which the statute punishes in the same way as adultery; as, for example, if he marries a woman who is detected in adultery and he declines to divorce her, or where he makes a profit from her adultery, or accepts a bribe to conceal illicit intercourse which he detects, or lends his house for the commission of adultery or illicit intercourse within it; youth, as I said, is no excuse in the face of clear enactments, when a man who, though he appeals to the law, himself transgresses it.

Digest 4, 4, 37

Augustus made a bid to increase marriage and the birth rate:

[Augustus] imposed heavier taxes on unmarried men and women without husbands; on the other hand, he offered awards for marriage and childbearing. Because there were more males than females among the nobility, he allowed anyone (except for senators) to marry freedwomen, and decreed that children of such marriages would be legitimate.

Dio Cassius, 54, 16, 1–1

He reformed the laws, completely overhauling some of them, such as the sumptuary law, and the laws on adultery and chastity, that on bribery, and marriage of the various classes.

Because of the greater severity in the emendation of this last one than the others, because of the active opposition he was unable to get it approved except by abolishing or mitigating the penalty, conceding a three-year grace-period before remarriage and increasing the rewards for having children… Moreover, when he found out that the law was being avoided through engagements to young girls and frequent divorces, he put a time limit on engagements and clamped down on divorce.

Suetonius, Life of Augustus 34

Syra, in Plautus' *Mercator*, vocalises the hypocrisy:

If a husband has been keeping a mistress without his wife knowing and the wife gets to know, the husband gets off with impunity; if the wife so much as goes outside the house without her husband knowing, the husband gets a pretext and the marriage is over. I wish the law was the same for the husband as for the wife; a good wife is happy with one husband so why shouldn't the husband be content with one wife? … if men were punished in the same way…as those women who are blamed for being guilty of one indiscretion, there would be more divorced men than there are women now.

Plautus, *Mercator* 823–9.

Ovid is all for adultery. To Ovid, the man who worries about his wife's adultery is nothing less than a peasant: *rusticus est* (*Amores* 3, 4, 37). Ovid can advise where to pick up all types of girls, including sophisticated women—*cultissima femina*; the games are literally crawling with sophisticated women:

Don't forget the races … no need here for sign language for secret messages, nor a nod of the head to tell you she's up for it: you can sit right next to your lady: nothing's forbidden, press your thigh against hers … the rows of seats force you close together, the girl is touched because of the rules of the place. Now find a reason for friendly conversation.

Ovid, *Ars Amatoria* 1, 135–163

Even more explicit are his instructions on how to conduct an adulterous affair in front of the husband at a dinner party:

Your husband too will be at the same dinner party as us. I only hope that it's that man's last meal! Shall I look at my beloved girl just like any other guest? ... When he sinks into the couch and when you recline there, put on the expression of modesty itself—and surreptitiously touch my foot! Watch me and my nods, and loquacious expression: pick up their furtive messages and respond in kind. I'll speak eloquent words without actually speaking, with eyebrows: you can read words from my fingers, words marked out in wine. When you recall the sexiness of our sex, touch your beautiful cheeks with your tender thumb. If you're silently complaining about anything pull your earlobe down gently. When what I do, and say, pleases you, light of my life, keep twisting your ring round with your fingers. Touch your hands on the table, as if you were praying, when you wish your husband much well-deserved malice.

Ovid, *Amores* 1, 4

At the imperial level, Scribonia was divorced by Augustus because she would not tolerate his affairs; her successor, Livia, was much more tolerant and lasted much longer. Claudius' erring wives were sensible enough to ensure that his bed was warmed by surrogates. The double standard was not lost on Plutarch: 'a husband who bars his wife from the pleasures in which he himself indulges is like a man who surrenders to the enemy and tells his wife to go on fighting' (Plutarch, *Moralia* 145a).

Suetonius tells us that Augustus' affairs were motivated not through lust but by a need for subterfuge, using the women to expose the intrigues of their partners, his political opponents. Lust, though, was probably the driving force:

> Mark Antony ... accuses him him of taking the wife of a consul from the dining table, in front of her husband, into a bedroom, and bringing her back to the meal, her ears very red, and her hair all over the place... But he always retained his sex drive, and, as he grew older, he would seduce young girls who were procured for him, from everywhere, even by [Livia], his own wife.
>
> Suetonius, *Augustus* 67, 69

In 18 BCE, Augustus, no doubt all the wiser from personal experience, was so concerned about the permissiveness in his Empire, particularly the growing infrequency of marriage, the increasing levels of adultery, and the falling birth rate, that he introduced the *Lex Julia de maritandis ordinibus* and other moral legislation in a bid to reduce adultery, encourage marriage, and increase the population in Italy. Romans needed to be reminded what marriage was for—producing children. Plautus said many years before: 'I believe that the reason for taking a wife is to produce children' (Plautus, *Captivi* 889).

We have already seen how the *Laudatio Turiae* highlighted the fact that the marriage that ended in the death of one of the partners rather than in divorce had become, it seems, something of a rarity. Augustus was intent on restoring the old ways.

Adultery (*adulterium*) had always been a private affair—a civil matter—often dealt with within the family; but now, it was open to glaring public scrutiny. A cuckolded husband had to divorce his wife within sixty days; failure to do so might result in prosecution for complicity and possible punishment as an adulterer himself. Where found guilty, the wife and her lover were exiled to separate islands; she lost half her dowry and one third of her property; he lost half his property. A man who subsequently married an adulteress committed a criminal offence; under Constantine, both parties were sentenced to death.[13] Augustus' own adulterous daughter, Julia, was a notable convict under this law, and was exiled to Pandateria (modern day Ventotene) in the Tyrhennian Sea.

Divorce

Divorce was not a very complicated procedure– it simply required the evaporation of *affectio maritalis* (the intention to be husband and wife) by one or both parties. By the end of the Republic, divorce was relatively common, probably much more so among the upper and middle classes than the lower classes for whom there is less information and evidence and little to be gained apart from the prospect of further poverty. We

have to treat the reports of rampant divorce with caution as some of the liter
evidence comes from Seneca, Juvenal, and Martial—not the most objective of soc
commentators—who misogynistically saw it as another sign of permissiveness among
women: 'the woman who marries so frequently doesn't actually marry—she's a legal
adulteress (*adultera lege est*)' (Martial 6,7).

Indeed, a prostitute offends him less than a serial divorcer does. Rapsaet-Charlier's
study of 562 women of senatorial rank and their marital activity between 10 BCE and
200 CE revealed only twenty-seven definite and twenty-four possible divorces, twenty
of which were in imperial families, mainly Julio-Claudians.[14] Five of the definite
divorces were claimed by one woman, Vistilla, who, Pliny the Elder tells us, had seven
children by six different husbands.[15] In Roman divorce, the father usually had custody
over the children, a situation that would be a powerful factor in a wife's decision to
make the break.

Marriage and divorce were often a political expedients for elite men. The merry-go-
round of political marriage is well-illustrated by a glance at the five wives of Pompey.
Antistia was his first wife, the daughter of a praetor called Antistius whom Pompey
impressed when defending himself against a charge of possessing stolen goods in 86
BCE. Antistius offered Pompey his daughter's hand, and Pompey accepted, but things
ended badly; Antistia's father was executed because of his connection with Pompey,
and her bereft mother committed suicide. In 82 BCE, Sulla persuaded Pompey to
divorce Antistia so that he could marry his stepdaughter, Aemilia. Aemilia was
pregnant by her husband, M. Acilius Glabrio, and reluctant to marry Pompey; she
eventually did, but died in childbirth. Q. Mucius Scaevola was the father of Pompey's
third wife, Mucia Tertia, whom he married in 79 BCE. Their marriage lasted until
62 BCE, and during this time they had a daughter, Pompeia, and two sons, Gnaeus
and Sextus. According to Asconius, Plutarch, and Suetonius, Mucia was unfaithful—
Suetonius and Cicero allege she had an affair with Caesar—and Pompey divorced her.
In 59 BCE, Pompey married Caesar's daughter Julia, who was already engaged to Q.
Servilius Caepio. Caepio took umbrage, so Pompey offered him his own daughter in
Julia's place—although Pompeia was engaged to Sulla's son, Faustus, at the time. Julia
miscarried soon after fainting at seeing blood-stained clothing, which she had taken
to indicate that her husband had been killed. In 54 BCE, Julia fell pregnant again, but
died in childbirth; her infant daughter died a few days later. Pompey's fifth wife was
Cornelia, daughter of Metellus Scipio and the widow of Publius Crassus.

Divorce (along with death) was a significant factor in spawning second and third
marriages. In the early days of the Republic, serial marriage was, however, rare; Plutarch
says that divorce was restricted to men divorcing women on certain specific grounds:

> [Romulus] also enacted certain laws, and among them one that was quite severe,
> which forbids a wife to leave her husband, but allows a husband to divorce his wife
> for using poisons, for substituting children, and for adultery; but if a man sues for
> divorce for any other reason, the law prescribes that half his estate shall go to his

vife, and the other half be dedicated to Ceres; anyone who sues his wife will make a sacrifice to the gods of the lower world.

Plutarch, *Romulus* 22

Translation adapted from *The Parallel Lives by Plutarch* Vol. I,
Loeb Classical Library 1914

According to Dionysius of Halicarnassus, such restrictions meant that were no divorces at all in the first 520 years of Rome's existence:

> Other offences, however, were judged by her relations together with her husband; among them was adultery, or where she had been found to have drunk wine—something which the Greeks would look upon as the least of all faults. For Romulus permitted the families to punish both these acts with death, them being the most serious offences a woman could be guilty of, since he looked upon adultery as the source of reckless folly, and drunkenness as the source of adultery. Both these offences continued for a long time to be punished by the Romans with merciless severity. The wisdom of this law concerning wives is attested by the length of time it was in force; for it is agreed that over 520 years no marriage was ever dissolved at Rome. But it is said that in the 137th Olympiad [231 BCE], in the consulship of Marcus Pomponius and Gaius Papirius, Spurius Carvilius Ruga, a man of distinction, was the first man to divorce his wife, and that he was obliged by the censors to swear that he had married for the purpose of having children (his wife, it seems, was infertile); yet because of his action, though it was based on necessity, he was ever afterwards despised by the people.

Dionysius of Halicarnassus 2, 25, 7

Translation adapted from *The Roman Antiquities of Dionysius of Halicarnassus* Vol. I,
Loeb Classical Library edition, 1937

Whether it is true or not, the case is interesting in itself: Ruga was not required to pay the penalty even though his grounds were technically spurious; a legal precedent was thus set, allowing men to divorce their wives, for any number of reasons, with virtual impunity. One of the consequences of this was the introduction of pre-marital contracts to legislate for the return and recovery of dowries (*actio rei uxoriae*).

The following settlement was made in 13 BCE between a couple, Zois and Antipater, living in Egypt, who 'agree that they have separated from one another and severed their arrangement to live together'—their *affectio maritalis* is no more; the dowry (120 drachmas worth of clothing and some gold earrings) is returned and they agree that the marriage contract is null and void. Both are free to remarry.[16]

Dowry recovery was, not surprisingly, open to abuse. Valerius Maximus tells how a Caius Titinius, married to Fannia, made a claim to retain her dowry when he divorced her on the grounds of her alleged *stuprum*—adultery. The judge, Caius Marius, knew that Titinius had foreknowledge of Fannia's louche character and had only married her in order to procure the dowry. Fannia got off with a nominal fine; Titinius received a fine equal in value to the dowry. Fannia was able to return the favour to Marius when she later concealed him during his flight from Sulla.[17]

At the highest level, the desire for successful political advancement was sufficient grounds for casual divorce. Plutarch tells how Quintus Hortensius Hortalus, the orator, tried to forge close links with Cato by requesting the hand of his daughter, then already married to Bibulus; Cato refused but did agree to divorce his wife, Marcia, so that Hortensius could marry her instead. Cato gave Marcia away at the wedding. Hortensius died a few years later, there were no children from the marriage and Cato remarried Marcia, then a very rich woman.[18]

We cannot know how frequent this wife swapping was, but it did recur. Suetonius cites an example of a political marriage merry-go-round of Byzantine complexity in his *Life of Augustus*: here, Octavian is either betrothed or married and divorced in rapid succession to three women. On this path of marital carnage were strewn: one fiancée, Claudia (stepdaughter of Mark Antony and barely of marriageable age) whom he divorced while she was still a virgin after relations broke down with Fulvia, his mother-in-law; Scribonia—married twice before to consuls—divorced when he grew tired of her nagging about his infidelity; and then Livia Drusilla, pregnant and already married and his eventual long-term wife. Julia, his daughter by Scribonia, is, in turn, married off three times to Marcellus, Octavian's sister Octavia's son, a mere boy; then to Marcus Agrippa, already married with children to one of Marcellus' sisters; and then to Tiberius whom he forced into a divorce even though he was then married with children to a pregnant wife.

Pompey, who had five wives, was another serial divorcee; he divorced his first wife to marry Aemilia, stepdaughter of Sulla—at the time, Aemilia was pregnant and settled in marriage.

So that adultery could be proven in law, divorce became notifiable and a divorce court was established in which seven adult males had to witness the formal declaration of divorce. Famous cases of adultery by women leading to divorce include Pompey *v.* Mucia, Lucullus *v.* Claudia, and Caesar *v.* Pompeia—after the Bona Dea scandal, not for adultery but for being implicated in a sacrilegious incident which brought ignominy on the state and on the sanctity of the Vestal Virgins, as the High Priest's wife must be above suspicion.

Under the new legislation, husbands lost the right to kill their wives and fathers their daughters; they still could still slay their wives' partners if the transgressor was a slave or freedman and if *in flagrante delicto* in the marital home. In what can only have caused a certain amount of dangerous confusion, fathers were still allowed to murder their adulterous daughters if they simultaneously killed the adulterer. Valerius Maximus provides one of the few recorded cases of women being put to death by their fathers:

> When [Pontius Aufidius, a Roman knight] found out that his daughter's viriginity had been betrayed to her teacher, Fannius Saturninus, not content that the slave

suffer the death penalty, Pontius Aufidius killed the girl too. So, far from celebrating a defiled wedding ceremony, he led the procession at a bitter funeral.

Valerius Maximus 6, 1, 3 and 6

A man could now be prosecuted if he committed adultery with a married woman, if he condoned his wife's adulterous behaviour, or if he indulged in *stuprum* with a mistress who was not a registered prostitute. The law was amended by Tiberius to put an end to the practice where 'respectable' women registered as whores to facilitate their extra-marital affairs.

Not surprisingly, Augustus' laws were generally unpopular—they amounted to what today we would term the workings of a 'nanny state'; consequently, they were diluted somewhat by the 9 CE *lex Papia Poppaea*, named after the consuls of that year.

Efforts were made to circumvent the legislation: Suetonius says that attempts by men to delay marriage and the birth of children through engagements to young, prepubescent girls were repulsed with stricter legislation relating to subsequent divorces and the length of betrothals. Fiancés had been exempt from the penalties paid by bachelors (*caelibes*); now, Augustus voided betrothals unless the marriage took place within two years. Tacitus confirms that the *Lex Julia* was unsuccessful:

Next it was proposed that the Papia Poppæa law be relaxed, which Augustus, in his old age, had passed after the Julian laws. The objective was to reinforce the penalties for being celibate and to get more money into the exchequer. And yet, there was no increase either in the number marriages or the raising of children—so powerful were the benefits of being childless.

Tacitus, *Annals* 3, 25

The attractions of a mistress—a woman of a young man's choosing and not his father's with the sexual freedoms she brought—or of a prositute, off-limits in the marriage market, or of an independent woman from a lower class, were all too apparent.

A more settled picture, and probably one that was much more typical, comes in the first century CE when Agricola married Domitia Decidiana:

From Britannia Agricola went to Rome, to go through the usual *cursus honorum*; and there he married Domitia Decidiana, a woman of noble birth. The marriage gave the ambitious Agricola both distinction and support. They lived in amazing harmony, through their mutual affection and by putting each other first.

Tacitus, *Agricola* 6

The same is true of Pliny's description of his love for his young wife Calpurnia Fabata whom he wed in 100 CE.

It is incredible how much I miss you, because I love you and we are not used to being apart. I lie awake for most of the night dispelling your image, and by day, I speak no lie, my feet take me to your house, at the times when I used to visit you; but then I leave the empty threshold, ill and sad like a locked-out lover; I return with as much sorrow and disappointment as an excluded lover. The only time I am not tormented is when I am in the Forum.

Pliny, *Epistles* 7, 5

4

Domestic and Sexual Abuse

The traditional power invested in the *paterfamilias* assumed a degree of domestic violence—physically against the child and psychologically against the mother—whenever the father exercised his right to expose his unwanted baby daughters. The *Twelve Tables* took things a stage further when one of the laws decreed that a father should raise all his sons, but only one daughter. A man could kill or thrash his wife for having a drink or for walking outdoors with her face uncovered. As we have seen, a cuckolded husband was entitled to kill his unfaithful wife and her lover if found *in flagrante*.

The personal epitaph left for Julia Maiana at Lugudunum in Roman Gaul by her brother and son is tragic: her husband, it seems, murdered her after a marriage that had lasted twenty-eight years. The couple's two children—a boy of nineteen and a girl of eighteen—are mentioned in the inscription.[1]

Nevertheless, Roman law later criminalised domestic abuse by a husband to his wife.[2] Cato the Elder said that the man who struck his wife or child laid violent hands on the holiest of holy things. He also thought it more laudable to be a good husband than a good senator.[3] Wife beating was grounds for divorce or other legal action against the husband.[4]

Counselling for alcohol abuse or wife-battering was doubtless unavailable but there was marriage guidance. The temple of Juno Viriplaca ('husband appeaser') on the Palatine Hill offered reconciliation between squabbling couples.

A 13 BCE marriage contract survives from Egypt and, although it probably owes as much to Egyptian legislation as it does to Roman, it is, nevertheless, interesting because domestic violence features as one of the seemingly routine things the husband will promise not to commit. Thermion and Apollonius, and Thermion's guardian, agree to share their lives together (*affectio maritalis*) and that Thermion has delivered a dowry, including a pair of gold earrings weighing three quarters and some silver drachmas. He will now feed and clothe her; he will not abuse her verbally or physically, kick her out or marry another woman—if he does any of these things, the dowry goes back. For her part, she will fulfil her obligations, she will not sleep away from the home without his permission, she will not wreck the house or have an affair—if she does, she loses the dowry.[5]

The Bona Dea rites have their mythical roots in domestic violence, provoked ominously by a woman taking a drink. Although Bona Dea was celebrated by men and women alike, in the domestic rite, which took place on 3 December, all males were banished, even male animals and pictures or statues of males. Only *matronae* and the Vestal Virgins were present; the Vestals brought in Bona Dea's image from her temple and a meal of sow's entrails was eaten, sacrificed to her on behalf of the Roman people, and sacrificial wine. The fun (*ludere*) lasted all night with female musicians, games, and wine, euphemistically called 'milk' from a 'honey jar'. This was not a weak attempt to conceal clandestine drinking; rather, it came about when Faunus, married to the Good Goddess, caught her drinking surreptitiously and beat her to death with a myrtle branch. Myrtle was also associated with Aphrodite and with sex, and so myrtle was alien to the rites and banned. The *matronae* refrained from sexual relations in the run up to the festival. According to Cicero, any man caught observing the rites could be punished by blinding.[6]

Causes of miscarriage can be found in the *Hippocratic Corpus* and include domestic violence: carrying too heavy a weight, being beaten up, jumping up into the air (an occupational hazard for acrobats and dancers), lack of food and fainting, fear, loud shouting, flatulence, and too much drink were all triggers for miscarriage.

Nero is probably the most renowned of the emperors for domestic abuse. He was alleged to have arranged for his first wife (and stepsister) Claudia Octavia to be murdered after he had subjected her to torture and incarceration (Tacitus, *Annals* 16, 6). Nero kicked Poppaea Sabina, his second wife, to death when she was heavily pregnant:

[Nero] loved Poppaea dearly; he married her twelve days after his divorce from Octavia, yet he killed her too by kicking her when she was pregnant and ill. She had rebuked him for coming home late from the races. He had a daughter by her, Claudia Augusta, but lost her when she was still a baby.

Suetonius, *Nero* 35, 3.

Commodus is also supposed to have killed his wife and his sister. On a more mundane level, we have seen how Julia Maiana was murdered by her husband after twenty-eight years of marriage.

Social breathalysing, harsh punishment, and financial penalties and death awaited women who had had a drink: Egnatius Mecenius clubbed his wife to death for drinking:

At Rome it was illegal for women to drink wine… the wife of Egnatius Mecenius was killed by her husband with a club, because she had drunk some wine. He was declared innocent of the murder by Romulus. Fabius Pictor, in his *Annals*, has stated that a woman was starved to death by her family for opening a purse in which the keys of the wine-cellar were kept; and Cato tells us that it was customary for male relatives to kiss the females of the family in order to establish if they smelt of *temetum*, wine, hence our word *temulentia*, meaning drunkenness. Judge Cn. Domitius once ruled that a woman appeared to him to have drunk more wine than was good for her, and without her husband knowing, so he relieved her of her dowry.

Valerius Maximus 6, 3, 9

Aspasia Annia Regilla was a rich, aristocratic, and powerful woman who was distantly related to several Roman emperors and empresses. She was the wife of the prominent Greek Herodes Atticus. Regilla was kicked in the stomach to death by one of Herodes Atticus' freedmen called Alcimedon. According to Philostratus, Appius Annius Atilius Bradua brought charges in Rome against his brother-in-law, alleging that Herodes Atticus was the murderer.

The frequency with which physical violence features in Roman love poetry might suggest that it was not uncommon; Catullus hates and loves his woman (*Carmen* 85)— *odi et amo*—and he has no qualms threatening Furius and Aurelius (*Carmen* 16) with some serious sexual violence: 'Fuck you, boys, up your arse and in your mouth!'

Here, Propertus is outlining the serious consequences of his mistress's infidelity:

But you will not get away: you should really die with me; the blood of both of us will drip from the same sword, the murder may well disgrace me but however much a disgrace it is, you are going to die anyway…

Propertius, 2, 8

Here, he rejects physical violence as being beneath him, but in doing so, gives us what sounds like his usual repertoire of physical abuse:

Is it true Cynthia that throughout all Rome you have a reputation for living a life of shame? Do I deserve this? You faithless woman, I will punish you… I won't tear the clothes from your duplicitous limbs, nor will my anger break down the doors you barricade against me; I would not dare in my anger to tear your plaited hair, nor bruise you with a cruel punch. Let some boor look for fights as demeaning as this.

Propertius 2, 5, 21–26; translation adapted from H. E. Butler, Heinemann 1912

Tibullus describes a scene of marital discord and domestic violence between a farmer and his wife:

The countryman drives home from the wood half-drunk half-sober, with wife and children in his cart, but then they evoke love's war, and the woman regrets her torn hair and the broken down doors. The battered woman weeps for her tender cheeks, but the victor weeps too that his hands were so strong in his mad rage … enough to have torn the thin clothes from her body, enough to have dishevelled her hair, enough to have made her cry.

Tibullus 1, 10, 51–8

Ovid echoes this although there is a hint that he derives some perverse pleasure from the violence:

Come on, if you're really friends, tie up these hands which, with unholy anger have wounded a mistress… I have broken the most religious ties, both to my parents and the gods: I tore (o god) her finely braided hair, how charming then looked the disordered fair… with streaming cheeks, and with dishevelled hair. Such lips were formed for kinder words than these, wounds made by lovers' furious ecstasies. Though like a torrent I was hurried on, a slave to passion which I could not shun, I might have only pierced her tender ear with threatening language, such as virgins fear. Fear having chilled the current of her blood, she pale as Parian marble statue stood.

Tears, which suspense did for a while restrain, gushed forth, and down her cheeks the deluge ran… and three times did she fight back against the criminal.

Ovid, *Amores* 1, 7
translation adapted from *Ovid's Art of Love, the Remedy of Love, the Art of Beauty, the Court of Love, the History of Love, and Amours*, by Anne Mahoney. New York. Calvin Blanchard 1855.

We find evidence for physical abuse in a woman's funerary inscription for Margarita, her dog; here, the statement that she was never assaulted may indicate that domestic violence was a normal facet of life: '[I was] never accustomed to being held in heavy chains or to suffer savage beatings to my snow-white body' (*CIL* 6, 29896). This papyrus describing an indictment by a Christian wife against her husband for various offenses has some disturbing details:

For seven whole days he shut up his own slaves and mine with my foster-daughters and his agent and son in his cellars, having abused his slaves and my slave Zoe and beat them half to death, and he set fire to my foster-daughters, having stripped them naked, which is against the law.

P. Oxy. 6, 903

Episodes of physical violence are sometimes evident in skeletal remains. In 2002, in excavations in the Collatina necropolis in Rome, the skull of a fifty plus-year-old woman exhibited a number of traumatic episodes suggestive of physical abuse throughout her life.

Of course, violence against women was not confined to the home. When the Romans sacked a city, the booty became the property of the victorious army; that booty included the women and girls of the town so we frequently find that they were raped or sold into slavery.

The ferocious sack of Cremona by Antonius Primus in 69 CE was notorious for the systematic rape and butchering of women, men, and the elderly on a prodigious scale:

> Forty thousand soldiers burst into Cremona with even more army suppliers and camp followers who were even more corrupted by lust and savagery. Age and dignity provided no protection as they interchanged rape with slaughter and slaughter with rape. Old men and aging women—useless as booty—were dragged into the 'fun'; any grown up girl or fine-looking man who came along was torn apart at the violent hands of the rapists.

> Tacitus, *Histories* 3, 32–4

In the 1930s, Eric Birley found two skeletons under the floor of a building during his excavations of Housesteads Roman Fort, on Hadrian's Wall in Northumberland. This is possibly one of the earliest instances recorded of domestic violence and murder in Britain. One skeleton was of a man with the tip of a knife in his ribs and the other was probably a woman. They had been buried in the clay floor beneath a rear room of what was probably an inn or brothel, and then concealed under a clean layer of clay.

More mystery surrounds the excavations in the armoury of the Pompeii gladiatorial barracks which unearthed eighteen skeletons in two rooms. Presumably these were the skeletons of gladiators, but they were not alone—the bones of a woman wearing gold and an emerald studded necklace were also found; she clearly was not there just to serve the rations.

Lifestyle Choices: Urban Living or Escape to the Country?

A pragmatic solution to the problems associated with Roman society and urban living was to move out to the country or the seaside. That's what those who could afford it sometimes did—failing that, they enjoyed the luxury of a weekend home somewhere more salubrious than Rome or similar urban hell holes, like some of us today. Horace's sheer delight at escaping the city to spend time at his place in the country is quite tangible. The huge difference between waking up on his Sabine farm and his noisy, busy, pressured daily grind in Rome is remarkable. Here Horace expatiates on the benefits of a life in the country compared with urban living:

This is just what I prayed for: a modest patch of land with a garden and, near the house a spring that always flows, and a bit further up a little wood. The Gods couldn't have done more or better for me. It's great. I ask for nothing more, son of Maia—make these gifts mine for ever.[1] If I have never improved my circumstances by evil ways nor diminished them by vice or crime, if I never offer up prayers as silly as these two: 'If only that little corner next door (which at present spoils the shape of my plot) could be added on to mine'. 'If Fortune could show me a crock of silver like the man who found treasure and then bought the very same plot of land to plough which he had worked as a hired labourer—rich in the friendship of Hercules'.[2] If I'm happy with what I have and I'm content, I pray to you like this: 'Fatten up the flocks I shepherd and everything else (except my head) and, as usual, be my biggest protector.'

So, now that I have moved out of the city to my citadel in the hills what should I celebrate first in my Muses' prosaic satires? Here there is no malicious canvassing to ruin me nor leaden sirocco nor oppressive autumn—all grist to sour Libitina's mill.[3]

Father of the dawn or Janus, if you are happier to be called that, you who control men's early-day work and the grind of life (such is the will of you Gods) be the prelude to my poem. At Rome you seized on me to stand as guarantor. 'Come on, get on with it before someone else takes on the job before you'. Whether the strong north wind tears over the earth or winter drags the snowy day into a tighter circle I've got to get on.

Afterwards (and it may one day come back to haunt me) when I have shouted loud and clear, I must struggle through the crowd and shove the shufflers out of the way. 'What do you want you idiot, what are you doing?' So some reprobate angrily swears at me. 'You push everything out of your way when you run back to Maecenas, thinking only of him'.

But I like that and I admit it. It's like honey to me but as soon as I get back to the gloomy Esquiline the problems of a hundred other people dance around in my head and surround me. 'Maybe you can meet Roscius tomorrow before seven at the Puteal Libonis'.[4] 'Quintus, the clerk begs you to remember to get back to him on that breaking news that everyone's waiting to hear'. 'Get Maecenas to fix his seal to these papers'. When you say 'I'll do my best'—they retort: 'You'd do it if you really wanted to'. Seven years—maybe eight—have flown by since Maecenas started to include me in his circle; he was even happy to carry me in his carriage on his journeys and make small talk: 'What's the time?' 'Is that Thracian Gallina a match for Syrus?'[5] 'The morning frost is biting now, so be careful' and other such nuggets you could safely drop into a receptive ear. Over all this time, for every hour of every day yours truly has endured so much envy. If Maecenas watches the games with me or plays with me on the Campus Martius, they all shout: 'Lucky lad!' When frigid rumour spreads from the Rostra to the crossroads, everyone I meet asks 'My good man,—you'll know because you are in close contact with the Gods—what have you heard on the Dacian question?'[6] 'Nothing'. 'You're always having a laugh at our expense' they say; so I say 'May all the Gods torment me if I have heard something'. 'Is the land Caesar has promised to give his soldiers going to be in Italy or in three-cornered Sicily?' When I swear that I know nothing about it they are certainly amazed that I can be such a singularly reticent man. Sadly, my daylight hours are wasted on such things and I pray: 'Oh countryside when will I see you again? When can I drink the happy oblivion of life's cares with my books of classic authors, with sleep and lazy hours? When will I be served beans—the relatives of Pythagoras—and cabbage greased up with fatty bacon?[7] Oh those nights and banquets were pure heaven when, in front of my own hearth, I made the offerings, feasted and fed the cheeky slaves. Each guest, according to his pleasure, drains his goblet be it large or small—no silly rules here—he drinks up depending on whether he is man enough to take the strong stuff or is happier with a more modest drink. So the conversation begins, but it is not about other people's houses and villas or whether Lepos is a good dancer or no –no, we deliberate on matters more relevant to us and stuff that it is good to know: does wealth or virtue make men happy, does self-interest or good behaviour forge friendships, what is 'the good' all about and what is its highest form?

Cervius, our neighbour, trots out old wives' tales in the middle of all this—old but relevant. For example, when someone, not realising the trouble they are causing, praises Arellius' wealth he begins thus:

'Once upon a time as the story goes a country mouse received a city mouse—old guest, old friend—in his poor mouse hole. Country mouse was a rough diamond and, though careful with his savings, he could, nevertheless, push out the boat and chill. He was generous with his chick peas though and his long stemmed oats and brought in his mouth a dry grape and half-eaten bits of bacon which he gave to his guest, whose distaste he was anxious to overcome by varying the menu. City mouse scarcely touched any of it though with his finicky teeth. Meanwhile the father of the house, stretched out on fresh straw, eats spelt and darnel, steering clear of the better courses.

At last the town mouse says: 'How can you be happy enduring this life lived on a rugged wooded mountain-side? Don't you prefer the company of men and the city to this wild wood? Believe me, let's hit the road together. All earth dwelling creatures have been allotted mortal souls—and there is no escaping death for great and small alike—so, good chap, live a happy life surrounded by the good things while you still can'. These words struck a chord with the country mouse; he sprang nimbly from his hole and they both set off on the journey they had agreed to make: their plan was to creep beneath the city walls under the cover of night.

It was the middle of the night when the pair entered a wealthy looking house. Here coverlets dyed in ruby red blazed on ivory couches; loads of courses had been left over from last night's feast, piled nearby in baskets. So when the town mouse had got the country mouse lying spread out on the purple drapes he ran to and fro and, got up like the host, kept the courses coming and just like a slave doing his job, tasted beforehand the dishes he brought in.

The country mouse, reclining and happy in his very changed circumstances was playing the happy guest when, all of a sudden, a mighty slamming of doors knocked them both off their couches. Terrified, they ran the length of the dining room and, scared half to death, they trembled as the lofty halls rang out with the baying of Molossian hounds. At this the country mouse said: 'I can do without this kind of life. So goodbye; my hole in the wood will keep me safe from ambush and simple pulses will keep me full.'

Horace, *Satires* 2, 6

Martial echoes this to some extent and, while appreciative of attempts to improve local services, is clearly exasperated by his life in the city, with its perils and its turgid monotony. Like Horace, he is clearly attracted towards a more otiose lifestyle outside Rome. Elsewhere, he gives us the real benefits of his Baian villa (3, 58), although country living can have its drawbacks too (7, 36). Martial deplores the noisiness of Rome—he can only get a good night's sleep at his country villa (12, 57). His annoyance at the inadequacies of his water supply should not be underestimated in a city that depended almost entirely on the sophisticated and enduring system of aqueducts for its sanitation and fresh water. For the last word on this, see Frontinus: *On the Aqueducts of the City of Rome* 2, 98–129 and Vitruvius: *Architecture* 8, 6.

Martial describes the daily grind that is life in Rome:

The first and second hours grind down the attendees at the morning court sitting, the third gets shouty lawyers going, up to the fifth Rome offers out her various tasks; sixth gives peace and quiet to the weary; the seventh brings an end. The eighth and ninth is just right for the oil-shiny wrestler; the ninth commands us to squash down on the heaped up couches.[8] The tenth hour, Euphemus, is poetry time when you carefully arrange the ambrosian feasts and good old Caesar relaxes with ethereal nectar and holds his temperate cup in his mighty hand. Now let's have some fun: Thalia my muse is scared to bother Jove in the mornings.[9]

Martial, Epigrams 4, 8

The sort of house or flat you lived in in Rome and in other cities and towns depended obviously on how well-off you were. The vast majority of people lived in small rented or freehold flats in blocks over shops or offices with shared kitchen and bathroom facilities on the landings. Families lived in very close proximity to one another.

Here is Martial's appreciation of some urban development that has uncluttered the streets of Rome:

That chancer of a hawker has robbed us of our Rome so that there are no longer any doorways on the doorways. Germanicus, you have ordered that our narrow alleyways be widened and that what were once tracks become streets.[10] None of the pillars are encircled by chained bottles any more and the praetor doesn't have to work mired in mud; no one flashes a blade at random in the dense crowd and the dingy take-away doesn't take up the whole street.[11] Barber, innkeeper, cook, butcher all stick to their own doorways. Now Rome is Rome again—not just one great big shop.

Martial 7, 61

Martial's flat is cold and draughty, like many others in Rome: 'I live in a tiny cell, with a window that doesn't close properly. Even Boreas, the north wind, would refuse to live here' (Martial 8, 14, 5–6).

Martial's town house is in need of some plumbing work:

I have (and I pray that it stays mine for a long time under your rule, Caesar) both a country cottage and a small place in Rome. My curved water pole makes hard work of pumping water from a small ditch but nevertheless it waters my thirsty place in the country. The town house, however, is dry and complains that there is no water to keep it going even though I can actually hear the fountain of Aqua Marcia nearby.[12] Augustus, any water at all you can give to my household gods will be a Castalian spring or a shower from Jupiter.[13]

Martial 9, 18

If we want the younger Pliny's take on the matter, then in letter 9, 36, he describes the perfect day out in Tuscany: a bit of work, some gentle exercise, a power nap, bath, quiet meal, and good conversation—the perfect way to recharge the batteries before returning to enjoy the more civilised pursuits of the city. In 2, 17 describes in some detail, and to our ears somewhat smugly, his country retreat and the pleasure it brings.

Such calm and balanced thinking is notably absent from Juvenal's analysis of the city versus country issue. His vituperative attack illustrates just how awful life in Rome could be. Partisan and somewhat exaggerated it may well be but it is quite likely that Horace, Martial, and Pliny would have agreed with him to a large extent. To Juvenal, Rome has nothing at all to commend it and he ends his rant as he begins it with a calm, reflective, and bucolic-tinged coda recommending a life in the country. But the diatribe in between is an excoriating attack on all things Roman, or rather non-Roman; moral bankruptcy and social turpitude are everywhere.

Juvenal's rant says it all about the horrors of urban life:

Although upset by the departure of my old friend, I nevertheless applaud his decision to set up home in quiet Cumae and to give the Sibyl her one and only citizen. It is the gateway to Baiae, a pleasing seaside resort and a pleasant retreat. I prefer even Prochyta to the Subura: a place so wretched and desolate but better than living in fear of fires, buildings falling down all the time and a thousand other dangers in this savage Rome—with its bloody poets reciting all through August.[14]

But while all of his belongings are being piled on to one four-wheeled wagon he pauses at the old arches at the dripping Porta Capena. Here Numa used to meet with his mistress in the night but now the same fountain, grove and shrine are let to Jews whose furniture amounts to straw and a basket.[15] This is because even every tree now is ordered to pay rent to the people; the muses have been evicted and the wood has taken up begging. We go down into the valley of Egeira and to the artificial caves. How much closer the spirit of spring would be if green grass bordered on the waters and if there was no marble invading the natural tufa.

Umbricus spoke at this point. 'There is no place any more in Rome for honest skill, no reward for your hard work, I have less today than yesterday and tomorrow will fritter away the little I have left—so I plan to go to the place where Daedalus pulled off his tired wings while my greying hair is still a recent event, while I'm still virile in early old age, while Lachesis still has something left of me to spin and I can still walk unaided without a stick in my hand.[16] Farewell homeland! Artorius and Catulus can live there; let the men who turn black into white stay and they who have no problem taking out contracts on temples, rivers and harbours, on drying up after floods or carrying corpses to the burial grounds and putting themselves up for sale at auction. These men played in horn sections once upon a time and could be seen as camp followers at every municipal fighting ground—their puffed out cheeks are well known in every town—now they put on shows themselves and kill to please whomsoever the mob orders with thumbs down. From here they go back to contracting for public toilets and why not for everything and anything. They are, after all, the sort of people whom Fortune raises up from the lowest of the low to the highest of the high whenever she wants a good laugh.

'What can I do in Rome? I don't know how to lie. If a book is no good I can't say it is good and want a copy. I don't do astrology, I won't and can't predict the death of someone's father, I have never examined the entrails of a frog and I am happy that others are good at bringing to the bride what she wants and what her adulterous lover sends. No thief will get help from me and I don't feature on any governor's staff so please think of me as crippled and physically useless. You're only held in high regard now if you're a conspirator—the type of man whose seething mind burns with secrets forever kept. No-one who has ever confided in you an honest secret thinks he owes you anything or will share anything with you. Verres only favours the man who accuses Verres at will. Don't rate the sands of shaded Tagus and the gold it rolls into the sea so much that you can't sleep, and unhappily take up bribes which must be surrendered, feared by your powerful patron.

'Now I must tell you about the people who are most acceptable to our rich friends, and from whom I particularly distance myself. I am not ashamed of it. I just can't bear, fellow Romans, a Grecian Rome: how many of our scum are Achaean? For a long time now Syrian Orontes has discharged into the Tiber and imports the language, customs, flautists and sambuca, foreign tambours and the girls pimped to ply their trade in the Circus. Go to them you whose pleasure is in foreign whores with their painted head-dresses. Quirinus, your country bumpkin puts on his Greek sandals and wears victory spoils on his greased-up neck.[17] This one comes from the heights of Sicyon, this one left Amydon, this comes from Andros, he from Samos, he Tralles or Alabenda—they all make for the Esquiline and the hill called Viminalis, destined to become our life blood and masters in the mansions of the mighty.[18] They are quick-witted and criminally impudent and as loquacious as Isaeus but even more gushing.[19] Tell me what you want that man to be: he brings to us all manner of men: grammar teachers, orators, mathematicians, artists, wrestling coaches, soothsayers, rope dancers, doctors, magicians. Your hungry little Greek is a know-it-all: tell him go to heaven and to heaven he goes. To sum it all up, the man who put on wings was neither a Moor nor a Sarmatian, nor a Thracian—he was born in central Athens.[20]

'I've got to get away from the purple cloaks. Will he sign before I do and recline propped up on a couch that's better than mine—he who is carried to Rome on the same breeze that brings in plums and Syrian figs? Please note that as a baby it was Aventine air that I breathed and I was nurtured on the Sabine berry.[21] What of the fact that these people are past masters at sycophancy, praising even the words of an uneducated friend, the looks of the deformed, equating the nape of a wimp to the thick neck of Hercules when he held Antaeus up off the ground, and marvelling at a voice that sounds as thin and as bad as a cockerel's when it pecks its hen? We too can extol the very same things but they it is who are believed. Is there any comic actor better at playing Thais or the part of a wife or some Doris without her green cloak?[22] Certainly it looked like a real woman speaking rather than a masked actor. I'd say that below his stomach everything was smooth and featureless, separated by a slender crack. And yet Antiochus will not be a celebrity in Greece nor Stratocles nor

Dimitrius nor gentle Haemus—they are a nation of comedians.[23] If you just laugh, he shakes with a guffaw; he weeps but without the grief if he sees a friend crying; if you want a fire in winter he puts on his woollen cloak; if you should say 'I'm boiling' he starts sweating. We are not therefore equal; he is the better because he can, night and day, assume the expression from someone else's face, he can throw up his hands and clap when his friend gives out a good belch or if he pisses in a straight line or if his golden bowls make a farting sound when he turns them upside down.

When it comes to matters of the groin nothing is sacred or safe: not the matron of the household, not the virgin daughter, not even her unbearded fiancé, not the prepubescent son—and if none of these is available he will lay his friend's grandmother. These men want to know your family secrets and are feared because of this. Since I have started going on about the Greeks, forget the gymnasia and listen to this much bigger outrage. That old Stoic who informed against and effectively killed his friend and disciple Barea, was born on that riverbank where the Gorgon's winged horse crashed to earth.[24, 25, 26] There is no place for a Roman in a Rome where some Protogenes or a Diphilus or a Hermarchus lords it and who by some genetic disorder never shares his friends but keeps them to himself. For when he has dropped drip by drip drops of his own and his country's poison into his receptive ear I am kicked off the threshold and my years of long service count for nothing. Nowhere is it easier to turf out a client.

'Moreover, lest I flatter us, what is the point of a poor man serving the state even if he is keen to run along in the middle of the night in his toga when the praetor compels the lictor to go flat out lest his colleague is the first to greet the childless Albina and Modia who have been awake for a long time already.[27] Here in Rome the son of free-born parents escorts the slave of a wealthy man because the slave can pay as much as a legionary tribune's salary to a Calvina or Catiena to throb away on top of her.[28] But you, attracted by the face of some tarted up whore, dilly and dally about bringing Chione down from her high pedestal.[29] At Rome you can produce a witness as squeaky clean as the host of the Idaean goddess—enter Numa or the man who saved trembling Minerva from the burning temple—but the first question will always concern his possessions, only the last would be about his character.[30, 31] How many slaves does he keep or how many fields has he got and how big and how many are the pudding dishes he eats from? A man gains trust in proportion to the money he keeps in his money chest. A poor man can swear on all the altars in Samothrace or in Rome but it is commonly believed that the poor man damns the gods and their thunderbolts and that this is even sanctioned by the gods themselves.

'What's more, that same poor man invites derision if his tunic is torn and dirty or if his toga is a bit soiled and one of his shoes is broken open where the leather has come away, if a piece of rough and recent thread shows more than one rip where a tear has been stitched up. The hardest thing about being wretchedly poor is the way it makes men look silly. 'Get out!' someone says, 'Have you no shame?' 'Get out of these seats—they're for the knights, you're too poor to meet the statutory requirement.' The sons of whores born in some brothel or another sit here; the sharply dressed son of an auctioneer applauds here with the educated sons of a gladiator on one side, the sons of the gladiator's coach on the other—empty-headed Otho was happy to segregate us like this. In Rome a prospective son in law who is short of cash and not up to his girl's dowry is never accepted. When was a poor man ever named as an heir? When was he ever appointed as an assessor to an aedile? Romans of slender means should have got out en masse a long time ago.

'Anyone whose small private fortune stands in the way of his good points will not find it easy to get on. In Rome it's an even harder struggle when a flea-pit of a lodging costs such a lot, where your slaves' bellies cost such a lot and where your lightest of snacks costs such a lot. You're ashamed to dine off earthenware dishes—but if transported suddenly to a Marsian or Sabellan table you'd be happy to wear their coarse Venetian hood.[32]

In most of Italy—if the truth be told—only dead men wear the toga. Even when the grand festival is celebrated again in the grassy theatre when the well-known farce at last is revived, when the gaping white-painted masks terrifies the country-born baby at his mother's breast—you will see the people in the stalls and orchestra all dressed the same or similar. White tunics are right for the posh aedile as a badge of high office. Here in Rome the dress is elegant enough but way beyond our means; here in Rome that little something extra—often more than is enough—is lifted from someone else's coffers. It's a common fault here—we all live in a kind of ambitious poverty. In short, everything in Rome comes at a price. How much do you pay to salute Cossus sometimes or for Veiiento to look tight-lipped at you?[33] This man trims a beard, another dedicates a lover's locks, the house is full of cakes for sale. Take your money and keep your cake. We clients are compelled to pay taxes and make good the savings of sophisticated slaves.

'Who in cool Praeneste fears or has ever feared that his house would fall down? The same goes for Vosinii situated on the wooded slopes, or rural Gabii, or the citadel of Tivoli on the hill. We live in a Rome shored up largely by lightweight props. That's how the bailiff stops his building from falling down, papering over the ancient cracks, and telling the tenants to sleep soundly while collapse is imminent. I need to live in a place where there are no fires, nothing to fear in the night. Ucalegon demands water now, now he's moving out his bits and pieces and there's already smoke coming from your place on the third floor—and you didn't know! If the alarm is raised at ground level the last man to burn will be the one who is protected from the rain only by the roof tiles where the delicate doves lay their eggs.

'This is what Codrus owned: a bed that would be too small for Procula, a sideboard decorated with six little jugs and a very small tankard below that, with a statue of Chiron the centaur, made from the same marble, lying flat out under the same and holding a box of little Greek classic texts in which the stupid mice were gnawing away at the divine verses. So, Codrus owns nothing then, who can deny that? However, the unlucky man has lost every bit of that 'nothing' and, to make matters worse, the nadir of his calamity is that while destitute and reduced to beggary no-one will to give him food or a roof over his head.

'On the other hand if the great house of Assaracus should fall down, his mother gets in a right state, the top brass are in mourning and the praetor postpones the bail bonds; then we bewail the disasters of Rome and despise its fires.[34] The fire is still burning when someone or other comes running to donate some marble and to offer building materials; one brings naked white statues, another something brilliant by Euphranor or Polyclitus, this one with relics of Asian gods, others will give books and book cases and a Minerva for the centrepiece, he a pile of silver.[35] So does Persicus, the most affluent of the childless replace his losses with more and better things and, with good reason, is suspected of torching the house himself.

'If you can be dragged away from the games in the Circus Maximus you can buy for cash the best of houses at Sora, Fabrateria or Frusino for the same price as your rent for one year for a black hole in Rome.[36] Out there you get a little garden, a shallow well which doesn't need to be worked with a rope and is emptied easily to water your seedlings. Live out here—as a lover of the hoe, a farm manager of a well-kept garden from which you can provide a banquet for one hundred Pythagoreans.[37] It is worth something, wherever and however remote the place, to be the master of even just one ... lizard.

'In Rome most of the sick die from insomnia: the languor itself is caused by undigested food clinging to a peptic stomach. What lodgings allow you to sleep? Only the very rich can sleep in Rome and here lies the root cause of the urban malaise. The constant criss-crossing of wagons in the narrow winding streets, the drovers shouting out loud when their herds are jammed up is enough to snatch sleep from Drusus or even a seal.[38] When duty calls the rich man is carried through the yielding crowd and in a huge Liburnian galley rides roughshod over their heads. On the way he reads or writes or sleeps (closed windows make you sleepy in a litter). But even though we hurry, he gets there before us because that tide of humanity up ahead gets in the way and the great queue behind us crushes my groin. One man smacks me with his elbow, another smacks me with a hard litter pole, but this one smashes a piece of wood, this one a jar, against my head. My legs are splattered with mud and it's not long before great big feet trample on me from all sides and a soldier stamps on my toe with his hobnail boots.

'Can you see the great plume of smoke where the people throng for the dole— hundreds of guests each followed by their own private barbecues? Corbulo himself could barely carry so many big pots and pans and all the paraphernalia which that unlucky slave carries on his head—ramrod neck—fanning the flames as he runs by. Newly patched tunics are torn, a tall fir tree wobbles on an oncoming cart, other wagons carry a pine tree tottering menacingly above the crowds. If that axle carrying Ligurian marble should snap it will unleash an avalanche on the queues of people. What would be left of their bodies? Who will be able to find the body parts, the bones? All the corpses are indiscriminately crushed and perish just like the soul.

Meanwhile back at home, oblivious to all this, they wash the dishes, blow on the cooking flame and clatter the oily skin scrapers, lay out the towels and fill the flasks. The slaves are hurrying about their various chores but the master now sits on the infernal riverbank—a novice petrified by the abominable ferryman; he hasn't a hope of a place on the boat over the seething mud; unlucky man, as he hasn't got an obol in his mouth to offer.

'Let's look now at the other different dangers of the night: look how high up the towering roof tops are—and from which a falling tile smacks my head. Leaky and broken vases are forever falling out of windows and smash onto the pavement with such force that they leave scratch marks. You might be thought of as careless, blind to the sudden accident, if you go out to dinner before making your will. There are as many ways of getting killed as there are open windows watching you as you pass by at night. So, the best you can hope for is to thank the gods that they are content just to empty out their shallow chamber pots.

'The drunken slob who luckily hasn't killed anyone yet doles out his torments just like Achilles the night he spent mourning his best friend, lying now on his face a moment later on his back. He wouldn't be able to sleep anyway since he can drop off only when he's had a fight. But however cocky he is and fired up with booze he still gives the man in the scarlet cloak a wide berth with his endless line of hangers-on carrying brass lamps and lots of torches and who orders him to get out of the way.

'But he despises me, I who usually go by the light of the moon or weak light of a candle whose wick I fiddle with to control. This is how the wretched brawl starts, if a brawl it is when he does the punching and I'm the punch bag. He squares up to me and commands me to stand still: I have to comply. What do you do when a madman calls the odds and he's harder than you? 'Where have you come from?' he bawls, 'Whose booze, whose beans are you full of? Which cobbler have you been eating leeks with, and boiled sheep's head? Nothing to say to me, eh? Speak up or you'll get a good kicking. Where do you stand, tell me, which synagogue will I find you in?' Whether you try to say something or leave in silence it's all the same: he hits you either way. Then, still furious, he serves a summons on you. Such are the civil rights of the poor man. Beaten up, soundly thrashed and punched, he begs and prays that he can go home just with a few teeth intact.

'There's more to frighten you; there will always be someone to rob you when your house is closed up, when your shops are chained and shuttered and everywhere is quiet. The gangster will all of a sudden go to work with his dagger: whenever the Pomptine marshes and Gallinarian pines are protected by armed guards they all come running into Rome as if it were a theme park. Every blacksmith's forge is hammering out heavy chains and with most of the iron going on the production of fetters you might well be worried about a shortage of ploughs, mattocks and hoes. Happy were our great great great grandfathers of great grandfathers, and you could say happy those days when Rome under the kings and tribunes could make do with one prison only.

I could add many other reasons but my cattle are calling and the sun is going down, it's time to go; my drover signals to me with a wave of his stick. So farewell and don't forget me; whenever you hurry out of Rome to your favourite Aquinum invite me over to join you from Cumae to your Helvius' Ceres and Diana and I will come over the icy fields in my boots to hear your satires, if indeed I don't embarrass them'.

Juvenal, Satires 3

The ubiquity of *delatores*—informers—receives special attention and reminds us uncomfortably of what Tacitus said about the corrupt nature of the state (*Annals* 1, 74, 1–2; 4, 30, 3–5; 3,3, 26; see also Seneca *De Beneficiis* 3, 26). Jews and especially Greeks feel the lash of Juvenal's tongue in a xenophobic attack that would not be out of place today in an argument over immigrants and immigration. Juvenal's urban world is a world turned upside down by these foreigners, the institutionalised sycophancy, effeminacy, corruption, gluttony, and arrogance of his fellow Romans.

Cicero's buy-to-lets have problems with subsidence: 'Two of my properties have collapsed and the others have wide cracks. Even the mice have left.' (Cicero, *Ad Atticum* 14, 9).

Despite the moanings of Martial and Juvenal, the Romans excelled in the provision of public services. Water supply was particularly impressive with some of their many aqueducts still standing today. Strabo, the Greek geographer (about 60 BCE–24 CE), marvels at the Romans' prowess in civil engineering:

So much, then, for the good things with which nature supplies the city [of Rome]; but the Romans have added still others, which are the result of their vision; for if the Greeks…went for beauty, strategic position, harbours, and fertile soil, the Romans had the best foresight in those projects which the Greeks made but little account of, such as the construction of roads and aqueducts, and of sewers that could wash out the effluent of the city into the Tiber. Moreover, they have also built roads which run throughout the country, with cuttings through hills and embankments across valleys so that their wagons can carry boat-loads; and the sewers, vaulted with close-fitting stones, have in some places left room enough for wagons loaded with hay to pass through them. So much water is brought into the city through the aqueducts that veritable rivers flow through the city and the sewers; and almost every house has cisterns, and service-pipes, and lots of fountains…in a word, the early Romans did not care much about the beauty of Rome, because they were busy with other, greater and more necessary projects.

Strabo, Geographica 5, 3, 8
translation adapted from Vol. II of the Loeb Classical Library edition, (1923).

There were public toilets in public places like the market place, at home, and in inns. However, chamber pots were used; the following graffito from Pompeii shows how essential they were: 'Dear host, sorry to say that I've wet the bed. Why did you do that you may ask? There was no chamber pot in my room' (*CIL* 4, 4957).

Good roads were, of course, absolutely essential for all sorts of reasons: commercial, military and administrative; as Strabo says, the Romans excelled at road building and constructed a system throughout the empire that was second to none; many Roman roads and routes are still in use today, albeit heavily disguised as motorways and trunk roads. The following milestones speak eloquently of the civil engineering challenges the Romans overcame and took in their stride: 'The emperor … Trajan [r. 98–117 CE] had this road built; construction involved cutting through mountains and flattening out sections which were not level' (*CIL* 3, 8267).

> The emperor … Antoninus Pius [r. 138–161 CE] repaired this road through the Numidian Alps which had deteriorated with age. Construction work entailed bridge building, draining marshes and reinforcing sections that had subsided.
>
> *L'Annee Epigraphique* 17 (1904) 21

'For sale' signs were simply the words 'For Sale', and a few details daubed on the wall of the property in question. These two were excavated in Pompeii:

> The Arrius Pollio Apartments…FOR RENT from 1 July: street-facing shops with counters, luxurious second floor apartments and a townhouse. Potential renters please contact…

> FOR RENT from 13 August, on five-year lease on the property of Julia Felix, daughter of Spurius, the elegant venus Baths with streetfront shops and booths, and second storey apartments.
>
> *CIL* 4, 138; 4, 1136

Many of the cheaper houses and apartment blocks were made of wood, so fire was a constant hazard. Insurance fraud was also a problem:

> Tongilianus, you had bought a house for 200,000 sesterces. A calamity all too frequent in Rome destroyed it. You collected ten times its value. I ask you, Tongilianus, is it just possible that you may have torched your own house?
>
> Martial 3, 52

City life inevitably involved experiencing theft and burglary. This graffito from Pompeii is short and to the point, and remarkably modern-sounding: 'A copper pot has gone missing from this shop; a reward of 65 sesterces is offered for its return, or a reward of 20 sesterces for information leading to its return' (*CIL* 4, 64).

The following crime report has a familiar ring to it as well, found in Tebtunis in Egypt from the second century CE:

When I got back from a trip out of town, I found that my house had been burgled and the entire contents stolen. I cannot just say nothing so I am filing this official complaint and ask that you file it in the registry so that if the guilty party is discovered I can deal with it.

Tebtunis Papyri 330

Turning back to Martial, we find him luxuriating in the joys of life at the seaside compared with Rome:

Frontinus—the peaceful retreat that is Anxur by-the-sea—a place nearer than Baiae with a house on the beach, a grove unknown to the bestial cicada when Cancer cooks, and the river and lake—while I frequented these places with you I had time to spare to celebrate the learned Muses—now mighty Rome wears us down. In Rome, when do I have a day I can call my own? I am knocked about in the depths of the city and life is frittered away in pointless work while I till unyielding acres in suburban fields just to have a household neighbouring yours, holy Quirinus. But the lover boy is not the only one who hangs around on thresholds by day and night; such time wasting isn't good for a poet. By the holy rites of the Muses—sacred to me—by all the gods I swear that I love you, unobliging as I am.

Martial, *Epigrams* 10, 58

However, provincial living has its dangers too. He describes a nocturnal, nearly fatal, accident due to drink:

Philostratus, a guest at the baths of Sinuessa, was making his way home after dark when he nearly did an Elpenor and died a cruel death when hurtling headlong down a long staircase.[39] This major accident would not have happened, Nymphs, if he had been drinking your waters instead.[40]

Martial 11, 82

Life on service oversees

By the time of the late republic and early empire, many men were absent from home for long periods of time and for much of their careers due to the demands of military service and provincial administration. This would also have had the important indirect social effect of fostering a degree of independence among wives left behind at home.

Statues of women started to go up in the late Republic, despite the best efforts of Cato the Younger to stifle the practice; Tiberius later advised moderation. Augustus honoured Livia with the Portico of Livia and the shrine of Concordia. In the provinces, a diluted version began to appear when the wives of governors were celebrated in statuary. In time, the statues were replaced by the real thing. Caecilia Metella led the way when she accompanied her husband, Sulla, to Athens in 86 BCE; in 49 BCE Cornelia went with Pompey to Lesbos and Egypt.

Aulus Caecina Severus adopts an extreme view, exaggerated in his unsuccessful speech of 21 CE, as recorded by Tacitus, but it contains within it the arguments which no doubt moulded the regulations relating to accompanied postings. Severus gets on with his wife and they have had six children together. However, he has left her at home for the forty years he has been away in the provinces because women encourage extravagance in peace time and weakness during war; they are feeble and tire easily. Left unrestrained, they get angry; they scheme and boss the commanders about. He cites instances of women running patrols and exercises, how they attract spivs, and embrace extortion.

Soldiers were not permitted to marry on service but many, no doubt, did, building relationships with local women and starting families with them.[41] One of the fascinating Vindolanda Tablets from around 100 CE shows that wives of officers clearly did accompany their husbands abroad: Claudia Severa sent a birthday party invitation to her sister Lepidina asking her to make her day by coming on 11 September. The body of the letter is written by a scribe but the postscript is written by Claudia and is the oldest example of a woman's handwriting in Latin in existence.[42]

6

Food and Feasting

The majority of Romans ate simply at home, without the pretentiousness and extravagance that came to characterise the middle-class dinner party. Three meals a day—breakfast, lunch, and dinner—was the norm, with the latter as the main meal taken late afternoon or early evening. Wheat-based food was the staple for the poorer classes; the price of grain was kept artificially low after the legislation of Gaius Gracchus in 122 BCE; the grain dole—free grain—was available to those who qualified after the law of Publius Clodius in 58 BCE. This grain might be crushed and boiled into a type of porridge or into a *puls*, a couscous; the Romans probably also made pasta noodles; these dishes were main courses, rather than side dishes. If a family could afford an oven, then the grain could be ground and made into bread. Other foods were beans, leeks, and sheep's lips; depending on your wealth, a selection of meats, cheeses, fruits, and vegetables were also an option. Wine was the drink of choice: the better off you were, the better the wine, with something approximating vinegar for the poorest people; it was usually mixed with water.

Fish sauce made from the blood and intestines of fish (*garum* or *liquamen*) was another popular staple which was enjoyed not just by Romans in Rome and Italy but by provincial officials, export businessmen, and soldiers all over the empire. It is possible that Lea & Perrins' Worcestershire Sauce has its origins in *garum*: it was exported to India by the Romans and still enjoyed there as Worcestershire Sauce in the 19th century by the British Raj. Anchovies are one of the ingredients. *Garum* factories proliferated in towns near to the sea and have been excavated at Barcino, Barcelona, and Pompeii. A recipe can be found in the *Geoponica* (20, 46, 1–5), a twenty-book collection of agricultural lore and animal husbandry, compiled during the 10th century in Constantinople for the Byzantine emperor Constantine VII Porphyrogenitus. *Garum* from Lusitania was particularly prized.

Ovid, in a roundabout way, describes for us a typical peasant meal in his story of Philemon and Baucis, in which Jupiter and Mercury are conducting some door-to-door research to measure the hospitality of the people of Phrygia in Asia Minor. One thousand doors were slammed in their faces when they knocked and asked for food and shelter; however, when they reached the humble abode of long-married and loyal

Philemon and Baucis, they were served a meal which, though frugal, was sumptuous by their own standards. The gods duly revealed their true identities and granted the couple a wish: Philemon and Baucis wished that they would die together so that neither one of them would ever have to live alone. Jupiter and Mercury obliged by changing them into trees when their time had come. The story not only emphasises the virtues of humility, parsimony, and hospitality, but it also celebrates marital harmony, lasting love, and affection—so often absent in Ovid's venal and permissive times.

> [Baucis] stripped some cabbage leaves, which her good husband had gathered for the meal. Then with a two-pronged fork the man fetched down a side of smoked bacon from a beam, and cut a small portion from the shank which had been smoked for ages. He tenderised it in boiling water… And here is set green and black olives, fruit of chaste Minerva, and the cornel berries, autumn-picked and pickled—these were served for relish; and endive, and radishes surrounding a large pot of cheese; and eggs not overdone but gently turned in glowing embers—all served up on earthen dishes. Then sweet wine served in clay, so expensive! all embossed… Again they served new wine, mellow this time; and a second course: sweet nuts, dried figs and wrinkled dates and plums, and scented apples, heaped up in wide baskets; and almost hidden in a wreath of grapes from purple vines, a glistening honey-comb. All these orchard treats were enhanced by a desire to please and with happy smiles… this aged couple, anxious to bestow their most valued possession, began quickly to chase the only goose they had—the faithful guardian of their little home — which they would kill and offer to the Gods. But swift of wing, at last it wore them out, and sought refuge with the smiling Gods.

Ovid, *Metamorphoses* 8, 646–678
Translation adapted from Brookes More, Cornhill Publishing Co. (Boston 1922).

A description of a schoolboy's typical day tells us that he went home for lunch: 'I ate some white bread, olives, cheese, dried figs and nuts, I drank cold water and went back to school' (*Corpus Glossariorum Latinorum III*, pp. 645–7).

The dinner party

The rich man's dinner party exemplified much of what some found repugnant and objectionable about Roman life and society. Horace highlights the toe-curling pretentiousness often to be found on such occasions: add to this the extravagance, gluttony, waste, one-upmanship, indulgent exoticism of the menu, bizarre entertainments, boring and boorish hosts, and we are left with a thoroughly dismal dining experience.

It is Petronius' *Cena Trimalchionis* which is the *tour de force*, encapsulating all the horrors of a meal at the flashy, trashy home of a *nouveau riche* in small town Italy.

Martial shows us just how vital a diary full of dinner invitations was in the social lives of some people, and how disastrous a day it was if it ended with a solitary meal at home. At 12, 82, he describes the lengths some people go to secure an invitation. The vulgar behaviour of some diners is described in the other poems: his doggy-bag guest is anticipated by Catullus' napkin thief (*Carmen* 112) and echoes his description of the gluttony of a guest in 7, 20. To Horace and Pliny, meanness is just as reprehensible as greed and extravagance. Elsewhere, Martial neatly sums up the excesses of one country house dinner party (3, 17) and, by contrast, describes his own menu, positively modest and restrained by a Trimalchio's standards (5, 78). For an example of what may constitute a meal enjoyed by the lower orders, see the meal provided by Philemon and Baucis just described.

Pliny reinforces the importance of protocol in Letters 1, 15 when he deplores the failure of an invited guest to show up. Martial's even-handedness and fairness in insisting on serving the same food to all the guests, whatever their social status, is reflected in Martial's attack on dinner time discrimination in 10, 49.

Here, Horace gives us an embarrassing yet hilarious dinner party hosted by a pretentious nouveau riche:

'How did you enjoy your dinner party with good old Nasidienus? Yesterday, when I was looking for you to be my guest they told me that you had been drinking there since midday.'

'I had the time of my life.'

'Tell me then, if it's not too much trouble, what was the first course to sate your grumbling stomach?'

'First up was a Lucanian boar. It was caught (as the master of the feast kept telling us) when a gentle southerly breeze was blowing. Around it were bitter-tasting turnips, lettuces, radishes—the sort of stuff that revives a tired stomach—skirrett, fish sauce and Coan tartar. A slave boy, wearing his tunic hitched up high, took these away and wiped the maple table dry with a purple and coarse woven cloth; another cleared away anything that was lying around, leaving nothing to annoy the diners. Next, like an Attic virgin bearing the sacred emblem of Ceres, dusky Hydaspes entered with Caecuban wine and then Alcon with Chian—and it hadn't been diluted with sea water.[2] Our master asked: 'Maecenas, if you'd prefer Alban or Falernian to this, we have both'.

'Wealth is obnoxious! But Fundanius, I really want to know who the diners were you were having such a good time with?'

'I was at the top table and next to me was Viscus from Thurii and, if I remember it rightly, Varius was further down. Then Vibidius and Servilius Balatro—the hangers-on whom Maecenas had brought with him. Nomentanus was up from him, down from him Porker—that buffoon who swallows his cakes in one go. Nomentanus' role was to point out with his forefinger anything that might have escaped our attention. The rest of the mob, us I mean, ate fowl, oysters and fish; it all tasted very different from what we were used to; this very quickly became apparent when he offered us livers of turbot and plaice—something we had not tasted before. After this he informed me that the honey apples were red because they had been picked by the light of a waning moon—why that makes a difference you'd best ask him.'

'Then Vibidius said to Balatro: 'If we don't drink him out of house and home we will die unavenged'—and he called for bigger goblets. At this our host's face turns white: nothing did he fear more than hardened drinkers—either because they're only too ready to bad-mouth you or because full-bodied wines blunt a delicate palate. Vibidius and Balatro decanted full jugs of wine into Allifan goblets; everyone else followed suit except those guests on the bottom couch who did the flagons no damage at all.[3]

'Then they brought in a lamprey sprawled on a platter with shrimps swimming around it. On this the master remarked: 'This lamprey was pregnant when it was caught; the flesh isn't so good after spawning. The sauce is mixed as follows: oil from Venafrum—the first pressing only—roe from the sauce of a Spanish mackerel, five year vintage Italian wine poured in while warm—warmed Chian is the best—white pepper and don't forget vinegar made from fermenting grapes from Lesbos. It was I who introduced bitter elecampane and greens boiled in the sauce. Curtillus uses unwashed sea urchins because the juices from the sea shells are better than just sea water.'

As he was speaking the curtains hanging above us crashed down weaking mass destruction on the dishes below, drawing up more black dust than the north wind raises on a Campanian plain. We feared the worst but, on finding there to be no danger, pulled ourselves together. However Rufus, head in hands, wept as if his son had died before his time. What would have happened if Nomentanus, playing the philosopher, had not reassured his friend: 'Fortuna—is any god crueller to us? You're always having fun toying with the affairs of man'. Varius could barely conceal a smirk behind his napkin; Balatro, turning his nose up at everything, said: 'These are the conditions by which we exist, you'll never get out of life what you have to put into it. To think that you have to drive yourself mad and torment yourself with every kind of worry just so that I might be entertained lavishly: is the toast burned, is the sauce served badly seasoned, are all your serving boys properly dressed and groomed? Then there are the unpredictable calamities: like the curtains crashing down just now or a dunderhead stumbling and smashing a dish. It's just the same with army generals: you only see their expertise when something goes wrong—it remains hiddenwhen things are going well.'

Nasidienus replied: 'May the gods give you everything you pray for. You're a good bloke and a convivial mate' and he then asks for his slippers to be brought.[4] At this point on each couch you could spot whisperers whispering in each other's ears.' 'I'd love to have been there, but come on, what was there to laugh at next?'

'Vibidius was asking the servant if they had smashed the wine jug ass well (he had not got the goblets he'd asked for) and while we were making up things to laugh at, aided and abetted by Balatro, Nasidienus came back in frowning, desperate to salvage some hope from adversity. Next the servants came in parading the carved up limbs of a crane on a huge platter, liberally seasoned with salt and lots of flour; the liver of a snow goose stuffed with juicy figs; and a hare with its legs ripped off—much nicer that way than with them still on.

Then we saw blackbirds, their breasts roasted and rumpless doves served up to us: special stuff this—our host told us all about the why and wherefore of each of them. We got our revenge by running out without trying any of it, just as if Canidia the witch had breathed all over the food—and her breath's worse than an African snake's.

Horace, *Satires* 2, 8

Here are excerpts from Trimalchio's famous feast—a picaresque description of small town *nouveau riche* Italy, with episode after vulgar episode of extravagance, pretentiousness, and outrageous ostentation as sumptuous dinner courses are punctuated by bizarre entertainments.

The third day arrived and with it the prospect of a free meal but, peppered as we were with so many wounds, we preferred to run away rather than rest. So, while we were gloomily deliberating how we might avoid the impending storm, one of Agamemnon's slaves interrupted us in our anxiety and said 'Why, don't you know where it's at today? Chez Trimalchio, a most splendid chap—he has a clock and in his dining room a decked out bugler so that he always knows how much of his life he has frittered away'. We dress carefully and all our problems forgotten, we order Giton, who up until now he had been playing the servant most willingly, to follow us to the baths… It would take ages to explain everything that happened; we went into the baths and as soon as we were hot enough to sweat went into the cold room. Trimalchio was now drenched in perfume and they rubbed him down not with linen but with towels made from the softest wool. Three masseuses meanwhile drank Falernian wine in front of him spilling much of it when they argued; Trimalchio said that this was them drinking to his health. He was then wrapped in a scarlet woollen cloak and put in a litter with four runners wearing medallions running before him; his squeeze rode in a hand cart: he was a bleary-eyed old looking boy, uglier even than his master. When they got going a musician moved up close to Trimalchio's head with some tiny pipes and played for the entire journey as if he was whispering a secret in his ear. We followed admiringly and reached the door with Agamemnon: on the post a notice was fixed with the inscription:

'Any slave going out without his master's permission will get a hundred lashes.'

In the entrance stood a porter dressed in leek green and wearing a cherry-red belt; he was shelling peas into a silver platter and a golden cage was hanging in the threshold in which a black and white magpie greeted anyone coming in. But while I was gawping at all these things I nearly fell back and broke my leg. On the left as you went in not far from the porter's lodge a huge dog tethered on a chain was painted on the partition wall and above it in block capitals:

'BEWARE OF THE DOG'.

My friends laughed at me but I got my breath back and began to look at the whole wall. There was a slave market with inscriptions painted on it: a long-haired Trimalchio was there holding the staff of Mercury and Minerva leading him into Rome.[5] We couldn't look at many more as we had now reached the dining room. At the entrance a cashier was doing his books. I was particularly struck by the rods and axes fixed onto the door posts of the dining room—one part of which was finished off like a ship's bronze beak; on it was inscribed:

'To Gaius Pompeius Trimalchio Priest of the College of Augustus from Cinnamus the Treasurer.'[6, 7]

We finally got to recline and some of the Alexandrian boys poured snow-cold water over our hands; others followed and at our feet skilfully gave us pedicures. Even in this irksome task they couldn't keep quiet but sang on regardless. I wanted to find out if all of the family slaves sang so I ordered a drink. A very attentive boy took this on with a shrill song—all of them did the same when asked to get anything. You'd think it was a pantomime dance and not the dining room of the head of the household. The *hors d'oeuvres* really whetted our appetites; everyone was reclining now except Trimalchio himself who was to be on the top table in the new fashion. A bronze baby saddle-back donkey stood on the tray, black olives on one side, white on the other. Two dishes hid the donkey, on the edge Trimalchio's name and their weight in silver were inscribed. There were even dormice seasoned with honey and pepper held up on little bridges that had been soldered on. Sizzling sausages had been placed on a silver grill and under the grill Syrian plums and Punic pomegranates.

We were enjoying these delicacies when Trimalchio himself was carried in to the room to musical accompaniment and propped up on a tiny pillar, much to the amusement of the impudent among us. His head was shaven and peeped out from a scarlet cloak; around the heavy scarf round his neck he had put on a purple striped cloth, its fringes hanging down.[8] On his left hand little finger he had a big golden ring and on the very end of his next finger a smaller one which I thought was solid gold but, as it turned out, was studded with iron stars.[9, 10] And these weren't the only extravagances he paraded: he bared his right arm to reveal a golden armlet and an ivory bangle buckled with shining gold plate; then he picked his teeth with a silver pin… We were still on the starters when a tray was brought in with a basket on it; in here was a wooden cockerel, its wings splayed out in a circle as they do when they are laying eggs. Two slaves came up now and with the music at full blast began to rummage through the straw; they plucked out pea-hen's eggs and shared them among the guests. Trimalchio turned to look at this scene and said: 'Friends, I told them to put the eggs of a pea-hen under an ordinary hen. And, good god, I am afraid they may have hatched out by now, but we'll try and see if they are still suckable.' We took up our spoons—each half a pound in weight—and tapped the eggs which were covered in fine flour. I nearly threw my portion away as it looked as if it had already turned into a chicken, but then I heard a guest who had seen it all before say: 'I've no idea how good this is going to be'. I poked the shell with my finger and found a plump blackcap inside wrapped in a peppery yolk.

Now Trimalchio… shouted at the top of his voice that we could have more mead if we wanted it. All of a sudden, signalled by a fanfare, a troupe of singing dancers cleared away the *hors d'oeuvres*. But in the tumult, someone dropped a starters dish—a boy picked it up from where it lay on the ground. Trimalchio spotted this and punished the boy with a thump ordering him to throw the dish down again. A porter followed him in and began to sweep up the silver with his broom with the rest of the rubbish. Then two long-haired Ethiopians with the tiniest of bags came in just like the men who sprinkle sand in the amphitheatre; they gave us wine for our hands because no-one was offering water. We complimented our host on such niceties. 'Mars loves a level playing field' he said 'So I said that everyone should be given his own table and these fetid slaves will fluster us less with their comings and goings.'

Then they brought in some glass amphorae that had been carefully coated with gypsum; the labels fixed to their necks bore the inscription:

Falernian of Opimius' vintage—100 years old.

While we were reading these Trimalchio clapped his hands and said 'Ah, wine lives longer than the little man; let's get pissed. Wine is life. I'm giving you genuine Opimian vintage. Yesterday the stuff I served was not nearly so good even though we were entertaining better men than you lot'. We drank up and carefully admired each extravagance in detail; then a slave brought in a silver skeleton made in such a way that its joints and vertebrae could be articulated and bent in every direction. He threw it down onto the table once or twice so that the moving joints took on different poses. Trimalchio intoned:

'Alas, we wretches; the man in the street is worth absolutely nothing.

And that's what we all will be after Orcus has carried us off.

Let us live life while it's still worth living.'

As we applauded this another course followed—clearly not as big as we'd hoped but its sheer originality had everyone agog. The twelve zodiacal signs were arranged in a circle on a round tray; on each of the signs the chef had placed food fitting and appropriate to the sign. Over Aries ram-shaped chickpeas; over Taurus a piece of beef; over Gemini testicles and kidneys; over Cancer a garland; over Leo an African fig; over Virgo the womb of a virgin sow; over Libra a set of scales with a tart on one side and a cake on the other; over Scorpio little sea fish; over Sagittarius a lamprey; over Capricorn a lobster; over Aquarius a goose; over Pisces a pair of red mullets. In the middle a honeycomb lay on a grassy clump of turf. An Egyptian boy was going round with bread on a silver bread tray.

Trimalchio then proceeded to murder a song from the mime Laserpiciario, his voice hideous. It was with some reluctance that we approached our low rent meal. Trimalchio said 'Come on let's dine—here's the menu.' As he spoke four dancers came in to a fanfare and lifted off the top part of the dish. This enabled us to see fat fowls and sows' udders at the bottom and in the middle a hare was dressed up in wings to look like Pegasus. Around the corners of the dish we picked out four figures of Marysas; the dancers drizzled a peppery fish sauce from their wine bottles over some fish which were swimming in a channel.[11] We all clapped (led on by the household slaves) and got stuck in to these delicacies with gusto. Trimalchio was pleased with this amusement and called out 'Carver'. The carver came forward at once and, gesticulating in time to the music, proceeded to hack up the fish in such a way that you'd think he was a gladiator fighting to the tune of a water organ grinder. Trimalchio repeated quietly: 'Carver, Carver'. I suspected more than once that his repetition of that word might be a conceit and felt no embarrassment in questioning the guest next to me about this. He had seen such sights many times before and explained: 'You see him who's carving the fish? He's called Carver, so whenever Trimalchio says 'carver' he's calling him and giving him orders with the same word

Petronius, *Satyricon*: *Cena Trimalchionis* 26–36

Trimalchio interrupted these great stories; the dishes had been cleared away and the merry guests had begun to guzzle the wine, chatting generally. Trimalchio lay back on his couch and said: 'Make this wine slip down nicely. Fish have got to have something to swim in. I ask you, do you think that I was happy with that dish you saw in the top part of the tray? Is this the Ulysses we all know? Is it not so? You must know your literature even at dinner. May the bones of my patron rest in peace, he who wanted me to be a man among men. There's nothing new in the world as that last course shows. The place where the twelve gods live in the heavens turns into the same number of figures. At one point it becomes a ram and so whoever is born under that sign has plenty of flocks and plenty of wool as well as a hard head, knows no shame, and has sharp horns. Lots of students and dunderheads are born under this sign.' We applauded the sophistication of his astrology; he went on: 'then the whole sky turns into a little bull and that's when heel kickers are born and ploughmen and people who have to provide for themselves. In Gemini, however, it's two-horse chariots, cattle and men with balls and those who just sit on the fence. I was born under Cancer. As such I have many legs to stand on and own many things on land and on sea—the crab is happy on either one or the other. Just now I didn't put anything on top of the crab in case I squashed my birth sign. Under Leo gluttons and tyrants are born; under Virgo, women, fugitives and shackled slaves; under Libra butchers and perfumers and anyone who weighs things out for a living; poisoners and assassins under Scorpio; under Sagittarius crossed-eyed people who look at the vegetables but take the bacon; under Capricorn the poor wretches whose troubles make them come out all prickly; Aquarius produces spivs and cabbage heads; under Pisces caterers and rhetoricians. So the world turns like a windmill— always bringing bad things: this is how mankind either lives or dies. You saw the turf in the middle of the plate and the honeycomb on the turf—everything I do has a reason. That's mother earth there in the middle, round as an egg and full of goodness like a honeycomb.

'Bravo!' we all shouted together and with hands raised high swore that Hipparchus and Aratus were no match for him.[12] The servants came in and placed valances over the couches; nets were painted on these and ambushers with hunting spears and all the paraphernalia of the hunt. We still didn't know what to expect next when a mighty roar came from outside the dining room and Spartan hounds began running round the tables. A platter was then brought in with the biggest wild boar on it you'd ever seen. It was wearing the felt cap of freedom, and two little baskets interwoven with dates hung from its tusks—one filled with nut-shaped dates, the other with Theban dates. Around it were little piglets made from cake looking as if they were about to suck the udders; this told us that we had before us a breeding sow. They were the gifts for the guests to take home with them. Carver, who had hacked up the fattened fowls, did not step forward to carve up the boar but instead a huge bearded bloke, his legs strapped with bands and wearing a woven hunting tunic, did the honours. He drew a hunting knife and slashed the flank of the boar hard with it. At this blow thrushes flew out from inside the boar. As they flitted around the dining room, fowlers who were ready with limed twigs for bird-catching caught them in a flash. Trimalchio then ordered that each guest should be given their own portion and added: 'Now you can see what splendid acorns the woodland pig has been eating.' Then the boys approached the baskets hanging from its tusks and shared the nut-shaped and Theban dates equally among the guests.

Meanwhile I had retreated to a corner on my own and tried to work out why the boar had come in wearing the cap of freedom. After I had exhausted every possible explanation, I steeled myself to ask my 'interpreter' about this conundrum. He said 'Clearly your humble servant could clear this up: there is no puzzle here, it's obvious. Yesterday this boar assumed itself to be the main course but the guests let him go free; so he returns today to the meal as a freedman.' I cursed my stupidity and let it rest in case it looked like I had never eaten with educated people before.

As we were speaking a good-looking boy with vines and ivy wreathed in his hair, appearing now as noisy Bacchus, then as Bacchus the Liberator, then as Bacchus Euhium, brought round grapes and fruit baskets and recited his master's poems in a piercing voice. Trimalchio turned round when he heard this racket and said 'Dionysus, you're free'. The boy removed the cap of freedom from the boar and put it on his own head. Then Trimalchio retorted: 'You can't say now that Bacchus the Liberator isn't my father'. We applauded Trimalchio's speech and snogged the boy as he did the rounds. After this course Trimalchio got up to go to the toilet. Finding ourselves free, our tyrant gone, we began to encourage conversation with the other guests. Dama was the first to speak up when he called for bigger goblets: 'Daytime is nothing; before you can turn round night has fallen. So, the best thing to do is go straight from your bed to the dining room. The world's a cold place and bathing scarcely warms me up; on the other hand a warm drink is like an overcoat. I have had a good drink and am obviously pissed. The wine has addled my brains'.

Petronius, *Satyricon: Cena Trimalchionis* 39–41

Martial shows the misery caused when those all-important invitations to dinner are not forthcoming:

> Rufus—look at Selius with his stormy frown, how his walking wears away the portico floor late into the night. His dejected expression betrays some unspoken misery. His ugly nose almost scrapes the ground and he beats his breast and pulls out his hair with his right hand. He is not grieving over the death of a friend or a brother though, each of his sons is still alive and I pray they go on living; his wife is safe too as are his belongings and his slaves. Neither his farm hand nor his neighbour are bankrupt. Why such misery then? Selius is dining at home!
>
> Martial 2, 11

Torianus has better luck when Martial invites him over with the promise of good food and some comparatively dull after-dinner entertainment:

> If you are bothered by the thought of a miserable dinner at home, Toranius, you can come and be hungry with me. You will have, if you are used to a starter, cheap Cappadocian lettuces and strong-smelling leeks; a piece of tunny fish concealed in sliced eggs… light green broccoli, fresh from the cool garden, and a sausage lying on white chick peas, and pale beans with ruddy bacon. If you wish for the rewards of a second course, bursting grapes will be offered and Syrian pears, and chestnuts which sophisticated Neapolis has grown, roasted over a slow heat; you will make the wine drinkable simply by drinking it. After all this, as Bacchus usually sharpens the appetite, select olives which Picenian branches have recently borne will satisfy you, and hot chick-peas and warm lupins.
>
> My meagre dinner is undeniably modest …nor will your host be reading a blockbuster, nor will girls from salacious Gades endlessly grind their sexy groins in well-practised rhythm; but the pipe of little Condylus will play something not too solemn nor trashy. Such is our little dinner. You will chase Claudia. Which girl do you wish to meet before me?
>
> Martial 5, 78; translation adapted from W.C.A. Ker, Loeb Classical Library (1919)

The invitation to Julius Cerialis (*Epigrams* 11, 52) is even more exotic, at least in terms of the dishes on offer: lettuce (good for the digestion), leeks, pickled tuna, eggs and rue leaves, cheese, and olives await Cerialis for starters. Fish, oysters, sow's udders, stuffed wildfowl and farmyard hens are, apparently, the main courses. There will be no post-prandial recitations.

Martial deplores a dinner guest's rude habit of stealing the meal:

> You hoover up whatever is served up for you: the udders of a sow, the rib of a pork, a hazel hen for two to share, a half eaten mullet and a whole sea bass, a side of murena, a chicken's leg, a wood pigeon dripping in its sauce. When you have concealed all this

in your soggy napkin you give it to your boy to carry home. We recline—an idle lot. If you have any shame—bring back our meal Caecilianus: I didn't invite you here today so that you can feast tomorrow.

Martial 2, 37

Here, we have Juvena's savage satire on the lothario Crispinus and his dinner party, ridiculously dominated by a huge turbot.

Enter Crispinus once again! A man who deserves to be cued often by me to play his role—a monster who has no virtues at all to redeem his vices; a sickly pleasure seeker whose only strong point is his sex drive, an adulterer who rejects only unmarried women. What does it matter the size of his porticos where he wears out his his donkeys, how big the shady grove is that he's carried around in, his acres of land and the mansions he has bought near the Forum? No charlatan is ever happy—especially when he is an incestuous corrupter who has just laid a vestal virgin; she will now be buried alive, her blood still coursing through her veins.

But now to lighter matters. If any other man had done these same things he would have been judged guilty by the censor on the grounds that what is repellent to good men like Titius or Seius was quite acceptable behaviour for Crispinus.[13, 14] What do you do when the man in question is crueller and more disgusting than any crime? He bought a red mullet for 6,000 sesterces and that's the same as 1,000 sesterces a pound, as they who exaggerate the exaggerated would put it.

I could endorse a crafty scheme like this if with such a fantastic gift he won top place in the will of some childless old man or, an even better ruse, sent it to a high and mighty mistress who drives around in her capacious, wide-windowed sedan. No chance, he bought it for himself. We're seeing lots of things nowadays which even miserly and penny-pinching Apicius never did.[15] Did you, Crispinus, who once upon a time dressed yourself in Egyptian papyrus pay such a price for ... fish scales? You could have bought a fisherman for less than you paid for the fish—land in the provinces sells for as much; you get even more in Apulia.

What banquets do you suppose our Imperator gobbled down when so many sesterces—a trifle, a mere side dish from a normal meal—were belched up by Crispinus—that purple toga'd dandy in the palace. Now he's in command of the knights, the same man who used to shout out the price of sprats from damaged cargoes to his fellow citizens, themselves sprats.

Begin Calliope—let's take our seats; this is no mere poetry recital, this is about the truth. Tell it you Pierian girls (and may I get some reward from calling you 'girls').[16]

At a time when the last Flavian was flogging a half dead world to death and Rome was enslaved to a bald headed Nero in the Adriatic Sea in front of the temple of Venus on Doric Ancon, a fabulously big flat fish fell into and filled a bulging net. It got stuck there, as big as the fish which icy Lake Maeotis conceals and which—the ice broken up by the sun—pour in a torrent out of the mouth of the Pontus, sluggish through sloth and fattened up through the long lasting cold.[17] This monstrous master of the Boat and Line is destined for the Pontifex Maximus; who would dare to sell or indeed buy such a thing when the shorelines are full of informers? Seaweed inspectors, all over the place, would go after the shirtless oarsman. They'd not hesitate to claim that this fish had fed for ages in Caesar's fish farm and, since it had escaped from there, must be returned to its former master. If Palfurius or Armillatus are to be believed, whatever is out of the ordinary and beautiful in the whole sea, wherever it swims, belongs to the imperial treasury and the fish will be given as a gift so that it doesn't go to waste.[18]

Then the man from Picenum says: 'Accept this fish, too big as it is for a private citizen's kitchen. Make this day a holiday. Hurry up and fill your stomachs with this feast of a fish; eat up this turbot reserved specially for your reign. It actually wanted to be caught.' What could be more blatant? The emperor's dander was up: there is nothing the divine potentate won't believe about himself when he is being praised.

But there wasn't a platter big enough for the fish. A council of top officials is convened—the Emperor hated them all, their pallid faces reflecting the miserable, majestic friendship...

Juvenal, Satires 4, 1–72

Pliny is riled by this rude no-show:

To Septicius Clarus

Hello there! You promise to come to dinner and then you don't show up! The law says that you must pay back my costs to the last penny, and it won't be cheap. This is what was prepared: one lettuce, three snails, two eggs, spelt mixed with honey and snow ... olives from Baetica, cucumbers, onions, and a thousand other equally sumptuous dishes. You would have heard a comedian, or a speaker, or a lyre-player, or all three—because I am such a generous host. But you preferred to dine somewhere else, I know not where—off oysters, sow's udders, sea-urchins, and to watch Spanish dancing girls. You will pay the penalty...

Pliny, Epistles 1, 15, 1–10

Martial shows his irritation at dinner party recitals:

Ligurinus I have no idea if Phoebus fled from the table at the feast of Thyestes but we're fleeing from yours.[19] It's certainly splendid and set with superb dishes but nothing can please us with you reciting. I don't want you to serve me turbots or two pound mullets; I don't want your wonderful mushrooms; I don't want your oysters: just shut up!

Martial 3, 45

We have already seen how Pliny abhors the insulting meanness and snobbery of a dinner host at *Epistles* 2, 6.

Recipes

Martial is something of a connoisseur when it comes to certain exotic dishes:

Goose livers:
    See how the liver swells bigger than a big goose![20] Amazed, you will ask 'Where did this come from, I want to know'.

Martial, Epigrams 13, 58

Ringed doves:
    Ringed doves slow and stunt your erection; no-one who wants to be horny should eat this bird.

Martial, Epigrams 13, 67

The *Apicius* is the place to go for a peerless Roman recipe book; compiled in the late 4th or early fifth century CE, it is often referred to as the *De Re Coquinaria of Apicius.* Here are some examples:

Rose Wine (*Rosatum*)
    Make rose wine in this manner: rose petals, the lower white part removed, sewed into a linen bag and immersed in wine for seven days. Thereupon add a sack of new petals which allow to draw for another seven days. Again remove the old petals and replace them by fresh ones for another week then strain the wine through the colander. Before serving, add honey sweetening to taste. Take care that only the best petals free from dew be used for soaking.

Brain Sausage (*Isicia de Cerebellis*)
    Put in the mortar pepper, lovage and origany, moisten with broth and rub; add cooked brains and mix diligently so that there be no lumps. Incorporate five eggs and continue mixing well to have a good forcemeat which you may thin with broth. Spread this out in a metal pan, cook, and when cooked cold unmould it onto a clean table. Cut into handy size. Now prepare a sauce. Put in the mortar pepper, lovage and origany, crush, mix with broth. Put into a sauce pan, boil, thicken and strain. Heat the pieces of brain pudding in this sauce thoroughly, dish them up, sprinkled with pepper, in a mushroom dish.

Smelt Pie, or, Sprat Custard (*Patina de abua sive apua*)
    Boneless pieces of anchovies or other small fish, either roast [fried] boiled, chop very fine. Fill a casserole generously with the same; season with crushed pepper and a little rue, add sufficient broth and some oil, and mix in, also add enough raw eggs so that the whole forms one solid mass. Now carefully add some sea-nettles but take pain that they are not mixed with the eggs. Now put the dish into the steam so that it

may congeal but avoid boiling. When done sprinkle with ground pepper and carry into the dining room. Nobody will be able to tell what he is enjoying.

Stuffed Pumpkin Fritters (*Gustum de cucurbitis farsilibus*)

A dish of stuffed pumpkin is made thus: peel and cut the pumpkin lengthwise into oblong pieces which hollow out and put in a cool place. The dressing for the same make in this way: crush pepper, lovage and origany, moistened with broth; mince cooked brains and beat raw eggs and mix all together to form a paste; add broth as taste requires. Stuff the above prepared pieces of pumpkin that have not been fully cooked with the dressing; fit two pieces together and close them tight holding them by means of strings or skewers. Now poach them and take the cooked ones out and fry them. The proper wine sauce for this dish make thus: crush pepper, lovage moistened with wine, raisin wine to taste, a little oil, place in pan to be cooked; when done bind with roux. Cover the fried pumpkin with this sauce, sprinkle with pepper and serve.

Treatment of Strong Smelling Birds of every Description (*Ad aves hircosasa omni genere*)

For birds of all kinds that have a goatish smell [add] pepper, lovage, thyme, dry mint, sage, dates, honey, vinegar, wine, broth, oil, reduced must, mustard. The birds will be more luscious and nutritious, and the fat preserved, if you envelop them in a dough of flour and oil and bake them in the oven.

For Flamingo and Parrot (*In phoenicoptero*)

Scald the flamingo, wash and dress it, put it in a pot, add water, salt, dill, and a little vinegar, to be parboiled. Finish cooking with a bunch of leeks and coriander, and add some reduced must to give it color. In the mortar crush pepper, cumin, coriander, laser root, mint, rue, moisten with vinegar, add dates, and the fond of the braised bird, thicken, strain, cover the bird with the sauce and serve. Parrot is prepared in the same manner.

Milk-fed Snails (*Cochleas lacte pastas*)

Take snails and sponge them; pull them out of the shells by the membrane and place them for a day in a vessel with milk and salt. Renew the milk daily. Hourly clean the snails of all refuse, and when they are so fat that they can no longer retire to their shells fry them in oil and serve them with wine sauce. In a similar way they may be fed on a milk porridge.

Stuffed Dormouse (*Glires*)

Is stuffed with a forcemeat of pork and small pieces of dormouse meat trimmings, all pounded with pepper, nuts, laser, broth. Put the dormouse thus stuffed in an earthen casserole, roast it in the oven, or boil it in the stock pot.

Apicius 1, 4; 2, 46; 4, 139; 4, 176; 6, 229; 6, 231; 7, 323; 8, 396

All translations by Walter M. Hill (1936).

Medicine, Death, and Dying

The medicine practised in Rome, particularly from the last hundred years or so of the Republic, was heavily influenced by Greek medical science and practice, and by Greek physicians. Before that, it was very much a domestic affair employing folk medicine, remedies, and therapies, reflecting the largely rural society that Rome was.

With the absence of formally trained and qualified doctors, the norm was for the *paterfamilias* or *materfamilias* to take lead in the provision of family medicine. Old Italic folk remedies, magic and divination formed the basis of early Roman medical practice with the focus on remedies for symptoms rather than anything sophisticated related to diagnosis, history taking or prognosis. The gods and the spirits looked after all of that: there was at least one divinity for every stage of life. Things began to change with the influx of Greek culture and science into Rome in the second and first centuries BCE; this brought with it scientists, including Greek doctors. In the first century CE, 90 per cent of doctors in Rome were of Greek origin. Access to libraries, such as Alexandria and the medical school there, led to improved surgical technique and progress in preclinical medicine: anatomy, physiology and pathology. In the first half of the third century BCE, two Greeks, Herophilus of Chalcedon and Erasistratus of Ceos, had been the first and only ancient scientists to perform systematic dissections of human cadavers; these probably included vivisections of condemned criminals.

In the second century CE, Galen attributed shortcomings in Roman medical training to the lack of practice available on cadavers because dissection and autopsy was forbidden by Roman law and urged students to visit Alexandria; failing that, to make good use of the corpses of robbers to be found on the roadside, or of bodies washed up on river banks.[1] On the assumption that their anatomy was similar to that of humans, Galen, for example, dissected the Barbary macaque and other primates.

Generally speaking, the medical profession received a bad press from the Romans, not least because many so-called doctors in Rome and other Italian places were Greek or freedmen or both. Medical training seems to have been alarmingly perfunctory and somewhat hit and miss—six months of trailing someone a bit more experienced than yourself in an extremely large firm was about as good as it got; no licence to practice was required. Galen's eleven years of training was probably the exception rather than the rule. Martial shows his contempt for the medical profession more than once—he complains that the 100-strong firm led by Dr Symmachus actually made him ill when before he had been quite well:

> I was a bit ill and you came to me at once Symmachus, with a firm of a hundred students. A hundred pairs of frosty hands mauled me: I didn't have a fever before, Symmachus; now I've got one.
>
> Martial 5, 9

> Andragoras bathed, and had a convivial drink with me; in the morning he was found dead. Fustinus, are you asking why so sudden a death? He had dreamt about Dr Hermocrates.
>
> Martial 6, 53

> Now you're a gladiator; before that you were an ophthalmologist. What you did as a doctor you now do as a gladiator.

> Not so long ago Diaulus was a doctor, now he is an undertaker. What he does now as an undertaker he used to do as a doctor.

> Diaulus was a surgeon, now he is an undertaker; he begins here where he left off as a doctor.
>
> Martial 8, 74; 1, 47; 1, 30

Pliny the Elder, uncle of Pliny the Younger, was a scientist who wrote about all things scientific, including medical science. Pliny bewails the Greek-ness of the practice of medicine and doctors' lack of accountability:

> Medicine is the only one of the arts of Greece, that, lucrative as it is, the Roman has so far refused to cultivate. The few fellow-citizens that have even attempted it soon become deserters to the Greeks: moreover, if they attempt practice in any other language than Greek, they are sure to lose all credibility... In fact, this is the only one of all the arts... which the minute a man declares himself to be qualified, is at once believed...To all this, however, we pay no attention, so tempting is the sweet influence of the hope of ultimate recovery.
>
> And then besides, there is no law whereby to punish the ignorance of physicians, no precedent before us of capital punishment. It is at the expense of our dangers that they learn, and they experiment by putting us to death, a physician being the only person that can kill another with impunity. Moreover, all blame is heaped on the patient; he is accused of not complying: it is the person who is dead that is put on trial.
>
> Pliny, *Natural History* 29, 8, 16–18

His nephew, Pliny the Younger, grieves over the suicide of his terminally ill friend; in so doing, he provides a moving account of a dignified end of life scenario.[2]

To Calestrius Tiro

I have suffered a great loss, if loss is the right word for the death of such a great man. Corellius Rufus is dead; he committed suicide and this makes my grief even more intense. The most lamentable type of death is that which is neither natural nor fated. When someone dies from disease there is much comfort knowing that it had to be, but in the case of those carried away by voluntary death, the grief is incurable because you believe they could have lived a long life. Indeed Corellius, rational as all philosophers must be, came to such a decision even though he had many reasons for living: the best of consciences, the best of reputations and an extensive authority. As well as this [he leaves] a daughter, wife, grandson and sisters as well as other relatives and true friends. But he was afflicted by ill health over such a long period of time that reasons for dying outweighed the rewards of life. I have heard him say himself that when he was thirty-two he developed gout in his foot. His father had it before him: many diseases, like other things, are hereditary. When he was in good health he overcame his illness and broke it through abstinence and a healthy lifestyle; but when it got worse recently in his old age he kept going by sheer determination, even though he was in excruciating pain and unbearable torment. The pain was not confined now to his feet as before but racked his whole body. I went to see him in Domitian's time on the outskirts of Rome where he lay ill. The servants left the room: (they routinely did this whenever his closer friends visited) and even his wife went out even though she was more than capable of being discreet.[3] He glanced around and said 'Why do you think I'm putting up with such great pain for so long—so that I might outlive that royal robber if only for just one day?'[4] If his body had been equal to his determination he would have got what he wanted. However, the gods heard his prayer and, his wish granted and free from care, he felt free to die and sever many of the less important aspects of his life. His illness got worse and although he tried to alleviate it through more careful living he was determined to escape from it. He fasted for two, three, four days. Hispulla, his wife, sent Gaius Geminus, a mutual friend, to me with the sad news that Corellius was intent on dying and would not be deterred by her or her daughter's pleas. I was the only one left who could bring him back from the brink. I ran to him and had almost got there when Julius Atticus told me from Hispulla that there was nothing even I could do as he had become even more obdurate. When his doctor prescribed food he simply said 'I have made up my mind'—words which remind me how much I admired him and how much grief he leaves in his wake. I keep thinking what sort of friend, what sort of man I have lost? He reached sixty-seven, a good enough age I know for the fittest of men. He evaded a terminal illness, I know. His family survived him, as did his country—and in fine fettle too—dearer to him than all else—I know all these things but I still mourn his death as if he were a young man in good health, I mourn too (and you may think me silly) for myself: for I have lost him, I have lost my mentor, the guardian who guided my life. To put it briefly I'll say what I said to my friend Calvisius when I first started to grieve 'I'm afraid I'm going to live a little more recklessly from now on'. Console me, but please don't just say he was old and ill (I know this); say something original and bold, something I haven't heard or read before. What I have already heard and read helps anyway but it is overwhelmed by such great grief. Farewell.

Pliny the Younger, *Epistles* 1, 12

On a more trivial level, Cicero describes his upset stomach to Marcus Fadius Gallus in 57 BCE, whether Gallus wants to know the details or not:

For the last nine days I have been suffering from severe stomach pains… in fact, for two days I fasted so strictly that I did not drink even a drop of water … the chefs … flavour mushrooms, pastries and every kind of stew so as to make them the most tempting dishes possible. Having succumbed to these at the augural banquet at the house of Lentulus, I was struck with violent diarrhoea, which, I think, is relenting for the first time today.

Cicero, *Ad Familiares* 7, 26

Seneca the Younger endured many illnesses but his asthma was the most difficult for him and his prognosis is rather gloomy:

There's one particular illness, though, for which I've always been singled out, as it were. I don't see why I should call it by its Greek name [*asthma*], difficulty with breathing is a perfectly adequate way of describing it. An attack doesn't last long at all—like a storm it's usually over within the hour. After all, you can hardly expect anyone to breathe his last for very long. I've had every troublesome or serious complaints there is but, if you ask me, none of them is more alarming than this one—hardly surprising, though when you consider that with anything else you're just ill, but with this one you're forever drawing your last breath. This is why doctors call it a 'rehearsal for death', since sooner or later the breath succeeds in doing just what it has been trying to do all the time.

Seneca, *Letters* 54, 1–4; 6

Here is what Pliny the Elder records about a range of conditions:

To cure jaundice, use the ashes from a stag's antlers or the blood of an ass's foal, taken with wine. The first manure excreted by the foal after its birth, taken in wine, in bean-sized pieces will effect a cure after three days. The dung of a new-born colt is just as good.

The flesh of cocks and capons, applied warm the moment it has been plucked from the bones, neutralizes the venom of serpents; and the brains, taken in wine, produce a similar effect… Poultry broth, too, is highly celebrated as a cure, and is found marvellously useful in many other cases. Panthers and lions will never touch people who have been rubbed with it, more particularly if it has been flavoured with garlic. The broth that is made of an old cock is more relaxing to the bowels; it is very good also for chronic fevers, numbness of the limbs, cold shiverings and maladies of the joints, pains also in the head, defluxions of the eyes, flatulency, sickness at stomach, incipient tenesmus (a bowel disorder), liver complaints, diseases of the kidneys, affections of the bladder, indigestion, and asthma. Hence there are several recipes for preparing this broth; it being most efficacious when boiled up with sea-cabbage, salted tunny, capers, parsley, the plant mercurialis, polypodium, or dill.

According to what the magicians say, glaucoma may be cured by using the brains of a puppy seven days old; the probe being inserted in the right side [of the eye], if it is the right eye that is being operated on, and in the left side, if it is the left. The fresh gall, too, of the asio is used, a bird belonging to the owlet tribe, with feathers standing erect like ears. Apollonius of Pitanæ used to prefer dog's gall, in combination with honey, to that of the hyæna, for the cure of cataract, as also of albugo. The heads and tails of mice, reduced to ashes and applied to the eyes, improve the sight, it is said; a result which is ensured with even greater certainty by using the ashes of a dormouse or wild mouse, or else the brains or gall of an eagle. The ashes and fat of a field-mouse, beaten up with Attic honey and antimony, are remarkably useful for watery eyes.

Scrofula, imposthumes of the parotid glands, and throat diseases, they say, may be cured by contact with the hand of a dead person, carried off by an early death: indeed there are some who assert that any corpse will produce the same effect, provided it is of the same sex as the patient, and that the part affected is touched with the back of the left hand.

For fractures, a great remedy is the ashes of the jaw-bone of a wild boar or swine: boiled bacon, too, tied round the broken bone, unites it with amazing speed. For fractures of the ribs, goats' dung, applied in old wine, is extolled as the first line treatment.

Pliny, Natural History 28, 64; 29, 25; 29, 38; 28, 11; 28, 65
all translations adapted from John Bostock, (Taylor and Francis, 1855)

Fertility

Soranus, the Greek physician practicing in Rome around 100 CE, concludes that 'women get married to bear children and heirs, and not for fun or pleasure'. To promote this, Soranus teaches that successful conception is all down to timing; he lists the best times:

The end of menstruation, when the urge and desire for sex is present, when the stomach is not full nor the partner drunk, after light exercise and a light snack, when the mood for sex is just right.

Soranus, *Gynaecology* 1, 34, 1.

These are the most promising conditions for making babies. Before him, Lucretius had taught that the best position for conception was for the woman to have *coitus more ferarum* (sexual intercourse like wild beasts do it), or from behind—*a tergo (kubra* in Greek).[5]

As she was unable to bear him children, Turia was happy not only to divorce her husband but also to find him another wife who was fertile; she would then act as a sister or mother-in-law in the new *menage a trois*. Turia's husband was wild with rage at her suggestion, preferring to stay married, even though it would mean the end of his family line.[6] Sulla divorced his allegedly barren wife, Cloelia.[7]

Trimalchio, in Petronius' *Satyricon*, has no such qualms and congratulated himself on not divorcing Fortunata because she failed to give him children.[8] Catullus, in his *epithalamium*, tells how you need to have Hymen's blessing in order to produce children—parents cannot rely on offspring without her blessing. Junia, the bride, must be sure to let her husband have sex with her, in case he goes looking for it elsewhere; indeed, Catullus urges the couple to mess around as much as they like and have children as soon as they can.[9]

Contraception

Contraception was all a bit hit and miss. Lucretius believed that women should wriggle their hips during sexual intercourse to divert the ejaculated semen—but, he adds, not all women should be so inelegant: *matronae* should not be so bold, just prostitutes.

For commonly 'tis thought that wives conceive more readily in the manner of wild-beasts, after the custom of the four-foot breeds, Because in such a position, with the breasts beneath and buttocks then upreared, the semen can take its proper place. Nor is there the least need for wives to use the motions of blandishment; For thus the woman hinders and resists her own conception, if too joyously herself she treats the Venus of the man with haunches heaving, and with all her bosom now yielding like the billows of the sea ... and courtesans are thuswise wont to move for their own ends, to keep from pregnancy and lying in, and all the while to render Venus more a pleasure for the men—which seems our wives have never need of.

Lucretius, *De Rerum Natura* 4, 1269–78
adapted from the quaint translation by William Ellery Leonard (1916).

Pliny the Elder, quoting Caecilius, recommended the use of an amulet:

> [It should be made from] the hairy spider which has a rather big head. If you cut this open you'll find two small worms which should be attached to the woman with deer skin: the woman will not then conceive…for one year.[10]

Pliny, Natural History 29, 27, 85

Non-vaginal sex is sometimes a form of contraception. Graffiti from Pompeii confirms its prevalence—with examples of sodomy and fellatio; Romula 'sucks her man here, there and everywhere', while Sabina sucks but doesn't get it quite right.[11] Seneca alludes to anal sex taking place on the wedding night, as does Martial, but just the once—nurse and mother forbid it from becoming a habit: the bride is his *uxor*, not a *puer*, a wife, not a boy.[12] Second century CE Manetho describes 'breast relief' in his *Forecasts*.[13]

In the first century CE, Dioscorides had twenty-four contraceptive potions, three of which were magic, including an amulet made of asparagus. Others involved the application of peppermint, honey, cedar gum, axe weed, and alum in various concoctions to the genitals. Soranus is equally unromantic: his contraception of choice is old olive oil, honey, or the sap from a balsam or cedar tree applied to the entrance of the vagina—on its own or (alarmingly) mixed with white lead and bunged up with wool. This has a coagulating and cooling effect which causes the vagina to close before sex, and acts as a barrier to the sperm. An alternative, just as inelegant, involved the woman holding her breath as her partner ejaculates, pulling away so that his semen does not penetrate too deeply, then getting up straight away and squatting and sneezing before wiping her vulva. He also recommends the use of vinegar, olive oil, ground pomegranate peel, and ground flesh of dried figs as vaginal suppositories.[14]

Things change very slowly: olive oil was still being advocated by the Marie Stopes Clinic as recently as 1931 along with other effective spermicides like lemon, alum, and vinegar.[15] Douches made from vinegar, alum, or lemon juice were still used by the working classes in New York in 1947, and lemons were still in use in 1970s Glasgow.[16]

Aetius vouches for the liver of a cat inserted inside a tube fitted to the woman's left foot, or a section from the womb of a lioness in an ivory tube.[17] In the fourth century CE, Oribasius advocated a cabbage pessary post-coitus.[18] These methods were hardly discrete or convenient and they certainly demanded consummate foresight and pre-coital preparation at the expense of romance and spontaneity. They all also indicate that it was up to the woman to organise contraception—although we do hear, from Pliny, of spermicides rubbed onto the penis and the use of goats' bladders as a primitive condom.[19] The 'safe' period seems to be unknown; no one mentions *coitus interruptus*, which may suggest that both methods were so common and obvious as to not merit comment. Withholding ejaculation was discouraged by Rufus of Ephesus because it damaged the kidneys and bladder; surgical sterilization only developed as far as experimentation on sows while vasectomy seems to have been carried out just on gladiators.

Juvenal, in his sixth satire rant against women, tells us that: 'Some women delight in impotent eunuchs with their soft kisses and failed beards, where there is no need for abortion' (Juvenal 6, 366–8).

Abortion & miscarriage

Dystocia (difficult labour), the chances of haemmorrhage, infection, puerperal sepsis, eclampsia, obstructed labour, and thromboembolism were all causes of the high rates of infant and maternal mortality and miscarriage in childbearing women of Rome.

Pliny the Younger offers consolation on a friend's grandaughter's miscarriage:

To Calpurnius Fabatus

The news that your grand-daughter has had a miscarriage will be even sadder for you to hear when you so much wanted a great grandchild. Being very young she did not know that she was pregnant and so failed to take certain precautions and avoid things she should have avoided. She paid for her mistake with the warning that she had put her life in mortal danger. Although you have to accept, reluctantly, that in your old age you are bereft of a descendent that was already on the way, you must thank the gods who, though they denied you a great grandchild for the time being, did after all take care of your grand-daughter. We can still hope that they are sure to bring us children because she has at least proven her fertility, albeit it with misfortune on this occasion. I urge, advise and encourage you as I do myself. I desire grandchildren as ardently as you desire great grandchildren and it would seem that their road to honour will be easier because they will be descended from you and from me. I will bequeath them a famous name and an established lineage. Only let them be born and turn this grief into joy. Farewell.

Pliny the Younger, *Epistles* 8, 10

If putting a positive gloss on the miscarriage like this seems rather insensitive and business-like, it is because the production of male heirs was a very serious business in Roman society and, from a man's perspective, represented a woman's main function in life. The perils of childbirth were all too real, as Pliny himself was himself aware: in another letter on the subject, he tells the tragic story of the Helvidius' daughters who both died giving birth (4, 21).

Unsurprisingly, inducing abortion involved taking the opposite advice to that given to avoid miscarriage.

In order to remove the embryo, the woman should take brisk walks or horse rides, jumping high into the air, have a massage, or lift weights that are too heavy for her;

if this fails the patient should be immersed in a boiled mixture of linseed, fenugreek, marsh mallow, and wormwood, using poultices and fusions of the same ingredients…

Soranus, *Gynaecology* 1, 64, 1–1

Take long baths and eat little. The woman is then bled aggressively and made to take a horse ride. A suppository may be inserted, made up from myrtle, snowdrop seeds and bitter lupines mixed with water, so long as it is not too powerful, and care must always be taken not dislodge the embryo with sharp instruments which may nick neighbouring organs.

Soranus, *Gynaecology* 1, 65, 1–7

Uterine sounds or dilators for probing the uterus through the cervix have been excavated at Hockwold in Norfolk and may well have been used to induce terminations.

Two of Ovid's poems clearly show that he was passionately opposed to abortion, particularly when it exposed his mistress' vanity:

The woman who first set about ripping out her foetus deserves to die midst the carnage she has started. Are you happy to inflict similar butchery just to avoid having wrinkles on your stomach.

Ovid, *Amores* 2, 14, 5–10

Ovid, mindful of the risks, can scarcely believe that his woman wants an abortion just to prevent later developing stretch marks on her stomach; if the mothers in the good old days had done this, the human race would be extinct, he splutters (Ovid, *Amores* 2, 14, 19–20). He questions how a woman can tear out her stomach with sharp instruments or administer *dira venena* (toxic drugs) to her unborn child.

The passage is significant for a number of reasons: these evil poisons are equated with the poisons used by witches and conjure up an association between abortion and nefarious activity; it highlights, as does the advice from Soranus nearly a century later, the prevalence of what we today call backstreet abortions; it demonstrates the obsession, a modern obsession Ovid would say, that some women had, as they do now, with self-image, even to the point of endangering their lives in the elusive pursuit of perfection. To Ovid, the whole issue is unnatural and he ends his poem with a salutary warning to the young girls of a tender age (*tenerae puellae*)—they can have their abortions but not with impunity; all too often they will die along with the unborn child they have murdered. Crowds watching the funeral procession will exclaim *merito!* (serves you right!); Ovid is only thankful that his girl has got away with it this time; if she does it again, though, let her pay the price. In the second poem, he seems too preoccupied with the dangers to be angry: Corinna's life was in the balance, *in dubio vitae,* and he does everything in his power to ensure her recovery.[20]

Ovid was not alone; Juvenal and Seneca both deplored abortion, as did Cicero, for socio-political reasons: abortions reduced the population and wiped out good families.

Juvenal talks of the powerful *medicamina* and the women who have industrialised sterility, killing human life in the stomach. Pliny regarded *abortiva* (abortifacients) to be more evil than poison. Domitian had no such reservations; he reputedly impregnated his niece, Julia, and arranged an abortion that killed her. Abortion was finally criminalised in the second century CE under Severus.

Soranus (*fl.* end of first century CE) authored more than twenty references and textbooks on biological and medical science, including the *Gynaikeia*, one of the first illustrated medical textbooks later abridged and translated into Latin probably in the sixth century CE by Muscio to produce his own *Gynaecia*. The first part is an early MCQ (multiple choice question) book with questions and answers on anatomy, embryology, childbirth and neonatal care; the second part covers pathology. Soranus' original book establishes the qualities which make the best of midwives—good midwives will recognise themselves here and students will find a model midwife to emulate. Here are a few of these guidelines:

> She should be experienced in theory and in practice, including therapy and special cases requiring dietetics, surgery and drug therapy; she will administer infection control and be able to spot symptoms and the necessary action deriving from them; she will be unflustered, reassuring and empathetic; she will always be careful and sober, as she never knows when she might be called to an emergency; she will be discreet as she will share with her patient in many secrets of life and she will not be prey to popular superstition or dreams, rituals or omens which may affect her clinical decision-making.
>
> Soranus, *Gynaecology* 1, 2, 4

This demonstrates how it was very professional, and indicative of the fact that in obstetrics and gynaecology much of the care and therapy was, by the first century BCE, the preserve of the midwife, *obstetrix*, rather than of the doctor, *medica* or *iatrina*; the midwife was, in effect, as much a doctor as a midwife, assuming a high level of literacy and scientific knowledge.

Funerary inscriptions for women doctors tell us that they were honoured in equal measure as men for their special skills. Medical books were dedicated to them by colleagues, and those who wrote medical textbooks and referencess were quoted and referenced as key opinion leaders and good authorities. The Romans, like the Greeks before them, welcomed women into the medical profession. We know of Claudia Trophima and Poblicia Aphe who probably met Soranus's criteria; the former lived to see seventy five years whereas Poblicia Aphe from Gaia lived only to her twenty-first birthday.[21] The aptly named thirty-year-old *obstetrix* Hygiae is commemorated on a tombstone by two of her tentmates (*contubernales*)—Marius Orthrus and Apollonius.[22]

Soranus knew what made a good wet nurse too, even though he believed that the mother's breast is best. She should be between age twenty and forty, and should have had two or three children herself; she should be a big woman and of a good complexion.

Her breasts should be of medium size, not rigid but soft with no wrinkles, and the nipples neither big nor too small; she should be calm, a Greek, and well turned out.

This insistence on a calm temperament perhaps indicates a concern regarding the physical abuse of infants; Soranus says that angry women are like maniacs when they drop the babies or handle them roughly when they cry endlessly. A letter has survived from the end of the second century BCE, advising a new mother on how best to select a competent wet nurse: she should be Greek, modest, clean, alert, and sober; she will offer the breast when she thinks it is time, not when the infant demands; she should be calm and induce a suitably equable environment for the baby, bathing him or her from time to time, not all of the time.[23]

Female genital mutilation (FGM)

Female genital mutilation was well known in the ancient world, and seems to have originated with the Egyptians. When the practice was adopted in Greece and Rome, it would appear that male anxieties about women, sexual pleasure, the obsession some males had surrounding the virginity of their brides, and the fidelity of their wives were the motivating factors for the mutilitating procedure. Strabo, the Greek geographer (*c.* 64 BCE–*c.* 23 CE) witnessed FGM on a visit to Egypt around 25 BCE:

> This is one of the procedures most enthusiastically performed by [the Egyptians]: to raise every child that is born and to circumcise [*peritemnein*] the males and cut [*ektemnein*] the females ... as is also the custom among the Jews, who are also Egyptians in origin.

> And then to the Harbour of Antiphilus [Naucratis in Egypt], and, above this, to the Creophagi [meat-eaters], of whom the males have their penises circumcised and the women are cut in the Jewish fashion.
>
> Strabo, *Geographia* 4, 16; 4, 9

Philo of Alexandria (*c.* 20 BCE–50 CE) agonises over the question of female circumcision, pointing out its prevalence in Egypt:

> Why orders he the males only to be circumcised? (Genesis 17:11). For in the first place, the Egyptians, in accordance with the national customs of their country, in the fourteenth year of their age, when the male begins to have the power of propagating his species, and when the female arrives at the age of puberty, circumcise both bride and bridegroom. But the divine legislator appoints circumcision to take place in the case of the male alone for many reasons: the first of which is, that the male creature feels venereal pleasures and desires matrimonial connexions more than the

female, on which account the female is properly omitted here, while he checks the superfluous impetuosity of the male by the sign of circumcision.

> Philo of Alexandria, *Questions on Genesis* 3, 47 in *Works of Philo*
> trans. F. H. Colson, Loeb Classical Library, 1937

On male circumcision, he asserts the following but we can safely assume that he advocates FGM for the same prudish reasons:

> To these [for circumcision] I would add that I consider circumcision to be a symbol of two things necessary to our well being. One is the excision of pleasures which bewitch the mind. For since among the love-lures of pleasure the palm is held by the mating of man and woman, the legislators thought good to dock the organ which ministers to such intercourse, thus making circumcision the figure of the excision of excessive and superfluous pleasure, not only of one pleasure, but of all the other pleasures signified by one, and that the most imperious. The other reason is that a man should know himself and banish from the soul the grievous malady of conceit.

> Philo of Alexandria, *Of the Special Laws* 3, Book I (ii),
> in *Works of Philo*, trans. F. H. Colson, Loeb Classical Library, 1937, Vol. VII, p. 105

A papyrus dated 163 BCE refers to the operation being performed on girls in Memphis, Egypt, to coincide with the time when they received their dowries, suggesting that FGM originated as a form of marital initiation of young women.

The Romans developed a procedure which involved slipping *fibulae* (broochs) through the *labia majora* of female slaves as a form of contraception. Galen (129–c. 200 CE) mentions it: 'When [the clitoris] protrudes to a great extent in their young women, Egyptians consider it appropriate to cut it out' (Galen, *Introductio sive Medicus* 10, 14, 76, 12–15) as does Soranus—'the enlarged clitoris and clitoridectomy' (*Gynaecologica* 4, 9).

Clitoridectomy is recorded by the Byzantine Greek physician Aëtius Amidenus (*fl.* mid-fifth century to mid-sixth century) citing the physician Philomenes. The procedure was performed in cases where the clitoris, or nymphê, grew large or triggered sexual desire when rubbing against clothing:

> For this reason, it seemed proper to the Egyptians to remove it before it became greatly enlarged especially at that time when the girls were about to be married.

> The surgery is performed in this way: have the girl sit on a chair while a muscled young man standing behind her places his arms below the girl's thighs. Have him separate and steady her legs and whole body. Standing in front and taking hold of the clitoris with a broad-mouthed forceps in his left hand, the surgeon stretches it outward, while with the right hand, he cuts it off at the point next to the pincers of the forceps.

> It is proper to let a length remain from that cut off, about the size of the membrane that's between the nostrils, so as to take away the excess material only; as I have said,

the part to be removed is at that point just above the pincers of the forceps. Because the clitoris is a skinlike structure and stretches out excessively, do not cut off too much, as a urinary fistula may result from cutting such large growths too deeply.

Aëtius Amidenus, *Tetrabiblion* 16

translations by Mary Knight, 'Curing Cut or Ritual Mutilation?: Some Remarks on the Practice of Female and Male Circumcision in Graeco-Roman Egypt,' *Isis*, 92(2), June 2001, pp. 317–338; p. 328

After the operation, the genital area was cleaned and sterilized with a sponge, frankincense, and wine or cold water, then wrapped in linen bandages dipped in vinegar, until the seventh day when calamine, rose petals, date stones, or a 'genital powder made from baked clay' might be applied.

Paulus of Aegina, a 7th century CE urologic surgeon, was something of an expert and gives his version of how to perform the procedure:

In certain women the nympha (clitoris?) is excessively large and presents a shameful deformity, insomuch that, as has been related, some women have had erections of this part like men, and also venereal desires of a like kind. Wherefore, having placed the woman in a supine posture, and seizing the redundant portion of the nympha in a forceps we cut it out with a scalpel, taking care not to cut too deep lest we occasion the complaint called rhoeas.

Paulus of Aegina, *De Re Medica Libri Septem* 6, 70

There is evidence that another form of FGM, female infibulation, was practised on prepubescent girls, if Strabo and Philo are to be believed. This is where the the labia are removed and the girl's legs are bound to allow the surgery to heal forming a skin over the vagina; a small hole is made to allow for urination and menstruation. Its purpose then, as now in some societies, was to reassure a husband that he is marrying a virgin.

Castration & circumcision

To the Romans, castration, eunuchs, and circumcision were barbaric, despite the best efforts of the Galli and Elagabalus to convince otherwise. Castration was more to be pitied than deplored. Diodorus mentions it in relation to the Troglodytes (3, 23, 2; 33, 7). Ammianus Marcellinus blames Semiramis for introducing such an unnatural practice (14, 6, 17); Lucian pities the castrated Galli and tells the story of the man who castrated himself to avoid the advances of his queen (*De Dea Syria* 19–27). To the Neoplatonic philosopher Sallustius, circumcision smacked of cannibalism and incest; he equated the snip with the Massagetae who 'eat their fathers' and the Persians who 'preserve their nobility by begetting children on their mothers'.

The Phrygian cult of Cybele was introduced into Rome during the late Republic and led by the Phrygo-Roman god, Attis. The priests were eunuchs who had castrated themselves and were known as Galli. This ritual castration took place during an ecstatic celebration called the *Dies sanguinis*, or 'Day of Blood'. The Galli wore women's clothes and a turban, together with necklaces and ear-rings. Their hair was long, and bleached, and they wore heavy make-up. They performed dances to the accompaniment of pipes and tambourines, and ecstatically flogged themselves until they bled. Catullus describes the emasculation of Attis under the intoxicating influence of Cybele:

> Roused by rabid rage and mind astray, with sharp-edged flint downwards dashed his burden of virility. Then as he felt his limbs were left without their manhood, and the fresh-spilt blood staining the soil, with bloodless hand she hastily took a tambour light to hold, your taborine, Cybele, your initiate rite'.
>
> Catullus 63, 4–8; translation by Sir Richard Francis Burton, 1894

'He' seamlessly becomes 'she' in the outcome of his self-inflicted castration.

By the end of the first century CE, bans against castration had been enacted by the emperors Domitian and Nerva in a bid to stop the burgeoning trade in eunuch slaves. Hadrian may have outlawed circumcision, on pain of death, while Antoninus Pius exempted Jews and Egyptian priests from the ban. Origen Adamantius (CE 184–CE 253) reports that only Jews were allowed to practice circumcision while Constantine freed any slave who had been subjected to circumcision; in CE 339, circumcising a slave was punishable by death. According to Eusebius, Origen reputedly castrated himself, after contemplating the book of *Matthew*:

> For there are some eunuchs, which were so born from their mother's womb: and there are some eunuchs, which were made eunuchs of men: and there be eunuchs, which have made themselves eunuchs for the kingdom of heaven's sake. He that is able to receive it, let him receive it.[24]
>
> *Matthew* 19, 12: King James Version.

Any successful civilising work was undone by the emperor Elagabalus (r. 218 to 222). He offered huge fortunes to any physician who could give him permanent female genitalia or in the words of Dio: 'to contrive a woman's vagina in his body by means of an incision'.[25]

If circumcision was loathsome to the Romans, it would be intriguing to know what they thought of the procedure performed to reverse circumcision. Some Jews resorted to a surgical procedure (epispasm) to restore the foreskin and cover the glans 'for the sake of decorum' and to make themselves less conspicuous at the baths or during athletics. Celsius describes how to raise the prepuce from the penis with a scalpel (and a steady hand), stitching the foreskin to its rightful place with a threaded needle. Apparently, it was not very painful:

The prepuce around the glans is seized, stretched out until it actually covers the glans, and there tied. Next the skin covering the penis just in front of the pubes is cut through in a circle until the penis is bared, but great care is taken not to cut into the urethra, nor into the blood vessels there. This done the prepuce slides forwards towards the tie, and a sort of small ring is laid bare in front of the pubes, to which lint is applied in order that flesh may grow and fill it up. It is seen that a large enough part of the penis has been bared, if the skin is distended little or not at all, and if the breadth of the wound above supplies sufficient covering. But until the scar has formed it must remain tied, only a small passage being left in the middle for the urine. But in one who has been circumcised the prepuce is to be raised from the underlying penis around the circumference of the glans by means of a scalpel. This is not so very painful, for once the margin has been freed, it can be stripped up by hand as far back as the pubes, nor in so doing is there any bleeding. The prepuce thus freed is again stretched forwards beyond the glans; next cold water affusions are freely used, and a plaster is applied round to repress severe inflammation. And for the following days the patient is to fast until nearly overcome by hunger lest satiety excite that part. When the inflammation has ceased, the penis should be bandaged from the pubes to the corona; over the glans the plaster is applied with the other end of the probe. This is done in order that the lower part may agglutinate, whilst the upper part heals without adhering.

Celsus, *Concerning Medicine* 7, 25
Translation from the Loeb Classical Library edition, 1935.

Martial refers to circumcision four times, all of them disparagingly.[26]

Urology in the male

Lucretius gives us a physiological description of sexual function in the male: according to him, physical maturity generates semen which manifests in wet dreams; seeing a beautiful body, be it a woman's or a boy's moves semen into the genitals and toward the object of desire. Erection creates an urge to ejaculate with its attendant pleasure. This human sex drive he describes as dumb desire, comparing ejaculation to the blood spurting from a wound. Love is just a by-product which taints sexual pleasure in the same way that life is tainted by the fear of death.[27] Women, on the other hand, are instinctively driven by affection, leading to mutual satisfaction. Falling in love should be avoided by men as it leads to physical, emotional, and financial ruin.

Too much semen was a bad thing. Cold baths and avoiding flatulence-causing foods were recommended to limit production.[28] In his *On Semen,* Galen describes semen as a concoction of blood and *pneuma* (the 'vital air' needed by organs to function) formed within the man's spermatic vessels, turning white through heat as it enters the testicles. Too much sex results in a loss of *pneuma* and, therefore, vitality; this was bad news for some Romans:

> those who are less moderate sexually turn out to be weaker, since the whole body loses the purest part of both substances, and there is besides an accession of pleasure, which by itself is enough to dissolve the vital tone, so that before now some persons have died from excess of pleasure.
>
> Galen, *De Semine* 1, 16, 30–32

Death was not the only outcome of too liberal a dissemination of semen. Before it got to that, mental acuity, masculinity, and a deep manly voice were all compromised.[29] The voice was particularly vulnerable with singers and actors resorting to infibulation to preserve their voices.[30] Roman doctors, dancers, and singers believed that infibulation was the answer. It obviously prevented erections while some believed it resulted in the patient becoming well-endowed. It was commonly believed that abstinence from sex also protected the voice or delayed its breaking. Quintilian taught sexual abstinence for the orator who wished to cultivate a deep masculine voice for court. Galen cautions, though, that too much abstinence leads to a loss of desire and capability—a wrinkling of the testicles as in old men—whereas the blood flow in men having sex often increased desire and a healthy sized set of testicles.[31]

Catullus's fellow new poet, Calvus, slept with lead plates over his kidneys to control his wet dreams. Pliny reports:

> When plates of lead are bound to the area of the loins and kidneys, it is used, owing to its rather cooling nature, to check the attacks of sexual desire and sexual dreams in one's sleep that cause spontaneous eruptions to the point of becoming a sort of disease.[32]

Lead plates were efficacious in other male sexual disorders: satyriasis, priapism (a chronic erection without a desire for sex), and involuntary ejaculation all benfited from the laying on of lead plates, cupping therapy, or the use of depilatories. Pliny gives us much detail on the knowledge of pharmacology acquired by men, suggesting that the origins of magic may lie in the early days of medicine.[33] Evidence to support this comes in popular remedies for impotence, plants used as aphrodisiacs, and as poisons.

Death & dying

The life expectancy for women was, on average, just less than thirty years, with men living a few years longer. Female mortality caused from underage pregnancy no doubt accounted for some of the difference: women could be married from the age of twelve and, in some cases could have been subjected to constant sexual activity before menarche, which would typically occur around age fourteen. The serial births that often soon followed would, over time, also have a deleterious impact on a woman's physical and mental health. There is little wonder that the expectation of life was generally short due to that and other causes of perinatal death, not least almost unbridled infection, and the fact that precocious sexual activity possibly led in time to cases of cervical cancer.

There are many epigraphical and funerary inscriptions for women who died in their twenties. Evidence from the Roman cemetery at Poundbury in Dorset may not be conclusive but it shows that fifty-one out of 281 females died in or around childbirth. Pliny the Younger writes with some irony about the tragic death of the Helvidiae sisters who both died in childbirth, giving birth to daughters (who survived): 'two great girls cut down in the bloom of youth by their own fertility' (Pliny, Epistles 4, 21).

There is inscriptional evidence for pain in childbirth in Egypt's Dosithea, aged twenty-five who, by dying from some disease or other, died 'in terrible pain, escaping the pangs of childbirth' (*Peek*, 1233).

Rusticeia Matrona died in childbirth and from 'malignant fate' at the same age in Mauretania; she urges her husband to look after their son (*CIL* 8 20288). Also twenty-five, Daphne, from Carthage, died giving birth; her epitaph records her aching concern for the baby: 'who will feed him, look after him for the rest of his life? (*CIL* 8, 24734)'

Veturia had a typical Roman woman's life, with the addition of those often fatal hazards involved in serial childbirth: 'Here I lie, a matrona called Veturia … I lived for twenty-seven years and I was married for sixteen years to the same man. I died after I gave birth to six children, only one of whom is still alive' (*CIL* 3, 3572).

Socratea died of a haemorrhage in childbirth aged thirty-six. This fifteen-year-old died giving birth in Tusculum in the first century BCE; the baby also died: 'the tomb [holds] two deaths in one body, the [urn] of ashes contains twin funerals' (*Lattimore* 1942, 270).

Funerary epitaphs reveal a sad litany of young girls who died: Lutatia Secundina age four years, six months, and nine days (*CIL* 6. 21738); Magnilla, aged eight—'a positive delight' (*CIL* 6. 21846); and Heteria Superba who died aged one year, six months, twenty-five days. Sosias Isas, twelve-year-old daughter of a 'desolate' father from Bologna in the second century CE (*AE* 1976, 202) and eighteen-month-old Irene from Ariminum (*CIL* 11, 466); thirteen-year-old Corellia Optata's headstone was uncovered in 2011 at the Hungate dig in York—perhaps, the victim of a too-early conception.

Pliny the Elder offers some reasons to explain the very high rate of maternal and infant mortality. Babies born before the seventh month (classified as premature today) do not survive; babies born in the seventh month only survive if they are conceived the day before or after a full moon or during a new moon. Eighth month babies are common, although Aristotle says otherwise; however, they are vulnerable until they are forty days old. He goes on to talk about how, for mothers, the fourth and eighth months are the most critical; abortions at that time are fatal. Babies are particularly vulnerable when they start to grow hair and during the full moon; if the pregnant mother eats too much salt then the baby will be born without nails; excessive maternal yawning can be fatal during delivery.

It has been estimated that the average early Empire Roman woman had to give birth to five babies if she was to ensure the survival of two and to do her bit to maintain the required birth rate.

The main causes of neonatal mortality—death within the first twenty-nine days of life—were insanitary conditions at the birth, and trauma; infant morbidity and deaths were often caused by intestinal disorders, particularly enteritis and dysentery. Celsus (*De Med* 2, 8, 30–31) recorded that the latter was particularly virulent in children up to the age of ten and in their pregnant mothers, when the unborn baby was also lost. Over-tight swaddling—where the limbs are confined and the heartbeat slows down dangerously—dirty laundry, and mastication of baby foods by wet-nurses who themselves might be carrying an infection may also have taken their toll, as indeed would goat's and cow's milk, as they contain infectious organisms and would have been used not just by reluctant breast-feeders but by poorer, undernourished women who were unable to feed and could not afford a wet nurse.

Generally, men and women may have died young from illness, infection and accidents. Many men would have been casualties of war; women and children would also have died as casualties of war—murdered, raped, burnt, and starved to death during and after seiges or in the enslavement that often followed the fall of their city.

Malaria (*plasmodium falciparum*) was widespread in much of Italy and in other parts of the empire, despite attempts to improve drainage of marshlands and river plains. In a fifth century CE cemetery near Lugnano, in Umbria, almost all of the forty-seven graves contained the skeletal remains of either infants, neonates, or foetuses. The foetuses were the result of miscarriages, particularly from *primigravida* mothers, caused by the immune suppression common in women in the final two trimesters of pregnancy, brought on by malaria; the female anopheles mosquito is thought to be attracted to certain chemical receptors found in the placenta of pregnant women. According to Diodorus of Ephesus and Diogenes Laertius (8, 70) Empedocles (495–430 BCE) blocked off a gorge in Acragas, Sicily and dammed a river at Selinus, because they were found to be funnels for a southerly wind bringing in mosquitoes which introduced placental malaria.

Obviously, there were exceptions to early death: in Britain alone, funerary inscriptions reveal that Tadia Vallaunius from Isca (Caerleon) (*CIL* 7, 126) survived until she was sixty-five, Julia Secundina from near Isca saw seventy-five (*CIL* 7, 124), and Claudia Crysis (*CIL* 7, 193) from Lindum (Lincoln) lived until the age of ninety. Among the celebrities, Cato the Elder (eighty-five), Augustus (seventy-six), Livia (eighty-six) and Tiberius (seventy-nine) all had very good innings.

Graves & Funerals

There were some strict laws pertaining to funerals and burials, as recorded by Paul:

A body, after it has been permanently buried and solemn sacrifices have been made, can be transferred by night to another place on account of the overflow of a river, or the fear of impending ruin.

It is not lawful for a corpse to be brought into a city, lest the sacred places of the latter may be polluted; and anyone who violates this law shall be arbitrarily punished.

A body cannot be committed to burial within the walls of a city, or be burned therein.

Anyone who strips a body permanently buried, or which has been deposited temporarily in some place, and exposes it to the rays of the sun, commits a crime, and therefore, if he is of superior station he is usually sentenced to deportation to an island, and if he is of inferior rank, he is condemned to the mines.

Anyone who violates a tomb, or removes anything from it, shall either be sentenced to the mines, or deported to an island, according to his rank.

Anyone who breaks or opens a sepulchre belonging to another, and places therein the body of a member of his own family, or that of a stranger, is considered to have violated the sepulchre.

When land is sold, consecrated ground does not pass to the purchaser, nor does he acquire the right to inter bodies therein.

Anyone who erases an inscription on a monument, or overturns a statue, or takes anything away which belongs to it, or removes a stone or a column therefrom, is considered to have violated the sepulchre.

A body cannot be placed in the same sarcophagus or vault where another has already been deposited; and he who does so can be prosecuted as guilty of violation of a sepulchre.

He who buries the body of a stranger and spends any of his own money for funeral expenses, can recover it from the heir, the father, or the master of the deceased.

A husband can recover out of the dowry of his wife whatever he has expended upon her funeral.

The right of residence near, or over a monument, does not exist, for a crime is committed even by the proximity of human habitation; and anyone who violates this law shall be punished either by being condemned to the public works, or by exile, according to his rank.

Parents and children over ten years of age should be mourned for the term of a year; minors up to the age of three years, should be mourned for one month for each year of their age at the time of their death; a husband should be mourned for ten months, and cognates, under the sixth degree, for eight months. Whoever violates this law is included in the class of persons who are infamous.

Anyone who is mourning should abstain from marriage, as well as from the use of ornaments, and purple and white garments.

Anything which is expended for the funeral occupies the first place among the debts of the estate.

Paulus, *Opinions* 1, 21

translation by S. P. Scott, *The Civil Law*, I, (Cincinnati, 1932)

Grave robbing was a serious problem: some, like Gaius Tullius Hesper, tried to deter it by having a curse etched onto their tombstones:

[Gaius] had this tomb built for himself as a place where his bones might be laid. If anyone damages or meddles with them may he live in perpetual pain and when he dies may the goods of the underworld deny entry to his spirit.

CIL 6, 36467

Apart from this, tombs were also vandalised by poorer people for burial gifts and the clothing of the dead; some people even opened tombs of strangers to bury members of their own families or dismantled them to use material with which to make their own new tombs. Grave monuments were also damaged to make milestones and for building walls. There were two ways to limit the violation of graves: fining and cursing; this from the end of 2nd, beginning of the third century CE:

Nicephoros, son of Moschion [made this grave] for his wife Glyconis and in his own memory while still living: if anyone buries another body [here] without my permission, he will be fined 2,500 denarii to the city and will be guilty of the crime of grave robbery.

Inv. 1225T from Istanbul Archaeological Museums

But this was decidedly tame stuff compared with a curse tablet found at Agios Tychon, Cyprus: 'Anyone who does anything bad to my tomb, then the crocodile, hippopotamus, and lion will eat him' or 'I will seize his neck like that of a goose. His face will be spat at. A donkey will rape him, a donkey will rape his wife. He will be cooked together with the condemned.'

I shall seize his neck like that of a goose (Inscription of Hermeru, Dynasty 6)
His wife shall be taken away before his face (Apanage Stele, Dyn. 22)
His face shall be spat at (El-Hasaia tomb, Dyn. 26)
A donkey shall rape him, a donkey shall rape his wife (Deir el-Bahri Graffito No. 11, Dyn. 20)
He shall be cooked together with the condemned (tomb of Khety II, Dyn. 9–10)

Another curses the thief so that he can no longer urinate, defecate, speak, sleep, or be well unless he brings back what he has stolen to the temple of Mercury. This was found in London, and is now in the British Museum.

In 2014, a dozen or so tombs were excavated at a site in Ostia, with some including lead tablets with inscriptions featuring curses to ward off potential looters.

Some graves had some rather sinister contents, apart from the corpse: voodoo dolls were made from a variety of materials including lead, bronze, and clay as well as wax, wool, and dough. The typical doll demonstrated a number of characteristics, including their legs or arms twisted behind the back as if bound; they were impaled with nails; the extremities and/or upper torso may be contorted back to front; they may be confined in a box or similar (like a coffin); and inscribed with the name of the victim.

Funerals were predominantly expedient affairs with the deceased buried, cremated, or entombed outside the city with due reverence and dignity. Only the wealthy and famous were buried with pomp: death masks (*imago*), processions, and the like were described here by Polybius:

Whenever a famous man dies, he is carried at his funeral into the forum to the so-called rostra, sometimes conspicuous in an upright posture and, less frequently, reclined. Here with all the people standing round, a grown-up son, if he has left one who happens to be present, or if not some other relative, mounts the rostra and discourses on the virtues and successful achievements of the dead... Next after the interment and the performance of the usual ceremonies, they place the image of the departed in the most conspicuous position in the house, enclosed in a wooden shrine. This image is a mask reproducing amazingly faithfully both the features and complexion of the deceased. These images are displayed at public sacrifices... and when any distinguished member of the family dies they take them to the funeral, putting them on men who seem to them to bear the closest resemblance to the original in stature and comportment. These representatives wear togas, with a purple border if the deceased was a consul or praetor, whole purple if he was a censor, and embroidered with gold if he had celebrated a triumph or achieved anything similar. They all ride in chariots preceded by the fasces, axes, and other insignia by which the different magistrates are usually accompanied according to the respective dignity of the offices of state held by each during his life; and when they arrive at the rostra they all seat themselves in a row on ivory chairs. There could not easily be a more inspirational sight for any young man who aspires to fame and virtue. For who would not be inspired by the sight of the images of men renowned for their excellence, all in one place, as if alive and breathing? What spectacle could be more glorious than this?

Polybius 6, 53–6; 6, 54, 3

translation adapted from *Histories* by Evelyn S. Shuckburgh. London, Macmillan, 1889.

Funeral clubs were set up to defray funeral expenses on the death of a member—an early form of life assurance. The clubs seem to have been anything but morbid or doom-laden as they involved a thriving social element enjoyed by members. A contract has survived on a marble tablet giving the details of the constitution of one of these clubs,

If any member of this club who was a slave should die and if his body is not handed over for burial because of the awkwardness of the master of mistress, or if he has not left a will, then a funeral will be held for an effigy of him…chairmen for dinners, four at a time…should provide one amphora each of good wine, and bread worth two asses, proportionate to the number of club members, and four sardines, and a room for the dinner, and hot water, and a waiter.

CIL 14, 2112

Causing a disturbance during a funeral by moving from seat to seat, and being abusive were punishable by fines: twelve sesterces was the penalty for being cantankerous to fellow members, twenty if to the president.

In literature, women were sometimes the subject of the *epicedion*, the funeral ode. In one respect this is something of an extended funerary inscription, where much of the praise is conventional. Nevertheless, the effect is like the tombstone—to bestow eternal recognition on the subject; Propertius' Cornelia and Statius' Priscilla were both honoured with *epicedia*. Cornelia is discussed in the section above on *matronae*: she was a *univira* to Paullus; she brought no shame to his achievements, his *res gestae*; indeed, she was a credit to his lineage; she was the perfect *matrona*.[34]

Statius's Priscilla was *quies* (calm) and *modesta* (modest), her table was unpretentious (*modica*) and she looked after Abascantus well, untouched by his success—he held an influential office with Domitian—she was a veritable *matrona*. This is how it starts:

Had I the skill to mould likenesses in wax, make lifelike features from ivory or gold, Priscilla, I'd fashion a work of solace welcome to your husband. For by his great devotion he deserves in his grief to have had Apelles pick out your face in paint, or to be reborn by Phidias' hand. So hard does he try to bring back your ghost from the pyre, fights a mighty contest with Death and exhausts the efforts of the artists when he strives to love you in every metal…

Statius, *Silvae* 5, 1, 1–9

8

Deformity and Disability

Generally speaking, the Roman attitude to deformity and disability was decidedly casual, and by our standards today, insensitive and inhumane. Before we deplore this, though, we should remember that what most people would today call proper and empathetic inclusion of disabled people into wider society is still a relatively recent phenomenon. Victorian freak shows ended not so very long ago, for example, and political correctness regarding disability is a development of the late 20th century.

We cannot know just how widespread disability and deformity were in ancient Rome although we can, with some certainty, assume that it was much more prevalent than it is today, at least in the west. The population was, of course, significantly smaller then than now and many fewer babies were born or survived birth. However, per head of population, the incidence of premature death, disability, and deformity will have been dramatically higher due to a number of factors which include: constant warfare (battlefield trauma and wound infection); dangerous sport (chariot racing, gladiator fights), being a slave and dying from extreme fatigue or being reduced to a physical wreck; perinatal death of child and mother (due to infection and poor hygiene); infection generally, including sexually transmitted infections, water-borne diseases and malaria; malnutrition; and mental illness—rarely diagnosed, never treated. It seems credible that the disabled were a relatively common sight in Rome.

Archaeology supports this. Five out of twelve Roman skeletons excavated in a group burial site near Cambridge were found to have a spinal deformity. Ailments and infirmities consistent with old age are evident from cemetery excavations. In Cirencester, for example, more than 80 per cent of the adult skeletons indicated osteo-arthritis, with more women than men afflicted. Alongside the existence of nodules on the vertebrae, this suggests that women were routinely engaged in heavy, manual work; the frequency of arthritis of the neck in female skeletons lends more support to this. Squatting facets—the remodelling of the bones at the front of the *talus* (ankle)—in women's bones found in York indicate that they spent much time squatting, presumably when cooking and tending fires. Arthritis and osteoporosis seem to have been common in the elderly in Pompeii, with postmenopausal osteoporosis commonly affecting the women. An example of leprosy has been found at Poundbury while Pott's

Disease (tuberculous spondylitis: extrapulmonary tuberculosis affecting the spine) has been traced in skeletons found in York and Cirencester. Excavations of Roman sewers in York reveal that worms and bowel parasites were pandemic.

Moreover, recent research has revealed that, contrary to the pleasant and pleasing images conveyed by many of the frescoes discovered in Pompeii, around ten per cent of the local women were obese and hirsute; furthermore, they have been found to have suffered from headaches and diabetes. Skeletal examinations revealed a small bony growth on the inside of their skulls behind the forehead, indicative of a hormonal disorder—hyperostosis frontalis interna (HFI)—which causes these symptoms.

War correspondence also helps: Julius Caesar reports that in one conflict during the civil war, four out of the six centurions in one cohort were blinded by enemy action—probably not that uncommon an incident, given the number of missiles that were flying about:

> So, there were six battles in that one day, three at Dyrrachium and three at the outworks; when we add them all up we found that about two thousand of the Pompeians had fallen…of our men no more than twenty were lost in all six battles. But in the redoubt every one of the men who was wounded and four centurions out of one cohort lost their eyes. As proof of their industry and the danger they were in, they counted out to Caesar about thirty thousand arrows which had been discharged at the redoubt, and when the shield of the centurion Scaeva was brought to him, one hundred and twenty holes were found in it.
>
> Caesar, *Bellum Civile* 3, 53

Deliberate blinding too was a popular form of torture inflicted on prisoners of war and a punishment for insubordination.

Juvenal reminds us of the trials and tribulations endured by gladiators when he describes the wounds and deformities suffered by Sergius, Eppia's young fighter for whom she is deserting home and family:

> A wounded arm promised a military discharge, and his face was covered in deformities: a scar caused by his helmet, a huge lump on his nose, a nasty humour always dribbling from his eye. But then he was a gladiator!
>
> Juvenal 6, 82–103

Vocabulary is often a good signpost to a society's attitude and cultural values. There is no exact word in Greek or Latin for 'disabled' but the Greeks use *teras* and the Romans *monstrum* to convey their meaning; linguistically, it is but a short step from 'a wonderful thing' to a 'monster'. Interestingly, the original meaning of *monstrum* was, according to *Lewis & Short* [*ad loc*], 'a divine omen indicating misfortune' but it can, more positively, also mean 'wonderful things'. The noun *monstrum*, though, is ominously related to the verb *monere,* meaning 'to give warning', and can, as in Tacitus, even mean 'to punish' (*Annals* 5, 9). Disability, then, was forever bad news. *Teras* elided from being a wonder or a marvel into 'a huge, unearthly creature, a monster' as in Homer and Plato. Linguistically, this means that disabled people are classed along with, and rub shoulders with, such mythological monstrosities as the Gorgon Medusa.

The Latin word *mutus* describes either something or somebody unable to speak, or, at the same time, a dumb animal or a brute. This may just be linguistic inadequacy, but the inevitable consequence is an association of the disabled with the monstrous and ugly. Pliny the Elder tells us that the Greeks also call such people *ektrapeloi* (freaks), a word which changed from meaning 'strange' or 'devious' to a description of people as monstrous, as in enormous children; however, the Romans have no word for them.

Columella (4–*c*. 70 CE) tells us about Cicero talking about tall people:

> For Cicero attests that there was once a Roman citizen, Naevius Pollio, who was a foot taller than the tallest of other men; and recently we ourselves might have seen, among the exhibits of the procession at the games in the Circus, a Jewish man who was taller than the tallest German.
>
> Columella, *De Re Rustica* 8

Pliny, though, is the last word on gigantism and dwarfism:

> Our histories do not tell us the height of Nævius Pollio; but we learn from them that he nearly died in the rush [of people] to see him, and that he was looked upon as a prodigy. The tallest man that has been seen in our times, was called Gabbaras, brought from Arabia by the Emperor Claudius; his height was nine feet nine inches. In the reign of Augustus, there were two people, Posio and Secundilla who were half a foot taller than him; their bodies have been preserved as objects of curiosity in the museum of the Sallustian family. In the reign of the same emperor, there was a man also remarkable for his extremely diminutive stature, being only two feet and a palm in height; his name was Conopas, and he was a big pet of Julia's, the grand-daughter of Augustus. There was a woman too, the same size, called Andromeda, a freed-woman of Julia Augusta. We learn from Varro, that Manius Maximus and M. Tullius, members of our equestrian order, were only two cubits in height; and I have myself seen them, preserved in their coffins. It is well known that children are occasionally born a foot and a half in height, and sometimes a little more; such children, however, have died by the time they are three years old.
>
> Pliny, *Natural History* 7, 16
> translation adapted from John Bostock's, Taylor & Francis, 1855. A cubit is 1.5 feet.

Hermaphrodites (*androgyni*) were originally thought of as prodigies but Pompey changed that when he made them figures of entertainment, putting them on the stage in his theatre (Pliny, *Natural History* 7, 34). They were joined in the limelight by such celebrities as: Eutyche, who was led to her funeral pyre by twenty children, to celebrate the thirty babies she had delivered to the world; Alcippe, who had given birth to an elephant; and the slave girl who was delivered of a snake (Pliny, *NH* 7, 3). Superstition and magic surely had a lot to do with sightings of centaurs (half man, half horse), which were not uncommon, it seems: Pliny (*NH* 7, 35) and Phlegon (*Mirabilia* 34) describe one immersed in honey. A baby was born in Saguntum, soon after the city was sacked by Hannibal: the baby took one look around, was not impressed, and immediately returned to its mother's womb. The fourth century CE Julius Obsequens describes monstrous children in his *Book of Prodigies*, taken from from Livy. Here is a sample:

> A two-headed lamb, and a boy with three hands and as many feet were born [at Atellae]... At Vulsinium ... a two-headed, four-footed, four-handed girl with twin sets of female genitalia was born dead... At Faesulae roaring was heard from the earth. A boy was born of a slave-girl without an aperture in his genitals through which urine might pass. A woman was found with two sets of genitalia. A torch was seen in the sky. A bull spoke. A swarm of bees settled on the rooftop of a private house. At Volaterrae a river flowed with blood. At Rome it rained milk. At Arretium two hermaphrodites were found. A farm-yard chicken was born with four-feet. Many places were struck by lightning.
>
> Julius Obsequens, *Book of Prodigies* 50, 51, 53
> Translation as at www.alexthenice.com/obsequens/

Phlegon of Tralles lived in the second century CE and wrote his bizarre *Marvels*—a half-serious compilation of ghost stories, congenital abnormalites, strange hybrid creatures, hermaphrodites, giant skeletons, and prophesizing heads. He records, for example, an hermaphrodite from 125 BCE who caused such a stir that the august Sibylline Oracles were consulted because no one knew what to do; a highly respected slave woman who in 49 CE gave birth to an ape; a four-headed child which was presented to Nero with eight arms and eight legs; and a child born with its head protruding from its shoulder (*Marvels* 20, 23).

Diodorus (in the late first century BCE) described hermaphrodites as 'marvellous creatures' (*terata*), who announce the future, for good or bad. Around 500 CE, Isidore of Seville described hermaphrodites as having the right breast of a man and the left of a woman, and after sex, can both sire and bear children. In Roman law, a hermaphrodite was classed as either male or female, not both. After Pompey made celebrities out of them, they had, by Pliny's time, become objects of delight and fascination (*deliciae*) and were highly sought after in the slave markets.[1]

Pliny insists on the phenomenon of instantaneous transgender transgression or gender reassignment—*non est speculum* (it is not a dream). In 171 BCE, a girl from Casinum instantaneously changed into a boy before her parents' eyes; the augurs banished them to an island. Licinius Mucianus records the case of Arescon from Argos who married a man as Arescusa; he then developed a beard and other male features and got married to a woman; there was a similar sighting in Smyrna. Pliny himself saw a bride turn into a man on their wedding day. Other oddities include the mother of a boxer, Nicaeus of Byzantium, was born from her mother's adulterous affair with an Ethiopian: the mother was born white but Nicaeus, one generation later, was born black. Another Ethiopian involved, or the same one? Pliny goes on to assert that certain Indian tribes bear children from age seven and are old by the time they reach forty while others conceive aged five and die three years later; the children of others go grey immediately after birth. Women who want a dark-eyed baby must eat a shrew during their pregnancy (*Natural History* 30, 134).

According to the *Twelve Tables* (4, 1), deformed babies of either sex should be disposed of as soon as possible after birth. As we have seen, Dionysius of Halicarnassus alleges that Romulus (in the so-called *Law of Romulus*) 'obliged the inhabitants to bring up all their male children and the first-born of the females, and forbade them to destroy any children under three years of age unless they were maimed or monstrous from their very birth'.[2]

In the ancient world, superstition often accompanied and shrouded deformity. Livy tells in 207 BCE of a 'monstrously' deformed child being cast adrift, alive in a box, to rid Rome of such a repulsive portent:

> a new report came, this time from Frusino, saying that a child had been born there in size and features equal to one four years old … it was impossible to say whether it was male or female. The soothsayers … said that this was a terrible portent, and the thing must be banished from Roman soil, not permitted to touch the earth, and buried at sea. They enclosed it still living in a box, took it out to sea, and dropped it overboard.
>
> Livy 27, 37

In Lucan's *De Bello Civili*, Arruns and the *matrona* were called on to interpret the series of terrible omens and repellent portents that appeared in Rome as Pompey and Caesar prepared to do battle at Pharsalia:

> The tongues of brutish animals uttered human speech; and women gave birth to monstrosities both in the size and number of their limbs, and mothers were horrified by the babies they gave birth to.
>
> Lucan, *De Bello Civili* 1, 584f

Disability in a baby told a parent that the gods were less than happy; a disabled baby was seen as a manifestation of divine punishment visited upon its parents. By extension, deformity in a newborn spelled doom for the state. The deformed baby presaged disaster and so the association of disability with misfortune served to fuel further the general suspicion and anxiety surrounding disabled people. As we have noted, *monstrum* is related to the verb *monere*, meaning 'to give warning'.

Many such infants were just abandoned after birth because Romans clearly saw the problems involved in bringing up a disabled child who was simply a financial and physical burden with no prospect of contributing to the family income.

Suetonius describes a decree in 63 BCE that all boys should be exposed; we have seen how Musonius Rufus in the first century CE deplored child murder and how Soranus, the gynaecologist, saw fit to provide a checklist for midwives to help them determine the newborn disorders which permitted exposure.[3, 4] Unwanted babies might be abandoned at the Temple of Pietas or the Columna Lactaria; those with serious abnormalities would be drowned or suffocated.

Generally speaking, the deformed and disabled were, as a worst case, decidedly odd, bad news, and something to be rid of; the best case was an object of fun, as with Pompey, or indulged as a pet or a *delicia*—as with Julia, living an apparently privileged life, but not without its sexual obligations.

It was not quite all doom for the upper class disabled. A couple of examples exist where kind and compassionate behaviour happened. Pliny the Elder comments on Quintus Pedius (not to be confused with his grandfather, the Roman general and great nephew of Julius Caesar):

[He] had a grandson [also Q. Pedius], who being dumb from his birth, the orator Messala, to whose family his grandmother belonged, recommended he should be brought up as a painter, a proposal which was also approved of by the late Emperor Augustus. He died, however, in his youth [about 13 CE], after having made great progress in the art.

Pliny the Elder, *Natural History* 35, 4
translation by John Bostock, Taylor & Francis, 1855.

Quintus has the distinction of being the first recorded deaf painter; his education is the first instance we know of the education of a deaf child. Octavia, Augustus's sister, was extremely solicitous and encouraged the boy's development and progress.

Claudius (emperor 41–54 CE), whom everyone delighted in mocking, was looked after to some degree by Augustus and his grandmother Livia, although much of this concern may have been triggered by their embarrassment. Suetonius shows this embarrassment, through various correspondence, notably in a letter from Augustus to Livia in which the emperor agonises over the extent to which he should allow Claudius to officiate at public events and be seen, indeed gawped at, in the imperial box with him. Nevertheless, the *Senatus Consultum de Cn. Pisone Patre* recognises the tuition and *discipulina* he received through Livia; she was clearly at pains to give him a chance to get on in life. The overbearing and ambitious Livia would have been involved in the selection of Claudius' first wife, Plautia Urgulanilla, granddaughter of her friend Urgulania.

Despite the disability—a limp, a stutter, and some deafness caused by his lifelong illness (probably cerebral palsy)—Claudius became a writer of some distinction and a student of Greek culture; he also introduced three new letters into the Roman alphabet. His teachers included Livy and Sulpicius Flavus:

> He began to write a history in his youth … while he was emperor he wrote a good deal and gave constant recitals through a professional reader. He began his history with the death of the dictator Caesar, but skipped to a later period and took a fresh start at the end of the civil war, realising that he was not allowed to give a frank or true account of the earlier times… He also composed an autobiography in eight books, lacking rather in good taste than in style, as well as a *Defence of Cicero against the Writings of Asinius Gallus*, a work of no mean learning. Besides this he invented three new letters and added them to the alphabet, maintaining that they were greatly needed…These characters may still be seen in numerous books, in the daily gazette, and in inscriptions on public buildings. He gave no less attention to Greek studies, taking every occasion to declare his regard for that language and its superiority…he even wrote historical works in Greek, twenty books of Etruscan History and eight of Carthaginian. Because of these works there was added to the old Museum at Alexandria a new museum named after him: in the one his Etruscan History was read out each year from beginning to end, and in the other his Carthaginian, by various readers in turn, as public recitations.
>
> Suetonius, *Claudius* 41–42
> translation adapted from *The Lives of the Twelve Caesars*
> published in the Loeb Classical Library, 1914

The new letters were Ɔ or ƆC/X (antisigma) to replace BS and PS, just as X stood in for CS and GS; ⅃, an inverted F or digamma to represent consonantal U; and Ⱶ, a half H—a short vowel sound used before labial consonants in Latin words such as *optimus*.

There is another side, though, to the way Claudius was treated. For whatever reason—frustration, disappointment, or embarrassment—Claudius' mother, Antonia Minor, was, to modern sensitivities, hurtful to Claudius, calling him a monster (*portentum*) and a half-complete creation (*nec absolutum a natura*); she also described others she considered stupid (*socordiae*) to be even stupider (*stultiorem*) than Claudius. Antonia may even have farmed him out as a boy to Salome I to be brought up with Agrippa I (Pliny *NH* 3, 2). His sister Livilla, on hearing that one day he might become emperor, is reported as saying that the Roman people did not deserve such a cruel misfortune. According to Suetonius (*Claudius* 3), Livia rarely spoke to him.

Work, and therefore self-sufficiency and dignity, was hard for the disabled to find in the Roman world. We have seen how Pompey, and no doubt others, put disabled people on the stage to sell their novelty value, for personal kudos and the titillation of the gawping, crowing masses; dwarfs and hunchbacks were presumably much in high demand as singers, dancers, musicians, jugglers, and clowns. Freak shows would have been all the rage. In his *Lapithae*, Lucian describes a buffoon (*morio*) called Satyrion as 'an ugly, shaven little fellow' who provides some of the mid-prandial dinner party entertainment:

Now came one of the usual short breaks in the procession of dishes; and Aristaenetus, to avoid the embarrassment of a pause, told his jester to come in and talk or perform, by way of putting the company even more at their ease. So in came an ugly fellow with a shaven head–just a few hairs standing upright on the crown. He danced with dislocations and contortions, which made him still more absurd, then improvised and delivered some anapaests in an Egyptian accent, and wound up with witticisms aimed at the guests.

Lucian, *A Feast of Lapithae* 18
translation adapted from *The Works of Lucian of Samosata* by H. W. Fowler,
Oxford: The Clarendon Press 1905.

Cicero, however, advises restraint because the ridicule can backfire:

In deformity, also, and bodily defects, is found fair enough matter for ridicule; but we have to ask the same question here as is asked on other points, 'How far the ridicule may be carried?' In this respect it is not only directed that the orator should say nothing impertinently, but also that, even if he can say anything very ridiculously, he should avoid both errors, lest his jokes become either buffoonery or mimicry.

Cicero, *De Oratore* 2, 239; translation by J. S. Watson

Suetonius tells how Augustus exhibited a man called Lycius who was under two feet tall, weighed only seventeen pounds and had a stentorian voice; however, Augustus was reported by Suetonius as studiously avoiding dwarfs and the like, believing them to be ill-omened (*Augustus* 83). According to Dio (67, 8, 4), dwarfs were recruited by Domitian to perform as gladiators against women as warm- up acts for the main event. However, Augustus was not typical, Domitian was and it seems that emperors of Rome generally led the way in exhibiting deformed people as objects of entertainment, curiosity, novelty, and amazement. Statius describes another Domitian extravaganza when hordes of dwarfs were deployed in the arena as pygmies to fight against a flock of cranes:

Here's a column of brave dwarfs, whom Nature suddenly paused in production, and tied forever in rounded knots. They wound and punch and threaten to kill each other. Mars and blood-stained Valour laugh while cranes swoop down at their wandering booty, amazed at their pigmy pugnacity.

Statius, *Silvae* 1, 6, 57–65

This, of course, was a precursor of the well-established *Geranomachy*, which first saw the light of day in Claudius Aelianus' (c. 175—c. 235 CE) *De Natura Animalium* (15, 29). Pygmies (*pugmaios*)—simply small people—are described most famously at the opening of Homer's *Iliad* Book 3. The exploitation of dwarfs continues apace today in 'dwarf-tossing' in Canada, the US, and France: a modern manifestation of people exploited as spectacle solely for their untypical physical form. At the most repellent end of the spectrum, Commodus (r. 180–192 CE) allegedly served up a pair of hunchbacks smeared with mustard on a silver platter (*Scriptores Augustae, Commodus* 11, 1).

It is but a short step from this cheap, voyeuristic sort of exploitation to sexual exploitation of the disabled. Pliny the Elder reports sex with a hunchback slave (*NH* 34, 11–12), while Martial launches an excoriating attack on a woman, Marulla, who apparently cultivated a predilection for sex with the facially deformed:

> To Cinna,
>
> Marulla has made you, Cinna, the father of seven children, I will not say freeborn, for not one of them is either your own or that of any friend or neighbour; but all were conceived on menial beds or mats, betray, by their looks, the infidelities of their mother. This, who runs towards us so like a Moor, with his crisped hair, avows himself the offspring of the cook Santra; while that other, with flattened nose and thick lips, is the very image of Pannicus, the wrestler. Who can be ignorant, that knows or has ever seen the blear-eyed Dama, that the third is that baker's son? The fourth, with his fair face and voluptuous air, evidently sprung from your favourite Lygdus. You may debauch your offspring if you please; it will be no crime. As to this one, with tapering head and long ears, like asses, who would deny that he is the son of the idiot Cyrrha? The two sisters, one swarthy, the other red-haired, are the offspring of the piper Crotus, and the bailiff Carpus, your flock of hybrids would have been quite complete, if Coresus and Dyndymus had not been incapable.
>
> Martial 6, 39
>
> translation Martial, *Epigrams* Book 6. Bohn's Classical Library (1897)

In another epigram he tells how Labulla exploits a dwarf by using him as an intermediary between her and her lover before the very eyes of her husband; she simply kisses the dwarf and then her lover kisses the dwarf, whose lips are still moist with Labulla's kisses (*Epigram* 12, 93).

Petronius, Martial and Juvenal casually poke fun at the disabled. Juvenal, in *Satire* 3, makes derogatory references to the appearance of the deformed; he highlights the insincerity of calling a 'little and deformed woman' Europa; Petronius, in the feast of Trimalchio (39), refers to people with convergent strabismus, or who are cross-eyed: 'Under Sagittarius are born cross-eyed people who look at the vegetables and take the bacon.'

On a slightly more constructive and less exploitative note, Tiberius, Claudius, Nero, and Domitian all admitted disabled slaves into their close circles of advisors and confidants. Suetonius says that Tiberius's dwarf court jester was particularly influential and, when he asked during a banquet about a man who had been charged with treason, Tiberius reacted and expedited the man's trial (Suetonius, *Tiberius* 61); Claudius enjoyed Julius Paelignus, 'despised alike for his stupid mind and contemptible body,' (Tacitus *Annals* 12, 49 1), appointing him as governor of Cappadocia. Domitian had a dwarf by his side at gladiatorial displays to be different and for the kudos: 'a boy dressed in scarlet with an abnormally small head', microcephaly, no doubt. These people were later to become the 'pinheads' in early circus sideshows and put on display as 'missing links'— the link between humans and lower mammals (Suetonius, *Domitian* 4, 2); Commodus named the slave Onos, 'Donkey', a priest of Rustic Hercules, due to his 'penis larger than most animals' (Lampridius, *Commodus* 10, 9). Elagabalus (r. 218–222 CE) retained so many human 'curiosities' that looking after them became a financial liability.

Some people with mobility issues could make a living as potters, teachers and metal workers; indeed, the lame Greek god Hephaestus was a blacksmith and something of a role model for the disabled, despite Hera's attempts to drown him at birth and forever being the butt of the other gods' ridicule. More lucrative, and certainly more dangerous, was employment as a spy or informer: Tacitus describes Vatinius:

> [He was] ranked among the filthiest prodigies of that court; the product of a cobbler, blessed with a misshapen body and a scurrilous wit, he had been taken on from the start as a target for buffoonery; then, by falsely accusing every decent man, he acquired a power which made him a leading villain, in influence, in wealth, and in the capacity to inflict harm.

> Tacitus, *Annals* 15, 34

In the reign of Domitian (81–96 CE), a blind man called Catullus Messalinus became a very successful informer, described by Juvenal as 'a great and renowned monster, a blind flatterer' (4, 115–6); he must have relied solely on what he heard rather than saw.

Pliny the Younger tells us about Domitius Tullus, a paralysed man who was sufficiently wealthy to be able to afford slaves to assist him with daily living. Pliny (*Epistles* 8, 18) says that Domitius Tullus did not feel lucky but rather somewhat humiliated at being so dependent on his slaves, and his dedicated wife, for the most basic functions and tasks: 'A quadriplegic, he could only enjoy his huge wealth by gazing at it and could not even turn in bed without help. He even had to have someone clean his teeth for him, a pathetic thing.'

However, begging on the streets, petty crime, fetishistic prostitution, seasonal work, and reliance on familial charity must have been commonplace for most disabled people who were usually consigned and confined to the margins of Roman society. Apart from in Athens, there was precious little in the way of welfare payments for disabled people in need in the ancient world. Seneca, however, does report a Roman law giving a one-off payment to visually impaired people, and writes that the Roman state 'comforts a man for his disability'.

Concern regarding the administration of care in our twilight years is by no means a modern anxiety. Indeed, a law was introduced in Rome in the second century CE, to make provision for care in old age when infirmity and disability were likely to take over. Some Romans adopted grown-up sons to ensure care and support in their later years.

The gods dealt a doubly devastating blow when a disabled person happened also to be a slave. There must have been many such unfortunates, due either to slaves being worked within an ace of death, or through injuries sustained in battle before being consigned as war booty to servitude as a defeated prisoner of war. It seems likely that when a slave became too weak or disabled to be of any further practical use to his master, he was simply killed: Claudius' law ruling that that disabled slaves should be abandoned rather than killed probably testifies to this. Manumitting a disabled slave was probably the cruellest act of all: in effect, that slave was being consigned to a life in penury on the streets; it did, however, save the master money.

Perhaps the most extraordinary, and untypical, story relating to a disabled person is left to us by Pliny the Elder when he describes what happened to the slave Clessipus, described by Pliny as 'an ugly hunchback' (*NH* 34, 11). A wealthy woman called Gegania went out shopping one day and decided to buy an expensive Corinthian chandelier for the prodigious sum of 50,000 sesterces; for good measure, the auctioneer threw in Clessipus as well, so she left the shop with a bronze candelabra and a deformed slave. Gegania showed him off at parties, and had him parade naked for the titillation of her guests. However, she also fell deeply in love with him, aroused possibly by his scoliosis, took him into her bed, and even changed her will to make him a beneficiary. On her death, Gegania's huge fortune came to Clessipus who presumably spent the rest of his days giving thanks to the candelabra. Whether Clessipus was just a very clever fortune hunter we will never know; we can only hope that he genuinely deserved his good luck.

Not surprisingly, some hunchbacks were very self-conscious about their condition. Suetonius tells that the notorious teacher of Horace, 'flogger' Lucius Orbilius Pupillusa, was rude to distinguished men; when he was unknown and was giving testimony in a crowded court-room, the lawyer on the other side, Varro Murena, asked what he did and what his profession was, he replied: 'I take hunchbacks from the sun and put them into the shade.' Murena was a hunchback.

There is even evidence that some Romans maimed their slaves out of sheer sadism, either to satisfy sexual deviance or just to create the unusual in order to impress—a kind of perverted status symbol for the home that had everything. There was nothing like a dwarf, hunchback, manic depressive, blind, death, dumb, or blind man or woman to impress the neighbours or dinner guests, all readily available from that special section of the slave market.

Plutarch describes this hideous place, the τεράτων ἀγορὰν—'monster market':

Therefore, just as at Rome there are some who take no account of paintings or statues or even, by Heaven, of the beauty of the boys and women for sale, but haunt the monster-market, examining those who have no calves, or are weasel-armed, or have three eyes, or ostrich-heads, and searching to learn whether there has been born some commingled shape and misformed prodigy, yet if one continually conduct them to such sights, they will soon experience satiety and nausea; so let those who are curious about life's failures, the blots on the scutcheon, the delinquencies and errors in other people's homes, remind themselves that their former discoveries have brought them no favour or profit.

> Plutarch, *De Curiositate* 10/*Moralia* 520c: translation W.C. Helmbold, 1939

An enlightened Longinus is yet more critical of this inhumane behaviour:

> And so, my friend adds, if what I hear is true, not only do the cages in which they confine the pygmies or dwarfs, as they are called, stunt the growth of their captives, but their bodies even shrink due to the close confinement, on the same principle that all slavery, however fair it may be, might be described as a cage for the human soul, a common prison.
>
> Longinus, *De Sublimitate* 44, 5

The incarceration and venality were bad enough in these places, but one gets the impression that they were also the place to go and gawp for the deviant and voyeuristic.

Children too were deliberately mutilated to ramp up the pity—and therefore the money—they would attract while begging on the streets; Seneca the Elder (*c.* 54 BC— *c.* 39 CE) tells the shocking story of a man on trial for snatching exposed children and mutilating them:

> Here roam the blind, leaning on sticks, here others carry round stumps of arms. This child has had the joints of his feet torn, his ankles wrenched; this has had his legs crushed. Another's thighs he has smashed, though leaving feet and legs unharmed. Finding a different savagery for each, this bone-breaker cuts off the arms of one, slices the sinews of another's; one he twists, another he castrates. In yet another he stunts the shoulder-blades, beating them into an ugly hump, looking for a laugh from his cruelty. Come on, bring out your troop half-alive, shaking, feeble, blind, crippled, starving; show us your prisoners. I want to get to know that cave of yours, that stripping-place for children.
>
> Seneca the Elder, *Controversiae* 10, 4
> translation by Michael Winterbottom, 1974

Nevertheless, the deformed slave was sometimes regarded as something of a talisman, a good luck charm, or a living force against malicious curses and evil spells. They also served to satisfy a sense of *schadenfreude* in the owner, or, more charitably, a living, daily reminder that 'there but for the grace of God, go I'.

Seneca the Younger's wife owned a dwarf named Harpaste who irked the philosopher:

> You know Harpaste, my wife's female clown; she has stayed in my house, a burden inherited from a legacy. I especially disapprove of these freaks; whenever I wish to enjoy the gags of a clown, I don't have to go very far; I can just laugh at myself. Now this clown suddenly went blind. Incredible as it sounds, I swear that it is true:

she does not know that she is blind. She keeps asking her attendant to change her quarters, saying that her apartment is too dark.

Seneca, Epistles 50, 2

To many Romans, the disabled and deformed were regarded in much the same way as they looked at exotic animals, such as hippos, rhinos, tigers, and apes. As such, they commanded a good price; Quintilian (*Institutio Oratoria* 2, 5, 11) asserts that Romans had higher regard for the deformed or for those acting the goat than for physically sound people—such was the premium they put on the strange and extraordinary. Martial tells how a man paid over the odds for a slave with learning difficulties, only to discover that he was actually quite intelligent; the buyer asked for a full refund. Pliny the Younger is tolerant, up to a point:

> To Genitor
>
> I got your letter, in which you complain of having been most disgusted lately at a very splendid dinner party, by a troupe of buffoons, actors, and wanton prostitutes, who were dancing about round the tables. But let me advise you to calm down. I confess, indeed, I don't allow anything of this kind at my own house; however, I put up with it in others.

Pliny the Younger, Epistles 9, 17, 1

9

Education

In the early days of Rome's existence, Romans were educated at home by father and mother and perhaps a literate slave. The goal was to inculcate in the child life skills and a solid grounding in the three 'r's, which would enable him or her to take their place in society as good Roman citizens, imbued with all the virtues that that assumed: respect, *pietas* with regard to family, country, and the gods, diligence, industriousness, and ambition. However, as Rome grew and expanded, a more formal education system developed with a broader curriculum and, for the boys at least, more focus on preparation for the *cursus honorum*—the political and military road map of service to the state.

For the children of the lower orders, though, there was little in the way of education of any sort. The *litterator* stage was as far as it went. Boys were needed to work the land or help in the family business; they would often automatically follow in their fathers' occupation, receiving on-the-job-training from an early age. Alternatively, a young boy would be contracted into an apprenticeship whereby he received no pay and lots of work; board and lodge were his only reward, with the hoped-for proficiency in a trade or manual job. Here is a papyrus from 53 CE found at Oxyrhyncus in Egypt showing an extract from one such contract:

> Pausiris, son of Ammonius, and Apollonius, a weaver, son of Apollonius, have come to the following agreement: Pausiris has given as apprentice to Apollonius his son Dioskus, still a boy, so that he may learn the trade of a weaver for one year from today. Dioskus will work for Apollonius and do everything he is told to do.
>
> *Wisconsin Papyrus* 16, 4

Apollonius agreed to feed and clothe Dioskus, for which he received a contribution of fourteen drachmae from Pausiris for the clothes and five drachmae per month for the food. Being lazy or not doing the work attracted a fine of one drachma per day, or working extra time to make up the loss. Taking the boy out of the apprenticeship would cost the father 100 drachmae plus an equal amount payable to the local treasury;

failure on the part of the weaver to provide the requisite training was punishable by the same fine. Lucian tells a story of an apprenticeship which, although full of good intentions, did not end well:

When I attained manhood, and had just left school, my father and I met to decide my profession. Most of his friends considered that a life of culture was very exacting in effort, time, and money: a life only for fortune's favourites; whereas our resources were few, and badly needed topping up. If I were to take up a trade, I should be making my own living immediately, instead of eating my father out of house and home; and my earnings would soon be a welcome contribution.

So the next step was to pick the best trade; it had to be one quite easy to acquire, respectable, inexpensive as regards tools, and reasonably profitable. ... my father turned to my mother's brother, an excellent sculptor of statues, and said to him: 'With you here, it would be a crime to prefer any other craft; take the boy, consider him your charge, teach him to handle, match, and engrave your marble; he will do well enough; you know he has the ability.' This opinion he had formed from certain tricks I used to play with wax. When I got home from school, I used to scrape off the wax from my tablets and work it into cows, horses, or even men and women, and he thought I did it well; my teachers used to cane me for it, but here it was taken as evidence of a natural ability, and my modelling gave them good hopes of my picking up sculpture quickly...

My uncle gave me a chisel, and told me to apply a gentle touch to a plaque lying on the bench... I brought down the tool too hard, and the plaque broke; he flew into a rage, picked up a stick which lay handy, and thereby gave me an introduction to the art which could have been gentler and more encouraging; I cried and absconded, reaching home still bawling and tearful. I told the story of the cane, and showed my bruises. I said a great deal about his brutality, and added that it was all envy: he was afraid of my turning out to be a better sculptor than he. My mother was very angry, and scolded her brother; as for me, I fell asleep that night with my eyes still wet, full of sorrow till the morning.

Lucian, *The Dream* 1–4
adapted from the translation by H. W. Fowler and F. G. Fowler
Oxford: The Clarendon Press (1905)

Young girls also followed a trade sometimes, as these two epitaphs attest:

In memory of Viccentia, a lovely girl, a worker in gold; she lived nine years.
CIL 6, 9213

In memory of Pieris, a hairdresser, she lived nine years
CIL 6, 9731

The curriculum

Initially, Roman education was, to all intents and purposes, thinly-disguised Greek education. In literature, until the Romans could provide their own critical mass of poetry and rhetoric written in Latin, all education was based on Greek works. By the end of the Republic, however, the burgeoning corpus of literature published in Latin allowed the work of Cicero and Virgil, Sallust and Terence, for example, to replace their Greek counterparts, providing gold standards in rhetoric, poetry, prose, and drama. The ultimate aim of 'primary' Roman education (conducted by a *litterator* or a *magister ludi litterarii* from around age seven) was to perfect self-expression: knowing how to speak properly in public and to interpret the poets were paramount skills. Painstaking and laborious work on the alphabet, first with letters, then with syllables, was inevitable and unavoidable according to Quintilian.

> As soon as the boy has learned to read and write without difficulty, it is the turn of the teacher of literature. My words apply equally to Greek and Latin masters, though I prefer that a start should be made with a Greek: in either case the method is the same. This profession may be most briefly considered under two headings: the art of speaking correctly and the interpretation of the poets; but there is more beneath the surface than meets the eye. For the art of writing is combined with that of speaking, and correct reading precedes interpretation, while in each of these cases criticism has its part to play.
>
> Quintilian, *Institutio Oratoria* 1, 4, 1–3;
> translation adapted from the Loeb Classical Library edition, (1920)

The grammaticus

From age eleven, the *grammaticus* took over and the equally painstaking and pedantic reading and analysis of literary texts began: the texts were studied less as an end in themselves and more as further preparation for the pupil's role as an orator in the courts or in the senate. Aptitude in public speaking was for many the be-all and end-all; it was the job of the *grammaticus* and then the *rhetor* to turn out a stream of adept public speakers. Subjects such as astronomy, music, philosophy, and natural science were also studied but, again, not as ends in themselves, rather to enable the student to understand better the use of these subjects in poetry or prose. Literary criticism, geography, mythology, and grammar were also on the curriculum.

Quintilian expatiates on the crucial role of the *grammaticus*:

> It is not enough just to have to have read the poets; every genre of writer must be carefully studied, not only for the subject matter, but for the vocabulary, for words

often acquire meanings from the particular writer using them. And that's not the end of the training: music must be studied because the teacher of literature has to talk about metre and rhythm; furthermore, if he he knows no astronomy he cannot understand the poets; for they, for example, often indicate time by reference to the rising and setting of the stars. Ignorance of philosophy is just as disadvantageous since there are numerous passages in almost every poem based on the most intricate questions of natural philosophy; among the Greeks there is Empedocles and among our own poets Varro and Lucretius, who expounded their philosophies in verse.

Quintilian, *Institutio Oratoriae* 1, 4, 4

The rhetor

By the end of the republic, a specific third stage had become established: instruction and practice in rhetoric, under the *rhetor*, which moved the fifteen or sixteen-year-old boy student yet closer to competence in declamation, that obsessive *sine qua non* of a successful life on the public stage and closer to the completion of a good *cursus honorum*. The boy pupil discarded the *toga praetexta* and donned the *toga virilis*: his first stage of the *cursus honorum*. He would pursue either the *tirocinium militia* (military cadetship) or the *tirocinium fori* (legal apprenticeship) for a year. If the latter, this may have been complemented by some philosophy, and perhaps a 'grand tour' of Greece or of a visit to a Greek colony.

In his *Brutus*, Cicero gives an account of his education from the age of sixteen when he was learning rhetoric and philosophy: listening to, watching and mixing with the experts was the way to success:

While he was in the height of his glory, Crassus died, Cotta was banished, our public trials were interrupted by the Marsic war, and I myself made my first appearance in the forum... The only trial we had, was that on the Varian Law; the rest, as I have just observed, were interrupted by the war. I regularly attended the courts, although L. Memmius and Q. Pompeius spoke in their own defence. They were far from being orators of the first distinction, but were yet tolerable ones, and Philippus, who spoke eloquently as a witness, displayed the full vigour and expressiveness of a prosecutor. The rest, who were esteemed our leading speakers, were then acting as magistrates, and I had the benefit of hearing their harangues almost every day. C. Curio was chosen a tribune of the people; though he left off speaking after being once deserted by his whole audience. To him I may add Q. Metellus Celer, who, though certainly no orator, was far from being short of things to say: but Q. Varius, C. Carbo, and Cn. Pomponius, were men of real eloquence, and might almost be said to have lived on the rostra. C. Julius Caesar too, who was then a curule aedile, was daily employed in making speeches to the people, which were composed with great neatness and accuracy. But while I listened to these speakers with eager interest, my first disappointment was the banishment of Cotta: after which I continued to hear the rest with the same keenness as before; and though I spent the remainder of my time every day in reading, writing, and private declamation, I cannot say that I much relished my confinement to these preparatory exercises. The next year Q. Varius was condemned, and banished, by his own law: and I, so that I might acquire a competent knowledge of the principles of jurisprudence, then joined Q. Scaevola, the son of Publius, who, though he did not choose to take on a pupil and by freely giving his advice to those who asked, he performed the function of a teacher to those who took the trouble to consult him. In the next year, in which Sulla and Pompeius were consuls [88 B.C.], Sulpicius was elected a tribune of the people, and spoke in public almost every day; therefore, I had an opportunity to acquaint myself thoroughly with his way of speaking. Then I became pupil to Philon, the leading philosopher in the Academy…and was much taken with his philosophy…

Cicero, *Brutus* 305–16

Translation adapted from that by by E.Jones (1776)

The system had not changed some 150 years later, according to Tacitus:

The usual practice with our ancestors when a boy was being trained for the bar, as soon as his home education was complete and his mind was full of culture, was to have him taken by his father, or his relatives to the orator who was at the top of his game. The boy would accompany and attend him, and be present at all his speeches both in the law-courts and the senate, picking up the skill of repartee…thus from the start they were imbued with true and real eloquence, and, although they were attached to one advocate only, they became acquainted with all advocates through a multitude of cases before the courts. He learnt the laws because he heard them every day; he knew the faces of the judges who were familiar to him; and he was continually exposed to the workings of the ways of popular assemblies.

Tacitus, *Dialogus de Oratoribus* 34, 1–6

translation adapted from A. J. Church and W. J. Brodribb

New York: Random House, (1942)

Suasoriae & controversiae

Once the basics had been mastered, the student moved on to case studies: *suasoriae* were exercises in which a speech was created to persuade an individual to take a particular course of action; *controversiae* were speeches arguing one side of a point of law. A famous example of a *suasoria* comes from Seneca the Elder:

Agamemnon is at Aulis warned by Calchas the seer that the gods forbid him to set sail [for Troy] until he as sacrificed his daughter, Iphigenia. Agamemnon deliberates whether or not to slaughter Iphigenia.

Seneca the Elder, *Suasoriae* 3, 6, 7.

An example of a Senecan *controversia*:

The law states that a priestess should be pure and chaste. A young woman was captured by pirates and sold to a pimp who brought her up as a prostitute; she persuaded her clients that the money they gave her was a gift [and no sex was involved]. One soldier, however, was not persuaded and tried to rape her. She killed him and was tried, acquitted and returned home to her family. She applies to become a priestess but is rejected.

Seneca the Elder, *Controversiae* 1, 2

The student has to present an argument saying why, or not, the woman should be admitted to the priesthood.

Many conservative Romans regarded the education of their children to be too precious to delegate or outsource. Cato the Elder is a good, if extreme example; we should consider him as an all-round good husband and father, with his childrens' best interests very much at heart:

He used to say that the man who struck his wife or child, laid violent hands on the holiest of holy things. Also, that he thought it more praiseworthy to be a good husband than a great senator; that there was nothing else to admire in old Socrates except that he was always kind and gentle in his dealings with a shrewish wife and stupid sons. After the birth of his son, no business could be so urgent, unless it was to the public good, as to prevent him from being around when his wife bathed and dressed the baby.

For the mother nursed baby herself, and even breastfed the infants of her slaves, that so they might come to cherish a brotherly affection for her son. As soon as the boy showed signs of learning, his father took him under his wing and taught him to read, even though he had an accomplished slave called Chilo, who was a schoolteacher and taught many boys. Still, Cato thought it not right, as he tells us himself, that his son should be told off by a slave, or have his ears boxed when he was slow to learn, still less that he should be indebted to his slave for such a priceless thing as education. He was not only the boy's reading teacher, but his law tutor, and his athletics coach and he taught his son not merely to hurl the javelin and fight in armour and ride the horse, but also to box, to endure heat and cold, and to swim strongly through the eddies and currents of the Tiber. His *History of Rome*, as he tells us himself, he wrote out long hand and in large characters so that his son might have in his own home a way of learning about his country's ancient traditions. He was careful never to swear in front of him, as if he was in the company of the Vestal Virgin.

Plutarch, *Cato Maior* 20, 2–5;
translated by Bernadotte Perrin, Loeb Classical Library (1914) with adaptations.

Girls' education

Roman education focused on the education of boys to prepare them for a life at the bar, in the senate, on the battlefield, or governing the provinces. Girls were schooled, usually by the *materfamilias,* in domestic duties—essentially working the wool and keeping the house—in preparation for their role as *matronae*, which would sometimes loom into their lives from as early as thirteen or fourteen years old. From then on, it was, ideally for the Roman, a succession of pregnancies producing boys for the bar and battlefield.

Women, of course, were largely excluded from public life; that naturally obviated the need to instruct them in rhetoric and declamation. The education of girls and young women seems, in general, to have been limited to a home-based instruction of the elementary stage under the *materfamilias* or a *litterator*, alongside her brothers. Marriage, too, was a limiting force: when a girl wed at twelve or thirteen, there was little time for education for the fledgling *matrona*; her concern in this regard would be the education of the children she was expected to produce. Boys were the focus of attention, but some young women, did, of course, excel and some, in the richer families, did move on to the grammar stage.

Cicero and Pliny remark on the purity of the Latin turned out by some women:

> Everyone has read the letters of Cornelia, the mother of the Gracchi; it seems that the education her sons received came not so much from their mother's bosom, as from her speech. I have often heard the conversation of Laelia, the daughter of Caius, and seen in her a marked hint of her father's elegance. I have likewise conversed with his two daughters, the Muciae, and his granddaughters, the two Liciniae, one of whom, the wife of Scipio, you, Brutus, I believe, have occasionally heard speaking. 'I have,' he replied, 'and was very taken with her conversation'.

Cicero, *Brutus* 211

She is erudite and attracted Greeks among the 'learned men' in her circle. Carneades of Cyrene found it quite normal to converse with her on philosophical things. It was the education she in turn gave her sons that accounted for their success, not their lineage; Cornelia also hired Blossius of Cuma and Diophanes of Mytilene to help out. Cornelia was bilingual in Greek and Latin, well-read, a good lyre player, a competent mathematician, and could hold a philosophical argument. Quintilian praised her literary style. She would certainly have benefited from the Greek library brought home to Italy by her uncle, Aemilius Paullus. Her namesake, Cornelia Metella (*c.* 73 BCE–48 BCE), daughter of Metellus Scipio, was similarly gifted: good at the lyre, good at mathematics, and good at philosophy.

Pliny writes in a letter of a gifted woman:

> TO ERUCIUS.
>
> Not long ago he [Pompeius Saturninus] read me some letters which he said his wife had written. When I heard them, I thought, that they must have been either prose versions of Plautus or Terence; whether they were composed, as he claims, by his wife or by himself, which he denies, he deserves the same credit either as the actual author of the letters, or as the teacher who has made such an educated and polished lady of his wife whom he took as a maiden.
>
> Pliny, *Epistles* 1, 16, 6

The suggestion in Pliny is that it was her husband who provided the education for his wife, rather than anything she had received as a girl. Nevertheless, the love poets from Catullus to Ovid and the letters of Pliny all attest to sophisticated and literate women—*doctae puellae*; on the other hand, Juvenal excoriates bluesockings and lady pedants.

While he had his grandsons educated in reading, swimming, and handwriting by the renowned teacher, Verrius Flaccus, Augustus attempted to inculcate domestic skills such as weaving and spinning in his granddaughters, and even in the wayward Julia, as a bid to resurrect traditional values. However, there is no reason to suppose that the girls did not benefit from the more academic tuition provided by Verrius Flaccus as well.

Educated women: *doctae puellae*

We have already seen how the home education, among the middle and upper classes at least, produced a number of exceptionally gifted and talented women among the teachers and the taught. Illiteracy among the upper classes was probably not that common but, all the same, these educated women are exceptional. Cornelia, Pliny's Calpurnia, and Sallusts' Sempronia were not the only beneficiaries of a more enlightened, Greek-influenced education for women that extended beyond Augustus's household management programme and the spinning of wool.

Sallust grudgingly acknowledges Sempronia's intellectual and artistic gifts:

> [She was] well-read in the Greek and Roman classics, able to play the lyre and could dance better than any honest woman needs to; she had many other accomplishments which made her very sexy … she could compose verse, tell a good joke, and use

language which was either modest, or gentle or filthy; in short, she was extremely witty and charming.

Sallust, *Catilina* 25

Cornificia (*c.* 85 BCE—*c.* 40 BCE) was a contemporary of Catullus and sister of Q. Cornificius, a neoteric poet friendly with Catullus and Cicero; she married Camerius, another friend of Catullus. None of her work is extant but her reputation as an epigrammist lasted well into the fourth century when St Jerome in his *Chronicle* described her work as 'remarkable': 'His [Cornificius'] sister was Cornificia, whose distinguished [*insignia*] epigrams survive to this day' (St Jerome *Chronicles*, for 41 BCE).

Praise confirmed later by Giovanni Boccaccio in his *On Famous Women* (*De Mulieribus Claris*, 1362 CE):

> She was just as glorious as her brother Cornificius, who was a much better known poet at that time. Not satisfied with excelling in such a superb art, inspired by the sacred Muses, she rejected wool-working and turned her hands, skilled in composition, to writing Heliconian verses ... With her genius and hard work she rose above her sex, and acquired an everlasting fame with her splendid work.

Boccaccio, *Concerning Famous Women* translation adapted from Guido A. Guarino (Rutgers University Press, 1963) p. 188

Ovid's step-daughter obviously benefited from a sound education: in a letter from exile, he envisages Perilla sitting with her mother 'her nose in a book and among the Muses' when his letter arrives. He refers to her polished poetry, *docta carmina,* and exaggerates how only Sappho is more gifted; he recalls how they used to read each other's poetry to each other, how he was her critic and teacher; Perilla is clearly most accomplished—*doctissima*. Ovid urges her to keep on writing because, come what may, she will always be read by posterity, like him.

> Off you go, hastily written letter, go greet Perilla and be the faithful servant of what I say. You will find her sitting with her kind mother or with her nose in a book and among the Pierian maidens, the muses, she loves... So if you are still doing the same work and, in a way that is different from your father, are writing clever poetry...only Sappho will be superior...I used often to read your verse to myself and mine to you; often was I your critic, often your teacher...

Ovid, *Tristia* 3, 7, 1–4, 11–12, 23–4

Pliny is delighted that Calpurnia, his wife, expresses her love for him by reading and re-reading his books, by closely following his court cases, and by singing his verses while playing the lyre (6, 7); in another letter (5, 16), a eulogy for the younger daughter of Fundanus, he describes her *anilis prudentia, matronalis gravitas*—her old-womanish prudence and matronly gravity—as well as her affection for her teachers, her avid and studious reading.

Agrippina, mother of Nero, wrote her memoirs (*commentarii*) in note form; Tacitus used them as a source for his histories as did Pliny for his *Natural History*.[1] We hear of two female philosophers: Magnilla, whose father, Magnus, and husband, Menius, were both philosophers, and Euphrosyne, versed in the nine Muses.[2] In the first century CE, Epidaurian Pamphile was a learned woman and wrote thirty three books of historical memoirs, summaries of various histories, controversies, and books on sex. The courtesans Astyanassa and Elephantine also wrote 'pornography'.[3] Martial recommends the works of Sulpicia to married couples if they want to please each other: like Ovid before her, she teaches *ars amatoria* (the art of love).[4]

> Let all girls who want to please only one man read Sulpicia. Let all husbands, who want to please only one wife, read Sulpicia...she teaches pure and proper love—fun and games, and wit. Anyone who assesses well her poems will say that no one is more mischievous, no one purer ... with Sulpicia as fellow-student, or as teacher, Sappho might have been cleverer and purer.
>
> Martial 10, 35, 1–4, 8–13, 15–6

Musonius Rufus, the Stoic philosopher of the mid-first century CE, showed an enlightened attitude when he remarked that he could see no reason why women should not study philosophy; indeed, philosophy equips the woman to be a good wife and *matrona*. Philosophy underscores everything; it enables her to run the house, rear her children, remain chaste, and be a devoted mother and wife—all the qualities and virtues a Roman looked for in his wife. It helps her to keep her emotions under control, be compliant, frugal, and modest.[5] Rufus also argues that men and women should be educated in the same way and to the same extent. A pupil of his, Epictetus, noted that Plato was popular with women because they believed that he advocated women's communes and promiscuity.[6] Plutarch argues that women should be well educated, if only to stop them filling their heads with nonsense: the woman who is studying geometry will have no time for dancing; the women who is reading Plato or Xenophon will reject magic:

> But it is even better for a man to hear his wife say 'My dear husband, but to me you are guide, philosopher and teacher in all that is most beautiful and most divine'. In the first place these studies will take away a woman's appetite for stupid and irrational pursuits. A woman who is studying geometry will be embarrassed to go out dancing and one who is enraptured by the words of Plato or Xenophon is not going to pay any attention to magic incantations. If women do not get the basis of a good education and do not develop this education in with their husbands they will, left to themselves, form a lot of ridiculous ideas and pointless aims and emotions.[7]
>
> Plutarch, *Moralia* 138a–146a;
> translation adapted from R. Warner, *Moral Essays*

In the late Republic, home-based education coincided with a growing independence among increasing numbers of better-off women, allowing them more freedom and independence outside the home. At the same time, a number of male poets were able to eschew the traditional *mos maiorum*, rejecting the *cursus honorum* for a life of *otium* in which they could while away their time penning poetry and pursuing the objects of their affection. Among these coteries we can recognise such poets as Licinius Calvus, Varro of Atax, Valerius Cato, Furius Bibaculus, Helvius Cinna, Cornificius, Ticidas and, most famously, Catullus. Collectively, they went under the name of *poetae novi, neoteroi* or *Cantores Euphorionis*.[8] Traditionalists regarded this otiose lifestyle as frivolous and un-Roman.

It is in such an environment that Catullus and his contemporaries flourished. Their educated women could mix with whomsoever they chose at the games, festivals, dinner parties or in the theatre enjoying, if they so chose, a degree of sexual freedom not dissimilar to that enjoyed by a *meretrix* (a prostitute) but with little of the social stigma.[9]

On a typical lazy day (*dies otiosus*), Varus invites Catullus to come over and meet his girl friend. First appearances show her to be elegant and well-mannered; however, a later indiscretion on her part that embarrasses Catullus renders her silly and annoying. On another occasion, Flavius' reticence about his girl leads Catullus to assume that she is 'common and a bit rough', 'a fever-ridden slag no less'.[10] When he invites himself over to Ipsithilla's place for an afternoon of sex, he sarcastically and sycophantically calls her: 'my delight, my clever one'.[11] Both Quintia and Ameana fall short: Quintia is indeed fair, tall and she holds herself well, but she is not beautiful (*formosa*), and she lacks charm and wit. As for Caecilius' girlfriend, she has begun reading his *Magna Mater* and is fired with passion for Caecilius as a result. To Catullus, she is thereby more refined than the Sapphic Muse.[12]

Catullus' Lesbia typifies the unattached, or readily detachable, sophisticated, rich, intelligent, and urbane ladies of the day who could exert considerable influence— sexual, psychological, and sometimes political—on their male friends: the recession of the *mos maiorum* allowed these sophisticated women to do that, and to provide the *milieux* for the *poetae novi* to write with conviction about their love for and of their relationships with them. Independent men of means were, for the first time, able to shrug off the traditional allegiance to bar and battlefield and to write personally and subjectively about independent and clever women of means.

It is Lesbia for whom Catullus reserves the highest praise: Claudia Pulchra Prima (b. 94 BCE), wife of Metellus Celer, brother of Publius Clodius Pulcher, and mistress of Catullus. She was also a lover of Marcus Caelius Rufus, the friend whom Cicero defended against charges of attempted poisoning and, in doing so, destroyed Clodia's reputation such as it was, calling her, among other things, the 'Medea of the Palatine', a witch in so many words. [13] Lesbia, though, has the *venustas* and *salis* Quintia lacks, and *Veneres*—'grace, elegance and charm'; this, and physical beauty, adds up to total beauty. Lesbia has literary talent; she can identify the 'best bits of the worst poet' as she demonstrates when she hands back the dreadful annals of Volusius—'pure unsophisticated doggerel, complete crap' (*pleni ruris et infacetiarum annales Volusi, cacata charta*).[14]

Propertius includes finesse in the fields of dance, music, and poetry, as well as intelligence, in the female competencies which drive his passion. Physical beauty is eclipsed by these more cerebral skills; Cynthia's lyre playing inspires his poetry. Cynthia is *docta*; she is a fitting companion to him in Helicon. Her conversation is fine, particularly when the couple are in bed together. She can compose poetry herself, and Propertius goes so far as to compare her with Corinna, a contemporary of Pindar. Intellectually, Cynthia is on a par with Propertius; it is reasonable to assume that a less intelligent or less accomplished woman would have held little attraction for him. At the same time, though, her *lepor* and sophistication are a double-edged sword: the attention she thereby attracts from other impressionable men, and her care not to be dependent on any one man may be reasons why he is unable to keep her.[15]

Propertius' contemporary, Albius Tibullus, is noticeably reticent on the intellectual qualities of both Delia and Nemesis; he favours the traditional, unobtrusive qualities and virtues in a woman. Indeed, the cosmopolitan life of a Catullus or a Propertius is not for Tibullus. He describes an ideal lifestyle more befitting a country *matrona*, which sees Delia sitting at home in the evening surrounded by seamstresses who one by one fall asleep working away at the loom. This itself is remimiscent of Lucretia, that paradigm of *matronae*.[16] By contrast, the author of the *Garland of Sulpicia* describes the poetess Sulpicia as *docta puella*.[17]

For Horace, writing about the same time as Propertius and Tibullus, any appreciation of the female intellect and artistic accomplishment is largely limited to the floor shows put on by the dancing girls at the drinking parties he attended: Damalis is leered at remorselessly, Lyde is summoned to play her lyre and Neaera is required to sing—all as a precursor to sex. Phydile is dismissed as simply *rustica*.[18] In a more general context, Licymnia is praised for her *dulces cantus* (sweet singing), Chloe is skilled on the cithara, and is good at gentle dance rhythms (*dulcis docta modos et citharae sciens*), while the *eburna* (ivory) and *curva* (curved) lyres of Lydia and the *scortum* Lyde are much in demand, as are Phyllis and *arguta* (melodious) Neaera for their singing, and Tyndaris for her lyre-playing and singing.[19] Horace appreciates accomplishment in the arts—music, dancing, and singing—but he seems quite indifferent to intelligence, wit, or social sophistication in his women.

Ovid is even less particular: to him, if a woman is *non rustica*, if she affects the resilience of the Sabine women, if she is bookish, or if she is common (*rudis*), if she attracts by virtue of her *simplicitas*, she is fine by Ovid. Shy girls, coquettish girls, tall girls, small girls, fashionable girls, frumpy girls, blonde girls, and black girls are all the same to Ovid. In the same poem however, he does single out the attractions of a woman who is literate and critical, who can sing, play the lyre, and dance well:

This girl sings sweetly, she has good range ... this one thrums the awkward strings with practised thumb—who could not adore such clever hands? This one delights

in the way she moves, her arms following the rhythm and her soft hips gyrating
with subtle skill.

Ovid, *Amores* 2, 4 25–31

Ovid confirms this in the *Ars Amatoria*.[20] His obsession with, and admiration of,
dancing girls and singers flew in the face of convention. Dancers were one short step
up from prostitutes to many, including Horace—ancient world lap dancers.

Ovid can advise where to find all types of girls, including sophisticated ladies
(*cultissima femina*)—the games are literally crawling with smart women—
confirmation that, generally, the educated woman was out and about and generally
much sought after. He acknowledges that some women appreciate good oratorical style
and oratory, and he himself consorts with women who are able to value his poetry, not
least Corinna. He advises his fellow men to get educated because women apparently
appreciate intellectual gifts in a man more than they do good looks.[21] He recommends
that men read widely in the Greek classics and in modern Latin literature, suggesting
clearly that women were similarly well-read and enjoyed literary discussion. Later
in the poem, though, he seems to reconsider when he admits that *doctae puellae* are
thin on the ground and that, generally, poetry is held in low regard. Clever women do
exist, though, and many aspire to culture; women can be seduced by verse or a piece of
declamation, be they clever or stupid.[22]

The urbanity and sophistication of the women courted by the love poets, the very
qualities which attracted the poets to these women in the first place, allow us to assume
that they read other genres such as epic, satire, history, tragedy, comedy and philosophy
both as leisure reading and for edification; Cicero, Propertius, Horace, Martial, and
Juvenal all corroborate this.[23] Varro, indeed, dedicated his *Res Rusticae, Country
Matters*, complete with exhaustive bibliography, to Fundania, his wife—fascinating
reading, no doubt, for the lay-woman. Whether she ever read it or not, we will never
know; the point is that she was patently capable of reading it and of understanding its
practical applications.

Two recommended reading lists, one aimed at women, exist. The first is compiled
by Ovid and is purportedly aimed at lower class rather than middle class women; it
is nothing if not erudite and includes Greek and Latin texts: Callimachus, Philetas,
Anacreon, Sappho, Menander, Propertius, Gallus, Tibullus, the *Argonautica* of Varro of
Atax and Virgil's *Aeneid*—as well as Ovid's own work. Quintilian's list for boys learning
grammar and rhetoric is completely different, with examples from tragedy; Virgil is the
only common author with Ovid's list. They confirm that women constituted a serious
market for books and that books 'for leisure' were seen as a very different commodity
from texts for the serious business of learning rhetoric. An example of a wife 'reading'
a husband's work pre-publication is given by Statius; it seems Claudia was up all night
sometimes hearing a first draft of his prolix *Thebaid*.[24]

Mothers had an important role to play in the education of their children. We have
noted how Julia Procilla was astute enough to steer her son, Agricola, away from his

infatuation with philosophy and helped him become the military and political success he was. Tacitus, we know, believed that child care was no substitute for a mother's influence. He cites the examples of Cornelia, Aurelia Cotta (Julius Caesar's mother), and Atia (the mother of Augustus) as role models:

> The mothers of the Gracchi, of Julius Cæsar, of Augustus, Cornelia, Aurelia, Atia, all took care of their children's education, bringing up the best of sons. In each the strict discipline produced a pure and good nature which vice could not corrupt.
>
> Tacitus, Dialogus de Oratoribus 28, 6

Schools & teachers

Schools themselves were very different from the purpose-built establishments we are used to today. They were usually *ad hoc* affairs in rented rooms in apartment blocks, or else *al fresco*, with lessons conducted on the pavement amid the noise and chaos of traffic and shoppers. An early start was essential if the worst of the cacophony was to be avoided, as we hear from a grumpy, sleep-deprived Martial:

> What is your problem with me, wretched schoolmaster, boss man loathed by boys and girls alike? Before crested cocks have broken the dawn silence, you thunder out your savage growls and lashes ... Us neighbours do not ask you for a full night's sleep for it is nothing to be woken up occasionally, but to be kept awake all night is a serious matter. Send your pupils away, prattler, and take as much for keeping quiet as you receive for making a din.
>
> Martial 9, 68 1–4, 8–12

Indeed, the teacher's lot was never a happy one, as we hear when Juvenal elucidates the issues and problems faced by the profession, many of which have a familiar ring today—low salary, pushy parents, and long hours:

> Whenever do Celadus and clever Palaemon [eminent *grammatici* of Juvenal's day] pocket what their hard work as a *grammaticus* deserves? ... give in Palaemon cut your losses so long as you get something for sitting from the middle of the night in a hole which no workman would tolerate, no one who teaches how to card wool ... And you parents certainly impose the harshest rules on the teacher: he must always be rigidly correct in his grammar; conversant with all historians…, and have all the authorities at his finger-tips…he must immediately tell you who Anchises' nurse was, what was the name and birth-place of Anchemolus' step-mother, how old Acestes lived, how many jars of Sicilian wine he gifted to the Trojans. You require that he mould the young impressionable minds as a sculptor moulds a face out of wax with his thumb;

you insist that he be a father figure to the whole mob so that they don't play nasty games and trick eachother. It's not an easy job to keep your eye on so many boys with their darting eyes and hands. 'That's your job', they say. At year end you get the same amount of money as the crowd demands for a single victorious victor in the arena.

Juvenal, Satires 7, 215–7; 219–224; 230–1; 234–243

Cicero tells us that there was no state requirement to provide either an education or public schools:

> As for boy-based education for free-born young men, a matter over which the Greeks have laboured so much in vain, and the only matter about which our guest Polybius accuses us of negligence with regards to our institution. No precise established system, or anything of a public nature that was the same for all was layed down in the laws.
>
> Cicero, Republica 4, 3

Aaccordingly, in 56 BCE, he made use of the services of a tutor for his son and nephew as revealed to his brother Quintus: 'Your son Quintus is an oustanding boy and an excellent student; I see this all the more because I now have Tyrannio here as a home tutor' (Cicero, *Letters to His Brother Quintus* 2, 4, 2).

Money for schools came from private investors, one of whom was a charitable Pliny the Younger, who describes his endowment for a school in a letter to the historian Tacitus:

> When I was last in my home town [Tusculum] a son of a fellow townsman of mine, an adolescent, came to pay his respects to me. I said to him, 'Do you keep up with your studies?' 'Yes,' he said. 'Where?' I asked. 'At Mediolanum,' he replied. 'But why not here?' I queried. Then the boy's father…, replied, 'Because we have no teachers here.' 'How is that?' I asked. 'It is vitally important to all fathers … that your children should receive their schooling right here where they can spend time pleasantly where they grew up… inexpensively at home. If you put your money together you could hire teachers at a pittance, using what you now spend on board and and travel and all the other costs of living away from home, which are not insignificant amounts. I have no children of my own, but still, in the interest of the town, which I may think of as my child or my parent, I am prepared to put in a third of the amount which you are happy to contribute… You cannot give your children a better gift than this, nor can you do your home town a better favour.
>
> Pliny the Younger, Epistles 4, 13, 3–6; 9

Boarding schools always brought with them cases of homesickness among some pupils. This plangent appeal for a parental visit comes from an unhappy, and increasingly desperate, boarder in third century CE Roman Egypt:

To my lord and father Arion from Thonis: greetings… Look, this is my fifth letter to you, and you have only replied once, not one word about how you are; nor have you come to see me although you promised to, saying 'I am coming'; you have not come to find out whether the teacher is looking after me or not. He himself asks about you nearly every day, asking 'Is he not coming yet?' And I just say 'Yes.' Try then to come soon… Goodbye, my lord and father, and keep well. [Postscript] Don't forget our pigeons.

Sammelbuch 6262;
Translation adapted from *Select Papyri (Non-literary Papyri)* in the Loeb series,
edited by A.S. Hunt and C.C. Edgar.

Some slaves were highly literate and bookish, not that surprising when it is considered that every slave has a backstory and can be relegated to servitude in any number of circumstances and situations:

Staberius Eros bought himself with his own savings at a public sale and was formally liberated because of his devotion to literature. He numbered Brutus and Cassius among his pupils. Some say that he was so noble that, in the times of Sulla, he admitted the children of the proscribed to his school free of charge and without any fee.

Suetonius, *On Grammarians* 13

Corporal punishment

Horace recalls the rote-learning he endured at school, especially the parrot fashion recitation of epic poetry of Livius Andronicus, drummed into him by *plagosus Orbilius*—Orbilius the flogger. None the worse for his flagellations, he advises a more discerning and critical view of old epic than was often found in his day:

Not that I think that Livy's [Livius Andronicus] epics should be destroyed or censured. I remember that the flogger Orbilius taught me them when I was a boy; but I am amazed that they should seem pure, beautiful, and just short of perfect … I am indignant that some work is criticised, not because it is clunky or inelegant, but simply because it is modern, while honour and rewards are demanded when it comes to the ancient writers.

Horace, *Epistles* 2, 1, 70–71

Suetonius gives a short biography of 'the flogger':

Lucius Orbilius Pupillusa of Beneventum was left alone in the world by the death of his parents…when he had completed his military service, he resumed his studies… After teaching for a long time in his native town, he eventually went to Rome when he was fifty years old…where he taught winning a greater reputation than reward. In one of his books he admits that he was poor and lived in a garret. He also wrote a book called *Perialogos*, full of the wrongs which teachers suffered from the indifference or selfishness of parents. Indeed he was bad tempered, not only towards rival scholars whom he attacked at every opportunity, but also with his pupils, as Horace implies when he calls him 'the flogger', and Domitius Marsus in the line: Whoever Orbilius thrashed with cane or with leather whip. He was even rude to distinguished men; when he was unknown and was giving testimony in a crowded court-room, when asked by Varro Murena, the lawyer on the other side, what he did and what his profession was, he replied: 'I take hunchbacks from the sun and put them into the shade.' Murena was a hunchback.

Suetonius, On Grammarians 9

An enlightened Quintilian was no advocate of corporal punishment, as he tells us below, suggesting that flogging was quite routine:

I do not approve of flogging, although it happens all the time; first, it is a shameful form of punishment and is fit only for slaves; it is insulting, as you will realise if you imagine how it is when inflicted at an older age. Secondly, if a boy is so opposed to being taught that being rebuked is pointless, he will, like the worst type of slave, merely become inured to the blows. Finally, there would be absolutely no need for such punishment if the teacher is a good disciplinarian.

Quintilian, Institutio Oratoriae 1, 3, 13–14

Educational methodology

As the Republic drew to an end, Latin rhetoric was introduced to run alongside the Greek and new, contemporary Latin literature. Virgil, Horace, and the elegiac love poets began to replace Plautus, Terence, and the old epic poets Naevius, Ennius, and Livius Andronicus.[25]

Quintus Caecilius Epirota … while he was teaching his patron's daughter, the wife of Marcus Agrippa, was suspected of improper conduct towards her and was fired. He then attached himself to Cornelius Gallus and lived with him on most intimate terms, a fact which Augustus used for one his heaviest charges against Gallus himself. After Gallus was convicted and executed Epirota opened a school, but accepted only a few pupils and only young adult men at that, admitting none under age, except those to whose fathers he could not say no. He is said to have been the first to hold extempore discussions in Latin, and the first to begin the practice of reading Vergil and other recent poets.

Suetonius, On Grammarians 16

This fairly typical funerary relief shows Lucius Vibius, his freedwoman wife Vecilia Hilara, and their son Lucius Vibius Felicius Felix, his last name a pun on his *cognomen*. They all attempt to display *Romanitas*, with father styled like Julius Caesar, mother with Livia-type hairstyle, and son like an Augustan boy. End of first century BCE; originally published in *Greek and Roman Portraits*, A. Hekler (New York, 1902); now in the Vatican Museum.

Funerary stele for the freedman Marcus Asellius Clemens, his wife Statia Statulla, and their freedman Marcus Asellius Latinus, exhibited in the Lapidarium. Archaeological Museum Milan. Second century AD; picture by Giovanni Dall'Orto, 2012.

A gold glass portrait of a Roman family once believed to depict Galla Placidia, politically influential daughter of the Roman emperor Theodosius I, and her children; the Greek inscription is either the name of the artist or the *paterfamilias* who is absent in the portrait. Alternatively, it may depict a family from Roman Egypt: the central knot worn by the woman in the centre suggests she may be a follower of the Egyptian goddess Isis. third century CE: from Santa Giulia Museum in Brescia.

Detail depicting a marriage from the Sarcophagus of the Dioscures. Made of marble, late 4th century. Musée de l'Arles et de la Provence Antiques. It shows a Roman couple joining hands. The bride's belt may show the knot symbolizing that the husband was 'belted and bound' to her; he would untie the knot in their nuptial bed. (*Ad Meskens*)

Right: Breastfeeding scene depicting a mother and her husband in close attendance.

Below: *Ex-voto* swaddled Roman baby; Musée Saint-Remi, Reims.

Head of an infant from the time of Antonine.

Funerary relief of a potter and his wife, late first century/early second century CE. Women often shared in the running of the family business. This relief probably shows the potter's wife helping out in the production of some pots. The man is glazing while the woman holds a palm fan and a piece of bread, symbolizing her domesticity. The characters were almost certainly freedman and woman, possibly brought to Rome with the numerous slaves who came as skilled craftsmen after Rome's conquests of Greece and Spain. All burials had to be outside city walls; this is one of many tombs which would have lined the roads around Rome and other cities. See J. J. Dobbins, A Roman Funerary Relief of a Potter and His Wife, *Arts in Virginia* 25:2/3 (1985) 24–33. With permission from Virginia Museum of Arts, Richmond, Adolph D. and Wilkins C. Williams Fund; VA (object #60.2).

Mummy portrait of a little girl in the
Egyptian Museum Cairo; first century CE.

The making of wool by women (*lanam
fecit*) was a powerful symbol in both
Greece and Rome, beginning with
Penelope in Homer's *Odyssey*. In Rome,
it came to be an emblem of the good
matrona, indicating chastity, fidelity,
and good house-keeping. This is a
copy of an Attic white ground *oinochoe*
(wine pitcher) from around 475 BCE,
hand-painted by P. Vasglis; the original
is in the Athens National Museum. It
clearly shows a Greek woman about
to start working at her wool, with her
basket (*kalathos*, κάλαθος) to the right.

Left: A *matrona* washes herself, in the Rheinisches Landesmuseum, Trier. Relief from a third century CE funerary monument which depicts four slaves: the first does the *matrona*'s hair, the second holds a perfume flask, the third shows a mirror, and the fourth carries a water pitcher.

Below: Mosaic from baths at Sidi Ghrib near Tunis. Here, the *domina* is being offered a mirror by one of her slave girls as she washes herself. By kind permission of Inga Mantle who took the photographs and Caroline Vout who published them in *Omnibus*, 65 (2013). They are now in the National Museum of the Bardo, Tunis.

A hair piece from a Roman woman found in a sarcophagus which contained a lead coffin and gypsum; presumably the hair was preserved because it was treated before burial. Two cantharus-headed hair pins are still in position. Courtesy of York Museums Trust YORYM 1998.695 [ID 1131]

Children playing ball games. Marble, Roman artwork of the second quarter of the second century CE. Louvre Museum Department of Greek, Etruscan, and Roman Antiquities. (*Marie-Lan Nguyen*)

Above: Children playing with nuts on a marble panel from a Roman sarcophagus, third century CE. From Vigna Emendola on the Via Appia. Museo Chiaramonti.

Left: Relief found in Neumagen near Trier, a teacher with three *discipuli*. Around 180–185 CE. Photo by Shakko of a casting in the Pushkin Museum, Moscow.

Woman poet, writer, or book-keeper? This image of 'Sappho' is in the Naples National Archaeological Museum.

Right: Roman bronze statuette
after a Hellenistic model showing
a young girl reading. Cabinet
des Médailles. (*Marie-Lan
Nguyen/Wikimedia Commons*)

Below: A scene from the fourth
century CE estate of Julius
found in a house in Carthage.
This shows a woman exhibiting
her credentials as a *matrona*
with one of the articles of
faith—she works the wool.

Left: Erotic scene fresco from around 50 CE in the Naples National Archaeological Museum Gabinetto Segreto. From Pompei, Terme Suburbane, VII.16.a.

Below: Altar of the twelve gods, perhaps the rim of a well or a Zodiac altar. The object represents the twelve gods of the Roman pantheon, each identified by an attribute: Venus and Mars linked by Cupid, Jupiter and a lightning bolt, Minerva wearing a helmet, Apollo, Juno and her sceptre, Neptune and his trident, Vulcan and his sceptre, Mercury and his caduceus, Vesta, Diana and her quiver and Ceres. Marble, found in Gabii, Italy, first century CE. Louvre Museum.

Side of a Roman sarcophagus showing the Dioscuri—Castor, Pollux, and horses. It was found in a garden in Middlesbrough and presented to the Dorman Museum in the town by the Middlesbrough Temperance Society in 1926.

Io is carried by a river god, setting her down at Kanopus near Alexandria. Roman fresco from the temple of Isis in Pompeii. Naples National Archaeological Museum.

Choregos and actors mosaic. Naples National Archaeological Museum. From the House of the Tragic Poet (VI, 8, 3), Pompeii.

A *retiarius* (left) and *secutor* do battle. The former's weapons consisted of a barbed trident and weighted net. They are attended by a trainer, either a *doctores retiarii* or a *doctores secutorum*.

A theatrical scene—two women consulting a witch with all three wearing theatre masks. Roman mosaic from the Villa del Cicerone in Pompeii, now in the Naples National Archaeological Museum. By Dioscorides of Samos.

Photochrom of the 'Circular Bath' at the Roman Baths in Bath between 1890 and 1905. (*Library of Congress, Prints and Photographs Division, Photochrom Prints Collection*)

Above: Dancers and musicians in the tomb of the leopards, Monterozzi necropolis, Tarquinia, Italy, in 475 BCE.

Below: *Cave canem*: Pompeii's 'beware of the dog' mosaic notice found in the House of the Tragic Poet.

Votive offerings including penises, breasts, and a uterus, now in the Naples National Archaeological Museum.

Fascinating scenes of everyday life from the fourth century CE estate of Julius found in a house in Carthage. This shows the *domina* selecting jewellery to wear from a box held by a slave. By kind permission of Inga Mantle who took the photographs and Caroline Vout who published them in *Omnibus*, 65 (2013). It is now in the National Museum of the Bardo, Tunis.

Above and below: Mercatus Traiani (Trajan's market), a semi-circular market in Rome built by Apollodorus of Damascus in 110 CE. (Upper image: *Elias Z. Ziadeh*)

After surviving Orbilius, Horace came to appreciate a more nuanced approach to education: the power of the bribe or incentive: 'what's to stop me telling the truth by way of a joke just as teachers give sweets to their pupils to get them to learn their ABC?' (Horace, *Satires* 1, 1, 25–26).

Sometimes, the incentive was a book rather than a cake; one wonders which was the more effective. The books certainly did Flaccus's career no harm:

Marcus Verrius Flaccus, a freedman, was famous for his teaching methods. In order to stimulate the scholarly efforts of his pupils, he would pit those of the same level against each other, not only setting the subject on which they were to write, but also offering a prize for the winner to take away. This was some antiquarian book which was either beautiful or rare. He was therefore chosen by Augustus to be tutor to his grandsons and he moved to the palace with his entire school.

Suetonius, *On Grammarians* 17

Quintilian has similar tactical, motivational advice:

Some believe that boys should not be taught to read untill they are seven years old—the earliest age at which they can benefit from teaching and cope with the rigours of learning…those, however, who hold that a child's mind should not be allowed to be inactive for one moment are wiser…most importantly, we must ensure that the child, who is not yet old enough to love his studies, does not end up hating them and, when older, dread the bitterness which he once tasted. His studies must be fun: when he is questioned he must be praised and taught to be glad when he gets things right; sometimes too, when he refuses to be taught, bring in someone else, a rival, to make him competitive and believe himself successful more often than not; encourage him to do his best with rewards which appeal to his age.

Quintilian, *Institutio Oratoriae* 1, 1, 15; 16, 20

In the *Ars Poetica*, Horace gives a typical lesson in arithmetic and money management; by comparison with the Greeks, he says, Roman education was much more practical:

The Muse gave the Greeks genius, polished eloquence in their speech, they were greedy for glory. Roman boys learn long division, and how to split a pound weight into a hundred parts.

Horace, *Ars Poetica* 325–30

Cicero had said as much when he observed that the Greeks studied geometry as an end in itself; the Roman, however, was much more pragmatic—he studied it so as to be able to measure out the land ahead of development. Pliny says that everyone's parent was also their teacher.[26]

Education in the early empire

From Vespasian's time (69 CE), the state was taking more responsibility for education: state funded rhetoricians and *grammatici* in both Greek and Latin were beginning to appear. Primary schools (*ludi*) were staffed by a *magister* or *litterator* and covered elementary education; secondary schools (*schola*), from about age twelve, were under a *grammaticus* and taught literature, Greek, and public speaking.

Suetonius records that there were twenty schools in Rome teaching grammar by the end of the Republic; Quintilian favoured schools to home tuition for the children of the elite.[27] A freedman at Trimalchio's dinner party in the first century CE declares that he learned no geometry but he is streetwise when it comes to money and percentages.

> No, I never learned geometry, or literary criticism, or any other such nonsense. But I know my capital letters, and I can do any sum ... Now I will show you that your father wasted the fees, even though you are a scholar in rhetoric.
>
> Petronius, *Satyricon* 58, 7

Roman education was shot through with moral advice and instruction. Instead of say, 'Janet saw the ball', the Roman pupil was more likely to learn to read with something like: 'From a wise man seek advice; do not blindly trust all your friends' (Catalogue of the Literary Papyri of the British Museum 253).

The World of Work

In the world of work, time was obviously important for a number of reasons: getting there on time, hours of working, time to go home. Before 263 BCE, the Romans relied entirely on the sun in the sky to perform this function. In 263 BCE, a sun dial was brought to Rome from Sicily and positioned in the forum. From then on, the Roman day was divided into twenty-four equal segments (*horae*)—the first hour, second hour, and so on—with the hours in winter markedly shorter than those in the summer. Plautus alludes to this:

> May the gods destroy that man who first discovered hours and who first set up a sundial here; who smashed up my day into fragments. When I was a boy, my stomach was my sundial…and so now the town is overflowing with sun dials but the people crawl around withered with hunger.
>
> Plautus, *The Boeotian Woman* (Fragment v. 21 Goetz)
> quoted by Aulus Gellius, *Attic Nights* 3, 3, 5

Cicero, from his privileged position, describes the most suitable occupations for a gentleman and sneers at the labours of the working classes; nowhere is snobbery and the divisive Roman class system more clearly portrayed:

> As regards trades and other ways of making a living, which ones are to be thought fit for a gentleman and which ones are vulgar? We have been taught, in general, the following. First, those means of livelihood which spark people's animosity are rejected as undesirable, for example, tax collectors and usurers. Also vulgar and ill-suited to a gentleman are all hired workmen whom we pay for manual labour, not for artistic skill; for in their case the very wage they receive is a pledge of their slavery. Those also who buy goods from wholesale merchants to sell on are vulgar because they would get no profits without a lot of bare-faced lying; and indeed, there is nothing meaner than misrepresentation. All mechanics are engaged in vulgar trades: no workshop can have anything liberal about it. Least respectable of all are those trades which cater for sensual pleasures: 'Fishmongers, butchers, cooks, and poulterers, and fishermen,' as Terence says. Add to these the perfumers, dancers, and anyone on the stage.

On the other hand, the professions in which either a higher degree of intelligence is required or from which society benefits—medicine and architecture, for example, and teaching—these are fine. Small scale trade is to be considered vulgar; but if wholesale, and on a large scale, importing large quantities from all parts of the world and distributing to many without misrepresentation, is not to be greatly disparaged but seems to deserve the highest respect, if those who are engaged in it are satiated, or rather, I should say, satisfied with the fortunes they have made, make their way from the port to a country estate, as they have often made it from the sea into port. But of all the occupations by which benefit is secured, none is better than agriculture, none more profitable, none more delightful, none more becoming to a freeman.

Cicero, *De Officiis* 1, 42
translation adapted from Loeb Classical Library edition (1913)

We get an idea of the vast range of occupations taken by both men and women from funerary inscriptions; this selection is fairly typical:

Publius Marcus Philodamus, construction worker, freedman of Publius.

Here lie the remains of Quintus Tibertinus Menelaus, freedman of Quintus, who made a living slaughtering animals for sacrifices.

Having left the famous city of Bithynia Nikaia as a young man, I came to the land of the Italians and in the sacred city of Rome I taught mathematics and geometry. This is the monument that I, Basileus, made, paying for the work by making a living with my mind.

CIL 9, 1721; 1, 1604; *IGUR* 1176

We have already met the nine-year-old worker in gold; to her, we can add the 'twenty-five-year-old short-hand writer in Greek, Hapate—Pittosus erected his monument to his most affectionate wife' (*ILS* 7760) and Thymele, Marcella's trader in silk (*ILS* 7600), and Turia Privata, mime artist, lived nineteen years (*ILS* 5215).

Plautus, too, gives us an idea of the range of occupations servicing the people of Rome: Megadorus bemoans the crowds of suppliers delivering and collecting payment:

there stands the launderer, the embroiderer, the goldsmith, the wool-weaver, fringe makers, dealers in lingerie, crimson dyers, violet dyers, wax colour dyers, sleevemakers or perfumers, wholesale linen drapers, shoemakers, slipper-makers; sandal- makers stand there; stainers all stand there; cleaners make their demands, boddice-makers and apron-makers stand there. Just when you think you've got rid of them along comes three hundred more ... weavers, lace-makers, cabinet-makers all turn up and the money's paid ... the dyers in saffron arrive.

Plautus, *Pot of Gold* 505–22

Workers in a particular trade commonly grouped themselves into associations, something like our guilds or trade unions. This gave them political power, particularly when it came to backing or endorsing politicians. One example of the endorsements daubed on walls in Pompeii states: 'The fruit sellers request that you elect Marcus Holconius Priscus as aedile.'

There are also mule drivers, goldsmiths, carpenters, fishermen, dyers, innkeepers, bakers, barbers, porters, fullers, millers, poultry sellers, mat makers, farmers, and grape pickers all canvassing votes for various local politicians (*CIL* 4, 206, 113, 710, 960, 826, 864, 336, 677, 743, 497, 7164, 7273, 373, 7473, 490, and 6672).

Some women were comfort workers, looking after the needs of lonely shepherds:

When it comes those who tend the herds in mountain valleys and woods…many have thought that it was a good idea to send along women to follow the herds, prepare food for the herdsmen, and thereby make them better at their work. Such women should, however, be strong and attractive. In many places they are just as good as the men at their work.

Varro, De Re Rustica 2, 10, 6
translation adapted from Loeb Classical Library edition, (1934)

Midwives and wet nurses were women's occupations, but most doctors were men. There were, though, female doctors, *medicae*, many of them slaves or freedwomen. Again, we know a number from the funereal and inscriptional evidence; many of them come from medical families. In the first century CE, Antiochis, daughter of the physician Diodotus, was so highly appreciated for her medical expertise by the people of Tlos in Lycia that they set up a statue celebrating her; Galen credits her with the discovery of effective drugs for sciatica and rheumatism.[1] Aurelia Alexandria Zosime was also honoured with a statue by her doctor husband in Adada, Pisine. There is Primilla, a physician who died at the end of the first century CE at the age of forty-four in Rome; four more Roman doctors: Iulia Pye, Minucia Asste, and Venuleia Sosis, all freedwomen, and a slave, Melitine; and Secunda Livilla and Terentia Prima. Wealthy *medicae* include Metilia Donata from Lyons.[2] Indeed, there is evidence of female physicians from all over the Empire: Hulia Sabina from Italy; Flavia Hedone from Gaul, Asylla Polia from Africa, Himertos of Marathon, and Iulia Saturnina from Merida in Iberia—she was not only a wife beyond compare but the best doctor.[3] The husband of Pantheia, a second century CE physician from Pergamum, is generous in praise for his doctor wife; apart from being 'the rudder of life in our home', she did much to enhance the family's medical reputation: 'even though you were a woman you were just as accomplished as me.'

To the departed spirit of Julia Saturnina, forty-five years old, wonderful wife, excellent doctor, faultless woman. Erected by her husband Cassius Phillius out of gratitude. Here she lies and may the earth lay lightly on her.

ILS 7802

Naevia Clara was also married to a doctor, in Rome in the first century BCE. Later in the second century CE Domnina from Neoclaudiopolis in Asia received virtual apotheosis because she 'saved her native fatherland from disease'. Theodore Priscianus, in the fourth century CE, dedicated his book on gynaecology to Victoria—the 'sweet teacher of my art'. Aspasia was a second century obstetrician and gynaecologist; we have an inscription referring to a *medica a mammis*—breast disease specialist.[4]

Women may not have had the vote in the legislative assemblies—the *comitia* and the *concilium*—but graffiti in Pompeii shows that they took an active interest in local politics and electioneering with examples of *programmata*, posters on which they endorsed candidates. Of the 2,500 *programmata* discovered, Savunen indicates that fifty-four (2.16 per cent) were posted by women, supporting twenty-eight candidates. There is, though, one striking example of women exercising real political influence. In 1955, an inscription dating from around 6 CE was found in Akmoneia (modern-day Ahat in central Turkey) by Michael Ballance, the English archaeologist. The inscription is now lost, but luckily Ballance photographed it and copied it down:

> The women, both Greek and Roman, honoured Tatia daughter of Menokritos ...
> the High Priestess who acted as their benefactoress under all circumstances, in
> recognition of all her virtue.

There then follows the names of the three men responsible for erecting the statue. Remarkably, we have here a unique example of women taking the initiative in, and responsibility for, an act of civic administration within local government, voting to finance, and raise the statue to one of their own. We cannot know if this political emancipation was a one-off or if there were other isolated instances now lost to us. What is important is that the women of Akmoneia proved beyond all doubt that women could have been actively involved in politics where the will existed to allow them.[5]

Tatia was not the Roman world's only benefactoress: Eumachia was a priestess who had married into one of the leading Pompeiian families after inheriting from her father, a successful brick manufacturer; she was patroness of the guild of fullers—a prestigious position in one of the most important local industries. During the reign of Tiberius, Eumachia gifted the fullers a large building for their head office, dedicated to Concordia Augusta and Pietas; it survives today as the Building of Eumachia.[6] The timing of the gift may not have been accidental; it coincided with her son's campaign for public office. Another Pompeian lady, Julia Felix, owned a local estate which comprised baths, shops with rooms above them, and flats on the second floor—all available for rent on a five-year lease. Junia Theodora is fondly commended by the citizens of Corinth in 43 CE for her largesse; likewise, Flavia Publicia Nicomachis was noted for her virtue, as benefactoress and founder of the city of Phocaea in the second century CE.[7, 8] Modia Quintia, a priestess in Africa Proconsularis, was honoured with a statue to recognise the fact that she furnished a marble patio in the portico, ceilings, and columns, and for paying for an aqueduct.[9]

Writers & writing

Given what we have already seen of the lifestyle enjoyed by Catullus, the other new poets, and the love poets, one might be forgiven for thinking that professional writing was the perfect way to spend one's time. However, as these excerpts demonstrate, this was not the case: plagiarism, apathetic audiences, and paltry royalties were problems for the Roman *literati*, just as they remain today.

Nevertheless, the market was there and seems to have included significant elements of the literate middle classes, including women.[10] For Martial and Pliny, writing and reciting were vital parts of their *otium*; Pliny describes just how seriously he took his writing in 5, 3; in 2, 34, he agonises over his literary credibility and his deficiencies in reciting poetry: should he hire the services of a freedman to deliver the poems for him—a kind of ghost speaking? Martial attacks plagiarism at 2, 20, while Pliny's obvious enjoyment of literary pursuits is echoed in 144 CE by Marcus Aurelius: 'I went back to my books ... and remained on my couch for two hours' (Fronto, *Letters to Marcus Aurelius* 415).

Martial rails against plagiarism, obviously a common problem:

You're making a big mistake, you greedy plagiarist, when you think you can actually be a poet for the price of a manuscript and a cheap book. You don't get a round of applause for six or ten sesterces. You seek out unpublished poems and works in progress known only to one man and which, as author of the unpublished page not yet scraped and hardened by rough chins, he keeps concealed in his writing desk. A bestseller can't pick its author. But if you find one with its edge not yet smoothed down and not yet published with spine and cover, then go ahead and buy it. I've got one for you which nobody else knows about. Whoever recites another man's work, and in so doing seeks fame for it, shouldn't just buy the book, but should buy my silence ...

Martial 1, 66

The rewards are derisory:

It's not just the city layabouts who enjoy my Muse, and my verses don't fall on deaf ears. My book is well thumbed through use in Getan frosts and amid the battle standards of hardened centurions and, it is said, my verses are sung in Brittania. What's the point though? My purse sees none of this. What all-conquering poems I could compose and how I could herald battles with my Pieiran trumpet if the holy spirits who have restored Nerva to the world were, Rome, to give you a Maecenas!

Martial 11, 3

Pliny complains about the public's apathy towards literary events; he could be talking about a twenty-first century book signing:

To Sosius Senecio

This year has produced a great crop of poets. Almost every day throughout April someone was giving a recital. I am pleased that literature is flourishing, that the talent is on display for all to see even if people are reluctant to come and listen. The majority just lounge about in public places wasting time, listening to gossip, giving out instructions that they be told from time to time when the reader has come on and read his preface or has almost finished the book. Only then and then slowly and reluctantly do they come in. But they don't stay but go out again before the end, some inconspicuously and furtively, others openly and obviously. Good god, our parents remind us of the time when the emperor Claudius was out strolling on the Palatine when he heard a din and asked what it was. When told that Nonianus was giving a recital he surprised everybody by going in, to the astonishment of the reader. Nowadays, any man with so much time on his hands is invited well in advance and reminded again and again, but he either doesn't turn up or, if he does, moans that he has wasted his day (for the very reason that he hasn't wasted it). So, all the more cause for praising and encouraging those keen to write and recite even though their audience is lazy and arrogant.

Personally I have let hardly anyone down; of course, most of them were friends anyway: there is scarcely anyone who likes literature who at the same time doesn't also like me. That's why I have to spend more time in Rome than I plan to. Now I can return to my retreat and do some writing. But I won't recite it to my friends in case I give the impression that I went to their recitals not to listen but to put them in debt to me. For, as in other matters, the duty of listening falls flat if thanks are demanded in return. Farewell.

Pliny, *Epistles* 1, 13

Pliny prepares meticulously for a dinner party recital:

To Maturus Arrianus

In life as in literature I think it is a fine and cultured thing to mix the serious with the humorous lest the one leads to doom and gloom and the other to ribaldry. That's why I pepper my more serious work with riddles and jokes. I choose the best time and place to introduce these and to accustom them to being heard in the dining room at leisure in July, which is the quietest time for lawyers. I gathered my friends together and settled them down on chairs in front of the couches. As it happened that morning I was unexpectedly summoned to court and this gave me the theme of my opening speech.

I prayed that no-one would say that I was being rude to those I had been about to read to, albeit a small number of friends, in that I had not freed myself from the court business for the sake of other friends. I added that I followed the same procedure in my writing where I put business before pleasure and serious matters before amusement and wrote first for my friends and then only for myself. The work in question comprised short pieces in different metres. We who lack confidence in our ability are accustomed to avoid the risk of over doing it. I recited over two days as demanded by the approving audience and although others who give readings miss out bits and expect credit for doing this, so I miss nothing out and I make it clear that I am missing nothing out. I read everything so that I can amend everything; selective readers can't do this. Theirs is a more restrained and perhaps more considerate way of working but mine is simpler and more kindly; the reader who is kind can believe he is liked when he doesn't have to worry about being tedious. What's the point of friends anyway if they meet just for their own pleasure? It is the indulgent and ignorant who prefer just to listen to a good book rather than help make it a good book. I am sure that because of your affection for me you will want to read my book as soon as possible before it goes out of date. You will get to read it but not before it's been revised, the very purpose of the recital. Some of you are familiar with it already. After it has been amended (or ruined as sometimes happens after a long delay) you will see it as a new work. When the majority of a text is changed the bits which remain untouched seem to have been changed too. Farewell.

Pliny, *Epistles* 8, 21

Most medical writers were men, but there were female authors. Metrodora was a second century CE author of a treatise on gynaecology, diseases of the kidney, uterus, and stomach. She is noted for the advances she made in gynaecological pathology and her expertise in digital examination and the use of the vaginal speculum. According to Galen, a lady called Cleopatra wrote the *On the Composition of Medicines by Place* (*Kosmetikon*) which included, among many other things, a remedy for baldness involving the topical application of pulverised mouse skulls; an alternative therapy required the use of mouse droppings—Cleopatra is more likely an example of clever branding than anyone of Ptolemaic provenance.

Pliny's *Natural History* names female practitioners as sources for his work: Elephantis, Lais, Olympias of Thebes, Salpe, and Sotira. Galen quotes Elephantis' cure for alopecia; she was also the author of a famous book on sexual positions—a Roman *Kama Sutra*. Suetonius tells that Tiberius packed a copy when he left for his retreat on Capri; Martial says it is [a book] 'with intriguing new ways of making love'. Aspasia in the sixth century CE wrote works on gynaecological surgery and abortion; she was reputedly even more empathetic with her patients than Soranus.

On being emperor

The top job in the empire was, of course, emperor. The following pieces give an insight into just some of the functions of *imperator*, the ways in which emperors went about their work, and attitudes and behaviour towards them. Martial's epigrams are peppered with praise for Domitian: whether Martial was really a sycophant or not is difficult for us to assess; one thing is certain, though—Martial would not have had too much leeway in the way he described Domitian in his verses. We can assume that the alternative to praise and eulogy would have been somewhat career- and life-limiting.

Pliny's letter to Trajan on the establishment of a fire brigade gives us an intriguing insight into how provincial machinery worked. Juvenal's satire here could have been included in any number of sections of this book but here it serves to underline his character assassination of monsters like Crispinus and his revulsion at Domitian's tyranny through the vehicle of a *consilium principis*—star chamber.

Martial hopes that Domitian will read his poetry:

If, Caesar, you happen to come across my verses, switch off the seriousness you show as master of the world. Keep all the messing about we get with your triumphs; there's nothing wrong for a leader to be the butt of jokes. Just as you watch Thymele and Latinus the satyr, so I pray that you read my verses with the same attitude. You, the censor can permit a bit of harmless fun: my pages are salacious, my life beyond reproach.

Martial 1, 4

Pliny recommends the setting up of a fire service:

Pliny to the Emperor Trajan

When I was visiting another part of the province an inferno broke out in Nicomedia and burned down a number of private homes and two public buildings—the Gerusia and the Temple of Isis—even though a road ran between the two. It would have been better contained had it not been, first for the strength of the wind, and then because of the apathy of the people who were quite happy to take no action, standing around doing nothing and just gawping at the inferno. What's more, there's not a fire engine to be found anywhere in the town, nor a fire bucket, nor any equipment for fire-fighting. These will now be provided on my orders. Emperor: do you think a fire brigade should be formed numbering about 150 men? I will see it to that no-one is recruited unless he is already a fireman and that the concessions they are entitled to are not abused; nor will it be difficult to keep such a small number in check.

Pliny, *Epistles* 10, 33

Trajan pours cold water on the idea:

Trajan to Pliny

Following precedents elsewhere, you believe that a fire brigade should be set up in Nicomedia. Remember that such groups have been the cause of disturbances before in your province and particularly in the cities. Whatever we call them and whatever reason we give them, whenever people assemble for a common purpose they soon become a faction. A better solution would be to provide the facilities needed for fighting fires and to advise residents to use them and, if needs be, call on the crowds that gather to use them too.

Pliny, *Epistles* 10, 34

Here is an example of Martial's sycophancy and obsequiousness toward the emperor:

In times gone by Rome hated the sycophants and the old- school crowd of leaders, and the arrogance you get on the Palatine. But now, Augustus, so great is the love of all men for what is yours that their very homes take second place. So calm are their tempers, so great is their reverence to you, so soothing is their peace of mind, so modest do they look. No-one (this is the way the corridors of power work) acts naturally any more but in the manner of Caesar, the master.

Martial 9, 79

11

The Moral High Ground,
Corruption, and the Good Old Days

These pieces clearly demonstrate the disdain writers felt for man's seemingly innate greed and dissatisfaction with life, and their own personal preference for a simple, uncorrupted, and unaffected lifestyle. Avarice can only lead to misery, Horace tells us, although miserliness, at the other extreme, has the same effect. Martial is more specific, deploring the rampant scandalising, informing, and sycophancy he sees all around him. Cheating and crime seem to pay in a world where, for example, flattering the emperor is quite the norm.

Pliny chimes in with his attack on professional legacy hunters (*captatores*)—a theme dealt with elsewhere by Horace in *Satire* 2, 5 and by Persius in his sixth satire. The high incidence of childless adults (*orbi*) at this time and the growing aversion to marriage only served to increase this practice, despite legislation by Augustus (Tacitus *Annals* 3, 25). Cicero, in his *Paradoxa Stoicorum* (5, 2, 39), refers to it, as does Horace in *Epistles* 1, 1, 77; Seneca, *de Beneficiis* 1, 1012 and Pliny *Historia Naturalis* talk about it as an established occupation. Martial 4, 56; Pliny 8, 18 and 1, 14, 9; and Juvenal 5, 131ff and 12, 93ff also make reference to the practice.

Juvenal characteristically treats us to a lengthy rant on everything that is repellent about Roman society: moral bankruptcy, political and commercial corruption, permissiveness, lawlessness, benefit fraud, institutional and private greed on an industrial level, a yearning for the 'good old days'—all facets of life that are eerily familiar to us today. Elsewhere, Juvenal attributes much of what is wrong with the women of his day to the tempting influx of luxury (6, 286ff). Seneca too highlights the virtues of earlier times after a visit to Scipio Africanus' baths—a symbol of old world simplicity and modesty (*Epistles*, 86). Pliny the Elder attempts to put a price on it all, assessing the cost of luxurious imports from the east at more than 100 million sesterces per year (*HN* 12, 41, 84).

Greed and excess in Roman society grew proportionately to Rome's expanding conquests and the spoils of empire that these brought: the more treasure found, the more cosmopolitan and exotic Rome became and the greater the impact on traditional Roman values, life, and culture. Historians writing of the period say that the rot started to set in around the first part of the Second Century BCE: Livy (39.6) dates it to 187 BCE when the army returned from Asia; Polybius (31, 25, 3) to 168 after Pydna; and Sallust (*Catiline Conspiracy* 10, 1 and *Jugurthan War* 41, 2) to 146 after Carthage and Corinth were vanquished—Pliny (*NH* 17.2.44) and Tacitus (*Annals* 3, 52–55; 1, 54) agree. There were official attempts to curb it all: sumptuary legislation was passed, including the *Lex Orchia* of 182 BCE to limit the number of guests at a dinner party, and the *Lex Fannia Sumptuaria* of 161 BCE that restricted the amount of money that could be expended on a routine meal. This was to no avail—the party just went on and laws enacted by Augustus and Tiberius were just as ineffective (Tacitus *Annals* 3, 52).

The concensus here seems to be that no one is happy with their lot; man is, by nature, greedy and his life is miserable as a result.

Maecenas, how is it that no one on this Earth is happy with what they've got—whether they have achieved it by design or have fallen upon it by accident—praising instead the very different lives led by others?

The soldier, his body already broken by long service and feeling his years, says 'those lucky old salesmen'. In reply the salesman, his ship tossed about in the southerly storm, says 'A soldier's life is better than this. Why? Because you join battle and in a flash you're either dead or enjoying victory.' The lawyer envies the farmer when he thinks of clients banging on his front door even before the crack of dawn. On the other hand the farmer, bound over to appear in court, is hauled into Rome from the country and exclaims that city-livers are the lucky ones. More examples, and there are many, would weary even big-mouthed Fabius.

So, I won't keep you—here's my point: what if some god says 'Look, I'll grant whatever you wish: soldier, you be a salesman now; lawyer, be a farmer now. Go on, get on with your new jobs; quick, what are you waiting for? 'They all decline the offer even though they could have been in clover. Why then should Jupiter not blast them away in anger and declare never again to be so obliging as to grant their prayers?

Besides, I won't make light of this like some comedian—but then again, what's to stop me telling the truth by way of a joke just as teachers give sweets to their pupils to get them to learn their ABC?—but, joking aside, let's be serious: you who till the heavy soil with your rough plough, you, a lying spiv, you soldier and the brave sailors who sail across every sea—all agree that they endure their daily grind safe in the knowledge that in old age, having made a pile of money, they can retire with some security. They're just like the tiny, industrious ant which, a good example this, drags in its mouth everything she can to add to the hill she's building, prudent and aware that the future could bring anything; and when Aquarius glooms the new year, she never creeps outside but uses up what she has wisely accumulated for her provisions.[1] A raging heat wave cannot deflect *you* though from your lucre, nor winter, nor fire, not the oceans nor war—nothing stands in your way while there is still someone out there richer than you.

Where's the pleasure in a ton of silver and gold if in fear you furtively bury it in a hole in the ground? You say 'But if you use it up you reduce it to a paltry pittance.' To which I say: 'But if you don't use it then it's just a nice looking heap and what's the point of that? If your threshing floor has ground out thousands of bushels of corn, your stomach still won't hold any more than mine; in the same way, as a slave, you happen to be the one hauling the bread basket on your overloaded shoulders but you're rewarded no more than the slave who carries nothing'.

Or tell me, what difference does it make to the man living off the land whether he ploughs 100 or 1,000 acres? You say 'But it's so much better to be able to make withdrawals from a big stash of money'. You leave us to take as much as you from our little piles so why do you think your big granaries are better than our small baskets? It's the same thing as when you only need a jug or ladle of water and then say 'I'd rather take the same amount from this big river as from this little spring'. So it is that those happy to have more than their fair share of wealth are swept away by the torrential River Aufidus, bank and all, while he who wants only as much as he needs neither swallows that water swirling with sludge, nor drowns in it.[2]

But lots of people, fooled by false desire, say 'You can never get enough because you're only as good as what you've got.' What do you do with people like that? Do you tell them to be miserable since that's what they're best at? They remind me of the squalid miser in Athens who used to mock what people said about him: 'The mob hisses at me but I just go home and congratulate myself when I think about the loot in my money chest'.

Thirsty Tantalus snatches at the streams that escape his lips—why are you laughing? Change the name and that story's about you. You heap up your bags on all sides, even sleeping on them, mouth gaping; you're forced to keep your hands off them as if they were sacred icons, to delight in them as if they were fine art.

Do you know what money is actually worth? What pleasure it brings? You can buy bread, vegetables, half a litre of wine and other things which cause man pain if he is denied them by Nature. Or would you prefer to lie awake rigid with fear dreading night and day, nasty robbers, fire, and slaves in case they rob you and run off? I would opt every time to be a pauper when it comes to material possessions.

If you catch a cold or are suffering for some other reason and are stuck in bed, is there anyone there to sit with you, prepare the poultice, call the doctor, to revive you and restore you to your children and next of kin? No. Your wife doesn't want you to get better, nor does your son. Everyone loathes you—neighbours, everyone you know, even little boys and girls. And you wonder, when you hold money in higher esteem than everything else, why no one gives you the love you don't deserve anyway. Even if you want to keep and preserve the affection of relatives which Nature has given you (no effort on your part) sad man, you are wasting your time in much the same way as the man who teaches a donkey to run in reins on the Campus Martius.

So, cut out this greed and, since you now have more than you could ever wish for and need fear poverty less, stop punishing yourself unless you want to end up like Ummidius. To cut a long story short, he was so rich that he used to measure out his money, so squalid that he never dressed better than a slave and feared that he would die a pauper up to the day he died.[3] As it happened a freedwoman cleaved him in half with an axe, bravest of the Tyndaridae.[4]

'What then do you advise? That I live like Naevius or Nomentanus?'[5]

You keep trying to throw contradictions in my face. When I tell you not to be a miser I am not saying be a slob or a scoundrel. There is a midway between a Tanais and the father in law of Visellius.[6] There *is* a middle way; there are certain boundaries beyond which you can't be in the right. But I digress and return to my main theme: no greedy man is ever satisfied but prefers to praise those living different lives and is consumed with jealousy because someone else's goat has a fuller udder. Rather than compare himself with the bigger crowd of poorer people he strives to go one up on him, and then one up on him. And so in such a rat race someone richer always gets in the way. It's like when chariots are launched from the gates and snatch after the horses' hooves in front and the driver challenges that other chariot which is beating his own and scorns the one he leaves behind. So rarely do we find anyone who says he has lived a happy life and who, his time up, takes his leave like a satisfied guest.

But that's enough: I'll not say another word or you'll think I've pinched the papers of bleary-eyed Crispinus.

Horace, *Satires* 1, 1

Horace expands on his beliefs here; he extols a simple life and a healthy lifestyle. Excess and meanness leads to misery; gluttony is bad for your health and your reputation:

Gentlemen: what is the benefit of plain living and just how good is it (not my words but the teachings of Ofellus the rustic, non-partisan philosopher who is big on home-grown common sense)? Let's find out, not surrounded by the gleaming dishes and tables, your vision blurred by crazy lights and your brain rejecting the real for the contrived; let's find out before we eat. 'Why?' you ask. I will tell you why, if I may:

All corrupt judges judge corruptly. Worn out after chasing a hare or by an unbroken horse or if Roman army athletics tire you when you're used to the Greek way, or perhaps when your sheer enjoyment of a fast ball game gently disguises the hard slog of it all, or maybe the discus (throw one through the air!) gets you going—when hard work has knocked the stuffing out of you and, parched and famished, you refuse cheap bread and don't drink mead unless it's diluted by Hymettan honey and Falernian wine.

Your butler has gone out for the day and there's no fish to be had from the stormy dark sea; salted bread calms your growling guts. Why do you think this is? The greatest pleasure is to be found not in the smell of expensive food but in you yourself. Build up an appetite through exercise. The man who is pale and podgy through excess can't possibly enjoy his oysters, scar fish or foreign grouse.

Yet if a peacock is served up I can hardly stop you wanting to taste it rather than a chicken. You are taken in by its appearance: it's a rare bird, is expensive and fans out its picturesque tail—as if that's relevant. Do you actually eat the plumage you like so much? It doesn't look so good when cooked! Although there is nothing between them in terms of their meat, you crave one more than the other, deceived by their appearance. OK. But how do you tell if the gawping pike was caught in the Tiber or in the sea, as if it was tossed between the bridges or at the river's Tuscan mouth. Idiot: you praise a three-pound mullet even though you've got to chop it up anyway into single portions. I can see that it's the appearance that drives you; why do you tend to scorn a long pike? No doubt because Nature makes it long and the mullet lighter. A hungry stomach rarely scorns common fare.

'I would rather see a big fish stretched out on a platter' comes the cry from a gullet worthy of a rapacious Harpy. But you, mighty gales, warm up their morsels. And yet the wild boar and fresh skate have already gone off since nasty excess churns the sick stomach which, full as it is, prefers radish and pickled gherkin. Simple food has not vanished completely from the banquets of kings for there is still a place today for black olives and cheap eggs. Not so very long ago Gallonius the auctioneer got a bad reputation when he served up a sturgeon.[7] Why? Did the sea sustain fewer skate then? Safe was the skate and safe was the stork in its nest until the praetor taught you how to cook them.[8] So if anyone should decree that roasted gannets are nice, our Roman youth—easy to deprave—will go along with it.

Ofellus maintains that there is a big difference between a stingy lifestyle and a simple lifestyle: for you will avoid the one vice in vain if you then just turn to the other depravity. Avidienus (to whom the name 'dog' has stuck for good reason) eats five-year-old olives and cornel cherries from the woods and is too tight to serve his wine until it has gone off. You can't stand the smell of his oil; he, when celebrating all dressed up in his white toga a wedding feast or some other such birthday or holiday, pours it out himself drop by drop from a two pound horn onto his cabbage. He is nevertheless generous enough with his malt vinegar. Which way of life then should the wise man adopt and whom should he imitate? On the one hand the wolf attacks, as they say, on the other hand, the dog. He will be clever enough not to offend by being mean and will be happy in his cleverness. He won't be cruel to his servants, as Albucius is when dishing out their duties nor, like homely Naevius will he offer oily water to his guests—another big mistake.

Now hear the great benefits of a simple lifestyle. First of all you'll be healthy: you know how bad a whole load of things are to man. Remember that plain food sits best in your stomach. As soon as you mix roasted with boiled, oysters with fieldfare, the sweet turns to bile and the thick phlegm makes you sick. Do you see how pale each guest is as they rise from the 'mystery meal'.[9] Indeed, burdened by last night's indiscretions the body oppresses the mind too and nails a particle of the divine mind to the ground.[10] The man who has taken care of himself falls fast asleep quicker than you can say boo and gets up fresh as a daisy for work. Occasionally it's alright for him to adopt a more extravagant lifestyle as when some holiday comes round or his weakened body needs sustenance or, as the years pass by, frail old age wants more gentle treatment.

But for you, when ill health or slow old age afflict you, how then will you be able to take indulgence for granted as you did as a healthy young man?

Our ancestors used to speak highly of rancid boar, not because they didn't have noses to smell with but because, I believe, they thought it was better that a guest arriving late could eat it even when off rather than a greedy master when fresh.[11] O that I had been raised among heroes such as those when the world was young!

You rate your good reputation highly—more musical to your ears than a good song. Big turbots and big platters mean big shame and big loss; now add in your uncle's anger, your neighbour's anger, your loss of self esteem, your vain hope to end it all even though you are so hard up you won't be able to afford the price of a rope. 'It's okay to tell Trausius off like that but I have a large income and riches enough for three kings.' Okay then, isn't there a better way of spending your wealth? Why should any good man be in need when you are so rich? Why are the ancient temples of the Gods falling down? Why, you charlatan, don't you donate some of your great piles of money to your country? Without doubt things will always turn out well for you, you of all people. But what a laughing stock you will be for your enemies later on. Who will have the more confidence in the ups and downs of life: the man who has allowed pride to consume his mind and body or the man who is content with little, who is cautious for the future and, in times of peace has prepared for war as wise men do.

So that you really believe me, when I was a small boy I knew this Ofellus well and he was no more extravagant when his fortune was intact than when it had all gone; you can still see him now, a hard-working labourer in his re-allocated allotment with his herd of cows and his sons.

'On a working day I did not eat just for the sake of eating—only vegetables and a leg of smoked ham—and if someone I hadn't seen for a while came to see me at home, or a neighbour on a welcome visit when rain had stopped work we would still have a good time—not eating fish brought from down town but with chicken or goat; dried raisins, nuts and split figs decorated the table for dessert. After that there'd be a drinking game where the loser takes charge and prays that Ceres rises up on the stem and smooths the furrows of a furrowed brow with wine.[12]

However much Fortune rages and stirs up more trouble she can't take away very much from that. How much more careful am I now—how much better shape are you lads in since the new landlord came along!

Nature has decided that neither he nor me or anyone owns the land. He drove us out: villainy, or ignorance of the cunning law or surely in the end, a long-living heir, will drive him out.

Today the land is called Umbrenus' when before it went under the name of Ofellus.[13] No-one actually owns it but I will work it now then someone else will. So live bravely and set your brave hearts against misfortune'.

Horace, *Satires* 2, 2

Martial describes a world of scandal-mongering, informing, and sycophancy:

Cinna, you're forever chattering in everybody's ear and you can even chatter about that
with the crowd listening. You laugh in whispers, you complain, you argue, you weep,
you sing in whispers, you judge, you keep quiet, you shout. This disease of yours is so
ingrained in you that, Cinna, you praise Caesar in whispers more often than not.

Martial 1, 89

Crime seems to pay: 'You are an informer and a charlatan, a fraudster and a banker, a
cock sucker and an agitator. I wonder, Vacerra, why you aren't loaded.' (Martial 11, 66)
Pliny is disgusted by the professional legacy hunter:

To Calvisius Rufus

Get your money out and hear this gem of a story, no, make it stories because this
new one reminds me of ones from before and it couldn't matter less which one I begin
with. Piso's Verania was lying gravely ill—I mean the Piso who Galba adopted. Enter
Regulus: the cheek of the man to intrude on her illness when he had been so hostile to
her husband and was so reviled.[14] If his presence there wasn't bad enough he sat down
on the couch next to her and asked her when her birthday was and at what time she was
born. When he heard the answers he looks intently, stares at her, moves his lips, taps his
fingers and counts.[15] Then nothing. He kept the poor woman hanging on in suspense
for ages and then said 'You're going through a crisis in your life but you'll get over it. To
make this clear I'll consult a soothsayer whom I often use.' Without delay he makes a
sacrifice and confirms that the entrails are in line with the star signs. Believing herself to
be in mortal danger Verania takes this in, demands a codicil and adds Regulus on to it
to receive a legacy. Soon her health deteriorates and as she dies shouts that the vile and
evil man is worse than a perjurer and has sworn falsely on the life of his son. Regulus
regularly does this kind of scandalous thing, calling down the anger of the gods (which
he manages to avoid himself on a day to day basis) onto the head of his unfortunate son.

Velleius Blaesus, famous for his wealth and a consul, was at death's door and wanted
to change his will. Regulus was hoping to get something from the new terms—he had
lately begun to hang around Blaesus; he begged and urged the doctors to prolong the
man's life somehow. After the will is signed he changed his tune and says the very
opposite to the very same doctors 'How much longer are you going to torture the
poor man for? And why do you begrudge him a good death when you don't have the
power to give him life.' Blaesus died: he must have heard it all because he left Regulus
a mere pittance.

Are two stories enough or do you want a third, so as to comply with the scholars'
rule?[16] There are certainly enough to choose from. The distinguished lady Aurelia
had done herself up in her best dress for the signing of her will. Regulus turned up at
the signing. 'I'm asking you to leave these clothes to me,' he said. Aurelia thought the
man was joking but he stood his ground, deadly serious and, to cut a long story short,

forced the woman to open her will and to bequeath the clothes she was stood up in to him. He watched over her as she wrote and checked that she had written the codicil. Aurelia is still alive today although he forced this on her as if she was at death's door. This is a man who helps himself to inheritances as if he had a right to them. But why do I get worked up when I live in a country which for a long time now has given the same or even larger rewards for depravity and wickedness as for decency and virtue. Look at Regulus who from penury and obscurity graduated to such affluence through vice; he himself told me that when he was trying to find out when he would be worth sixty million sesterces he found two sets of entrails portending that he would be worth twice that—and so he will be if he carries on like this, stipulating the terms of other people's wills to their owners—the very worst kind of deception. Farewell.

Pliny, *Epistles* 2, 20

Juvenal justifies his satirical writings; the sheer awfulness of all aspects of life in Rome with all its sycophancy, immorality, danger, vice, corruption and drudgery make writing satire a necessity and inevitable:

Am I always going to be stuck in the audience? Will I never get my own back for all the times raucous Cordus' *Theseid* has annoyed me? Will this writer get away with reciting his Roman comedies, this one his love elegies; will this one get away with taking the whole day over an epic *Telephus*; or an *Orestes* when he's filled the margin at the end of the roll, he's written on the back and it's still unfinished? No-one knows his own household better than I know the groves of Mars and the cave of Vulcan near to the Aeolian mountains; what the winds are playing at, which ghosts Aeacus is torturing, where that other bloke steals the golden fleecelet from; the height of the ash trees hurled by Monychus.[17, 18] Fronto's plane trees, his echoing marble halls and cracked columns cry out loud from the interminable recitations.

You'll get exactly the same thing from all poets, good and bad. I too have been caned and I too have advised Sulla to retire and get a good night's sleep; it's a daft indulgence when you're bumping into poets everywhere to save paper that's going to be wasted anyway.[19]

If you have the time, let me explain logically why I choose to run along the same plain as the one where great Lucilius gave rein to his horses. When a girly eunuch takes a wife, when bare-breasted Mevia shafts a Tuscan boar with her spear, when the one man who shaved me as a youth and made my heavy beard rasp challenges the whole patrician class with his wealth, when Crispinus—a Nile pleb and slave of Canopus—his Tyrian cloak hitched up on to his shoulder, wears his gold ring on his finger sweating in summer unable to endure the weight of a heavier stone, when we have all this it is difficult not to write satire.[20, 21] Who can tolerate this mean city that is Rome, who is so iron-willed as to restrain himself when the brand new litter of the lawyer Matho comes along full of … Matho himself, and after him the bloke who informed on his powerful friend and who soon will rapidly rape all that's left of our nobility—the bloke whom Massa is scared of, whom Carus softens up with gifts and Thymele sent secretly by scared Latinus; when they who win legacies by their nocturnal acts barge you out of the way and are raised to the heavens by the best route to high office: the fanny of a little old rich woman.[22, 23] Each heir's share is measured out according to the size of his prick: Proculeius thereby gets a little; Gillo a lot. By all means let them get them get the reward for their virility and turn pale like the man who treads on a snake in his bare feet or the orator about to speak at Caligula's Lugdunum altar.[24]

Why should I tell you how much my spleen seethes with rage—when I see the people crowded out by a herd of hangers on: this one has robbed and prostituted his pupil; the other is condemned by a meaningless judgement. But infamy is fine if the money's safe? Marius in exile starts drinking at the 8th hour and takes delight in annoying the gods when you, Africa, weep in victory.

Am I not to believe these horrors are worthy of Horace, the light of Venusia? Can't I have a go at these horrors too? Is it better that I write about Heracles or Diomedes, or the Minotaur's howling labyrinth, or Daedalus the flying carpenter and his boy Icarus smacking into the sea; is it better that I write about such things at a time when a husband pimps his wife and takes gifts from her adulterer because she can't legally inherit—he a born ceiling gazer, a born snorer with his nosy nose in his drinking cup—at a time when someone who frittered away his fortune in brothels and squandered his family's possessions, presuming it right and proper to have hopes of commanding a cohort, a boy Automedon hurtling down the via Flaminia at full pelt, holding the reins himself and showing off to his great-coated mistress.[25]

I'd love to fill my voluminous notebooks while standing at the crossroads watching the forger carried high on six shoulders, half naked and exposed in his lady's chair on both sides, reminiscent of cool Maecenas, with his scrap of paper and a forging seal, and makes himself into a squeaky clean and splendid chap.

Here comes the mighty matron who, just before she offers her thirsty husband a mellow Calenian, mixes toxic toad into it; better even than Lucusta she teaches her stupid neighbours to carry off their blackened husbands for burial despite the mob and its rumours.[26, 27] If you want to be anyone who is anyone be brave enough to do something that'll get you exiled to the confines of Gyara and its dungeon.[28] Honesty is held in high esteem—but left out in the cold. It's Crime that they have to thank for their gardens, and their palaces, tables, their antique silver goblets with goats standing out in high relief. You can't sleep for worrying about your greedy daughter in law being seduced, about shameful brides and juvenile adulterers? If I am denied natural ability, indignation will push my verse to the limit and produces the kind of poems either I or Cluvienus write.[29]

From that time when Deucalion raised the waters with his rain clouds and climbed the mountain by boat to demand an oracle, when boulders gradually grew soft and warm with life and Pyrrha showed off naked girls to married men—everything a man does—his prayers, fear, anger, pleasure, joy, comings and goings—is fodder for my anthology.[30] When was the abundance of vice more abundant, when did the gape of greed gape wider? When was gambling so rife? Gamblers place their bets at gaming tables now not with purses on hand but with money chests nearby. You'll see some great battles there between cashier and armour bearer. Is it not plain madness to lose 100,000 sesterces when you can't afford to give a tunic back to a shivering slave? Which of our ancestors built so many villas or dined alone on seven courses? Now the daily dole that sits on the edge of the threshold for the toga'd throng to snatch at is a pittance. The patron first scans your face fearing you might come under false pretences making your claim using a false name and only recommending that you get your dues when he recognises you. He orders the herald to summon even those of Trojan stock and they rattle the threshold too just like us. 'Pay the praetor first, then give to the tribune'. But a freedman was there first: 'I was here first' he says. 'Why should I be bullied or hesitate to stand my ground even if I was born on the Euphrates, a fact proven by my earrings though I myself deny it. But my five shops bring in 400,000 sesterces. What more can the purple confer that is worth having if a Corvinus shepherds his rented sheep in the Laurentian countryside while I own more than a Pallas or a Licinus? [31, 32, 33, 34] So let the tribunes wait, let lucre conquer. The man who just came to the city with his feet whitened should not give way to the sacred magistracies since with us the majesty of wealth is most sacred.[35] Death-bringing Money doesn't yet occupy a temple and so far we haven't erected altars to Money in the way that we cultivate Peace, Honour, Victory, Virtue and Concord which clatter when we salute their nests.[36]

But when the consul calculates at year end what the dole contributes and how much it adds to his income, what are we clients to do who must from this dole find money for togas, shoes, bread and heating the home? A traffic jam of litters seeks out the hundred quarter dole. A husband does the rounds with his sick or pregnant wife in tow. This man claims for his absent wife—experienced in this familiar scam, pointing to her clothes and the empty litter instead of a wife. 'My Galla is in there' he says. 'Hand it over quickly. What's the hold up? Galla—look out the window. Don't wake her, she'll be sleeping.'

Every day is distinguished by a remarkable sequence of events: the dole, then the courts and law-schooled Apollo, then triumphal statues among which some Egyptian taxman has had the audacity to set up goodness knows what inscriptions and it's okay not just to piss on his statue. The clients leave the threshold older and more tired, abandoning their hopes and prayers although the greatest wish a man has is for a dinner: the poor still have to buy their own cabbage and firewood.

Meanwhile your patron will be devouring the best the forest and sea can give reclining alone on an empty couch and devouring whole fortunes in one sitting from his fine and expensive antique round tables. No parasites now! Who can bear such sordid opulence? How big has a gullet got to be to accommodate a whole wild boar—a beast born for the feast? Yet the price you'll pay for all of this isn't far off: you throw off your cloak and with full stomach carry your undigested peacock to the baths. And then? Sudden death and old age spent without a will. The news does the rounds of all the dinner tables—a not so sad story—and the funeral procession goes out amid his friends' angry applause.[37]

Posterity can add nothing worse to our ways: our offspring will do the very same things and desire the very same things. Every kind of vice totters on the brink. Fill your sails, spread your wings! It's at this point that you might ask where my skill comes from for this subject? Where do I get our forefathers' bluntness from for writing passionately about whatever they pleased? Is there anyone I dare not name? Does it matter if Mucius ignores me.[38] But if you cite Tigellinus for example, you will burn on that torch in which men stand blazing and smoking—their throats throttled while your corpse ploughs a wide furrow across the arena.[39]

Is the man who has administered aconite poison to three uncles to ride on by, looking down on us from his swaying couch, without me saying anything? Yes, and when he approaches you, button your lip because if you say 'That's him' you'll be labelled an informer. You can set Aeneas against ferocious Turnus with a clear conscience; it's no big deal to hear how Achilles was slain, how they searched for Hyla pursuing his water carrier, but whenever Lucilius rants and rages as if with sword drawn, he whose soul is frozen in crime reddens when he hears it and his heart sweats with tacit guilt. It may all ends in tears of rage for you. So think these things over before the trumpet sounds. When you've got your helmet on it's a bit too late to regret your decision to do battle. I will try and see what I'm allowed to say against those whose ashes are concealed under the Via Flamina and the Via Latina.[40]

Juvenal 1

While a deficiency in public morals and permissiveness certainly characterises aspects of the Roman world, there were various checks and balances in place to curb the worst excesses: it was never all vice, corruption, and sensational depravity, despite the best efforts of some of the emperors and their empresses to make it so. Indeed, one of the responsibilities of the Censors, an important office in Rome, was to look after public morality and to keep the state on the rails by promoting marriage and acting as guardians of public morals.[41] This power earned them reverence and fear in equal measure; they were known as the *castigatores* (the chastisers). Their ultimate weapon against transgressors was the withdrawal of rank and citizenship in response to a failure to uphold the *mos maiorum*: the code of behaviour, ethics, and character that embodied everything that distinguished the Roman from what was considered to be barbarian. Living as a single celibate, divorcing casually, treating a wife and children badly, spoiling children and allowing them to be naughty with their parents, sumptuous living, neglecting the fields, being cruel to the slaves, and being an actor or engaging in similar disreputable professions all attracted the censure of the *censores*, winning the accused a dreaded *nota censoria*, and, to some extent, modulating public behaviour and private life.[42]

The good life and the good old days

The alternative, of course, to all this corruption was, as Horace has recommended, a much more ascetic and moderate lifestyle. The 'good life' can either be a moral and good way of conducting one's life or it can be a good and enjoyable lifestyle. The extracts here look at both. Sentimental and rose-tinted reminiscence over the 'good old days', when everyone and everything apparently was always better and much nicer, was probably as common a pastime in early imperial Rome as it is today. Persius, *Satires* 2, 59–61, Juvenal 11, 77–81 and Statius *Silvae* 4, 6 all join in, but here Martial takes the opposite view and questions the all too easy inclination to criticise contemporary life and culture.

It is, however, *otium*—leisure time—that Martial craves; to Pliny too, it is an essential part of his life in the country (1, 9, 4–6). *Otium* was the new *officium* and *negotium*; it was the world of non-work. It was important to be busy doing nothing because doing nothing allowed you time to contemplate, to cogitate, to meditate, to read, and to write. Martial's idealised prescription for a life worth living is instantly recognisable, recommending as it does virtual antitheses to the greed and excess of urban living: no litigation, no official engagements, plenty of unpretentious and affable dinners and diners, and marital bliss—in short, a stress free life completely the opposite to that deplored above in Horace *Satires* 2, 6 and *Satires* 1, 1.

Martial criticises the vogue for rubbishing the present in favour of the 'good old days.'

'How can I explain the fact that you can never be famous if you're still alive and that it's a rare reader who actually likes the times they are living in?' These are days freighted with great jealousies, Regulus, demonstrated by the fact that we always prefer the men of old to today's men. So, we're being ungrateful when we pine for Pompey's old shaded portico and when old men say they like Catulus' low-rent temples. You read Ennius even though Virgil is perfectly okay, O Rome! and even Homer's contemporaries ridiculed him. Theatre-goers hardly ever applauded the garlanded Menander. Only Corinna knew her Ovid. But you, books of mine, don't rush, if glory comes only posthumously then I am in no hurry.

Martial 5, 10

Martial yearns for a life of leisured ease away from all the litigiousness and bureaucracy:

If you and I, dear Martial, were allowed to enjoy carefree days and to pass our time at leisure and have time as well for some real living, we would know nothing at all about the corridors of power and the houses of powerful men, nor depressing law suits and the intimidating forum, nor proud statues. Instead we'd know all about strolls, plays, books, the open countryside, porticos, shade, cold baths from the Aqua Virgo, warm baths—this is where *we* would be at, this would be our work. Nowadays neither of us lives our own lives and we each feel that the good times are flying by into the distance—time which is ticking away and is held to our account. Does anyone delay who knows what living is all about?

Martial 5, 20

Martial's recipe for the good life:

> The things which make life more enjoyable, most pleasing, Martial, are as follows: wealth acquired not by hard work but from a legacy; a field that is easy to till, a home fire that never goes out; no litigation, rarely having to put on a toga, calm of mind, the strength of a free born man, a healthy body, real prudence, good friends, easy going dinner guests, an unpretentious table, nights not drunken but nights free from care, a happy bedroom that hasn't been sullied, sleep which makes the nights go quickly. Be happy with what you are and crave nothing else. Don't fear your last day on earth and don't yearn for it.

Martial 10, 47

An example of outstanding character and conduct:

To Attius Clemens

If ever the liberal arts flourished in Rome they're flourishing more than ever now. There are many famous examples but one will do: Euphrates the philosopher. When in Syria as a young man doing military service I got close to him, even going to his home; I worked hard to win his friendship although you couldn't really call it particularly hard work since he is affable and accessible, full of the good breeding he expounds. I wish that I could have fulfilled the hope he had for me then just as he has added substantially to his own virtues! Or is it that I admire them more because I understand them better. But I still don't understand them well enough because, just as only an artist can judge art, engravings or sculpture, so you don't recognise wisdom if you're not wise yourself. However, I fully appreciate the many qualities which Euphrates exhibits and which shine out from him so that even averagely educated people can see them and are influenced by them. He argues subtly, seriously and elegantly so that he often even affects the depth and range of Platonic expression no less. His conversation is wide-ranging and discursive, in particular it is seductive and he can persuade and influence even his detractors. Added to this he is physically tall, good-looking, has long flowing hair, a full and white beard—things which you might think are just fortuitous and of no consequence but they bring him much respect for all that. He dresses not to shock, he shows *gravitas* but is never melancholy; when you meet him you'll be in awe rather than fear of him. The life he leads is without blemish but he is amiable all the same. He censures faults—not men; he doesn't castigate those who have strayed from the straight and narrow but seeks to rehabilitate them. You would follow his advice, wrapt and hanging on every word, and you'd want him to win you over even after he has already won you over. He has three children, two boys whom he has brought up with great care. His father-in-law, Pompeius Julianus is distinguished and has generally lived an outstanding life; but there's one thing about him that stands out: as a peerless leader in his province in the face of the best of offers, he chose a son-in-law who was notable not for his official achievements but for his wisdom.

Mind you, I don't know why I go on about a man whose company I'm unable to enjoy unless it is to distress myself even more because it's not permitted? I'm tied up with my official duties: important but extremely irksome. I sit as a magistrate, sign petitions, do accounts, write lots of official letters. I complain about these duties to Euphrates whenever I can. He makes me feel better when he says that the man who performs public duties, knows the law, dispenses and exercises justice and actually practises what philosophers preach—that's the most wonderful kind of philosophy. But this one thing he can't persuade me of: that doing my job is more satisfying than spending the whole day listening to and learning from him.

You have the time so I urge you all the more when you next come to Rome (and you'll come sooner now because of this) to allow him to improve and polish you up. For I, like most people, don't begrudge others the good things I can't have myself. Quite the opposite: I feel good when I see my friends getting what I am denied. Farewell.

Pliny, *Epistles* 1, 10

Slaves, Freedmen, and Freedwomen

We have heard much of slaves and slavery throughout the book so far—this is hardly surprising because slaves were an integral part of Roman society, particularly from the third century BCE when Rome's expansionism and conquests brought an inexorable influx of foreign slaves into Rome and other Roman cities and towns from conquered regions. Julius Caesar alone is said to have been responsible for bringing in a million or so slaves from his conquests in Gaul between 58 and 51 BCE. War was the main source of supply, but there were others, including those unfortunates kidnapped by pirates, political and common criminals, debtors, abandoned or exposed children, and the children of slaves. By the early years of the empire, up to 30 per cent of the population of Rome was made up of people in servitude.

Some were employed by the state, building and maintaining public buildings, and running services, many were privately owned, usually as household slaves. Some were bought or hired to haul all manner of loads and freight from one place to another; at the lowest end, some were enlisted as gladiators to fight in the arena, often to the death, or as fodder for wild animals, always ending in death; others still were bought as prostitutes, freaks, or even pets. Farm slaves were probably worse off in many ways than city slaves, as agricultural work was physically exhausting and their absent masters delegated control to slave overseers who would have been extremely demanding if only to keep their jobs. A farm slave was barely higher than the farm animals in the agricultural labour food chain; a standing threat in Roman comedy was 'I'll send you to work on the farm!'

Slaves were employed in the crucial business of keeping the water flowing in towns and cities; this from the expert:

> It remains for me to speak of the maintenance of the aquaducts ... there are two of those [slave] gangs, one belonging to the State, the other to the emperor. The one belonging to the State ... numbers about 240 men. The number in Caesar's gang is 460 ... Both gangs are divided into several classes of workmen: overseers, reservoir-keepers, inspectors, pavers, plasterers, and other workmen; of these, some must be outside the city for purposes which do not seem to require any great amount of work,

but yet may demand immediate attention; the men inside the city at their stations at the reservoirs and fountains will devote their energies to the works, especially in case of sudden emergencies, in order that a plentiful reserve supply of water may be diverted from several wards of the city to one afflicted by an emergency.

Frontinus, *De Aquis* 2, 116–7
translation adapted from Charles E. Bennett's in the Loeb edition, 1925

Columella, writer on agricultural and agronomical matters, is quite specific with regard to what type of slave to hire on his farm; certainly no attractive, weak boy from the permissive city—an illiterate cretin is preferable to that:

So my advice at the start is do not appoint an overseer from those slaves who are physically attractive, and certainly not from that lot which has been preoccupied with the voluptuous attractions of the city. This lazy and dopey class of servants, used to ambling off to the Campus, the Circus, and the theatres, to gambling, to cookshops, to brothels, never stops dreaming of these pecadillos; and when they bring them into their farming, the master suffers not just a loss with the slave himself but also with his whole estate. Choose a man who has been hardened by farm work from his infancy, one who has been tested by experience. If, however, you can't find one, put one in charge who has slaved patiently at hard labour … He should be, then, middle aged and physically strong, skilled in farm operations … Even an illiterate person … can manage affairs well enough … he should be given a female companion to keep him under control and in certain matters to be of help him; and this same overseer should be warned not to have affairs with members of the household, and much less with an outsider … he must not allow in soothsayers and witches, two types who incite ignorant minds through false superstition to spending and then to disgusting practices.

He must have no acquaintance with the city or with the weekly market, except to make purchases and sales in connection with his duties. For, as Cato says, an overseer should not … go off site except to learn something new about farming … as far as the care and clothing of the slaves is concerned he should look to practicalities rather than appearance, taking care to protect them against wind, cold, and rain with long-sleeved leather tunics, garments of patchwork, or hooded cloaks … It is customary for all cautious men to inspect the inmates of the workhouse, to establish they are chained up properly, whether the places of confinement are safe and properly guarded, whether the overseer has put anyone in fetters or removed his shackles without his, the master's, knowledge … he also tests their food and drink by tasting it himself, and inspects their clothing, their gloves, and their shoes. In addition he should give them frequent opportunities for making complaints against those who treat them cruelly or dishonestly.

Columella, *De Re Rustica* 1, 8
translation adapted from the Loeb Classical Library edition, 1941

Hard labour in a silver mine was particularly brutal:

> The slaves who work in [the silver mines] produce for their taskmasters revenues
> beyond belief, but in doing so they exhaust their bodies day and night in their
> excavations, dying in droves due to the exceptionally bad reatment they endure.
> There is no respite or break from their work, but they are driven on under the blows
> of the overseers to endure the most severe of plights, exhausting their lives in this
> wretched way…indeed to them death is preferable to life, such is the enormity of the
> hardships they must endure.
>
> > Diodorus Siculus 5, 38, 1

Mill work was no better; here, the life of the slaves was unspeakably atrocious,
comparable to that of the donkey into which Lucius had been transformed in Apuleius'
second century novel, *Metamorphoses*:

> Dying of hunger as I was I was nevertheless curious and anxious and fascinated to see
> the routine of that terrible baker's mill … good God, what pathetic slaves they were!
> Some had skin black and blue all over from the beatings, some had their backs striped
> with lashes merely covered rather than clothed with torn rags, some had their groins
> barely concealed by a loin cloth; so ragged were they that they might as well have been
> naked; some were branded on the forehead; some had their hair shaven; some had
> shackles on their ankles; their skin was an ugly sallow; some could barely see, their eyes
> and faces were so black with the smoke, their eye-lids all glued up with the gloom of
> that fetid place, half blind and sprinkled black and white with dirty flour like boxers …
>
> > Apuleius, *Metamorphoses* 9, 12

Due to their invisibility in the eyes of the law, slave owners could get away with such
treatment. Slaves had no rights; they were merely their owners' property, no more than
living labour-saving machines. Misconduct or alleged criminal activity could lead to
crucifixion or being burned alive. Psychological torture was applied when an owner
threatened to sell off a slave's spouse or children to another owner. It took until the *Law
Code of Theodosius* in 438 CE for this repellent practice to be repudiated.

Not surprisingly, some slaves did rise up and revolt. In 134 BCE, there was an
insurrection of slaves at the Laurium silver mines in Attica. Attalus, the heirless king of
Pergamum, bequeathed his state to Rome to prevent a simmering slave revolt. In Lydia
in 399 CE, hordes of slaves joined the Ostrogoth army. Slaves plundered Thrace in
401 CE. In the siege of Rome by the Goths in 408–9 CE, most of Rome's slaves—40,000
in all—went over to the Goths.

The first major uprising became known as the First Servile War (135–132 BCE);
it began on a large farm owned by a Greek from Henna, called Damophilius. In 136
BCE, Eunus, a slave from Apamea in Syria occupied Henna (modern Enna) in central
Sicily with 400 other runaways. The extensive *latifundia* on the island meant high

populations of slave workers from the mid third century onwards. Some were prisoners of war, some had been bought on the slave markets of the eastern Mediterranean such as Rhodes and Delos. The *latifundia*, huge tracts of land, had come onto the property market after the Romans expelled the Carthaginians and opened the door to speculators. Not unusually, the new owners—mainly *equites*—treated their slaves badly, which fomented rebellion and banditry. The Roman armies sent to crush the revolt in 134 and 133 BCE were themselves defeated; it was not until 132 BCE when occupied Messina fell to the Romans that the slave army was defeated, as Florus records:

> At last punishment was inflicted on them under the leadership of Perperna, who, after defeating them and finally besieging them at Henna reduced them by famine as effectively as any plague and punished the surviving rebels with fetters, chains and the cross.
>
> Florus, *Epitome of Roman History* 3, 20

Over time, numerous slave revolts followed and the problems on the *latifundi* continued to worsen. Many landowners went bankrupt; many sold up, no doubt at depressed prices, to those increasingly wealthy patrician landowners. Many farm labourers were made redundant, replaced by the surge of free labour slaves who were increasingly available in the wake of Rome's conquests. The ethnic Romans sought work in the towns and cities; slaves took over their farm jobs. Appian summarizes this economic and social revolution:

> The rich…used persuasion or force to buy or seize property which adjoined their own, or any other smallholdings belonging to poor men, and came to operate great ranches instead of single farms. They employed slave hands and shepherds on these estates to avoid having free men dragged off the land to serve in the army, and they derived great profit from this form of ownership too, as the slaves had many children and no liability to military service and their numbers increased freely. For these reasons the powerful were becoming extremely rich, and the number of slaves in the country was reaching large proportions, while the Italian people were suffering from depopulation and a shortage of men, worn down as they were by poverty and taxes and military service. And if they had any respite from these tribulations, they had no employment, because the land was owned by the rich who used those slave farm workers instead of free men.
>
> Appian, *Civil Wars* 1, 13
> translation by Horace White, Loeb edition 1913

A one-thousand-acre farm would be on the small side. As an example of the immense size of this landowning, one owner died in 8 BCE, leaving 4,000 slaves, 3,000 yoke of oxen, and 257,000 other farm animals. The lands of Marcus Licinius Crassus (115–53

BCE) were valued at 50 million denarii. In 49 BCE, Lucius Domitius Ahenobarbus owned 270,000 acres.

One of the many lucrative sidelines and benefits of owning slaves was their potential role as gladiators—or as wild animal fodder in gladiatorial conquests. Money could be made here, particularly with the celebrity status won among the more successful survivors of the arena. One such celebrity was a slave by the name of Spartacus.

Gladiatorial contests were serious business. The gladiators had to be good if the baying crowds which flocked to the shows all around the empire were to be satisfied. Gladiators, then, underwent training in gladiatorial schools. In 73 BCE, seventy-eight of them escaped from the fighting school of Gnaeus Lentulus Batiatus at Capua. According to Plutarch, the gladiators were only armed with meat cleavers and spits stolen from the kitchen. As luck had it, they came upon a wagon filled with gladiatorial weaponry; now heavily armed, they occupied a slope on Mount Vesuvius.

Plutarch gives us some detail:

> Spartacus was a Thracian from the nomadic tribes and not only had a great spirit and great physical strength, but was, much more than one would expect from his condition, most intelligent and charismatic, being more like a Greek than a Thracian.
>
> Plutarch, *Life of Crassus* 8; translation by Rex Warner (1958)

Despite initial successes, Spartacus ultimately was defeated. The Romans captured six thousand of his unfortunate slaves alive. As a stark, rotting reminder of the fate that awaited the rebellious slave they were all crucified on crosses placed every forty metres or so along the 150 miles of the Via Appia between Rome and Capua; the corpses were gradually eaten away by wild dogs and carrion. Pompey butchered a further 5,000 'survivors'. By contrast, 3,000 Roman prisoners of war were found at Spartacus's camp at Rhegium, alive and well. Spartacus was no angel, and was quite capable of committing his very own atrocities, but the reprisal against his slave army was especially savage.

If joining a rebel army was not an option then the slave could always run away. Masters soon got wise to this, though, and branded their slaves or else tagged them in much the same way as we tag paroled prisoners or dogs today; one such give-away tag reads: 'I have run away. Capture me. You will get a reward when you have retuned me to my master, Zoninus' (*CIL* 15, 7914).

Not surprisingly, a healthy trade in professional slave-hunting soon sprang up; this extract from Petronius' novel evidences this:

> a herald came into the dive with a public official and a small crowd of people; he shook a torch which gave out more smoke than light, and made this announcement: 'Wandered off just now from the public baths, a boy aged about sixteen, curly hair, effeminate, good looking, name of Giton. A reward of a thousand pieces will be paid to any person willing to bring him back or reveal his whereabouts.'
>
> Petronius, *Satyricon* 97

It is easy to gloss over Roman slavery—and it often is glossed over or, at best sanitised, in our history books—as just another stratum in Roman society, glibly and casually dismissed as just something that was part of the Roman experience, described with a veneer which takes little account of the horrors involved and endured, often for life, by ordinary people whose only mistake often was to be in the wrong place at the wrong time. In war, particularly after a siege, the conquered population were at the mercy of the victors. By the first century BCE, it was axiomatic that 'It is a law established for all time among all men that when a city is taken in war, the people and property of the inhabitants belong to the captors' (Xenophon (d. 354 BCE), *Cyrus* 7, 5, 73).

The vanquished were just another spoil of war; combatant prisoners of war were often enslaved, as were the women and children and the infirm and the elderly. Women might become prostitutes or concubines, considered no better than just another item in the war booty inventory. They suffered unspeakable and abhorrent abuse—physical, sexual, and psychological—they might be raped; they might be gang-raped or repeatedly raped over long periods of time. They may be plagued with sexually transmitted infections, they endured *ad hoc* abortions with the attendant infections that often killed them; there was the possibility of unwanted pregnancies, the half-foreign offspring which are a lifetime's haunting reminder of the violence and trauma they had endured. All of this came with enslavement. On the other hand, they might be spared slavery when they were summarily tortured, horribly mutilated and murdered—sometimes in front of their husbands and children as they awaited a similar fate.

The situation in Rome becomes all the more shockingly commonplace when it seems that familiarity started to breed contempt. If the historians and rhetoricians are to be believed, the endless descriptions of sacked cities, raped women, pillaged temples, and enforced evacuation or enslavement were actually becoming somewhat tedious. It had, of course, all started many centuries earlier with the sack of Troy—the study of which was a staple of Greek and Roman rhetorical school education—and had been relentless ever since. Polybius, writing before 118 BCE, deplored the 'ignoble and womanish' style used by the historian Phylarchus to excite the emotions of his readers, what with all those 'clinging women with their hair dishveled and their breasts bare ... weeping and lamenting as they are led away into slavery' (Polybius 2, 56, 7).

Sallust, in the first century BCE, complains that 'arms and corpses, gore and grief are all over the place' (*Ad Catilinam* 51, 9); the orator-teacher Quintilian (35–100 CE), though, gives a master class in the effect of hyperbole, recommending the use of descriptions of women shrieking and mothers fighting desperately to keep hold of their children (*Institutio Oratoria* 8, 3, 67–70).

Captured inhabitants might be spared slavery if they could afford to pay a ransom. Diodorus Siculus gives us an example in 254 BCE during the First Punic War at Panormus (modern Palermo):

[The Romans] went to Panormus where they moored their ships in the harbour close to the walls, and after disembarking their men, invested the city with a palisade and a trench... Then the Romans broke down the city wall by repeatedly attacking and by deploying siege engines, and having taken the outer city killed many [inhabitants]; the rest fled for refuge to the old city, and sending envoys to the consuls asked for assurances that their lives would be spared. It was agreed that those who paid two minas each should go free, and the Romans then took over the city; at this price fourteen thousand persons ... upon payment of the money, were released. All the others, thirteen thousand of them, were sold by the Romans as booty along with their household goods.

Diodorus Siculus 23, 18, 4–5

Translation adapted from *The Library of History of Diodorus Siculus* published as Vol. XI of the Loeb Classical Library edition, 1957

The selling of slaves was carefully regulated:

The edict of the curule aediles, in the section relating to stipulations about the purchase of slaves, reads as follows: 'Ensure that the invoice of each slave is written so that it is clear what disease or defect each one has, which one is a runaway or a vagabond, or is still on probation for some offence.'

Aulus Gellius, *Attic Nights* 4, 2, 1

Here it is in practice in 129 CE:

At Oxyrhynchus ... Agathodaemon ... acknowledges to Gaius Julius Germanus ... that he hereby confirms the signed contract ... for the sale of a female slave called Dioscorous, aged about 25 years, with no distinguishing marks, who became his property by purchase and formerly belonged to Heracleides ... which slave Julius Germanus did then take over from him just as she was, non-returnable except for epilepsy or seizure by a claimant, for the price of 1200 silver drachmae of silver ...

P. Oxy. 95 [*Select Papyri* 1, 32]

Slaves evoked widely diverging attitudes. Martial's defence of his brutish treatment of his cook (8, 23) betrays what seems to be the standard attitude towards the servile classes. Cato had taken Aristotle's description of slaves as 'human tools' very literally and ill treatment of slaves was clearly endorsed by Quintilan (1, 3, 13–14): 'flogging is shameful, fit only for slaves.' However, it was not just the odd flogging; things could be much worse: eye-gouging, branding, limb smashing, and psychological and sexual abuse were seemingly all quite common. In addition, both female and male slaves often had to endure rape on a regular basis. Martial 3, 94 anticipates 8, 23 when he accuses Rufus of preferring to cut up his cook than the hare on his plate. Pliny the Elder tells us how the sadistic Vedius Pollo was in the habit of throwing convicted slaves into a pool of *muraenae* to see them being torn to pieces:

> Vedius Pollio, a Roman equestrian and a friend of the late Emperor Augustus, found a way of practicing his cruelty by means of the muraena (a large eel): he had any slave condemned by him thrown into pools filled with muraenæ. Not that any land animal would have done the job: he would not then see a man so efficiently and instantly torn to shreds by any other kind of animal.
>
> Pliny the Elder, Natural History 9, 39, 77

Martial, however, is not altogether, or always, as cruel as 10, 31 demonstrates; here, Martial deplores the venality of an acquaintance who sells a slave to pay for a sumptuous dinner party. Pliny's compassion in 8, 16 echoes Seneca's Stoic view at *Epistles* 47, while Suetonius tells us that the emperor Claudius was sympathetic to cruelly treated slaves:

> Some people abandoned their sick and devoted slaves on the island of Aesculapius, because thy could not be bothered with curing them; [Claudius] declared that all of those who were so exposed could go free, never more to return, if they got better, to their former servitude; and that if any master chose to kill straight off, rather than expose, a slave, he should be liable for murder.
>
> Suetonius, Claudius 25, 2

Hadrian (r. 117–138 CE) also showed compassion and legislated accordingly:

> He forbad masters to kill their slaves, and ordered that any who were guilty should be sentenced by the courts. He forbad anyone to sell a slave or a female slave to a pimp or trainer of gladiators without giving a good reason… He abolished work houses of hard labour for slaves….He issued an order that, if a slave-owner were murdered in his house, no slaves should be tortured except those who were near enough to be complicit in the murder.
>
> Scriptores Historiae Augustae,
The Life of Hadrian, 18, 7–11
translation adapted from Loeb edition (1921)

The extract reveals how it was not unusual practice for a slave to be tortured before giving evidence in court on the assumption that a slave was incapable of freely telling the truth.

Pliny, once again, has a balanced approach to the whole issue, recommending caution in 3, 14 where he describes the murder of Larcius Macedo by his slaves. In *Annals* 14, 42–45, Tacitus tells a similar story. In law, if a slave murdered his master then all of the household slaves (including women and children) were guilty by association and executed along with the murderer.

Martial beats his chef for his bad cooking:

> I seem to you, Rusticus, to be cruel and a bit of a slob because I clout my cook for his cooking. If this seems too trivial a reason for a flogging, tell me why you would wish a cook to be beaten?

> Martial 3, 94

Playing the hypocrite, he complains that Rufus is not much better: 'You say the hare is not cooked properly, and call for a whip. Rufus, you would rather whip your cook, than your hare' (Martial 8, 23). Martial takes a swipe at the venality in valuing a life less than a sumptuous meal to show that he is not all bad:

> Yesterday, Calliodorus, you sold a slave at auction for a huge sum just so that you could dine well just one time. You didn't dine in 'well' though did you? The four pound mullet you bought was the *pièce de résistance*, the highlight of the meal. But you could say, 'This is not a fish, you charlatan, it's a man—Calliodorus, you're eating a man.'

> Martial 10, 31

This complete life story—from rags to riches almost—is encapsulated on a gravestone and neatly shows just how fortunes, even for slaves, can change:

> Gaius Julius Mygdonius, born a free man in Parthia was captured as a boy and sold as a slave in Roman territory. Once I became a freedman and citizen of Rome I saved up some money, thanks to Fate, when I was fifty years old.

> *CIL* 11, 137*

Slavery does not always get in the way of close friendship:

> Aulus Memmius Urbanus set up this memorial for his very dear friend and fellow freedman Aulus Memmius Clarus. We never argued and I held you in the highest regard … you and I were sold as slaves at the same time, we became freedmen at the same time in the same household … nothing has ever separated us until the day death took you.

> *CIL* 6, 22355a*

Some masters made their slaves part of the family, as this tombstone attests: 'Gaius Calpenius Hermes built this tomb for himself and his children and his freedmen and freedwomen, and for his wife Antistia Coetonis' (*CIL* 14, 4827*).

Some slave owners admired and appreciated their slaves:

> Here lies Marcus Canuleius Zosimus; he was twenty-eight years old. His master erected this to a well-deserving freedman. In his lifetime he never spoke ill of anyone; he did

nothing without his master's consent, there was always a lot of my gold and silver in his possession but he never stole any of it. He was a skilled master of Clodian engraving.

CIL 6, 9222*

Others loathed some of them:

Marcus Aemelius Artema built this tomb for his honoured brother ... his wife ... for himself and his children and for his freedmen and freedwomen and their descendants except for freedman Hermes whom he forbids, because of his ungrateful and obnoxious behaviour, to approach, walk round or come near to this tomb.

CIL 6, 11027*

translations adapted from those on

www.worldhistory.biz/ancient-history/57767-funerary-inscriptions.html

There was a thriving trade in slave-hire, organised in much the same way that we hire cars today; rented slaves would have been treated with even less compassion and care than they would by their original owner who would have gone some way at least to protect his investment:

Glaukios ... has rented out to Achillas ... for one year his female slave Tapontas to work as a weaver. Glaukios ... will ensure that she is absent neither day nor night, that she will be fed and gets other essentials, clothing apart, from Achillas who will clothe her. The rental fee for the whole year will be 420 silver drachmae...

P. Wisc. 16, 5

Pliny's letter describes the murder of a master by his slaves:

To Acilius

This atrocious affair needs more than just a letter. Larcius Macedo—a man of praetorian rank—has suffered at the hands of his slaves. Admittedly, he was a bullying master and a thug who often forgot that his own father had been a slave—or perhaps he remembered it all too well? He was bathing in his villa at Formiae. Suddenly his slaves surrounded him. One grabbed him by the throat, another punched him in the face, another in his chest and stomach and even (and this is shocking to say) his balls. When they believed him to be dead they threw him out onto the baking patio to ensure that he was not still alive. Whether he was actually senseless or because he just pretended to be so, he lay there motionless and flat out to give the impression that he was dead. He was then carried out to make it look as though he had been overcome by the heat. The slaves who had remained loyal to him picked him up; his concubines came running wailing and bawling. Woken up by their shouting and by the cool air, he opened his eyes and moved about to show that he was alive (now that it was safe to do so). The slaves who had revolted had scattered in all directions; most of them have been caught while the others are still being hunted. Macedo revived for a few days but it was a struggle: he died, though, with the consolation that he was avenged in the same way that those who are murdered are avenged. This shows just how great the dangers and insults are and the ridicule we are exposed to. Even if you're indulgent and kind you're still not safe because it is not good sense but criminality which makes slaves murder their masters.

Enough of this. What else is new? What? Nothing—otherwise I'd have mentioned it; I still have some paper left and the holiday today allows me to deal with more things. I will add something that happened about that same Macedo which I have luckily just remembered. When he was bathing in the public baths in Rome a remarkable thing happened which, as his death tells us, was ominous. One of his slaves gently touched a Roman knight to indicate he wanted to get past. The knight turned and slapped—not the slave who had touched him—but Macedo and he did so with such force that Macedo nearly fell over. So, baths have been the place where, as if by progression, he was first insulted and then murdered. Farewell.

Pliny, Epistles 3, 14

The consequences of murdering your master were dire in the extreme, but not just for the perpetrator despite popular opinion to the contrary, as Tacitus reveals in this ancient version of complicity law:

The city prefect, Pedanius Secundus, was murdered by one of his own slaves; either because he had been denied freedom after Pedanius had negotiated the price, or because he was burning with passion for a rent boy and could not bear to have his master as a rival. According to ancient law, all the slaves living under that same roof should have been executed, but a demonstration by the people wanting to protect so many innocents started a riot and the senate house was besieged. Even here there was a faction keen to reject such great severity but the majority believed that there should be no change.

Tacitus, Annals 14, 42–5

Pliny is upset by the illness and deaths of some of his slaves; he is consoled only by the generosity he has shown them:

To Plinius Paternus

The illness of my slaves and freedmen and indeed the deaths of some of the younger men has upset me greatly. Two things give me comfort, although in no way is it equal to my grief: one was my readiness to grant them their freedom (so their deaths seem less premature because they died as freedmen); second, I allowed my slaves to make a kind of will which I regard as legally binding. They make their stipulations and requests as they see fit: I fulfil them as ordered. They can share out, donate and bequeath their possessions so long as it's within the household—the house is to the slaves a kind of state and country.

Although I can be comforted by these consolations I am weakened and torn by the same considerations which led me to make these allowances. Not that I would want to be less lenient; I am aware that other people see this kind of misfortune as nothing more than a financial loss and thereby think themselves great men and philosophers. Whether they are great men and philosophers I don't know—they are certainly not men, for a true man is affected by grief and has feelings—even though he may resist them—and gives way to consolation and actually needs consolation. Indeed, I have perhaps said enough on this matter but less than I would like. There may even be pleasure in grief, particularly when you weep in the arms of a friend who is ready for your tears with approval or sympathy.

Pliny, *Epistles* 8, 16

An enlightened Seneca has some humane advice with regard to the treatment of slaves:

I am glad to learn ... that you live on friendly terms with your slaves. This is right for a sensible and well-educated man like yourself. 'They are slaves,' people declare. No, rather they are men. 'Slaves!' No, comrades. 'Slaves!' No, they are unpretentious friends. 'Slaves!' No, they are our fellow-slaves, if one reflects that Fortune has equal rights over slaves and free men alike.

That is why I smile at those who think it degrading for a man to dine with his slave. But why should they think it degrading? It is only because purse-proud etiquette surrounds a householder at his dinner with a mob of standing slaves. The master eats more than he can take, and with monstrous greed fills his belly until it is stretched and at length ceases to do the work of a belly so that he is at greater pains to discharge all the food than he was to stuff it down. All this time the poor slaves may not move their lips, even to speak. The slightest murmur is repressed by the rod; even a chance sound,—a cough, a sneeze, or a hiccup,—is accompanied by the lash. There is a grievous penalty for the slightest breach of silence. All night long they must stand about, hungry and mute.

The result of it all is that these slaves, who may not talk in their master's presence, talk about their master. But the slaves of former days, who were permitted to converse not only in their master's presence, but actually with him, whose mouths were not stitched up tight, were ready to bare their necks for their master, to bring upon their own heads any danger that threatened him; they spoke at the feast, but kept silence during torture...

I shall pass over other cruel and inhuman behaviour towards them; for we mistreat them, not as if they were men, but as if they were beasts of burden. When we recline at a banquet, one slave mops up the vomit, another crouches beneath the table and gathers up the left-overs of the drunken guests. Another carves the priceless game birds; with unerring strokes and skilled hand he cuts choice morsels along the breast or the rump. Hapless fellow, to live only for the purpose of cutting fat capons correctly... Another, who serves the wine, must dress like a woman and wrestle with his advancing years; he cannot get away from his boyhood; he is dragged back to it; and though he has already acquired a soldier's figure, he is kept beardless by having his hair smoothed away or plucked out by the roots, and he must stay awake throughout the night, dividing his time between his master's drunkenness and his lust; in the chamber he must be a man, at the feast a boy. Another, whose job it is to evaluate the guests, must ... watch to see whose flattery and whose immodesty, whether of appetite or of language, is to win them an invitation for tomorrow... With slaves like these the master cannot bear to dine; he would think it beneath his dignity to associate with his slave at the same table! Heaven forfend!

Kindly remember that he whom you call your slave sprang from the same stock, is smiled upon by the same skies, and on equal terms with yourself breathes, lives, and dies. It is just as possible for you to see in him a free-born man as for him to see in you a slave...

I do not wish to involve myself in too big a question, and to discuss the treatment of slaves, towards whom we Romans are excessively haughty, cruel, and insulting. But this is the nub of my advice: treat your inferiors as you would be treated by your betters. And as often as you reflect how much power you have over a slave, remember that your master has just as much power over you.

Seneca, *Moral Letters to Lucilius* 47, 1–11
Translation adapted from *Moral Letters to Lucilius (Epistulae Morales ad Lucilium)* translated by Richard Mott Gummere (Loeb 1917–1925)

It is always as well to remain cautious:

TO PLINIUS PATERNUS.
I think the slaves which I bought on your recommendation look decent enough. It now remains to be seen whether they are honest; because in judging value for money in a slave, your ears are a better judge than your eyes. Farewell.

Pliny, *Epistles* 1, 21

Freedmen & freedwomen

Enslavement was by no means always a life sentence. The Roman practice of manumission—setting a slave free—provided some slaves not just with yearned for liberty but also with Roman citizenship, social and financial independence, and (in some cases in the empire) high office in Roman administration or even a place in the emperor's bed. We have already met a number of freedmen and women in funerary inscriptions.

Slaves could buy their freedom if they saved up enough money from gifts and tips, or through bribes if in public service, or from even what they could steal; they would then repay the master the original price he paid or something deemed reasonable. Once released, the freedman would sometimes become the ex-owner's client, showing him loyalty and doing a specified number of days work for him each year. They might continue doing the same work they did as a slave, but with the crucial difference that they were now paid, and had to feed and clothe themselves.

Manumission was just as important a weapon in the master's armoury as flogging. The very real threat of flogging was used to encourage hard and conscientious work; manumission was equally important as an indicator of the reward that awaited the slave who worked hard and well.

Some masters freed their slaves out of genuine generosity or because they believed they deserved it and would work better when freed. Cicero's Tiro is a famous example of a talented slave and an appreciative master:

> You have made me very pleased with the news about Tiro, that he doesn't deserve his bad luck and you prefer to have him as a friend rather than a slave. Believe me when I tell you that when I read your letter and his I jumped for joy and I both thank and congratulate you, for if the loyalty of my Statius is a delight to me, how much greater must those same qualities be in Tiro since we can add that he is conversant with literature, is a good conversationalist and is cultured—qualities which have more clout even over those agreeable virtues.
>
> Cicero, *Ad Familiares* 16, 16

Not all freedmen associated with Cicero were so lucky. Pomponia—the widow of Cicero's brother (Quintus Tullius), and sister of Atticus—exhibited shocking sadism in her extreme torture of the freedman who betrayed the Cicero brothers:

> [Antony] handed over Philologus to Pomponia, the wife of Quintus. And she, with the man in her power, besides other dreadful punishments which she inflicted upon him, forced him to cut off his own flesh bit by bit and roast it, and then eat it.
>
> Plutarch, *Cicero* 49, 2
> translation by Bernadotte Perrin in the Loeb edition (1919)

Dionysius of Halicarnassus is concerned about the abuse of the manumission system and the very real danger of introducing men of dubious character with criminal records into the Roman citizenry:

> Most of these slaves obtained their liberty as a gift because of good conduct—the best kind of discharge from their masters; and a few paid a ransom raised by lawful and honest labour. Not so today: things have got so confused and the noble traditions of the Roman empire have become so debased and stained, that some who have made

their fortune by robbery, housebreaking, prostitution and every other base means, purchase their freedom with their ill-gotten gains and immediately become Romans. Others, who have been complicit and accomplices in their masters' poisonings, receive from them their freedom as their reward. ... And others owe their freedom to the whim of their masters and to their vain thirst for popularity. I, at any rate, know of some who have allowed all their slaves to be freed after their death..., some of whom... had committed crimes worthy of a thousand deaths. Most people... condemn the custom, regarding it as not right that a dominant city which aspires to rule the whole world should make such men citizens.

Dionysius of Halicarnassus, Roman Antiquities 4, 24, 4–8
translated adapted from Earnest Cary's in the Loeb Classical Library (1937–1950)

There were, of course, restrictions on what a freedman or woman could or could not do: no public office, no elevation to the equestrian or senatorial orders, and they had to live with the indelible stigma of having been an ex-slave and put up with the prejudice and frequent xenophobia aimed at them by fellow citizens. These, with astonishing similarities to what some immigrants face today in western societies, begrudged them their employment and were uncomfortable with their foreign ways and religions, oblivious to and dismissive of any cultural richness and diversity they brought to Roman society. However, the restrictions died with the freedman: his children were free, just like any other free Roman.

We have already seen how Petronius gives us a satirical stereotype of the freedman made good in the shape of Trimalchio:

He is so fabulously rich that he does not know himself how much he has... Trimalchio has estates wherever the red kite flies, he is a millionaire's millionaire. There is more silver plate in his doorman's cabin than anyone else has in their entire fortune... don't sneer at his fellow freedmen. They're dripping with money. That one you see at the end of the sofa is worth eight hundred thousand today.

Petronius, Satyricon 37, 8; 38, 6–7

When Augustus disbanded the old aristocratic crony and class-based system, which favoured the senatorial and equestrian classes, he effectively threw open the doors of political influence to virtually anyone clever enough or sufficiently sycophantic to catch an emperor's ear, and that included freedmen. Furthermore, the increasing bureaucracy—civil service if you like—caused by a burgeoning empire enabled freedmen to impress, excel in their various departments, and move closer to the seat of power by deploying varying levels of loyalty and obsequiousness. Upward mobility had never been more mobile. Narcissus and Pallas, both closely associated either with the emperors' first ladies Antonia, Messalina, or Agrippina the Younger, are examples of the highly successful imperial freedman who became embroiled in the imperial power politics of the first century CE.

Agrippina allegedly had an affair with Marcus Antonius Pallas (b. *c.* 1 CE), a former slave of Antonia Minor and now one of Claudius' most powerful freedman advisors, in charge of the treasury, *a rationibus*—Chancellor of the Exchequer no less. He was so influential that he convinced Claudius to marry his niece Agrippina Minor and adopt her son Nero. Pallas also initiated the law that allowed a free woman who married a slave to keep her freedom so long as the slave's master approved, a law for which he received much acclaim.[1]

Tiberius Claudius Narcissus (d. 54 CE) was another of Claudius' former slaves and was no less powerful in Claudius' inner circle. He was the emperor's correspondence secretary (*ab epistulis*) and amassed a fortune of about 400 million sesterces. He planned Agrippina's downfall by revealing her affair with Pallas. Narcissus then allied himself with Britannicus, Nero's rival for the succession. Nero had him arrested and compelled him to commit suicide soon after Claudius' death.[2]

Marcus Antonius Felix was Pallas's brother and procurator of Samaria; he took over as procurator of Judaea from 52–58 CE, the first freedman to attain such a senior provincial post.

Back in the late Republic, Terentia married Cicero in 79 BCE when she was about nineteen and he was twenty-seven. Her substantial dowry would have passed to Cicero's family but Terentia seemed to have kept control of her other financial interests, with the help of Philotimus—her guardian and freedman family financial advisor—whom Cicero disliked and distrusted.

We have already met Phlegon of Tralles, the eccentric freedman of Hadrian's. Phlegon's *magnum opus* was the *Olympiads*, a sixteen book history of Rome from 776 BCE to 137 CE. Other publications included *On Long Lived Persons*, a diverting list of Italian and Roman centenarians culled from the censuses; but it is his paradoxographical *Marvels* which records, for example, that highly-thought-of slave woman who in 49 CE gave birth to an ape; a four-headed child which was presented to Nero; and a child born with its head protruding from its shoulder.[3]

Freedmen were frequently to be found in Nero's bed. After Nero had kicked his pregant wife (Sabina Poppaea) to death, he became even more psychotic and unbalanced. He apparently missed Poppaea so much that he detained and debauched a woman who resembled her.

> Later he caused a boy freedman, whom he used to call Sporus, to be castrated, since he, too, resembled Sabina, and he used him in every way like a wife. In due course, though already 'married' to Pythagoras, a freedman, he formally 'married' Sporus, and assigned the boy a regular dowry according to contract; and the Romans as well as others publicly celebrated their wedding.
>
> Dio Cassius 62, 18 translation adapted from Loeb Classical Library edition, (1925)

The wedding to Pythagoras in 64 CE had also been celebrated with full nuptial regalia; Nero wore a bridal veil, and the dowry, marriage bed, and torches were all on public view. Now, Nero had two freedmen in his bed: Pythagoras played the role of husband to him, and Sporus that of wife. The latter was called 'lady', 'queen', and 'mistress'.

> [Nero] became, in the full ceremony of a legitimate marriage, the wife of one of that herd of low-lifes, by the name of Pythagoras. The veil was drawn over the imperial head, witnesses were sent to the scene; the dowry, the nuptial bed, the wedding torches, were all there: everything, which night conceals in the marriage bed, was there for all to see.
>
> Tacitus, *Annals* 15, 37

Much of Nero's depravity took place at the notorious banquets of Tigellinus, where another freedman, Doryphorus, got in on the act:

> [Nero] made up a game, in which, draped with the skin of some wild animal, he was released from a cage and attacked the genitals of men and women who were bound to stakes. When he had satisfied his mad lust, he was buggered by his freedman Doryphorus; for he was married to this man just as he had married Sporus, even going so far as to imitate the cries and wailing of virgins being raped.
>
> Suetonius, *Nero* 29

13

Roman Women in Roman Society

Women, of course, are everywhere in this book. In particular, we have met them in the chapters on family, marriage, and education. Women, in common with slaves and children, were second-class, marginalised citizens, and they were subordinate to men—whether father, husband, brother, cousin, or guardian. They were excluded from public office and the military, were politically anonymous because they had no vote, and they had little or no voice or stake in most aspects of state religion or in political, historical, or philosophical writing that was largely written by men. Women's education was limited by early marriage, the rigours and tedium of domesticity, and serial childbirth. Much of what we know about Roman women we derive through the prism of middle-class, educated, or powerful men. Many of the women we do hear about populate the elite classes; the lower and servile orders are largely absent and anonymous although they do, as we have seen, figure prominently in funerary inscriptions.

There are many books available on the position of and attitude to women in Roman society; this chapter looks specifically at attitudes to women by Roman and early Christian men, thereby isolating the roots of misogyny in subsequent cultures.

Livy sums it all up well in the debate on the repeal of the Oppian Law in 195 BCE, where he seems to encourage women to confine themselves to shopping:

> Women cannot hold magistracies, priesthoods, celebrate triumphs, wear badges of office, enjoy gifts, or booty; elegance, finery, and beautiful clothes are women's emblems, this is what they love and are proud of, this is what our ancestors called women's decoration.
>
> Livy, *Ab Urbe Condita* 34, 7

This sentiment is echoed in the conservative Cato's speech, in which he spits out his disgust at the women who had the temerity to voice a political opinion and attempt to extend the democratic process to include them:

If all of us men had made it our business to assert his rights and authority as the man of the house in relation to his own wife, we should have less trouble with women in general; as it is, our freedom at home is destroyed by the violence of women, and even here in the Forum it is crushed and trampled underfoot; and because we have not controlled them as individuals we are terrified of them when they club together... For myself, I could not hide my embarrassment just now, when I had to make my way to the Forum through a crowd of women... I should have said, 'What kind of behaviour is this, running out into the streets and blocking the roads and speaking to other women's husbands?'... Our ancestors did not allow a woman to conduct even personal business without a guardian to intercede on her behalf; they wanted them to be under the control of fathers, brothers, husbands; we (God help us!) now allow them now to interfere in public affairs, yes, and to visit the Forum...

Livy, Ab Urbe Condita 34, 2, 1; 2, 8–11

According to many Roman men, the role of women in Roman life was quite simply to produce male children to extend the family line and provide a ready supply of administrators, bureaucrats, and soldiers. Marital sex for a women was nothing to do with pleasure; their role was a domestic one: producing babies, rearing children, looking after the household, and working the wool. Soranus, the Greek physician practicing in Rome around 100 CE, neatly sums it up when he remarks 'women are married to bear children and heirs, and not for pleasure and enjoyment' (Soranus, *Gynaecology* 1, 34, 1).

The Stoic philosopher Musonius Rufus strengthened the procreation argument when he reasoned in his first century CE work *Whether Marriage is an Impediment to Doing Philosophy* that the whole point of having genitals, and of marrying, was to have children and ensure the survival of the human race (320).

The archetypal description of a woman's role in life could be represented by this inscription:

Stranger, my message is short. Stand here and read it through. Here is the unlovely tomb of a lovely woman. Her parents called her Claudia. She loved her husband with her whole heart. She had two sons; one she leaves on earth; under the earth she has placed the other. She was charming to talk with, yet proper in her manner. She kept house, she made wool. That's all I've got to say. On your way.

CIL 1, 1211

According to Philo of Alexandria, a Hellenistic Jewish philosopher in Alexandria in Roman Egypt writing soon after Livy, woe betide any woman who acted intemperately—indeed behaved anything like a man—even in defence of a husband being assaulted. He says:

If any woman, out of love, should yield to the feelings which overpower her and rush forth to help him, even then let her not be so bold as to behave like a man, going beyond the nature of a woman; but even while aiding him let her still be a woman. It would be a very terrible thing if a woman should expose herself to insult, by revealing a life full of shamelessness and be liable to great reproaches for her incurable boldness; for should a woman be abusive in the marketplace and give vent to bad language? And if a man uses foul language, should she not cover her ears and run away?

For Philo, things have already gone too far:

Nowadays, some women have reached such a level of shamelessness that, though they are women, use intemperate language and abuse among a crowd of men, and even strike men and insult them, with hands more used to working the loom and spinning than in blows and assaults ... but it is shocking if a woman were to be so bold as to grab the balls of one of the men quarrelling ... so, let the punishment be to chop off of the hand which has touched what it ought not to have touched.

> Philo, *De Specialibus Legibus* 172–175
> Translation by C. D. Yonge: *A Treatise on Those Special Laws Which Are Referrible to Two Commandments in the Decalogue, the Sixth and Seventh, Against Adulterers and All Lewd Persons, and Against Murderers and All Violence,* (London 1854).

Plautus had earlier said that there was nothing more miserable than a woman (*Bacchae* 41). Whether he is simply giving his jaundiced opinion on half the human race, or sympathising with the lot of women, we will never know. A nostalgic Cicero had already famously pronounced that his ancestors, in their wisdom, wanted all women, because of their feebleness of mind, to be in the power of guardians (*Pro Murena* 12, 27). In the second century CE, not that much had changed when Martial asserted that a *matrona* will never be equal to a man while she remains *inferior marito*—under the thumb of her husband (8, 12).

However, the chauvinism and insistence on deference was not confined to the pagans. Origen Adamantius (185–254 CE), the theologian, was one of Christianity's earliest misogynists. He erased the femininity of the 'honest' Tatiana, a third century saint who was martyred in Rome under Alexander Severus, describing her as 'manly'—a woman with such sound virtues must surely owe these qualities to masculinity, not femininity. Tertullian, a third century convert to Christianity, confirmed:

[Women should be] walking about as Eve mourning and repentant, in order that by every garb of penitence she might the more fully expiate that which she derives from Eve,—the ignominy, I mean, of the first sin, and the odium (attaching to her as the cause) of human perdition. 'In pains and in anxieties dost thou bear (children), woman; and toward thine husband (is) thy inclination, and he lords it over thee.'

And do you not know that you are (each) an Eve? ... You are the devil's gateway: you are the unsealer of that (forbidden) tree: you are the first deserter of the divine law: you are she who persuaded him whom the devil was not valiant enough to attack

Tertullian, *On the Apparel of Women* 1, 1, 1–3; 2, 2, 4–6
Translation by the Rev. S. Thelwall

Long before him, Paul (Saul) of Tarsus, a Jew with Roman citizenship who converted to Christianity on the famous road to Damascus in the early first century CE, made the following influential statement:

A woman should learn silently and submissively. I permit no woman to teach or have authority over men. Woman should remain silent. Adam was created first, then Eve ... she became a sinner. However, woman shall be saved by bearing children, if she behaves modestly, in faith, love and sanctity'.

I Timothy 2, 11–15

The die was cast, the damage was done—for many, a woman was officially consigned to subservience to men and to providing sex for child-rearing. Chrysostom, the fourth century CE Archbishop of Constantinople, said it all when looking back on Greeks, Romans, and Christians in his *The Type of Women Who Ought to be Taken as Wives*: 'a woman's role is exclusively to care for her children, her husband, and her home ... God assigned a role to each of the sexes: women look after the home, men take care of public affairs, business and military matters—in other words, everything outside the home' (*PG* 51, 230).

Women and drink did not always make a happy mix—or that is what the men say. Whatever its effect on men, alcohol was seen as a catalyst for sexual infelicities in women. Juvenal probably spoke for many contemporary men when he asked 'What does love care when she is drunk?' (Juvenal 6, 300).

Servius (*Ad Virgil, Aeneid*, 1, 37) says that in the old days, women were forbidden to drink wine, except at a few religious festivals, citing Egnatius Metennius as evidence who whipped his wife to death for drinking from a pitcher; he literally got away with murder when tried by Romulus. According to Valerius Maximus, women in the old days did not drink because it led to depravity: a drunk woman was only one step removed from a fornicating woman (Valerius Maximus 2, 1, 5).

We have already alluded to Pliny the Elder's unfortunate drink-related stories in his chapter on viticulture: the consensus was that women should not drink because that set them on the road to depravity and infidelity.

Aulus Gellius quoted an extract from the speech delivered to the people by Quintus Caecilius Metellus Macedonicus when he was censor, urging them to marry, and support the *Lex Julia* (Augustus' moral legislation) in 17 BCE. According to Livy (*Per.* 59), Augustus read out this speech in the senate in support of his own legislation encouraging marriage and childbearing:

If we could get by without wives, Romans, we would all do without that irritation; but since nature dictates that we can neither live very comfortably with them nor at all without them, we must consider our well-being in the long term rather than our immediate pleasure.

Aulus Gellius, Noctes Atticae 1, 6, 2

We can almost hear Varro sigh with an air of resignation when, in the Menippean Satire that he called *On the Duty of a Husband*, he sagely declared:

A husband must either put a stop to his wife's faults or else he must put up with them. In the first case he makes his wife a more likeable woman, in the second he makes himself a better man.

Aulus Gellius, Noctes Atticae 1, 17, 4

Martial shows us two very different attitudes towards women. The first finds him sniping at the permissiveness of women seduced by the pleasures of Baiae (see also Propertius 1, 11) and critical of modern day sexual *mores*; sex at the seaside, it seems, was not for Martial. This is echoed in his complaint that modern girls are all too decadent and cannot, or will not, say no. In the second, we get a change of view and hear him first celebrating the dignity and devotion of a lady recently widowed and then, in another, extolling the virtues and grace, the matronly qualities of a lady of 'British' descent as discussed in our treatment of the Roman *matrona* above.

Pure, and more than a match for the Sabine women of old, Laevina was straighter than her straight-laced husband. But she succumbed to the Lucrine lake and then to Avernus, and acquired a taste for the waters of Baiae; she fell into the fires of passion, chased after a young man and left her husband. You could say she arrived as a Penelope and left as a Helen.

Martial 1, 62

For a long time now, Satronius Rufus, I have been searching all over Rome for a girl who says no. But no girl says no. As if it was wrong, as if it was rude to say no, as if it wasn't allowed for any girl to say no. Does it mean that no girl is chaste then? No! There are a thousand chaste girls. What then does a chaste girl do? She may give nothing away but she still doesn't say no.

Martial 4, 71

So it was not all misogyny and chauvinism. Pliny reflects an appreciation of the finer qualities exhibited by women in a letter in which he eulogises Macrinus' wife of thirty-nine years who has recently died:

Our Macrinus has suffered a serious wound. He has lost his wife; a lady whose virtues would have made her an outstanding example even in ancient times. He lived with her thirty-nine years without a quarrel, without recrimination. How did she respect her husband and how did she win the highest respect! How she collected and combined so many valuable virtues at evey stage of her life!

Pliny, Epistles 8, 5

Quintilian's eulogy on his wife (*Institutiones Oratoriae* Praefatio 6, 3–6), discussed above, is similarly respectful to a woman who demonstrated every virtue a woman could. Pliny extols the virtues of Calpurnia, and doubts very much whether they will see another of her kind—the perfect model of a wife:

To Calpurnia Hispulla [his wife's aunt]

You are a paragon of dutiful conduct and you love the best and most devoted of brothers as much as he loves you; you love his daughter as if she was your own, and your affection for her is not so much as an aunt but more as the father she lost. It will no doubt be a great joy to you to know that she, [Fannia], has turned out worthy of her father, worthy of you and worthy of her grandfather. She is very clever, very prudent, and her love for me is a mark of her chastity. You can add to these qualities her study of literature which has been developed by her devotion to me. She has all my books, reads them and even learns them by heart. She is very concerned when she sees me going to court to plead and is glad when it's all over! She sends men to report to her the outcome, the applause I get and the judgement. And when I give a recital she sits nearby hidden behind a curtain and listens avidly to the praise I get. She has even set my verses to music and sings them accompanied with a lyre, taught not by a musician but by love—the best teacher.

All of these things give me great hope that our happiness will grow by the day and will last for ever. She loves me not for my age or my appearance (which will gradually grow old and die) but for my glory. Nothing else would be worthy of a woman educated in your hands, steeped in your ideas and who had seen nothing but purity and integrity in your company; she has grown up to love me on your recommendation. You respected my mother as if she were a daughter and you have praised and guided me since my childhood; you always did predict that I would turn out like this in my wife's eyes. We compete in our thanks to you—I because you have given her to me, she because you have given me to her as if you chose us for each other. Farewell.

Pliny, Epistles 4, 19

The epigram here portrays a prostitute sympathetically while his compassion shines through with considerable pathos, and sympathy too for the bereaved Nigrina, whom we have already met:

A girl whose reputation was not the best, the sort who sits in the middle of the Subura, was being sold off by Gellianus the auctioneer. For a while the bidding was low; he wanted to prove to everyone that she was clean, so he sidled up close to her. Although she motioned to him to stop he kissed her twice, three times, four times. You ask what he gained by kissing her? Nothing. Except that a punter who was offering six hundred sesterces pulled out of the bidding.

Martial, Epigrams 6, 66

14

The Games, Circus, Theatre, and Baths

Venari, lavari, ludere, ridere, hoc est vivere!
Hunting, bathing, playing, laughing—that's living!
CIL 8, 1793

The games and other forms of public entertainment were integral to the Roman way of life and, if Juvenal is to be believed, as crucial as the provision of bread to the populace: it was just as important for the authorities to entertain as well as feed the masses. The origin of the games (*ludi*) lies in the Roman system of holidays; these were originally based around religious festivals mainly concerned with getting on the right side of gods who were responsible for life-changing events such as good harvests, good weather, and livestock fertility. Over time, the religious and agricultural elements receded but the games endured, augmented by celebrations in honour of military victories and significant dates in the life of the current, and past, emperors.

The pieces here demonstrate the exoticism and excitement of the games: bursting fruits, wild and strange beasts from the east and south, exotic dancers, sea battles, gladiators, athletics contests, chariot races, public torture, mutilation, and death were all on show for a largely appreciative public that was baying for blood.

To some, though, the whole thing was distasteful: Seneca gives us a more civilised view and may well speak for the more educated and compassionate Roman, dwelling on the damaging effects of such gratuitous violence:

I went to the games one mid-day hoping for a little wit and humour there. I was bitterly disappointed. It was really just butchery. The morning's show was merciful compared to the afternoon when men were thrown to lions and to bears...'Kill him! flog him! burn him alive' went up the cry: 'Why is he such a coward? Why won't he rush on the steel? Why does he fall so feebly? Why won't he die willingly?' Unhappy I certainly am, what have I done that I deserve to look on such a scene as this? Do not, my Lucilius, go to the games, I beg you. Either you will be corrupted by the masses, or, if you show disgust, be hated by them. So stay well away.

Seneca, *Epistles* 7, 3–5
translation adapted from William Stearns Davis, ed., *Readings in Ancient History: Illustrative Extracts from the Sources, Vol. II: Rome and the West,* (Boston 1912–13)

The principal forms of public entertainment were chariot races, theatre, wild animal hunts, wild animal fights, and later, gladiatorial contests. Mock sea battles were also staged:

It was Augustus' doing to organise these naval battles and to roughen up the seas with the sound of naval war trumpets. Such a small part of Caesar's work though. Thetis and Galatea saw strange beasts in the sea; Triton saw in the sea spray fervent chariots and thought that his master's, Neptune's, horses had fled; and Nereus arranged fierce battles for the savage ships and trembled as he paddled in the flowing waters. Whatever we see in the Circus and the amphitheatre—these treasures, Caesar, these waves are down to you. Don't mention the Fucine lake and the stagnant pools of cruel Nero: future ages will know only about your sea battle.

Martial, *De Spectaculis* 28

Suetonius gives us vivid descriptions of lavish spectacles at *Caesar* 10 and *Nero* 11–12, the latter apparently even featuring bestiality and fatal flying:

He also put on a naval battle in salt water with sea monsters swimming about in it, as well as Pyrrhic dances by some Greek youths, to whom he handed certificates of Roman citizenship at the close of his performance. The Pyrrhic dances represented various scenes: in one a bull mounted Pasiphae, who was concealed in a wooden image of a heifer—or at least many of the spectators thought so. Icarus at his very first attempt [to fly] fell close by the imperial couch and spattered the emperor with his blood.

Suetonius, *Nero* 12, 1–2
translation adapted from *The Lives of the Twelve Caesars*
by C. Suetonius Tranquillus, Loeb Classical Library, 1914

The Circus Maximus was the main venue for chariot racing with its 1,968-foot track and 250,000 capacity; we know that for Ovid this was the place to pick up a woman (*Ars Amatoria* 312); for a thrilling commentary on a chariot race go no further than Sidonius Apollinarius writing in the fifth century CE:

Brightly gleam the colours, white and blue, green and red, your several
badges. Servants' hands hold mouth and reins and

with knotted cords force the twisted manes to hide
themselves, and all the while they incite the steeds,
eagerly cheering them with encouraging pats and in-
stilling a rapturous frenzy. There behind the barriers
chafe those beasts, pressing against the fastenings,
while a vapoury blast comes forth between the wooden
bars and even before the race the field they have
not yet entered is filled with their panting breath.
They push, they bustle, they drag, they struggle,
they rage, they jump, they fear and are feared;
never are their feet still, but restlessly they lash the
hardened timber. At last the herald with loud blare of trumpet calls
forth the impatient teams and launches the fleet chariots into the field...
The ground gives way under the wheels and the air
is smirched with the dust that rises in their track.
The drivers, while they held the reins, ply the lash;
now they stretch forward over the chariots with
stooping breasts, and so they sweep along, striking
the horses' withers... everywhere the sweat of drivers and flying
steeds falls in drops on to the field... Thus they go once
round, then a second time; thus goes the third lap,
thus the fourth... Now the return half of the sixth course
was completed and the crowd was already clamouring
for the award of the prizes... Then the enemy in reckless
haste overtook you and, fondly thinking that the
first man had already gone ahead, shamelessly
made for your wheel with a sidelong dash. His
horses were brought down, a multitude of intruding
legs entered the wheels, and the twelve spokes were
crowded, until a crackle came from those crammed
spaces and the revolving rim shattered the entangled
feet; then he, a fifth victim, flung from his chariot,
which fell upon him, caused a mountain of manifold
havoc, and blood disfigured his prostrate brow.

Sidonius Apollinaris, Poems 23, 323–424
translation from *Poems and Letters* by W.B. Anderson, Loeb Classical Library 1936

Like Seneca, the bookish Pliny just didn't get the excitement:

To Calvisius

   I have spent these last few days reading and writing, with the most pleasing peace imaginable. You will ask, 'How that can possibly be in the middle of Rome?'

It was the time of celebrating the Circensian games: an entertainment for which I have not the least taste. They have no novelty, no variety to recommend them, nothing, in short, one would wish to see twice. It surprises me even more that so many thousand people should be possessed with the childish passion of desiring so often to see a pack of horses gallop, and men standing up in their chariots. If, indeed, it were the swiftness of the horses, or the skill of the men that attracted them, there might be some pretence of reason for it. But it is the dress, [the colours of the factions], they like.

Pliny, *Epistles* 9, 6

Cicero, too, had had his doubts (*Ad Familiares* 7, 1, 1–3).

Despite this, the popularity of public entertainment continued unabated among the masses. In 100 BCE, there were sixty-eight days given over to festivals without games and fifty-seven days with games in six separate celebrations; by the fourth century CE, there were 177 days of actual games in one year. Gladiatorial events really took off in the early days of the empire with the first purpose-built venue built in Rome in 29 BCE. In 80 CE, when the Flavian Amphitheatre opened, 9,000 animals were slaughtered over 100 days; Trajan's games in 108 CE saw 10,000 gladiators in combat of whom 1,100 died. In *History* 17, Fronto emphasizes the political and social importance of such entertainments, echoing Juvenal's *panem et circenses* (10, 78–81), a satire which gives us graphic accounts of gladiator fights, chariot races and athletic contests.

The amphitheatres around the Roman world and the spectacular games held within were associated with sex on a number of levels. First, as we have just seen, Ovid recommends the games as the best place to pick up a sophisticated lady; the place is crawling with them. Valeria 'accidentally' met with Sulla there, and later married him. However, unless you were a Vestal Virgin or a member of the imperial family, you were subjected to a pecking order when it came to seating in the amphitheatre or the theatre; women, along with slaves and foreigners, found themselves stuck high up at the back, while men enjoyed seats at the front allocated according to their rank. Also, some women were physically attracted to some of the bronzed and muscular gladiators who performed in the arenas, occasionally as celebrities in their own right. By the same token, some men would have found the bouts fought by *gladiatrices*, women gladiators, erotic and sexually exciting.

This chimes with Ovid's assertion that some elite women were partial to 'a bit of rough', and with Petronius in his *Satyricon* who has Chrysis describe how some well to do women burn with desire for men of the lower orders:

There are some women, you see, whose lust is triggered only by the sight of slaves or messenger boys with their tunics belted right up high. Gladiators in the arena, a mule driver covered with dust, an actor in the shameful exposure of this performance — that's what it takes to get some females heated up. My mistress is one of this tribe:

her taste goes fourteen rows back from the reserved seats and looks for a lover at the fringes of the mob.

Petronius, Satyricon 126

Some women even going so far as to lick the wounds of the flogged. Juvenal includes this distasteful libido for gladiators in his tirade against women.[1] Martial wrote of Hermes, the famous gladiator, 'Hermes spells riches for the ticket touts'. Some women bribed guards to allow them access to the gladiator billets. Elagabalus 'married' his blond haired chariot driver, Hierocles.

The gladiator, although usually a slave and on the lowest level of Roman society, was something of a fascinating paradox with magical qualities. His blood was used as a remedy for impotence, an aphrodisiac, and any traditional bride would have her hair parted by a spear to ensure a fertile married life—ideally one which had been dipped in the blood of a defeated and dead gladiator. Medical authorities had it that drinking a gladiator's blood or eating his liver cured epileptics. Gladiators, apparently, were the only males who were given vasectomies.

Ironically, given that they were considered the equivalent of 20th century *untermenschen*, some gladiators won admiration for their bravery, and for their willingness to die—true Roman qualities, *Romanitas* indeed, and indicative of the *virtus* to which every man, every Roman worth his salt, aspired to. Despite their lowly social station, some became celebrities and were depicted in mosaics and sculptures, on lamps and tombstones: graffiti was scrawled by them and about them: 'Celadus the Thracian, thrice victor and thrice crowned, the young girls' heart-throb' (*CIL* 4, 434) and 'Crescens the Netter of young girls by night' (*CIL* 4, 353).

Gladiators, then, were all the rage. But, even in victory, a gladiator remained what he was: *infamis* and a slave, unable to escape his classification alongside criminals, whores, actors, dancers and similar so-called dregs. The paradox and irony was not lost on Tertullian:

> Men surrender them their souls, and women their bodies, too…On one and the same account, [men] glorify them and degrade and diminish them—indeed, they openly condemn them to ignominy and the loss of civil rights, excluding them from the senate house and rostrum, the senatorial and equestrian orders, and all other honors or distinctions of any type. The perversity of it! Yet, they love whom they punish; they belittle whom they esteem; the art they glorify, the artist they debase. What judgment is this: on account of that for which he is vilified, he is deemed worthy of merit!

Tertullian, De Spectaculis 22–23

In the second century CE, Calpurnius Flaccus ranked gladiators below slaves: 'There is no meaner condition among the people than that of the gladiator.'[2]

Despite it all, they still won the admiration and adulation of some women in the crowds: the gladiator was what the Roman lady yearned for, what her husband, son, and brother surely envied. The elite gladiator exuded virility: archaeological evidence for the sexualisation of gladiators has been found in the shape of a multitude of objects depicting phalluses: a phallus-shaped terracotta gladiatorial helmet; a stone relief from Beneventum, showing a heavily armed gladiator in combat with a huge penis. The very word *gladius*, meaning sword, carries unmistakeable sexual connotations and is sometimes slang for penis. The famous bronze figurine from Pompeii shows a menacing gladiator using his sword to fend off a dog-like beast that is growing out of his huge erect penis. Five bells (*tintinnabula*) are suspended from his body: every Roman's perfect doorbell.

Juvenal spits out this sorry tale of family desertion as we meet Sergius and Eppia again:

> Eppia, the senator's wife, [who] ran off with a gladiator … And what were the youthful charms which captivated Eppia? What did she see in him to allow herself to be called 'a she-Gladiator'? … a wounded arm promised a military discharge, and his face was covered in deformities: a scar caused by his helmet, a huge lump on his nose, a nasty humour always dribbling from his eye. But then he was a gladiator!
>
> It is this that transforms these fellows into Hyacinths! It was this that she preferred to children and to country, to sister and to husband. What these women love is the sword: had this same Sergius received his discharge, he would have been no better than a Veiento'.
>
> Juvenal 6, 82–103

Faustina, the wife of Marcus Aurelius, was smitten by a gladiator and finally confessed her passion to her husband. On advice from the Chaldean magicians, the gladiator in question was executed and Faustina was made to bathe in his blood. She then had to have sex with her husband while still covered in the blood—all thoughts of the gladiator apparently disappeared.[3]

We have seen how excavations in the armoury of the Pompeii gladiatorial barracks unearthed eighteen skeletons and the bones of a woman wearing expensive jewellery. While the performing arts were held in high regard by the Romans *per se*, those who performed them—dancers, actors, musicians and gladiators—were despised. Dio is disgusted by members of the elite classes getting up and performing on stage and in the amphitheatre.[4] Women gladiators shared their particular stage with an elephant walking on a tightrope at games arranged by Nero in honour of his mother, Agripinna the Younger, whom he had recently murdered. Tacitus is just as outraged as Dio: 'Many ladies of distinction, however, and senators, disgraced themselves by appearing in the amphitheatre' (Tacitus, *Annals*, 15, 32).

The fact that these women were rich women and were not doing it for the money suggests that they did it for the adrenalin, the sexual high. Dio tells of another spectacle when Nero, entertaining king Tiridates I of Armenia, gave a gladiatorial show featuring Ethiopian men, women, and children.[5] Petronius describes a woman who fought from a chariot just like the male *Essedari*, possibly armed with bow and arrow.[6]

Women gladiators were just one of many variations on a theme used to keep the baying crowds entertained. In the hundred-day games put on by Titus they competed with a battle between cranes and one between four elephants—just a handful of the nine thousand beasts slaughtered in one single day, 'and women took part in despatching them'.[7] They must surely have participated in Trajan's games in in CE 108 which lasted 123 days and in which 'eleven thousand or so animals both wild and tame were killed and ten thousand gladiators fought'. Martial, in his *De Spectaculis*, describes women battling in the arena, one dressed as Venus herself. Another overcomes a lion: 'Caesar, we now have seen such things done by women's courage'.[8] Domitian put on 'hunts of wild beasts, gladiatorial shows at night by the light of torches, and not only combats between men but between women as well' and, Dio adds, 'sometimes he would pit dwarfs and women against each other'.[9] Statius sums it all up: 'Women untrained to the *rudis* take their stand, daring, how recklessly, virile battles!'[10] The *rudis* was the wooden sword given to a gladiator when he was freed after a series of conspicuous victories.

Juvenal sardonically describes 'Mevia', hunting wild boars in the arena 'holding her spear, breasts exposed'.[11] Elsewhere, he was scathing:

> How shameful is a woman wearing a helmet, who shuns femininity and loves brute force ... If a sale is held of your wife's effects, how proud you will be of her belt and arm-pads and plumes, and her half-length left-leg shin-guard! Or, if instead, she prefers a different form of combat how pleased you'll be when the girl you love sells off her greaves! ... Hear her grunt while she practises thrusts from the trainer, wilting under the weight of the helmet.
>
> Juvenal, *Satires* 6, 252f

Nicolaus of Damascus mentions women gladiators.[12] Nero dealt with annoying senators by threatening to have their wives thrown into the arena to do combat.

In 19 CE, a *senatus consultum* from Larinum stated that elite women cannot appear on the stage or become gladiators. In 11 CE an attempt to ban senators and women performing in amphitheatres and on the stage was unsuccessful.[13] The law decreed that 'no female of free birth of less than twenty years of age and for no male of free birth of less than twenty-five years of age to pledge himself as a gladiator or hire out his services'.

Nearly 200 years later in 200 CE, Septimius Severus barred any female from fighting in the arena, μονομαχεῖν: to fight as a gladiator. Dio reports that, 'women took part, vying with one another most fiercely, with the result that jokes were made about other very distinguished women as well. Therefore, it was henceforth forbidden for any freeborn woman, no matter what her origin, to fight in single combat'.[14] This came about after Severus' visit to the Antiochene Olympic Games where he would have seen traditional Greek female athletics. His attempt to impress the mob in Rome with a similar extravaganza was met with derision from the crowds in the Colisseum.

A second century CE marble relief from Halicarnassus (modern Bodrum) in Turkey (now in the British Museum) shows two women, Amazon and Achillia, fighting as gladiators. They are heavily armed, like a *secutor*, (a chaser of the *retiarius*—net man) with greaves; the right arm is protected and carrying a large oblong shield; their hair is cropped in the style of a slave and their breasts are bare. Such a spectacle must have been important for it to commemorated in this way. An epigraph from Ostia praises Hostilianus as the first to 'arm women' (*mulieres*) in the history of the local games.[15]

In September 2000, the Museum of London announced that they had discovered the grave of a female gladiator from the first century CE—the first ever to be found. A piece of red pottery has been discovered with the inscription *VERECVNDA LVDIA LVCIUS GLADIATOR*, 'Verecunda the woman gladiator, Lucius the gladiator'.

It seems likely that female gladiators came to the arena by a number of different routes. Some would have been slaves coerced by their masters—the *lanistae*; others would have volunteered and received the requisite training in the gladiator schools; others still may have just been thrown in there as a punishment—*damnati ad gladium* (damned to the sword). Women would not have faced men; rather, as we have seen, they would fight from chariots with the bows and arrows characteristic of the Amazons (*mulierem essedariam*) Diana and Atalanta; alternatively, they may well have been pitched against dwarfs.

The female gladiator with her breasts revealed would have an erotic impact on the male members of the audience, heightened by the arousing appearance of a woman wealding a weapon—something a typical Roman woman obviously never did, except for a handful of military exceptions or when a woman stabbed a man in a domestic setting. Women trained in combat were usually foreign women from foreign lands—this exotic mystique must have stimulated further the sexual overtones of the spectacle and the libido of the male spectators. Ovid, we know, says that the sight of a female leg, rarely seen outside the home, was exciting; the half-naked, weapon-wielding female gladiator with breasts exposed would have been more exciting still.[16]

Here is Statius' celebration of the spectacle given by Domitian for the Saturnalia:

The Kalends of December
    Father Phoebus, over-serious Pallas and holiday-time muses—get lost! We will call you back on 1 January. But Saturn, slip your shackles and come here, and December, well sloshed and joking Jester and shameless Wit—all of you come here while I tell of good old Caesar's happy holiday and the drunken feast that ensued.
    It was barely dawn when fruit and nuts rained down from the ropes—the prevailing south easterly was spreading the dew: noble fruit from Pontic nut groves or dates from the fertile fields of Idume, or the plums which pious Damascus grows on its branches, figs which bibulous Caunus ripens, all fall freely like great big booty.[17, 18] Biscuits and soft pastries; apples and pears from Ameria—masses of them, their ripeness just right, and laurel cake and bursting nut-shaped dates—all fell down from palm trees you couldn't see. The downpours with which stormy Hyades rushes

over the earth and soaking Pleiades—neither were as severe as this 'winter weather' hailing down on the Latin people from a storm free sky. Jupiter can lead his storm clouds over the world and threaten the wide open fields with floods all he wants while our own Jove brings on these showers.

Look, more people are coming through the benches—a marvellous sight—they're all very well turned out and are as many as the people already sitting down in there. Some carry bread baskets and white napkins and even more sumptuous fare; others lavish languishing wine, you'd think they were as many as the servants of Ida! You are feeding, blessed Emperor, so many people; the circle of the great and good and, at the same time, the people who wear the toga—so let proud Annona not know about this day.[19] Come now Ancient of Days and compare our age more with the Golden Age of antique Jove: the wine didn't flow as freely then and the harvest didn't last the lazy year. One table feeds every rank: little ones, women, the common people, knights, senators: liberty has relaxed the usual reverence. Indeed, even you Emperor (what god could have so much time or promise as much you) even you come and share our banquet with us. Now Everyman, needy and fortunate alike, glories in the fact that he is the guest of the Emperor. Amid such clamour and unaccustomed luxuries the pleasure of the spectacle flew by. Women who have no inexperience in and who knew nothing about sword-craft got up and without embarrassment took on men's battles. You'd think that this was Thermodon's troops seething at Tanais or savage Phasis.[20] A brave company of dwarfs comes on: Nature finished off creating them too soon and left them short and all bound up in a knotty lump. They take and dish out wounds in close combat and threaten to kill—what hands they have! Father Mars and bloody Bravery have a laugh at this and cranes waiting to fall on scattered booty are amazed by such ferocious fighters.

Now night's shadows draw in. What a tumult accompanies this distribution of largesse! Cheap girls come in now; you can see everything and anything fine and impressively skilful which the theatre audiences like. Here a crowd of big breasted Lydian girls clap their hands, there the tinkling symbols of Gades, there columns of Syrian soldiers raise a din, ordinary theatre goers and those who exchange common sulphur for powdered glass.[21]

In among all of this great flocks of birds all of a sudden swoop down from the sky: birds from the sacred Nile and freezing Phasis, birds which the Numidians pick off in the dripping south.[22, 23] There aren't enough people to grab them all but they rejoice in filling the folds of their togas with their new booty. Voices, too many to count, are raised to the stars singing the praises of the Emperor's Saturnalia and they come to acclaim their Dominus with devoted affection. It had just got dark when a fireball fell glowing into the middle of the arena through the dark shadows brighter even than the starlight of the Gnosian coronet. The heavens were lit up like fire driving away the darkness of the night. Seeing this, lazy Quiet fled, and inert Sleep left for other cities. Who can sing of this spectacle, the endless fun, the partying, the free food, the floods of wine? Now that I am wasted by you Baccus, I drag myself drunk to sleep at last.

For how many years from now will this day be remembered for? This holy day will never die out. For as long as the hills of Latium and old father Tiber remain, while your Rome still stands with the Capitol you have given back to the world, it will endure.

Statius, *Silvae* 1, 6

Martial marvels at the sight of a rhinoceros:

The trainers were aggravating a rhinoceros and they were worried because it was taking so long for the mighty beast to get angry; they all despaired for the battle and the war that was on the programme. But in the end the fury they had seen before returned. The rhino tossed a heavy bear with his twin horns just as a bull throws stuffed dummies into the air, just like young Carpophorus lets loose the Noric hunting spears with sure aim from his strong right hand. The rhino, its neck swivelling, hurls a pair of cows; overcomes a fierce oxen and a bison; a lion flees from him and runs straight onto the spears. Go now you mob and heckle any long delays!

Martial, *De Spectaculis* 22

Pliny, obsequiously, praises a gladiator show, although it did not go entirely to plan:

To Valerius Maximus

Well done for putting on that gladiator show for the people of Verona; for a while now they have loved, esteemed and honoured you. Your dearly beloved and excellent wife came from Verona and it is in her memory that you must devote some civic work or other: this spectacle is especially fitting as a funeral tribute. Besides, so many people have asked for it, that to refuse would have looked not so much single-minded but hard-hearted. You have come out of this admirably by producing a show with such facility, generosity and magnanimity.

I only wish that the African panthers which you had bought in such numbers had featured on the appointed day; but they didn't show because they were detained by a storm—you, however, deserve credit and it was not your fault that you couldn't display them. Farewell.

Pliny, *Epistles* 6, 34

The absence of animals, however, was a minor inconvenience. Seneca reminds us of two rather more pressing incidents when the participants are so determined to escape the dreadful fate which awaits them that they commit suicide in the most horrible of ways; there is little glory or adulation here:

For example, not long ago in a training-school for wild-beast gladiators a German, who was getting ready for the morning display withdrew in order to relieve himself,—the only thing which he was allowed to do in private and without the presence of a guard. While so engaged, he grabbed a stick of wood with a sponge fixed on the end which was used for cleaning excrement. He stuffed it, just as it was, down his throat blocking his windpipe, and choked to death…

a gladiator who had been sent out to the morning exhibition was being carried in a cart along with the other prisoners. He was nodding as if he were fast asleep and then he let his head fall over the side far enough so that it was caught in the spokes of the cartwheel; he kept his body there long enough to break his neck as the wheel went round.

Seneca, *Epistles* 70, 19–21, 23
translation adapted from Lucius Annaeus Seneca, *Moral Epistles*. Translated by
Richard M. Gummere. The Loeb Classical Library 1917–25. Volume II.

The Campus Martius

The geographer Strabo gives us his version of a travel brochure describing the Campus Martius and the leisure activities to be enjoyed there:

Indeed, the size of the Campus is remarkable, since it can accomodate with ease, not just the chariot-races and all other equestrian exercise, but also all those crowds of people who take exercise by playing ball games, hoop-trundling, and wrestling. The works of art dotted around the Campus Martius, and the ground, covered with grass throughout the year, and the tops of those hills above the river extending as far as its banks—when you look at all these they take on the appearance of a painted stage set which you can barely take your eyes off.

Strabo, Geographia 5, 3, 8
translation adapted from *The Geography of Strabo* Vol. II
Loeb Classical Library edition, 1923

The Theatre

It is difficult to assess just how far the plays of Plautus and Terence reflect actual Roman experience since these plays are coloured by Greek *mores,* as portrayed in Menander and the many other playwrights of the New and Middle Comedy. However, if Plautus or Terence were going to raise a laugh from the audience, then they would surely have imbued their characters with traits and mannerisms that were recognisable to their audiences as being part of their own everyday experience; their plots would reflect Roman life to some degree and their characters would be recognisable as Romans. In short, the Roman playwrights would have to bring their Greek originals home to the Romans if they were to be successful. The prologue to the *Poenulus* is a case in point with Plautus playing to a strictly Roman audience; here he admonishes the *matronae* in the audience for their irritating laughter, and then requests that the wet nurses do not bring in crying babies:

> Let nurses keep children, babies, at home, and don't let anyone bring them to see the play lest both the nurses themselves get thirsty [for booze] and the children die of hunger. Don't let them squeal about here, in their hungry fits, just like kids. Let the *matronae* watch the play in silence, and laugh in silence, and don't let them scream here with their shrill voices; let them keep their gossip for home, so as not annoy their husbands here as well as at home.
>
> Plautus, *Poenulus* 32–35, 28–31
> translation adapted from *The Comedies of Plautus* by Henry Thomas Riley.
> (London 1912)

Terence tells us more about the playwright's problems with noise and disruptions from the audience in a second attempt to present his *Hecyra* (*Mother-in-Law*):

> Second Prologue
> I again present the *Hecyra*, which I have never been allowed to act before you in silence; so many calamities have overwhelmed it…the first time when I began to act this play, the boastings of boxers, the expectation of a tightrope walker, along with their noisy followers, the shrieking of women—all this caused me to leave the stage prematurely… I brought it on again: the first Act went down well but then a rumour spread that gladiators were about to go on—the crowd flocked to them in a clamorous tumult, fighting for their places, and I had to leave the stage. Now there is no confusion: there is attention and silence—this is a chance to act my play.
>
> Terence, *Hecyra* 28f

These comedies are particularly important because they shed light on aspects of non-elite Roman family life; unlike much of the rest of the literary evidence they describe domestic situations in the lower classes.

The Baths

The baths and bathing have cropped up already throughout many of the sections in the book. Like other forms of public entertainment they were an essential facet of Roman life for men, women and children, rich and poor, slaves and free. Baths were as ubiquitous as temples and bars. Socialising in the baths was as routine as worshipping or drinking in those bars.

Seneca the Younger writes to Lucilius describing life in an apartment above a public baths; in doing so, he gives us a fascinating glimpse into what went on in these places:

Imagine what a cacophany reverberates in my ears! I have lodgings right over a bathing establishment. So picture the assortment of sounds, which are so loud as to make me hate my very powers of hearing! When your strongman, for example, is exercising himself by wielding lead weights, when he is working hard, or else pretends to be working hard, I can hear him grunt, and whenever he exhales his imprisoned breath, I can hear him panting in wheezy and hissing tones. Or perhaps I notice some lazy fellow, content with a cheap rubdown, and hear the crack of the pummeling hand on his shoulder, varying in sound according as the hand is laid on flat or hollow. Then, perhaps, a professional comes along, shouting out the score; that's it! Add to this the arrest of the odd drunk or pickpocket, the din of the man who always likes to sing out loud in the bath, or the keen men who plunge into the swimming pool splashing loudly. Besides all of these whose voices are at least normal, imagine the hair-plucker with his penetrating, shrill voice,—for purposes of self-advertising,— continually giving it vent and never holding his tongue except when he is plucking armpits and making his victim yell instead. Then the cakeseller with his different cries, the sausageman, the confectioner, and all the vendors of food hawking their wares, each with his own individual cry.

Seneca the Younger, *Letters* 56, 1, 2
translation adapted from Lucius Annaeus Seneca. Moral Epistles. Translated by
Richard M. Gummere; The Loeb Classical Library. 1917–25. Volume I.

15

Religion

State religion was, as the name suggests, state controlled and its rites and functions were performed by priests who were state officials. The proper and dutiful observance of state religion was believed to be necessary for the preservation and prosperity of the Roman state. Certainly, with hindsight, the diligence afforded religious practice was considered a major factor in Rome's past military successes. The Roman only had to look back on the centuries of military and political victories and domination to be assured that his or her state religion was a viable and effective adjunct of the machinery of the state. Matters of state were inextricably bound up in religion and vice versa. A politician and a priest had the same objectives—to look after the state: Julius Caesar, for example was both consul and Pontifex Maximus in the same year, 63 BCE. By the same logic, the *paterfamilias* played the same role in looking after his family as the state priests did for the local community; the latter was an extension of the former. The many temples and festivals around the Roman world were state funded.

State religion was built around and based on a large and incestuous pantheon, where the superhuman gods and goddesses governed and controlled everything that happened to Romans in the Roman world, in their current life and in the next. For example, all aspects of farming, conception, weather, travel, death, and warfare were amply represented by deities and spirits—male and female—in that pantheon.

Augustine describes how wedding night sex is meticulously controlled by the gods down to the very last detail.[1] Virginiensis, or Cinxia, is there to loosen the bride's girdle (*cingulum*), along with Subigus who yields the bride to the groom; Prema, goddess of the sex act itself, attends as does Inuus or Pertunda who helps with penetration; Venus provides the passion and Priapus the erection. Juno is the goddess for women's sexual function and has a multifunctional role in marriage: as Iterduca, she is specifically responsible for leading the bride to the groom's house and, as Unxia, oversees the annointing of the bride; she is a bridesmaid, as Pronuba, and performs a midwifery role as Lucina. Janus opens the way for the semen to enter, leading, hopefully, to conception, while Saturn looks after the semen. Consevius is the god of insemination; Liber Pater enables the man to ejaculate, Libera does likewise for the woman. Mena (Juno) produces menstruation, which in the pregnant mother is diverted to feed the foetus. Fluonia is Juno, who keeps the nourishing blood in the womb. Vitumnus gives the foetus life; Sentinus or Sentia develop cognitive faculties in the newborn.[2]

However, it was not just the minutiae of human activity that were controlled by the gods and goddesses, each with a very specific sphere of activity and responsibility: animism ensured that deities and spirits looked after every stream, river, forest, mountain, and meadow. Every aspect of the home had its spirit too: the *lares* were there in the hearth, the cupboards, and the rooms—the *lares* also had religious jurisdiction in the local community—*lares compitales*—and in the wider city—*lares publici*. Seneca puts it all beautifully into words:

> If ever you have come upon a grove that is full of ancient trees which have grown to an unusual height, shutting out a view of the sky by a veil of intertwining branches, then the loftiness of the forest, the seclusion of the spot, and your wonder at the thick unbroken shade in the midst of the open spaces, will convince you of the presence of a deity. Or if a cave, made by the deep crumbling of the rocks, holds up a mountain on its arch, a place not built with hands but hollowed out into such spaciousness by natural causes, your soul will be deeply moved by a certain intimation of the existence of a God. We worship the sources of mighty rivers; we erect altars at places where great streams burst suddenly from hidden sources; we adore springs of hot water as divine, and consecrate certain pools because of their dark waters or their immeasurable depth.
>
> Seneca the Younger, Letters 41, 3
translation adapted from Moral Epistles by Richard M. Gummere,
Loeb Classical Library 1917–25 Volume I. 2

Cato shows how even cutting back a grove of trees or ploughing the land followed a meticulous religious procedure:

> The following is the Roman formula to be observed in thinning a grove: a pig is to be sacrificed, and the following prayer uttered: 'Whether thou be god or goddess to whom this grove is dedicated, as it is thy right to receive a sacrifice of a pig for the thinning of this sacred grove, and to this intent, whether I or one at my bidding do it, may it be rightly done. To this end, in offering this pig to thee I humbly beg that thou will be gracious and merciful to me, to my house and household, and to my children. Will you deign to receive this pig which I offer thee to this end.'
>
> If you wish to till the ground, offer a second sacrifice in the same way, with the addition of the words: 'for the sake of doing this work.' So long as the work continues, the ritual must be performed in some part of the land every day; and if you miss a day, or if public or domestic feast days intervene, a new offering must be made... If favourable omens are not obtained in response to all, speak thus: 'Father Mars, if anything has not pleased you in the offering of those sucklings, I make atonement with these victims.' If there is doubt about one or two, use these words: 'Father Mars,

inasmuch as you were not pleased by the offering of that pig, I make atonement with this pig.'

Cato the Elder, *On Agriculture* 139–41
translation adapted from *De Agricultura*
by Cato the Elder, Loeb Classical Library, 1934

Martial, often cynical and sardonic, is genuinely sad to leave behind his deities when he sells his farm. This illustrates their importance in rural communities where the old agriculture-based religion prevailed much longer than in the sophisticated and cosmopolitan cities. Here is what he says to Marrus, his buyer:

To you, Marrus, lover of the quiet life… to you I entrust these twin pine trees, the centre-piece of a rustic grove, these holm oaks sacred to the Fauns, and these altars dedicated to Jupiter and shaggy Silvanus, erected by my half-taught manager—altars which the blood of lamb or kid has often stained. I entrust Diana to you too, the virgin goddess of this sacred temple; to Mars who rules my year, his chaste sister's guest; and the laurel grove of gentle Flora, into which she fled taking refuge when chased by Priapus. Whenever you propitiate these kindly divinities of my little property, whether with blood or with incense, you must remember to say to them, 'Behold, the right hand of your absent votary, wherever he may be, unites with mine in offering this sacrifice. Imagine him to be here, and grant to each of us whatever we pray for.'

Martial 10, 92

Where the Romans did not have a god for a particular event or place they simply imported and adopted one from the Etruscans or Greeks, as in the case of Aesculapius, the Greek god of medicine, during an outbreak of plague around 269 BCE. The story is recorded in the anonymous *De Viris Illustribus*, 22.

Warfare was conducted under the influence of the gods; whether or not to join battle or declare war should always have been subject to the gods' bidding, while the taking of a besieged city saw the Romans persuading the local divinities to defect according to an ancient ritual (Macrobius, *Saturnalia* 3, 9, 7, 8).

Everyone had recourse and access to the divinities; they were there for all to see, all around—painted on walls, embodied in statuary, stamped on their coins, laid out in mosaics on the floor. If they could read, the Roman could learn about them from, for example, Homer's *Odyssey*, Lucretius' *De Rerum Natura*, Cicero's *On the Nature of the Gods,* or Ovid's *Metamorphoses*. If illiterate, then published theology or mythology could be read to them verbatim or communicated in stories. They could see them on the stage, comedic or tragic. The Roman would also observe their gods at countless festivals and in temples. In short, Roman gods were omnipresent and ubiquitous. Both Cicero and Virgil say so: 'God covers all things: the earth, the open seas and the vast skies.'[3]

Maintenance and proper observance of what was called the *pax deorum* (being at peace with the gods) was crucial; keeping the gods on your side through prayer and propitiation was essential. It came with an obsessive requirement to do it all methodically and exactly right—*cultus deorum* (cultivation of the gods). This, with *pax deorum,* kept everything as it should be—all in order—harmonious and functioning well, ensuring productivity and success. *Pietas* was a cornerstone of Roman life and conduct; it was the proper devotion to family, state, ancestors and fellow citizens—and to the gods, and the rites conducted for those gods. A frequent epithet applied to Aeneas, founder of Rome and the race of Romans, was *pius*, a hero dutiful in all aspects.

Prayer, vows, sacrifice, and divination were among the ways in which the Romans sought to appease or influence the gods. Divination involved the interpretation of signs sent by a god, for example thunder and lightning, volcanic eruption, storms—or else through augury (*auspicium*) where the flight, feeding behaviour or cries of birds were analysed. The close examination of entrails of sacrificial animals (*extispicium*) was also common practice. Both forms of divination were taken very seriously and were performed by specialists—augurs and haruspices respectively; both were elected from the senatorial class and were as much political as religious offices.

Here is an example of divination from Livy, illustrating a case where military expediency led to an economical use of the sacred truth:

> The soldiers were annoyed that the battle was postponed until the following day... Papirius got up silently in the third watch of the night and sent a *pullarius* [an augur in charge of the chickens] to observe the omens. There was not one man, whatever his rank or status, in the camp who was not consumed by passion for battle, the highest and lowest ranking soldiers were keenly looking forward to it. The general could see the excitement on his men's faces, the men could see it in their general. This overall excitement extended even to those who were busy observing the sacred birds. The chickens refused to eat, but the *pullarius* had the audacity to lie and told the consul that they had eaten so greedily that the corn dropped from their mouths on to the ground. The consul was delighted at the news, and announced that the omens could not have been better; they could now proceed under the direction of the gods. He then gave the signal for battle.
>
> Livy, *Ab Urbe Condita* 10, 40, 1–5, 14

The *pullarius* was found out and duly slain; the consul was able to announce that they had done everything they could to rectify the sacrilege.

Claudius Pulcher is notorious for barging into Julius Caesar's Bona Dea women-only ritual dressed as a woman. His behaviour during a naval battle off Sicily was no less iconoclastic, with serious consequences:

> Claudius Pulcher was off the coast of Sicily when the chickens used for taking the auspices declined to eat; in contempt of this omen, he chucked them overboard, declaring that if they would not eat then they should at least drink; Claudis Pulcher engaged in his naval battle and was routed.
>
> Suetonius, *Tiberius* 2, 2

Failure to observe or to perform with absolute precision the various religious festivals throughout the year also came with its consequences. The gods would be angry and, for example, the crop might fail in rural communities. Two writers, literally and socially as far apart as they could be—Cato (*On Agriculture* 141) and Tibullus (2, 1, 1–26)—describe the Ambarvalla in their different ways and in so doing underline the importance of religious festivals and their proper execution right across Roman society.

Thus, official Roman religion essentially started founded on and catering for a primitive agricultural society: for example, Jupiter made the crops grow with his rain and sun; Saturn encouraged sowing; Ceres promoted growth. As Rome's overseas possessions increased and more of the world was Romanised, as Rome became more urbanised, then, with the gradual syncretisation of exotic and mysterious foreign gods and goddesses, traditional religion slowly but surely lost its relevance to many aspects of Roman life and culture. Varro, in 47 BCE, was so concerned by the decline of and indifference to state religion that he wrote a book about it, lest it all be forgotten. His *Human and Divine Antiquities* contains sixteen books describing the festivals, rites, priests, temples, divinities, and institutions. Ovid, too, lists the various festivals and liturgies in his *Fasti*.

State religion became staid, humdrum, and unappealing, so men and women began to turn to and embrace the new, oriental, mystery religions that they came into contact with and were percolating into Roman society.[4] With the exception of Mithraism, which was exclusively for men, these cults—particularly the cult of Isis—offered women an active role in the priesthood, something denied to them in state religion. The cults could be personalised and customised to meet the needs of individuals, be they man or woman, and, because their eschatology often enshrined birth and rebirth, they offered hope of life after death.

In keeping with the absence of women from civil and political affairs, a woman's religion in the state system was considered irrelevant. On marriage, women were expected to renounce their own religion and follow their husband's. Priesthoods, sacerdotal reponsibilities and Sibylline Books were mainly controlled by men. Only in the exceptionally rare opportunities for being a Vestal Virgin or a Sibyl could a woman exert any religious power, and that was limited and subject to male authority and punishment.

Ovid's *Fasti* exemplifies the intensely detailed focus the Romans applied to the proper observance of festivals throughout the year. For example, Robigus was the spirit of mildew or grain rust and it was imperative to keep him on side if you wanted a decent harvest. The festival took place on 25 April and included games (*ludi*) and a sacrifice of the blood and entrails of an unweaned puppy (*catulus*) Ovid explains:

On that day, as I was coming back from Nomentum to Rome, a white-robed crowd blocked the middle of the road. A *flamen* [priest] was on his way to the grove of ancient Robigo to throw the entrails of a dog and a sheep onto the flames. I immediately went up to him in order to learn something about the rite. The flamen, O Quirinus, said:

'Scaly Mildew, spare the sprouting corn, and let the smooth plant tops burst through the soil; let the crops, nursed by the heaven's propitious stars, grow till they are ripe for the sickle. You have considerable power: the unhappy husbandman gives up for lost the corn which you have blighted, neither winds, nor showers, nor glistening frost, that nips the sallow corn, harm it as much as when the sun warms the wet stalks; then, dread goddess, is the hour to wreak your wrath. Spare, I pray, and take your scabby hands off the harvest! Don't damage the fields; it's enough that you have the power to do harm. Don't grip the tender crops, but rather sieze the hard iron. It is better that you should gnaw at swords and baneful weapons.

There is no need of them: the world is at peace… Do not damage the corn, and ever may the husbandman be able to offer up prayers to you while you are away.' So he spoke. On his right hand hung a loosely woven napkin, and he had a bowl of wine and a casket of incense. He put the incense, and wine, and sheep's guts, and the foul entrails of a filthy dog on the hearth — we saw him do it. Then to me he said, 'You ask why such an unusual victim is assigned to these rites? Learn why,' the *flamen* said. 'There is a Dog (they call it the Icarian dog), and when that constellation rises the earth is parched and dry, and the crop ripens too soon. This dog is put on the altar instead of the starry dog'.

Ovid, *Fasti* 4, 905–941
translated adapted from Sir James G. Frazer in the Loeb edition, 1931

The desire for fertility, of course, included women. The Lupercalia was a popular festival that took place around 15 February and doubled as a purification ceremony and a fertility rite. After some spring cleaning, the women left their houses to watch scantily-clad young men running round purifying the town or city. The hope among the womenfolk was not just for purification but for fecundity as well. Plutarch has the details:

The priests slaughter goats, and then, after two boys of noble birth have been brought to them, some of them touch their foreheads with a bloody knife, and others wipe the stain off at once with wool dipped in milk. The youths must laugh after their foreheads are wiped. After this they cut the goats' skins into strips and run about, with nothing on but a loin cloth, striking all who meet them with the strips. Young married women make no attempt to avoid their blows, believing that they promote conception and easy child-birth. A peculiarity of the festival is that the Luperci sacrifice a dog as well.

Plutarch, *Romulus* 21, 3–5

The pagan Lupercalia was so popular that it endured until 494 CE, through years of Christianity until Pope Gelasius I declared 15 February the Festival of the Purification of the Virgin Mary.

The Saturnalia took place on 17 December and was a time of much feasting, partying, and dressing up, with the exchange of presents between friends. Even slaves were allowed the day off, and were encouraged to join in the fun. Martial captures the atmosphere:

> Now, while the knights and the senators get dressed up, and Domitian dons the cap of liberty; and while the slave, as he rattles the dice-box, has no fear of the Aedile, seeing that the ponds are so nearly frozen, see what gift you have drawn, whether it be from a rich man or a poor man. Let each give suitable presents to his friends ... I offer you an ear pick to stop the tickling of your ear, when it annoys you with troublesome irritation... If your slave does something wrong, do not smash his teeth out with your fist; give him some of the (hard) biscuit which famous Rhodes has sent you...The pig fed on acorns among slavering wild boars, will get you a merry Saturnalia... Breast-band! confine my mistress' heaving breasts, so that I may stroke and squeeze them.
>
> Martial 14, 1, 23, 68, 70, 134

The Romans had always been broadly receptive to new and foreign religions, absorbing them from here and there as their possessions and dependancies, both within and beyond the Italian peninsula spread. Aspects of Etruscan and Greek religions were among the first to be syncretised over time. Once such popular import was the Bona Dea.

Bona Dea

The foreigness, notably the Greekness, and the involvement of women in these religions brought its detractors. Plutarch presents a relaxed and objective account.[5] In vivid contrast, Juvenal launches an excoriating attack on the patrician women performing the rites of the Bona Dea, describing them as drunken maenads, crazed with desire for sex, which, if it cannot be satisfied by an *adulter*, can be sated by the *adulter*'s son, or by slaves, or the water carrier, or as a last resort an ass will sodomise them: *inposito clunem sumittat asello.*

> We all know about the mysteries of the Good Goddess, when the flute stirs the groin and the Maenads of Priapus sweep along, frenzied alike by the horn-blowing and the wine, tossing their hair and howling. What filthy desire burns within their breasts! What cries they utter as the passion throbs within! How wet are their thighs from torrents of old wine! ... And now impatient nature can wait no longer: woman shows herself to be as she is, and the cry comes from every corner of the den, 'Bring on the men!'
>
> If one adulterer is asleep, his son is told to put on his hood and get in quick; if no luck there a slave is hurried in; if this too fails, the water-carrier will be paid to

come in. If he cannot be found and there are no men then without further delay she'll surrender her arse to a donkey.

Juvenal 6, 314–334
translation adapted from *Juvenal and Persius*
translated by GG Ramsey in the Loeb edition 1918

The cult first appeared in Rome around 272 BCE, during the Tarentine War; Bona Dea was, despite what we hear from Juvenal, associated with chastity and fertility and the protection of Rome; as Fauna, she could prophesy the fates of women. She had two festivals: one at her temple on the Aventine; the other at the home of the Pontifex Maximus. Her Aventine cult, in which a blood sacrifice took place on 1 May, was re-dedicated in 123 BCE by the Vestal Virgin Licinia. This was annulled as unlawful by an anxious Senate; Licinia was later charged with unchastity, and entombed.

Although Bona Dea was celebrated by men and women alike, in the domestic rite which took place on 3 December each year all males were excluded, even male animals and pictures or statues of males. According to Cicero, any man caught observing the rites of Bona Dea could be punished by blinding.[6] This did not seem to bother Publius Clodius Pulcher when, as we have seen, he sacrilegiously gatecrashed the rites of 62 BCE dressed as a woman; the rites which were being held *chez* Caesar, that year's Pontifex Maximus. Pulcher was hell-bent on pursuing Pompeia, Caesar's wife, with whom he was allegedly having an affair. The ensuing scandal was huge, not least because of the presence of Caesar's mother, Aurelia Cotta, Pompeia his wife, and his sister, Julia, and the Vestals. According to Juvenal, any sexual propriety that was left in Rome evaporated that night: Juvenal described Pulcher as the 'lute girl sporting a penis'. The scandal led to Caesar divorcing Pompeia; she was implicated in the outrage, and Caesar's wife must not be under suspicion.

But every Moor and every Indian knows how Clodius, the lute girl sporting a penis, forced his way into a place from which every mouse flees, only too conscious of his testicles, and in which a veil must be drawn over any image of the male form.

Juvenal 6, 336–342

Cybele

An early, officially sanctioned import from Asia Minor was Cybele, or Magna Mater—a universal earth mother who looked out for all things maternal and represented rebirth and immortality through the resurrection of Attis, a castrated adherent. Cybele was brought to Rome in 204 BCE after consultation of the *Sibylline Books* revealed that victory over the Carthaginians could be ensured by her presence at Rome; according to Livy, the *Books* decreed that any enemy would be expelled if the Idaean mother is brought from Pessinus to Rome. Once the cult was established, however, the

Roman authorities must have wished that they had thought a bit harder about what they had wished for. The orgiastic, frenzied rites, the eunuchs, the dancing, the self-castration, and other acts of self harm by adherents (the Galli) were all quite alien and objectionable to the Romans. Therefore, measures were taken to control the cult and to marginalise it as far as possible. Lucretius has a fine and vivid account of a display of Cybelean rites where he describes the Galli as crazy eunuch priests, and their violent frenzy:

> *And hollow cymbals, tight-skinned tambourines*
> *Resound around to bangings of their hands;*
> *The fierce horns threaten with a raucous bray;*
> *The tubed pipe excites their maddened minds*
> *In Phrygian measures; they bear before them knives,*
> *Wild emblems of their frenzy, which have power*
> *The rabble's ingrate heads and impious hearts*
> *To panic with terror of the goddess' might.*

Lucretius, *De Rerum Natura*. 2, 594ff
translation by William Ellery Leonard. E. P. Dutton 1916[7]

The Bacchanalia

The cult of Bacchus was also, at first, exclusively female, and notorious for the frenzy and shrieking of its adherents, the beating of drums, and the clashing of cymbals. It had huge popular appeal even before men were admitted. Livy described its spread as an epidemic; like other exotic religions, it excited the sexual emotions in women.

There were initiatory rites which at first were revealed only to a few, but then began to be known among men and women generally. To the religious element in them were added the delights of wine and feasting, so that a larger number of adherents might be attracted. When wine had inflamed their minds, and night and the mingling of males with females, youth with age, had destroyed every ounce of modesty, all sorts of corruption began to be practised…

the promiscuous intercourse between free men and women, perjured witnesses, forged seals and wills and evidence, all were contrived here. Likewise poisonings and secret murders, so that sometimes not even the bodies were found for burial. Much was ventured by guile, more by violence. This violence was hidden because amid the howlings and the crash of drums and cymbals you could not hear the cries of victims suffering as the debauchery and murders went on and on…many are women, and they are the source of this mischief; then there are men just like the women, debauched and debauchers, fanatical, with senses dulled by wakefulness, wine, noise and shouts in the night. The conspiracy so far has no strength, but it has a huge source of strength in that the adherents grow more numerous day by day.

Livy, *Ab Urbe Condita* 39, 8; 39, 15, 6
translation adapted from Livy, *The History of Rome*, by Evan T. Sage

Plutarch has some equally interesting details regarding the role of women in the Bacchanalia: frenzied women go straight for the ivy and chew it to bring on 'a wineless drunkenness and joyousness; [it] has an exciting and distracting breath of madness, deranges persons, and agitates them'[8].

Officially, the Bacchanalia was regarded as an unsettling conspiracy against Rome in which an Etrurian initiate was suspected of secret and mysterious nocturnal sacrifices and soothsaying. In its earlier days, it was relatively harmless with daytime rites three times a year and *matronae* as priestesses; we know from Cicero that nocturnal rites were illegal, as was initiation, except in the rites of Ceres.[9] Things changed dramatically when a priestess called Paculla Annia started initiating men, the rites were moved to night time, and took place a frequent five times every month. This heady mix of wine, darkness, women, and then men was explosive, with *orgia* on a grand scale involving hetero- and homosexual sex, all of which provided a platform for perjury, forgery, poisoning, and murder. The initiation of men was seen officially as tantamount to removing them from the sanctity of and responsibility for the *familia* and of the state.

It all came to a head in 186 BCE when Publius Aebutius was targetted by his greedy stepfather who, with the boy's mother, Durenia, conspired to dispose of him by enrolling him in the Bacchanalia. Aebutius' girlfriend, Hispala Faecina, a reforming prostitute who had witnessed the orgiastic rites as an initiate, was horrified when she heard this and dissuaded Aebutius from joining. The cult was known for its notoreity and the extreme dangers involved; ritual male rape was routine, with any resistance met by summary sacrifice. According to Livy, 7,000 Bacchantes were eventually prosecuted under the *Senatus Consultum de Bacchanalibus*, many of whom fled Rome or committed suicide.[10]

Isis

The oriental cult of Isis spread to Italy from Egypt at the end of the second century BCE and had immediate appeal to women, not least because Isis was associated with a number of other female deities such as Athena, Aphrodite, Hera, Demeter, and Artemis. Unlike her Olympian predecessors, she was also seen as being caring and compassionate, making time for each of her initiates. Moreover, Isis was flexible and versatile—she was all things to all men, and all things to all women; one inscription describes her perfectly: 'goddess Isis, you who are one and you are all' (*CIL* 10, 3800).

Above all, Isis was a woman and a mother; she was perceived to know what it was to be a woman. Mortal women empathised with her because Isis appeared to empathise with them. She had known grief and bereavement; she had also been a prostitute in Tyre and therefore had appeal across the whole range of female Roman society. She was benificent and came to be associated with fertility; every year when she saw famine encroaching on Egypt, she wept in sorrow so that her tears replenished the Nile and irrigated the flood plains. She was responsible for the Egyptian practice of honouring queens above kings, as exemplified by Cleopatra; most crucially, 'she made the power of women equal to that of men'.[11] Women would have sympathised with Isis' role as a mother, as she is often depicted with a baby in her arms—namely Horus, the offspring of her incestuous relationship with Osiris, her brother. Death and resurrection could be recognised in the rejuvenated Egyptian lands and the death and rebirth of Osiris, also her husband. Her good works and the adulation she received in Egypt were soon to be repeated in Rome.

The first century BCE love poets were particularly put out by the endless devotion their mistresses gave to this new faddish religion. Tibullus is frustrated with the time his Delia spends worshipping Isis: all that clean-water bathing, and sleeping alone in laundered sheets:

> *What good is your Isis, to me now Delia, what use*
> *the bronze that you shook so many times in your hand,*
> *or, while you cultivated the holy rite, I remember,*
> *you bathed in pure water, sleeping in clean sheets ?*
> *Now, Isis, help me now, for the many pictures*
> *in your temples tell me that you have the power to heal,*
> *that my Delia in discharging her votive vows*
> *might sit before your sacred doors, dressed up in linen*
> *and twice a day speak your praise, her hair loosened*
> *among the Pharian crowd.*

Tibullus, 3, 23–34

Propertius is also indignant and resents the fact that Isis keeps him and Cynthia apart:

Those bloody rites are back again: Cynthia's been tied up for the last ten nights. To hell with these sacred things that Inachus's daughter sent from tepid Nile to the women of Italy ! This goddess, whoever she may be, who separates desirous lovers all the time, was always a nasty piece of work ... Haven't you got enough dusky followers in Egypt? Why do you bother with such a long journey to Rome? What do you get out of having girls sleep in empty beds? ...

But you Cynthia, for whom my pain is less than pleasing, let's have sex three times on those nights when we're free.

Propertius 2, 33, 1–22

Ovid is less than convinced by the devotion apparently showed to the cult; he hints at the freedom women enjoy, pretending to be out celebrating Isis when they are really having a girls' night out at the races or in the theatre: 'Can spies avail when you to plays resort, Or in the circus view the noble sport? Or can you be to Isis' fane pursu'd, Or Cybele's, whose rights all men exclude?' (Ovid, *Ars Amatoria* 635–8; translation from Ovid's *Art of Love* Anne Mahoney; New York, Calvin Blanchard 1855)

Elsewhere, when he is describing the way Dipsas, a procuress, teaches the art of deception, he recommends that Isis be used as an excuse for refusing sex: 'Deny him nights often. Pretend you've got a headache, or it's the days of Isis' (Ovid, *Amores* 1, 8, 73).

Apuleius has a colourful description of the initiation of Lucius into the rites of Isis in his *Metamorphoses*: these extracts give a taste of the exotic, un-Roman nature of the cult:

> *Then came a great throng, of men as well women, with lamps, candles, torches, and other lights, doing honour to her that was born of the heavenly stars. After that came the musical harmony of instruments, pipes and flutes in most pleasant rhythm. Then came a fair company of youths dressed in white singing both metre and verse with a lovely grace which some studious poet had made by favour of the Muses... then arrived the trumpeters ...then came a great company of men and women of all ranks and every age who were initiates and had taken divine orders, whose garments, being of the whitest linen, glistened all through the streets. The women had their hair annointed, and their heads covered with light linen; but the men had their crowns shaven and shining bright... Another [initiate] carried the secrets of their glorious religion, enclosed in a coffer.*
>
> Apuleius, *Metamorphoses* 11, 7ff
> translation adapted from W. Adlington (1566) and revised by S. Gaselee 1922

The inclusiveness of the cult of Isis set it apart from official Roman religion; it allowed women to aspire to high religious office and become priestesses. One inscription shows six female Isis *sacerdotes* (out of twenty-six), one of which was a woman of senatorial rank, another the daughter of a freedman, Usia Prima.[12] Around one third of Isis devotees mentioned in Italian inscriptions are women.

As the popularity of the cult spread and grew, so did the official suspicion and paranoia. Augustus saw a worrying reincarnation of Cleopatra in Isis, and a threat to his license-curbing, moral legislation. In 28 BCE, he banned the building of temples of Isis within the city of Rome and seven years later in 21 BCE he extended this to an exclusion zone outside the city. The anti-Isis fever reached its zenith under Tiberius after a scandal involving a well-to-do *matrona*, Paulina, and the equestrian Decius Mundus. The priests of Isis had told Paulina that Anubis, the Egyptian god, wanted to have sex with her in the temple; Anubis, of course, was none other than Decius Mundus who had paid the priests to assist him. The tactless equestrian boasted of his conquest and word inevitably reached Tiberius: Mundus was exiled, the priests were crucified, and thousands of Isis worshippers were expelled from the city to Sardinia. The scandal is interesting because it shows that it was quite usual for a Roman *matrona* to visit a temple of Isis.

Caligula was the first to spot the political kudos to be gained from support for such a popular cult; he built a temple to Isis in the Campus Martius within the walls of Rome. The goddess remained popular until the arrival of Christianity.

Vestal Virgins

The hearth was literally the *focus* of the Roman household, traditionally tended by the daughters of the family. Vesta was the goddess of the hearth, attended by virgin priestesses (the Vestal Virgins) who kept the sacred flame (*ignis inextinctus*) alight in the Temple of Vesta. This flame symbolized the preservation of the Roman state; the *Virgo Vestalis Maxima* symbolized the wife of old Roman kings (represented in turn by the *Pontifex Maximus*) while the others (the College) were the symbolic daughters of the king. The kings were said to originate from sparks in the ground. Any Vestal careless enough to allow the flame to go out on her watch was whipped; tending the flame occupied the Vestals for around eight hours every day. There is something of a paradox whereby Vesta was also associated with agricultural productivity and with fertility. The Vestals' virginity embodied the safety of Rome: Rome was safe while their virginity remained intact; when it was violated, Rome was under threat. When a Vestal was ill, she was treated by a *matrona* away from the temple.

The last known *vestalis maxima* was Coelia Concordia, appointed in 380 CE. The Vestals were finally disbanded in 394 CE but not before ten or so had been entombed alive; this was the awful penalty for a Vestal who lost her virginity (*incestum*), or was suspected of having lost it. The entombment took place in a cellar under the Campus Sceleratus; the male partner involved was flogged to death in the Comitium like a slave, *sub furca*, a fork-shaped gallows or yoke. The rationale behind entombment was that Vesta would still be able to rescue the 'Virgin' if she really were innocent; Vesta never did. Plutarch wonders if entombment was decided upon because the Romans thought it somehow inappropriate that one charged with looking after the flame should be cremated, or that one so sacrosanct should be murdered. He graphically describes the solemn process where the condemned Vestal is bound, gagged, and carried to her subterranean prison in a curtained litter; she is unbound and, after a prayer, the Pontifex Maximus puts her on a ladder that leads to the small chamber below. The ladder is hauled up, then the entrance closed and covered with earth. The chamber has a bed, lamp, bread, water, milk, and oil. To Plutarch, this is the most shocking spectacle in the world; when it occurs, it is the most horrific day Rome has ever seen.

> For minor offences the virgins are punished with lashings, the Pontifex Maximus sometimes scourging the culprit on her bare flesh, in a dark place, with a curtain drawn. But she that has broken her vow of chastity is buried alive near the Colline gate. Here a little ridge of earth extends for some distance along the inside of the city-wall…Under it a small chamber is built, with steps leading down from above. In this are placed a couch with its coverings, a lighted lamp, and very small portions of the necessaries of life, such as bread, a bowl of water, milk, and oil… Then the culprit herself is placed on a litter, over which coverings are thrown and fastened down with cords so that not even a cry can be heard from within, and carried through the forum… No other spectacle is more appalling, nor does any other day bring more gloom to the city than this. When the litter reaches its destination, the attendants unfasten the cords of the coverings. Then the high-priest, after stretching his hands toward heaven and uttering certain mysterious prayers before the fatal act, brings forth the culprit, who is closely veiled, and places her on the steps leading down into the chamber. After this he turns away, as do the rest of the priests, and when she has gone down, the steps are taken up, and great quantities of earth are thrown into the entrance to the chamber, hiding it away, and make the place level with the rest of the mound. Such is the punishment of those who break their vow of virginity.
>
> Plutarch, *Numa* 10, 4–7
>
> translation adapted from *The Parallel Lives* Vol. 1 Loeb Classical Library edition, 1914

Vestal Virgins sometimes took the blame when catastrophe struck: for example their alleged *incestum* was held responsible for the slaughter that was the Battle of Cannae in 216 BCE; two Vestals, Opimia and Floronia, were duly convicted: one was entombed, the other committed suicide.[13] Lucius Cantilius, the secretary of the Pontiffs who had deflowered Floronia, was beaten to death.

On the other hand, their sacrosanctity was clearly evident, for example in their role as intermediaries between emperor Claudius and Messalina, and as envoys for Vitellius during the battles in 69 CE, the year of the four emperors. Important state papers and the wills of eminent statesman and emperors were kept in their building, the Atrium. The Vestal Virgins were the stuff of legend and provided a fertile source of copy for the historians. One Vestal, Aemilia, let the flame go out, provoking questions about her chastity. She reacted by praying to Vesta and threw a cloth onto the cold embers; when this burst miraculously and spontaneously into flame, all questioning ceased. Tuccia endured the same calamity but absolved herself by fetching a sieveful of water from the Tiber without losing a single drop.[14]

Domitian was particularly suspicious of the moral rectitude of the Vestal Virgins: he brought a number to trial in 83 CE and 90 CE in a bid to improve the moral climate— *correctio morum*, particularly as it seems the Vestals had lost their moral compasses under Vespasian and Titus, and were running what was virtually a brothel. In 83 CE, the Oculata sisters and Varronilla were given the option to commit suicide—*liberum mortis arbitrium*—while their lovers were exiled; seven years later, Cornelia, the Chief Virgin, was condemned to the living death that was entombment; her lover was whipped to death.[15]

Vestal Virgins were sometimes sacrificial lambs in games of political intrigue. In 114 BCE three were charged with *incestum* and running a brothel—one was convicted; the other two were condemned the following year after a retrial was demanded by Sextus Peducaeus who accused the Pontifex Maximus, L. Metellus Delmaticus (his political rival) of partiality.[16] In 73 BCE, two Vestals were embroiled in the Catiline conspiracy: Fabia, the half-sister of Terentia, Cicero's wife, was accused of having an affair with Catiline, while Licinia was similarly accused of consorting with Crassus, her cousin. Both were acquitted but mud sticks: soon after, neither Vestal was present at a religious event described by Macrobius although their four colleagues were; no doubt they were selected to stay back at the temple fanning the flames.[17, 18] In 215 CE, Caracella seduced a Vestal and had her, and two others, entombed. In 220 CE, the depraved Elagabalus divorced his wife and married a Vestal, Aquilia Severa, after arranging special dispensation for her to renounce her vows of chastity.[19]

What to do with the Christians proved, at times, a near intractable problem. Pliny's letter to Trajan here is a fascinating insight into the challenges facing the Romans in deciding how best to treat refractory Christians. The often tolerant and syncretic Romans struggled with this new, troublesome offshoot of Judaism with its dogmatic monotheism. The unwillingness of Christians to accept Roman polytheism exposed them to discrimination and exacerbated the problem for everyone. Nero had fanned the flames when he encouraged the rumour that it was the Christians who started the great fire in Rome in 64 CE; Tacitus tells the story in *Annals* 15, 44. 120 years later, Tertullian exposed the ambivalence in Trajan's reply to Pliny's suggestions (*Apologia* 2, 7–9). Popular rumour and propaganda increased over the years discrediting Christianity and Christians: the most outrageous claims against them included atheism, baby-eating, sexual orgies, and incest, as described here by Minucius Felix in his passionate denial:

> And now I should wish to meet him who says or believes that we are initiated by the slaughter and blood of an infant. Think you that it can be possible for so tender, so little a body to receive those fatal wounds; for any one to shed, pour forth, and drain that new blood of a youngling, and of a man scarcley come into existence? No one can believe this, except one who can dare to do it. And I see that you at one time expose your begotten children to wild beasts and to birds; at another, that you crush them when strangled with a miserable kind of death. There are some women who, by drinking medical preparations, extinguish the source of the future man in their very bowels, and thus commit a parricide before they bring forth.
>
> Minucius Felix, *Octavius* 30
> translation Peter Kirby in *Early Christian Writings*, with permission.

Pliny is in a dilemma over the treatment of Christians:

> It is usual for me, my Emperor, to consult you on anything I am unsure about. For
> who is better able to deal with hesitancy or to inform my ignorance? I have never
> attended a trial of Christians before. Consequently I don't know anything about
> them or how far it is customary to punish or cross-examine them. And I am more
> than hesitant over whether any distinction should be made on age or whether
> young and old should be treated differently, whether a pardon be given to those
> recanting or whether you don't get away with having been a Christian even if you
> renounce it; whether the name itself should be punished, even where no crime has
> been committed or whether it is the crimes clinging to the name which should be
> punished. Up until now this is the procedure I have followed whenever Christians are
> brought before me. I have asked them if they are Christians and to those confessing
> to be so I ask again and then a third time, threatening them with punishment. Those
> who persist I order to be led away to be executed. For whatever they say in admission
> I have no doubt that such stubbornness and obstinate inflexibility should certainly be
> punished. Others who are similarly fanatical (and because they are Roman citizens)
> I have ordered be sent back to Rome to stand trial. In dealing with these cases, as
> often happens, the offences increase and differ in nature. An anonymous book has
> been circulated listing the names of many accused people. I believed that I ought to
> dismiss those who denied they were Christians or ever had been. They followed me
> in prayer to the gods and made offerings to your statue with incense and wine which
> I had ordered be brought into the court for this very purpose along with the statues of
> the gods; besides they blasphemed against Christ—true Christians, it is said, cannot
> be induced to do any of these things.
>
> Others named as Christians by informers first confess and then soon deny it
> saying that they ceased to be Christians three or more years previously, some even
> twenty years ago. They too all worshipped your statue and the images of the gods,
> and cursed Christ. They admitted that the full extent of their guilt or error of their
> ways amounted to just this: they normally meet before dawn on a fixed day and took
> it in turns to chant to Christ as if to a god and to bind themselves by oath—not with
> criminal intent but so as never to commit theft, robbery or adultery, not to betray
> trust or refuse to guarantee a deposit when it's requested. After this it was usual for
> them to go their own ways and meet up later for a perfectly legitimate and harmless
> meal. This all stopped, though, after my edict had been passed which, following
> your orders, outlawed political meetings. I thought it all the more necessary because
> of this to extract the truth through torture from two slave women whom they call
> deaconesses. I got nothing out of them apart from twisted and excessive superstition.
>
> I have for this reason postponed further examination and hasten to consult you:
> it seems to me to be worth your consideration particularly in view of the number of
> people under suspicion. Many people of all ages and class and of both sexes are being
> compromised and will go on being compromised. This contagion infects not only

towns but also villages and rural areas although it does seem to me that it can still be checked and brought under control. It is certainly clear that people have started crowding back in to the temples which until recently were deserted, the sacred rites for a long time neglected are being performed again and the flesh of sacrificial victims is back on sale everywhere, though up until now buyers have been extremely rare. From this it is easy to conclude that a great throng of humankind might be reformed if they are given chance to recant.

Pliny, *Epistles* 10, 96

Trajan reassures Pliny that he's got it just about right:

You have followed the correct procedure, Pliny, where Christians have been brought before you, for I have decided that it is not possible to apply a one size fits all judgement to an issue which is so variable. The Christians should not be hunted down. If they are brought before you and the case is proven then, of course, they must be punished. But for those who deny the Christian faith and demonstrate they are not Cristians by praying to our gods, even if they have been under suspicion before, they should be pardoned on the grounds of their penitence. Anonymous pamphlets must have no place in any case because they set the worst example and are out of step with our times.

Pliny, *Epistles* 10, 97

There is no such dilemma for Segius: for Martial, atheism pays: 'There are no gods, the heavens are empty, Segius declares. He's right because while he is making these denials, he's made himself rich' (Martial 4, 21).

Magic and Superstition

Magic and superstition were just as much a feature of Roman life as religion, although many social histories of Rome give them short shrift, glossing over their importance and ubiquity. Magic is all around and, it seems, it always has been. People sometimes say that magic is in the air, which is everywhere. The dark arts too have been dabbled in for as long as religions have been practised, in all societies. Roman magic and Roman involvement in the various aspects of the occult, and the thereafter are merely developments of what had gone on in earlier civilisations and societies, particularly from Greece and Egypt, reaching far back into prehistoric times.

What exactly is magic and what were the dark arts? Where on earth did it all come from? Essentially, magic is the art (some might say science) of meddling with the natural course of events through occult agencies such as witches or sorcerers. The dark arts embrace all things related to the occult: necromancy, certain kinds of divination, sacrifice, life after death, journeys through the underworld, potions, curses and charms, witchcraft, exorcism, ghosts, and haunting. The practice of magic and the dark arts was fuelled by deep-seated, ubiquitous superstition in both ancient Greece and Rome.

'Grey areas' and 'thin lines' are often what separate established and official from the magical and marginal in ancient societies. To make matters even more complicated, these lines themselves are often blurred; they show up particularly in ancient religions and in medicine—two areas fundamental to any civilised society. Gynaecology and male impotence, for example, seem to be two specialities where 'good medicine' often elides with herbal, folk medicine, and magic—sympathetic and apotropaic; this of course reflects the importance of fertility in any civilisation and the extremes to which a society will go to guarantee procreation. The Greek word *pharmakon* exemplifies and amplifies the confusion, as it can refer to magic, poison, and medicine.

When does divination, divine possession, sacrifice, spell-making, and eschatology in general stop being religion and become dabbling in the dark arts? One difference between magic and religion is that in religion, the religious person is submissive to his gods and subject to them, while the purveyor of magic is often controlling and sometimes even tells the gods what to do. We see this blurring in ancient Egypt and in Mesopotamia; this lack of distinction passed into the worlds of ancient Greece and Rome.

The plethora of Roman occult material and literature alluding to or describing magic, witchcraft and the afterlife, reflects the ubiquity of and preoccupation with the magical, mystical and occult in the Roman world. Roman literature can offer any number of poets, philosophers, playwrights or historians who refer to or expatiate on these subjects, based on their own contemporary experience or on works by earlier authors. In addition, there were evolving beliefs about magic, witches, and life after death. We have a fertile, extensive, and detailed commentary on Roman chthonic practice throughout the whole extent of the Roman period. Even the material that originates from the later Empire describes activity and events that probably took place centuries before and had become part of the fabric of Roman life and society.

Plutarch's *De Superstitione* suggests, by implication, that obsessive superstition (*deisidaimonia*) was endemic in Roman society. Lucian deplored the ready acceptance of superstition by the gullible; he wrote a satirical account, *Alexander*, or *The Pseudoprophet*, on the founding of a new cult by Alexander of Abonuteichus, which was closed to Epicureans and Christians.

Pliny the Elder asks all the right questions:

Why on the first day of the year do we wish one another cheerfully a happy and prosperous New Year? Why do we also, on days of general purification, choose persons with lucky names to lead the victims? Why do we meet the evil eye by a special attitude of prayer, some invoking the Greek Nemesis, for which purpose there is at Rome an image of the goddess on the Capitol, although she has no Latin name? Why on mentioning the dead do we protest that their memory is not being attacked by us? Why do we believe that in all matters the odd numbers are more powerful, as is implied by the attention paid to critical days in fevers? Why at the harvest of the first-fruits do we say: 'These are old,' and pray for new ones to take their place? Why do we say 'Good health' to those who sneeze? This custom according to report even Tiberius Caesar, admittedly the most gloomy of men, insisted on even in a carriage, and some think it more effective to add to the salutation the name of the sneezer. Moreover, according to an accepted belief absent people can divine by the ringing in their ears that they are the being talked about. Attalus assures us that if on seeing a scorpion one says 'Two,' it is checked and does not strike. The mention of scorpions reminds me that in Africa nobody decides on anything without first saying 'Africa,' whereas among all other peoples a man prays first for the approval of the gods. But when a table is ready it is a universal custom, we see, to take off one's ring, since it is clear that scrupulous actions, even without words, have their powers. Some people, to calm mental anxiety, carry saliva with the finger to behind the ear. There is even a proverb that bids us turn down our thumbs to show approval. In worshipping we raise our right hand to our lips and turn round our whole body, the Gauls considering it more effective to make the turn to the left. All peoples agree in worshipping lightning by clucking with the tongue. If during a banquet fires have been mentioned we avert the omen by pouring water under the table. It is supposed to be a most unlucky sign for the floor to be swept while a diner is leaving the banquet, or for a table or dumbwaiter to be removed while a guest is drinking. ... Medicines set down by chance on a table before being used are said to lose their efficacy.

To cut the nails on the market days at Rome in silence, beginning with the forefinger, is a custom many people feel binding on them; while to cut the hair on the seventeenth day of the month and on the twenty-ninth prevents its falling out as well as headaches. A country rule observed on most Italian farms forbids women to twirl their spindles while walking along the road, or even to carry them uncovered, on the ground that such action blights the hopes of everything, especially the hope of a good harvest. Marcus Servilius Nonianus, a leading citizen of Rome, who was not so long ago afraid of ophthalmia, used to tie round his neck, before he mentioned the disease himself or any one else spoke to him about it, a sheet of paper fastened with thread, on which were written the two Greek letters rho and alpha; Mucianus, three times consul, following the same observance, used a living fly in a white linen bag. Both avowed that by these remedies they themselves were kept free from ophthalmia. We certainly still have formulas to charm away hail, various diseases, and burns—some actually tested by experience.

Pliny the Elder, *Natural History* 28, 5
translation from Pliny's Natural History by H. Rackham (vols. 1–5, 9) and
W.H.S. Jones (vols. 6–8) and D.E.Eichholz (vol. 10) from the 10 volume edition
published by Harvard University Press, 1949–54.

As already noted, Plutarch probably sums up the typical Roman attitude to magic in his *Moralia* where he offers advice on how to achieve a good marriage. Education of the wife by the husband is crucial—he is her mentor, philosopher, and teacher; part of his responsibility is to urge the study of Plato or Xenophon, leaving no room for silly and aimless pursuits like dabbling in magic incantations.[1]

By definition, it is impossible to gauge just how much occult activity went on in Rome. However, the sheer number of references in the literature and the prodigious number of curse tablets found would, on its own, suggest that magic, superstition and cursing were prevalent. The number of women actually, or allegedly, engaging in witchcraft at any one time was no doubt insignificant, but the frequent appearance of witches in poetry and anthropology cannot be accounted for by the exigencies and traditions of literery genres alone. Roman epic, satire, love poetry, and tragedy are populated with witches and other female peddlers of the occult: it seems plausible that audiences will have been familiar with their practices and would recognise them from everyday experience, stories, or by traditional superstition.

Then there is the insinuation of the bogeywoman into the lives and psyches of children. The bogeywoman often appeared as a big bad wolf that ate naughty boys and girls alive and always had one freshly devoured in her stomach. The ubiquitous bogeywoman took the shape of Mormo in ancient Greece—she was either queen of the Lystraegones who had lost her own children and now murdered others, or a child-eating Corinthian. Another was Empusa who variously took the form of a cow, donkey, or beautiful woman; yet another was Gello, an evil female spirit and child snatcher. To Diodorus Siculus, Empusa was a beautiful child-eater. The Roman equivalent was Lamia—a vivacious Libyan woman whose children by Zeus were murdered by Hera; like Mormo, she was a cannibal and exacted revenge by murdering other women's babies, eating them alive.[2] In the late second century CE, Flavius Philostratus talks of Lamia and Empusa as *phasma*—ghosts or nightmares.

Lucretius was sufficiently concerned about irrational fear and over-active imaginations that he attempted to explain it all away:

> Such are the extremes of wickedness to which men are driven through superstition.
> And there will come a time when even you,
> Forced by the soothsayer's tales of doom, will seek
> To escape us. Ah, many a dream even now
> Can they concoct to wreck your life plans,
> And destroy all your good fortune with fears.
> And for good reason: because, if men saw a
> end to their ills, they would be strong enough to find a way
> to endure the mumbo jumbo and the menacings of seers. As things
> stand, they are powerless because they are haunted by the dread of
> eternal punishment when they die.
>
> Lucretius, *De Rerum Natura* 1, 132

Horace includes the fear of dreams, the terrors of magic, miracles, and night-time ghosts in a catalogue of events those strong in mind should have nothing to do with: 'Is you heart free… from horror, indignation at death? Do you scoff at dreams, miracles, magical terrors, witches, ghosts in the night, and Thessalian portents?' (Horace, *Epistles* 2, 2, 209).

Persius singles out god-fearing grandmothers and aunts in his satire on the uselessness of men's clandestine prayers to the gods. Prayers may be said to be expert in averting the evil eye and may predict a life of extravagant wealth and a good marriage—an altogether rosy life. However, Persius is far from convinced, and no nurse will ever hear a prayer from Persius. Juvenal too satirises the *anxia mater* at the temple of Venus for optimistically wishing her daughter's beauty.[3]

Superstition played a part in Roman weddings. A sizeable number of days of the year were avoided by betrothed couples when choosing their wedding day; the groom always carried his bride over the threshold to avoid any chance of an unlucky stumble.

Superstition, then, was rife and omnipresent. It was considered unlucky if: a black cat entered your house; a snake fell from the roof into your garden; a statue of a god was seen to sweat blood ; a horse was born with five legs, a lamb with a pig's head or a pig with a human head; a rampant bull ran up three flights of stairs and a cow talked; a statue laughed uncontrollably; a horse cried hot tears; a person sneezed in the presence of a waiter holding a tray; someone swept the floor when a guest was standing up; or one did not whistle when lightning flashed.[5, 6, 7, 8] It was *de rigeur* to only cut your nails on market days, starting with the forefinger and doing it in silence, but never at sea. In certain Italian towns, it was forbidden by law for women to walk through the streets carrying a spindle.

It is important to put this into some sort of context and remember that the Romans were probably no more superstitious than other cultures and societies. Indeed, if we look at the old wives' tales recounted by George Orwell from a rural childhood around 1900 in *Coming Up for Air*, can we say that they are any more rational than the Romans'?

> Swimming was dangerous, climbing trees was dangerous ... all animals were dangerous ... horses bit, bats got in your hair, earwigs got into your ears, swans broke your leg ... bulls tossed you ... raw potatoes were deadly poison, and so were mushrooms unless you bought them at the grocer's ... if you had a bath after a meal you died of cramp ... and if you washed your hands in the water eggs were boiled in you got warts ... raw onions were a cure for almost anything.[9]

The Sibylline Books, a compendium of oracular responses, were consulted in times of crises and their prognostications acted upon. Generally, women had a vital role to play in Roman divination (*divinatio*) by virtue of the Sibyl and her *Sibylline Books*. The originals of the *Books* were a collection of oracular responses in three books brought to Rome by Tarquinius Priscus, after some haggling about their value with the Sibyl at Cumae. Virgil dignifies them by including them in the list of religious initiatives Aeneas will take when he establishes Rome: 'A great sanctuary awaits you too in our kingdom; for this is where I will put your oracles and the mysterious prophecies told to my people; here I will ordain chosen men, propitious Sibyl' (Virgil, *Aeneid* 6, 71–4).

The *Books* were kept underground in a stone chest under the temple of Jupiter Optimus Maximus on the Capitoline and guarded by ten men; they could only be accessed by fifteen specially appointed augurs (*quindecimviri sacris faciundis*). Consultation took place by Senatorial decree at a propitiatory ceremony in times of civil strife, external threat, military disaster, or on the appearance of strange prodigies or phenomena. Unfortunately, the temple and the oracles were lost in a fire in 83 BCE. A new collection was compiled from various sacred sites and kept by Augustus in the temple of Palatine Apollo. They were last consulted in 363 CE.

We have seen how if a Vestal Virgin was found to have lost (or was just suspected of losing) her virginity, it was a terrible omen for the Roman state and that she was entombed alive; at the same time, if Rome was threatened in any way, or suffered a disaster, it was because it was universally believed that at least one of the six Vestal Virgins was guilty of *stuprum*: sexual depravity.[10]

Magic had been a problem right from the start for the Romans. We know this because the *Twelve Tables* deals with it; these laws were drawn up in 451 and 450 BCE— some 300 years after the foundation of Rome in 753 BCE—so there had been plenty of time to identify the problematic areas of Roman life that would benefit from formal legislation. *Table VII, law three* interests us here: it outlaws the casting of harmful spells on another man's crops, crop-charming; this rural crime was obviously a serious and frequent problem: guilty parties were sacrificed to Ceres. 'Anyone who, through incantations and magic arts, prevents grain or crops of any kind belonging to another man from growing, will be sacrificed to Ceres' (*Twelve Tables* VII, 3).

We have an example of the crime from the first half of the second century BCE when C. Furius Cresimus was indicted on a charge of crop-charming. Cresimus was a clever man, though: he turned up at court with all of his agricultural equipment and with some burly slaves in train. These, he pleaded, were his 'spells'; no magic could explain the blood, sweat, and tears he routinely invested in his work on the land. Cresimus was unanimously acquitted.

Magic, superstition, witchcraft, and other manifestations of the occult were under continual suspicion by the state, not least because of its innate mysteriousness; officialdom was always nervous about it and extended its anxieties to class it alongside other extraordinary crimes: tomb-raiding, human sacrifice, philters, sex crimes, foreign and exotic rites, and sacrilege were all tarred with the same brush as the practice of magic and witchcraft. These strange activities led to, or were believed to be one step removed from, sedition, treason, paganism, and adherence to the burgeoning heretical religious sects. In the end, all magic was prohibited by the monotheistic Christian authorities.

In the event, either the anti-magic law in the *Twelve Tables* was ineffective, or magical practice was just becoming more widespread and uncontrollable as Rome's hegemony spread further east and south, sucking in exotic influences as it went.

In 331 BCE, 116 women were condemned when they assembled for a mass potion- and poison-fest. As alluded to above, in 186 BCE, the rites (and rights) of the exciting, exotic Bacchanals were severely restricted by the *senatus consultum de Bacchanalibus*, with around 7,000 followers of Dionysus thrown into jail or executed for druggery— *veneficia*, according to Livy.

Things came to a head with the passing of a law criminalising assassins and poisoners; Sulla's *Lex Cornelia de Sicariis et Veneficis* in 81 BCE made it illegal to administer a love potion or abortifacients; the penalty for the lower classes was hard labour in the mines although this soon changed to crucifixion or being thrown to ferocious animals. Banishment to an island awaited the upper classes with property forfeited. If the recipient of the magic died, the only option was execution regardless of class.

The *Lex Cornelia de Sicariis et Veneficis* is as unequivocal as it is unforgiving:

Persons who celebrate or cause to be celebrated impious or noctural rites so as to enchant, bewitch or bind anyone, shall be crucified or thrown to wild beasts... Anyone who sacrifices a man, or attempts to obtain auspices by means of his blood, or pollutes a shrine or a temple, shall be thrown to wild beasts, or, if he is of superior rank, shall be punished with death. ... It has been decided that persons who are addicted to the art of magic shall suffer extreme punishment; that is to say, they shall be thrown to wild beasts or crucified. Magicians themselves shall be burned alive. ...

No-one shall be permitted to have books of magic in his possession, and when they are found with anyone they shall be publicly burned and those who have them, after being deprived of his property, if they are of superior rank shall be deported to an island, and if they are of inferior station shall be put to death; for not only is the practice of this art prohibited, but also knowledge of the same.

In the late republic and early empire, magical practices were further criminalised by Agrippa in 33 BCE when he banished astrologers (*astrologoi*) and sorcerers (*goetoi*), fearful that they were polluting established religion and having an unsettling effect on social order by fomenting revolution. Maecenas also tried to introduce legislation in 29 BCE in his recommendations to Augustus. Augustus had criminalised divination to individuals and any divination on the subject of death (particularly an emperor's death) in 11 CE, although the historians are quick to point out that he himself published his own astrological birth chart. He had also indulged in some injudicious book-burning when, in 31 BCE, he destroyed around 2,000 Greek and Latin books of an 'unsuitable' nature—prophetic writings—and of questionable authorship even though many had been published anonymously. Some of the highly revered *Sibylline Books* were included in the panic bonfires.

Augustus' successor, Tiberius, ever paranoid and saturnine, suppressed druids and outlawed the clandestine consultations of soothsayers (*haruspices*). In 16 CE, Tiberius got personal when he charged a man called Libo Drusus for a crime he saw as tantamount to treason: divining the date of the emperor's death. Much of the case rested on the allegation that Libo had conducted necromancy with the usual incantations, indulged in the interpretation of dreams (oneiromancy), consorted with Chaldeans (notorious magic-dabblers), and had scribbled strange, mystical signs next to the names of the imperial family, including Tiberius'. Libo denied all charges but was forced to deliver two sword stabs into his own stomach. He had tried to explain his actions away by a desire to know if he would ever be rich enough to pave with money the Appian Way the whole distance to Brundisium (Tacitus, *Annals* 2, 27–32).

At the same time, Tiberius banished a number of astronomers (*mathematici*) including Lucius Pituanius who was helped off the Tarpeian Rock, and Publius Marcius, who was grandiosely executed at the Esquiline Gate to a fanfare of trumpets. Altogether, 130 sorcerers died in Tiberius's reign, eighty-five of whom were women. The most celebrated was Claudia Pulchra, great niece of Augustus, who was accused of an attempt to poison Tiberius, using magic, binding curses, and spreading immorality. She died in exile.[11]

Tacitus tells of the suspicious death in in 19 CE of Germanicus, the adopted son of Tiberius who was tipped to succeed to the imperial throne. The assumption was that Germanicus had been poisoned by Gnaeus Calpurnius Piso and his wife, Plancina; some, though, suspected black magic—a suspicion which was confirmed when workmen searching Germanicus' quarters made sinister discoveries under the floor and between the walls. There, they found human remains, spells (*defixiones*) inscribed with Germanicus' name, bloody ashes, and other magical paraphernalia:

> The cruel virulence of the disease was intensified by the patient's, Germanicus's, belief that Piso had given him poison; and it is a fact that explorations in the floor and walls brought to light the remains of human bodies, spells, curses, leaden tablets engraved with the name Germanicus, charred and blood-smeared ashes, and others of the implements of witchcraft by which it is believed the living soul can be devoted to the powers of the grave. At the same time, emissaries from Piso were accused of keeping a too inquisitive watch upon the ravaging progress of the disease.
>
> Tacitus, *Annals* 2, 69

A Syrian witch, Martina—famous for her *veneficia*—was summoned to Rome by those preparing charges against Piso and Plancina. However, before she could get there, she was found dead at Brundisium, poisoned it seems by her own poison, knotted into her hair.[12]

In 26 CE, more foreigners were deported: Chaldeans and Jews were removed from the country, the former for confusing impressionable Roman minds and publishing false astrology. Even more hypocritically, the Jews, ever considered secretive, were accused of corrupting Roman morality. Christians too were viewed with great suspicion, with their signing of the cross, the Eucharist, and their clandestine, nocturnal prayer meetings.

The book burning continued, the bonfires lit this time by converted Christians under the auspices of St Paul. Apparently, sorcery books to the value of 50,000 pieces of silver were torched in public.

In 54 CE, the emperor Claudius banned druids. During Nero's reign, Suetonius Paulinus, the Roman governor of Britannia, was busy trying to take Mona (modern Anglesey). The objective was to eradicate the exiled druid community there and end the island's status as a haven for disaffected refugees. Druidism was feared by the Romans, not least because of its reputation for focusing opposition to Roman rule and the mystery surrounding the arcane rites; druids were also known for their veneration of the human head, which often resulted in the routine decapitation of corpses after battles. According to Tacitus, the druids had a reputation for 'soaking their altars in the blood of prisoners and using human entrails in their divination'. Tacitus takes up the lurid story:

> On the beach stood the adverse array, a serried mass of arms and men, with women flitting between the ranks. In the style of Furies, in robes of deathly black and with dishevelled hair, they brandished their torches; while a circle of Druids, lifting their hands to heaven and showering imprecations, struck the troops with such an awe at the extraordinary spectacle that, as though their limbs were paralysed, they exposed their bodies to wounds without an attempt at movement. Then, reassured by their general, and inciting each other never to flinch before a band of females and fanatics, they charged behind the standards, cut down all who met them, and enveloped the

enemy in his own flames. The next step was to install a garrison among the conquered population, and to demolish the groves consecrated to their savage cults: for they considered it a duty to consult their deities by means of human entrails.

Tacitus, *Annals* 14, 30

translation from *The Annals of Tacitus* Vol. V of the Loeb Classical Library edition, 1937

Once she became Claudius' fourth wife, Agrippina's absolute priority was to install Nero (r. 54–68), her son, onto the throne. Rivalry came from Britannicus, son of Claudius. One woman who got in the way, Lepida, had to go; she was charged with the attempted murder of Agrippina by magical means, and sentenced to death. Agrippina now saw her chance to murder Claudius; the only question was the type of poison to use. Anxious that Claudius might recant on his death bed and rehabilitate Britannicus if a slow-working poison was used, and aware that an aggressive, instantaneous toxin would be incriminating, she compromised with a venom that would drive him insane before delivering a slow death. Locusta, a lady proficient in pharmacology with a criminal conviction hanging over her for poisoning—*veneficii damnata*—was enlisted. The poison was prepared; it was to be administered by a eunuch, Halotus, a regular dish taster. Tacitus says that a particularly juicy mushroom was smeared with the poison but failed to be effective; a terrified Agrippina called in Claudius' physician, Gaius Stertinius Xenophon, who was in on the plot, so that he could thrust a poisoned feather into Claudius' throat, pretending to try and make him vomit. The feather worked.

[In 51 CE] a number of prodigies took place during the year. Birds of ill omen perched on the Capitol; houses were flattened by the shocks and after shocks of an earthquake, and, as the panic spread, the weak were trampled underfoot by the terrified crowd. Another shortage of corn, and the resulting famine, were construed as another supernatural portent.

Tacitus, *Annals* 12, 43, 1

The year 54 CE was also a bad year for the omens:

In the consulate of Marcus Asinius Marcellus and Manius Acilius Aviola, it was obvious from a run of prodigies that things were taking a turn for the worse. Fire from heaven played round the standards and tents of the soldiers; a swarm of bees settled on the pediment of the Capitol; it was reported that semi-bestial babies had been born, and that a pig had been produced with the talons of a hawk. That each of the offices of state found its numbers reduced, since a quaestor, an aedile, and a tribune, together with a praetor and a consul, had all died within a few months, was considered another portent.

Tacitus, *Annals* 12, 64

With Claudius out of the way, Nero resolved to poison Britannicus. The captain of the guard, Julius Pollo, and the famous professional, convicted poisoner, Locusta, were in on the plot; Locusta administered a poison which proved ineffective, acting only as a strong laxative. She was duly flogged by Nero who, not unreasonably, demanded to know why she had dispensed a medicine and not a poison, so a second much more powerful toxicant was selected from her *pharmacopeia*; this was tested on a goat, which took a disappointing five hours to die. Nero ordered that the potency of the potion be increased; it was then trialled on a pig, which died immediately—Nero had his poison. The customary royal tasting and the taster were circumvented by serving Britannicus a beverage which was too hot for him to drink; the cooling water poured into his cup was laced with poison that rendered him speechless and breathless. A disinterested Nero attributed these symptoms to the epilepsy which, he said, had afflicted Britannicus from childhood, and that the choking boy would soon recover. Britannicus, of course, never did recover, but the meal went on regardless. His peremptory cremation took place that very night during a heavy rainstorm, during which the rain conveniently washed off the gypsum which had been smeared on his corpse to camouflage the skin darkening caused by the poison. Locusta was rewarded with a free pardon and a ready supply of 'students' from Nero for her sinister experiments. When it looked as though all was up for Nero, he took a selection of Locusta's poisons with him when he fled Rome but, perhaps wisely, chose death by other means. Locusta lives on in Alexander Dumas' *The Count of Monte Cristo* in which the poisoner Madame de Villefort is compared to Nero's witch; one of the chapters is entitled 'Locusta'.

Nero was ambivalent about magic. In the early years of his reign, he made great use of divination but, by 51 CE, he followed Tiberius by exiling those who consulted Chaldeans, particularly those who tried to divine the date of his death. He had Agrippina murdered at Baiae in 59 CE, appropriately near Lake Avernus, gateway to hell; he was then forever scared out of his wits by her ghost and by the torch brandishing and whip wielding Furies—female chthonic deities of vengeance—which crowded his imagination. Suetonius relates how when fuelled by drink, he paid an unhealthy interest in his mother's corpse, thus substantiating allegations of incest and necrophilia. In a bid to rid himself of her spectre he enlisted magicians to call up her ghost and exorcise the evil. While travelling in Greece, he declined the offer to partake in the Eleusinian mysteries because he knew that it would involve a descent to the underworld—and an awkward meeting with his dead mother.

Vitellius, one of the emperors in 69 CE, was particularly hostile to astrologers and would frequently have them executed without trial. They did little to help their cause, however, when they responded to Vitellius' edict that all Chaldeans be banished by 1 October with a pamphlet wishing for Vitellius's death on the same day, for the good of the state.

Dio Cassius describes the emperor Hadrian as a dabbler in divination and sorcery (*manganeiai*), particularly in his attempt to come to terms with the mysterious and untimely death of Antinous, his lover.

In Roman Egypt, in 189 CE, an edict went out from the Prefect banning all magical divination, oracles and sorcery, on pain of death. Any governor not prosecuting this ruling would find himself subject to the same penalty. Execution too awaited those in 357 CE who, under the emperor Constantius II, wore amulets for the eradication of disease or illness, or pilfered the 'horrible contents' of tombs at night.

The second century novelist Apuleius is best known to us for the tales of magic, witchcraft, shape-changing, and bestiality that he regales us with in his *Metamorphoses,* written in 158 CE. His *Apologia,* or *De Magia,* by is a mine of information on magic; it forms the basis of his real-world defence against charges of practising magic, of being a *magus,* brought against him by the family of Pudentilla, a rich and attractive widow whom he had married. The in-laws were anxious not to lose Pudentilla's fortune to a foreigner and Apuleius accordingly found himself in the dock, defending himself for his life. He also makes the point that, over the years, a trumped up charge of witchcraft has often been used to legally dispose of one's enemies. This is the opening of his spirited defence:

> Cease, I say, to bring forward these empty slanders. Prove your indictment, prove that I am guilty of ghastly crimes, detestable sorceries, and black art-magic. Why is it that the strength of your speech lies in mere noise, while it is weak and flabby in point of facts? I will now deal with the actual charge of magic. You spared no violence in fanning the flame of hatred against me. But you have disappointed all men's expectations by your old wives' tales, and the fire kindled by your accusations has burned itself out.

Apuleius, De Magia 25–43;
adapted from the translation by H. E. Butler

All manner of alleged magical practice was brought before the court including Apuleius's black Hermes voodoo doll. Apuleius had to make the defence of his life to prove his innocence. His magical and witchy stories may indeed be warnings to his readers of the serious consequences inherent in practicing sorcery: dangerous, illegal, and anti-social.

The actions of the emperor Valens (r. 364–378) show how paranoia continued to haunt the authorities throughout the later Empire. In an act of socio-political cleansing, ostensibly designed to rid the Empire of sorcerors, Valens executed, mainly by strangulation or by burning to death, all the pagan philosophers in the eastern empire. Ammianus Marcellinus gives us a catalogue of murders, informers, evidence obtained under torture, planting of evidence, panic burning of potentially incriminating books, (many of which were written on the fine arts, or were law books) and the burning of personal libraries in an attempt to avoid incrimination:

> For having gained leave to name all whom he desired, without distinction of fortune, as dabbling in forbidden practices… he entangled many persons in his lamentable

nets, some of them on the ground of having stained themselves with the knowledge of magic, others as accomplices of those who were aiming at treason. And in order that even wives should have no time to weep over the misfortunes of their husbands, his men were immediately sent to put the seal on the houses, and during the examination of the furniture of the householder who had been condemned, to introduce privily old-wives' incantations or unbecoming love-potions, contrived for the ruin of innocent people. And when these were in a court where there was no law or scruple or justice to distinguish truth from falsehood, without opportunity for defence young and old without discrimination were robbed of their goods and, although they were found stained by no fault, after being maimed in all their limbs were carried off in litters to execution. As a result, throughout the oriental provinces owners of books, through fear of a like fate, burned their entire libraries; so great was the terror that had seized upon all.

Ammianus Marcellinus, *History* 29, 1–2
translation from *The Roman History of Ammianus Marcellinus*,
Loeb Classical Library edition, 1939

Efforts to divine the date of the emperor's death and, indeed, the name of his successor, would not go away despite the penalties. Valens heard report that a necromancy had been held in which the name of his successor was sought. The letters 'e', 'o', and 'd' emerged as parts of a compound name. The astonishing result was the wholesale slaughter of all those in the empire answering to Theodorus, Theodotuse, Theodosius, Theodolus and anything remotely similar—despite frantic attempts on the part of many to change their names to anything 'theodo-less' (Ammianus Marcellinus, *Res Gestae*, 29, 1, 29).

The *Digest of Justinian* adds that peddling or possession of *venena* and *medicamenta*—evil drugs—was outlawed; a woman who gives a drug to aid conception and kills the recipient is executed; irresponsible distribution by perfumers (*pigmentarii*) of hemlock, salamanders, aconite, pine caterpillars, bubrostis insect, mandrake, or Spanish fly also became a criminal offence.

This litany of official anti-magic and its malevolent use illustrates a number of recurrent themes. First, it confirms that magic and occult practice generally was inherent in society and ubiquitous; second, it highlights the apparent association of magic with treason and revolution; third, it reinforces the xenophobic association of foreigners with things chthonic and magical; fourth, it exemplifies the use of accusations of peddling magic to secure unsound convictions for both men and women; and finally, it highlights the fabricated association of women, magic and sexual depravity. We have already noted one of the most celebrated uses of this was by Cicero when he called Claudia Pulchra Prima the Lesbia of Catullus's love-hate poems, 'the Medea of the Palatine'.

The literature is awash with references to aspects of the occult. Ennius provided an early link between Greek and Latin literature with his adaptation of Euripides'

Medea. Plautus contrives a ghost story in the *Mostellaria*; and Lucretius, in *De Rerum Natura* Book 3 teaches us Epicurean eschatology and Cicero, in the *Somnium Scipionis,* Stoic eschatology. [13, 14] His *On Divination* gives us a description of a ghost at Megara; a necromancy is described in *In Vatinium*.[15] Strabo describes the oracle of the dead at Avernus as the location for Odysseus' *nekyia* in the *Odyssey*; Varro lists the various forms of divination. [16, 17, 18]

All provide a rich vein of sources for Virgil, whose Book Six of the *Aeneid* was the tour de force of infernal description and Roman eschatology. As well as the extensive coverage of the underworld in *Aeneid* 6, Virgil himself reflects Theocritus with his description of the sorcery of Amaryllis in *Eclogues* 8 and gives his version of the *katabasis* of Orpheus in *Georgics* 4.

Tibullus gives a vivid description of death, Elysium, and Tartarus; he also colourfully describes an execrable witch (*nefanda*), the black arts, one other witch, and ghosts, divination, and Aeneas' Sibyl.[19] Horace is a frequent dabbler in the occult. In the *Odes*, he describes life after death and, specifically, the after-life of Augustus, Archytas' ghost and Hades; in the *Satires*, we have necromancy and witches, the celebrated Canidia, and Odysseus and Tiresias in the underworld; the *Epodes* bring a reprise of Canidia, this time with her witchy cabal.[20] The author of the *Culex* provides a *katabasis,* a description of the underworld, and a parade of mythological heroes.[21] Propertius gives us ghosts and chthonic curses.[22] Ovid's *Metamorphoses* is rich in infernal and eschatological material: it describes Pythagoreanism, Orpheus' *katabasis*, and Medea.[23] She re-emerges in the *Heroides*, while in the *Fasti* he describes the rites of Tacita. In the *Amores*, we meet the witches Circe and Dipsas. Medea takes centre stage in his lost eponymous tragedy.

We have then a social phenomenon which is not only rich in terms of literary heritage but dynamic, highly topical, and contemporary as well. No wonder that Lucan, Statius, Silius Italicus and Valerius Flaccus went on to incorporate the chthonic into their epics given the convention established by Homer and Virgil, and the apparent modishness and popularity of such *topoi* as evidenced further by Lucan's lost works, the *Catacthonia* and the *Orpheus*. [24, 25] In other genres, Petronius features witches among the characters in the *Satyricon*, and Seneca the Younger describes metempsychosis in his *Epistulae*, another *Medea*, Hercules crossing the Styx in his *Hercules Furens* and a possessed Cassandra in his *Agamemnon*. [26] His *Oedipus*, with its necromancy, was probably an important source for Statius along with the works of Ovid, both lost and extant.[27] Martial describes witches and Tacitus, as we have seen, records evidence of magic, witchcraft, and witches, most notably in the mystery surrounding the high profile death of Germanicus.[28, 29] Statius describes the *katabaseis* of Aeneas, Theseus, Alcestis and Protesilaus in his *Silvae*.[30] Suetonius also provides evidence of the ubiquity of magic and sorcerers: as well as his description of Nero using magic to placate the ghost of his mother, Agrippina the Younger, whom he had just had murdered, he also pictures Caligula driven mad by a love potion, and describes various legislation against and expulsions of sorcerers by Augustus, Tiberius and Vitellius.[31]

Curse Tablets

Curses and charms were very popular throughout the Roman world. Here are a few examples of the 1,600 or so curse tablets that have been found; *defixiones* reach back as far as the fourth century BCE in Greece and were traditionally consecrated to the gods of the underworld. Predominantly a practice of the lower classes, the curses were often provoked by unfortunate, disappointing and untoward events such as commercial disputes, failures in law suits, or unrequited love: they gave vent to the curser's vengeful wrath, malice and vindictiveness.

Typically, the victim's name was written on a lead tablet, although gold, silver, and marble are not unknown; blanks have been found, suggesting that there was a steady ongoing trade. The consecration was made and a nail stuck through the name; this was often followed by the name of the target's mother, to avoid any mistaken identity, which would invalidate the curse. Magic words and symbols were added to enhance the chances of success. Some tablets featured a portrait of the victim that is also pierced with nails; the texts were anonymous. In tablets inspired by jilted love, a lock of the intended's hair was sometimes attached. By the Hellenistic period, a variant— 'vindictive prayers'—appears: these usually bore the name of the author. One of the biggest finds was at Aquae Sulis (Bath) where 130 were discovered; many are angry retorts about clothes stolen while their owners were bathing.

The *defixio* which brings down all manner of calamity on the recipient is typical:

> May burning fever seize all her limbs, kill her soul and her heart; O gods of the underworld, break and smash her bones, choke her, arourarelyoth, let her body be twisted and shattered, phrix, phrox.
>
> Ziebarth 24, 1–4, pp. 1042ff.

This very angry man was clealy leaving nothing to chance. A bitter and broken-hearted Marcus Junius Euphrosynus, obviously torn between grief for a daughter and hatred for her mother, set up a tomb to the eight-year-old daughter, Junia Procula, in the first century CE. On it he curses Acte, his 'treacherous, tricky, hard-hearted poisoner' of a shameful wife, hoping that she gets in the next life as good as she gave in this. He leaves the adulteress a nail and a rope for her neck, and 'burning pitch to sear her evil heart'.[32] A late second century curse on Rufa Pulica found in an urn along with her ashes in Mentana near Rome lists a number of her body parts: the prurient focus on sexual organs suggests that illicit sex was involved somewhere. Ticene of Carisius suffered a similar *post mortem* fate on a tablet found at Minturnae, south of Rome; her curser wishes that everything she does goes wrong: his catalogue of her body parts is less sexual than Rufa's, but is anatomically quite methodical, running as it does more or less from head to toe. Philo may have had something to hide when he cursed Aristo; he ties up her hands, feet, and soul, condemns her to silence, and wishes her tongue be bitten off. The wife of Aristocydes curses him and his lovers, hoping that he will never marry another woman or a boy.

It was not all fire and brimstone, however. There are occasional examples of love *defixiones* where a lover will invoke chthonic deities to help him win the love of his life. The optimistically named Successus dedicates his wife in a bid to see his love for her requited: 'May Successa burn, let her feel herself aflame with love or desire for Successus.'[33]

Considerably less romantic, excessively malevolent, and obsessively perverted love charms targeted at women appear in the *Greek Magical Papyrus*. This originates from the fourth century CE, but undoubtedly describes practices that were prevalent much earlier.

Some men went to extraordinary lengths to ensure the fidelity of their women: the following (*PGM* 4, 296–466) is one of the most notorious and takes a typically prescriptive, recipe form: 'take wax or clay from a potter's wheel and form it into two figures, a male and a female ... her arms should be tied behind her back, and she should kneel.' There then follows directions: to write magical words on her head and other parts of her body, including the genitalia, to stick a needle into her brain and twelve others into other parts of her body; tie a binding spell written on a lead plate to the figures; dedicate it to gods of the underworld; and leave it at sunset near to the tomb of someone who has died violently or prematurely; invite them to rise from the dead; and bring 'X' [the object of the charm], daughter of 'Y', to him and make her love them. There then follows a litany of instructions to deprive the girl of food and drink, sexual intercourse, sleep and health, all designed to make her make love with the curser forever.

Sarapammon (*Suppl Mag* 47) invokes a whole pantheon of underworld gods in his efforts to ensure the fidelity of Ptolemais; he asks the *daemon* Antinous to tie Ptolemais up to prevent her from having intercourse or from being sodomised.

> [She should] give no pleasure to any man but me ... and let her not eat, nor drink, nor be happy, nor go out, nor sleep with anyone but me ... drag her by the hair and entrails until she does not reject me ... submissive for her entire life, loving me, desiring me.

This tablet (the Louvre Doll) was found in a vase which also contained a voodoo-type clay figure of a kneeling woman, her hands tied behind her back and body pierced with needles.

The spell cast by Akarnachthas was found in Egypt and probably dates from the early first century CE: the ingredients are the egg of a crow, the juice of a crow's foot plant, and the bile of an electric catfish from the Nile; these are to be ground up with honey and rubbed on the penis while chanting the spell, which goes:

> womb of NN, open and receive the semen of NN and the unconquerable seed of ... let NN love me for all of her life ... and let her remain chaste for me, as Penelope did for Odysseus. And you womb, remember me for the whole of my life.

Have intercourse after this, and the woman will love you and sleep with no one else.
Another papyrus aims to render the woman sleepless until she relents.

> Take the eyes out of a bat and release it alive. Take unbaked dough ... or wax and
> shape a puppy dog. Put the right eye of the bat into the right eye of the puppy and
> the left eye of the bat into the left eye of the puppy. Take a needle and stick the magic
> substance into it. Prick the eyes of the puppy ... Pray: 'I conjure you to ... make X lose
> the fire in her eyes or become sleepless and have no one in mind except me ... and
> love me passionately'.

The Papyri were not exclusively heterosexual; one from the second century CE
describes a lesbian curse where Heraias brings and binds the heart and soul of
Sarapias.[34]

Love potions in literature appear in Virgil's Eighth *Eclogue* (adapted from Theocritus'
Idylls 2) where Amaryllis concocts a potion (*herbae* and *venena*) and spells to win
back Daphnis: 'by these magic rites I'll try and bring Daphnis back to his senses: all
I need now are some spells'. A less than idyllic love potion recommended by the *magi*
and scorned by Pliny the Elder involved the wearing of an amulet which contained a
hyena's anus.[35]

Endnotes

Introduction

1. Quoted in *Ductor Dubitantium*, or The *Rule of Conscience* (1660) by Jeremy Taylor 1, 1, 5
2. Cicero, *In Verrem* 2, 5, 162 used as an expression of rights under Roman law. American president John F. Kennedy quoted the phrase in 1963: 'Two thousand years ago, the proudest boast was 'civis romanus sum'. Today, in the world of freedom, the proudest boast is 'Ich bin ein Berliner'. www.columbia.edu/itc/german/korb/3001-06/berlin-pilot/tempelhof-schoen/jfk-berliner-website.html accessed 19 June 2016. The *Constitutio Antoniniana*, or the Edict of Caracalla or the Antonine Constitution, allowed all free men in the Roman Empire Roman citizenship and all free women the same rights as Roman women. Before 212, mostly only inhabitants of Italy had Roman citizenship.
3. As Montesquieu wrote, '[I]t should be noted that the main reason for the Romans becoming masters of the world was that, having fought successfully against all people, they always gave up their own practices as soon as they found better ones.' From *Considerations on the Causes of the Greatness of the Romans and Their Decline*, ed. David Lownthal, Hackett Publishing, 1999, p. 24.

Chapter 1

1. It is not in Lewis & Short, *A Latin Dictionary*, because its first use falls beyond the 200 CE date limit set by the lexicographers.
2. Incidentally, *De Pallio* is described by E. J. Brill, publishers of Huninck's *Commentary*, as one of the strangest and perhaps most difficult texts ever written in Latin.
3. See Adams, J. N. 'Romanitas and the Latin Language.' *Classical Quarterly* 53.1 (2003) 184–205.
4. Plutarch, *Cato* 23, 1–3; Polybius 31, 24.
5. Livy 24, 2–4; Aulus Gellius 7, 6–8. Cf Arkins, *Aspects of Sexuality* p.8ff.
6. See G. Colin, *Rome et la Grece*; J. Griffin *Augustan Poetry* p. 88ff and the Appendix, *Some Imperial Servants*. Various suggestions for the start and or cause of the decline have been made: Polybius, 31, 25 ascribes it to the victory over Macedonia; L. Calpurnius Piso (Pliny *NH* 17, 38, 244) goes with 154 BCE; Appian, *Bellum Civili* 1, 7 for the end of the war in Italy; Livy 39, 6, 7 prefers 186 BCE; Valleius Paterculus, *Historiae Romanae*, and Sallust, *Catilina* 10 opt for the end of the Third Punic War. See also Putnam, *The Roman Lady*; Reinhold, *The Generation Gap* p.52ff.
7. See also Dio Cassius 57, 15, 2
8. Valerius Maximus 2, 2, 2
9. Putarch, *Cato* 12, 4–5

Chapter 2

1. For infanticide see Brunt, *Roman Manpower* pp. 148–154.
2. Livy 27, 37.
3. Suetonius, *Augustus* 94, 3; Musonius Rufus, *Reliquae* 80f.
4. Soranus, *Gynaecology* 2, 10.
5. *The Gnomon of the Ideologue* (41 and 107) provides for male foundlings—children of the dung heap but there is nothing for females.
6. Pomeroy, *Goddesses* p. 164–165 points out the short-sightedness of the exposure policies, delimiting as they do the supply of child bearers and their male offspring, much needed for the army; the comparison with Spartan policy is stark. See Golden, p. 155. Cicero, *Tusc.* 1, 39, 93; *IG* 5, 2, 43. Marcus: see G. Patriarca (1933), 'Epitaffio Grec Recentemente Scoperta a Roma', *Bullettino della Commissione Archaeologica Comunale* 61, 211–15
7. Cicero, *Ad Atticum* 1, 8 for *deliciolae*. For a reply see Servius Sulpicius Rufus' at *Ad Familiares* 4, 5, 1, 4–6. Dolabella: *Ad Atticum* 7, 2.
8. *CIL* 6, 38605 and *CEG* 153.
9. *CIL* 6, 8517. Other instances of the deaths of young daughters recorded on tombstones are Lutatia Secundina age four years, six months and nine days (*CIL* 6. 21738); Magnilla, aged eight—*a positive delight* (*CIL* 6. 21846); and Heteria Superba who died aged one year, six months, twenty-five days. Sosias Isas, twelve-year-old daughter of a 'desolate' father from Bologna in the second century CE (*AE* 1976, 202) and eighteen month old Irene from Ariminum (*CIL* 11, 466); Minicia's epitaph can be seen on the family tomb now in the Terme Museum in Rome. See also thirteen-year-old Corellia Optata whose headstone was uncovered in 2011 at the Hungate dig in York. See also the gifted Menophilia from Sardis from the same time (*Peek*, 1881) and five-year-old Politta from Memphis at the end of the second century CE (*Peek* 1243)—blameless and without fault in her parents' eyes.
10. Valerius Maximus 2, 4, 5.
11. For Julia, Revocata and Murra see *CIL* 3, 2399; 3, 3017; 13, 2219.
12. Tacitus, *Agricola* 4, 2–4
13. *CIL* 6, 10230
14. Valerius Maximus, *Facta et Dicta Memorabilia* 4, 4.
15. Dio Cassius, *Historia Romanae* 78, 2.
16. See also *CIL* 8, 8123 where a twenty-five-year-old mother's last wish is that her daughter is chaste.
17. See also *CIL* 1, 2, 1221 where Lucius Aurelius Hermia similarly praises his faithful, devoted, happy, dutiful wife—for better or for worse. See also *CIL* 6, 6593 from the tomb of the Statilii in Rome and the epitaph to Urbana in third century CE Rome (*CIL* 6, 29580). Other similar inscriptions include *CIL* 6, 29149; 11, 1491—to Scribonia Hedone with whom her husband lived for eighteen years without a quarrel. *ILA* 175, p.54; *CIL* 5, 7453.
18. Also Nepos, *Fragmenta 1–2 de Viris Illustribus*.
19. Pliny *Historia Naturalis* 7, 69. It is as well to bear in mind his caveat that he has no responsibility for the veracity of anything he writes; this is down to his sources, the original authors (*op cit* 7, 8).
20. 4, 3; 19, 1–3. Translation by Ian Scott-Kilvert in *Plutarch, Makers of Rome*. 1, 2–5;
21. Paullus was consul in 34 BCE and Censor in 22.
22. Livy 2, 13, 11
23. *Ad Marciam* 16, 1 and *Ad Helviam* 16, 5.
24. Pliny 7, 24.
25. Martial 1, 35, 8–9; Valerius Maximus 8, 3.
26. *Sammelbuch* 3, 6263.
27. Tacitus, *Agricola* 7

28. Seneca the Younger, *Ad Helviam* 2,4
29. See also a similar refrain in 7, 5 and Pliny's concern about his wife's illness in 6, 4. See the letter on Macrinus' perfect wife and marriage *(concordia)*—8, 5, 1–2.
30. 'Mother's breast is best' seems to be another badge of the good matron, *CIL* 6, 19128; presumably thought by some as preferable to the use of wet nurses.
31. Livy 1, 58, 7.
32. Ovid, *Fasti* 2, 720–58.
33. Pliny, *ibid*, 7, 19. Tacitus, *Histories* 1, 3.
34. Tacitus *Annals* 16, 34.
35. Appian, *The Civil Wars* 4, 39
36. Valerius Maximus, *Memorable Deeds and Sayings*, 6, 7, 1–3.
37. See Grmek, *Les Maladies* pp 214–225.
38. Appian, *Bella Civilia* 4. 39–40.
39. Sallust, *Catilina* 25. See Balsdon, *Roman Women* pp. 47–49 for the controversy surrounding Sallust's description of her.
40. Seneca *Ad Marciam* 1, 1; *Ad Helviam* 16, 5.
41. Pliny, *NH* 6, 24.
42. Plutarch, *Brutus* 13 and Dio 44, 13–14. See also Valerius Maximus 4, 6 and 6.7 on brave and faithful wives; Appian *BC* 4, 39–40 and Tacitus, *Annals* 16, 34, on wives in civil wars.
43. Tacitus, *Annals* 6, 29; 16, 10.
44. *Ibid* 6, 40.
45. *Ibid* 6, 29.
46. *Ibid* 15, 63, 2–4.
47. *Ibid* 16, 34
48. Pliny, *Epistles* 3, 16, 7–9.
49. Livy, 8–11, 14.
50. *Aulularia* 498–550. Translation is by E.F. Watling, Penguin 1965
51. Cicero, *Att.* 15, 11.
52. Cicero, *Ad Fam* 14, 4–6. *Att.* 3, 19.
53. Suetonius, *Augustus* 73,1; 64,2
54. Balsdon, *op cit* p. 270 and n. 59.
55. Ovid, *op cit* 3, 817–820.
56. Columella, *praef* 1–3; 7–9.
57. Aelius Aristides, *Roman Oration* 71b.
58. Petronius, *Satyricon* 37, 67
59. Columella 12, 3
60. See Cicero, *Pro Murena* 12, 27, where he asserts that women require guardians because of their inferior intellect.
61. Tacitus *Annals* 13, 32.
62. *Twelve Tables* 4, 2.
63. Livy 48, 12 -13.
64. Seneca, *Ad Marciam* 12, 2.
65. Petronius, *op. cit.* 46, 5.
66. Martial 7, 87.
67. See, for example, *IG* 14, 56 (Sicilia) and *CIG* 3559.
68. Pliny, *NH* 10, 42; 10, 121–2.
69. Varro, *Rerum Rusticarum,* 3, 5. Cicero *Epistulae ad Quintum Fratrem* 3, 1, 1
70. Apuleius, *Florida* 12.
71. Persius *Prologus* 8–14; Pliny *NH* 10, 42, 118–9; Petronius, *op.cit.* 28, 9; Statius 2, 4, 19.
72. 4, 6.
73. Pliny, *op. cit.* 10, 120
74. Apicius 5, 6, 1; *Lampr. Heliog.* 20, 6.

75. Ovid, *Metamorphoses* 5, 33; Seneca, *Epistles* 121; Pliny, *NH* 10, 73; 11, 37.
76. Plutarch, *Moralia* 959f; Pliny *NH* 18, 17.
77. Juvenal 15, 7; Hyginus, *De Astronomia* 2, 28; Aulus Gellius 20, 8.
78. *AP* 7, 189; 190, 192–8, 200, 201.
79. Pliny, *NH* 3, 82; Plutarch, *Sertorius* 11; Aulus Gellius 15, 32; Appian, *Bellum Civile* 1, 13, 110; Frontinus, *Strategematon* 1, 11, 13.

Chapter 3

1. Dio 54, 16, 7.
2. *AE*, 1971, 534.
3. See Harkness, *Age at Marriage*.
4. See also Pliny, *Ep* 1, 10; 6, 26; 6, 32.
5. Cicero *Att.* 6, 6, 1 and *Fam* 8, 6, 2 for his reported sanguine resignation over the issue.
6. Cicero *Att.* 1,3,3 and 6,6,1; *Ad Q. Fratrem* 2,4,2; 2,6,2; See also Collins, *Tullia's Engagement*.
7. 4, 10
8. Cicero, *Att.* 11, 2, 2; 11,23,3.
9. *Ibid* 16, 15, 5.
10. Pliny, *NH* 7, 48, 158.
11. Plutarch, *Aemilius Paullus*.
12. Aulus Gellius, *Noctes Atticae* 4, 3, 2.
13. Paul, *Sent. Recept* 2, 26, 4; *Digest* 48,5,30.
14. Rapsaet-Charlier, M. –Th. *Ordre Senatorial*.
15. Pliny, *NH* 7,5
16. *BGU* 1103.
17. Valerius Maximus 8, 2, 3.
18. Plutarch, *Cato Minor* 25, 52; Lucan, *Pharsalia* 326–371.

Chapter 4

1. *CIL* 13, 2182
2. *A Casebook on Roman Family Law*, Frier and McGinn p. 95.
3. Plutarch, *Cato the Elder* 20, 2.
4. G. G. Fagan, Violence in Roman Social Relations, in *The Oxford Handbook of Social Relations* (Oxford, 2011), p. 487.
5. *BGU* 1052.
6. *De Haruspicum Responsis* 17, 37; 18, 38.

Chapter 5

1. Mercury, god of luck.
2. Hercules, god of treasure trove.
3. Libitina = Proserpine, goddess of things funereal.
4. Situated in the forum, enclosed by a wall; it was considered sacred after it had been struck by lightning.
5. Gladiators
6. In the forum from which speakers addressed the public.
7. Pythagoreans were not permitted to eat beans because they believed the souls of the dead inhabited them.
8. i.e. dinner
9. The muse of epigrams.
10. The emperor Domitian.

11. A common sight on the outside of wine shops.
12. An aquaduct in Rome.
13. On Mount Parnassus, sacred to the muses.
14. Prochta is a small island off Baiae; the Sabura was Rome's busiest street.
15. Numa maintained that the nymph Egena inspired his religious institutions.
16. *Cumae.*
17. Romulus.
18. All Greek towns or islands.
19. A rhetorician.
20. Daedalus.
21. The olive.
22. The three stock female characters in comedy: wife, whore, slave girl.
23. Greek actors working in Rome.
24. Publius Egnatius Celer.
25. Tarsus.
26. Pegasus.
27. Childless women would be more likely to leave him a legacy.
28. Aristocratic women.
29. Chione was a prostitute.
30. Publius Cornelius Scipio Nasica.
31. Lucius Caecilius Metellus.
32. Models of frugality.
33. Nobles.
34. The king of Troy and therefore from one of the families which claimed descent from the house of Troy.
35. Fourth and fifth century sculptors.
36. Towns in Latium.
37. Pythagoreans were vegetarian.
38. Seals were believed to sleep very soundly.
39. See Homer, *Odyssey* 10 552ff for Elpenor's accident.
40. Instead of wine; the waters at Sinuessa in Campania were sobering and medicinal, and they cured even insanity. Pliny *H N.* 31, 2
41. See Phang, *Marriage.*
42. *Bowman and Thomas* No 5, 1987.

Chapter 6

1. Boar was often very expensive and a symbol of extravagance; see Pliny *Ep* 8,210
2. Fine Roman and Greek wines respectively.
3. i.e. Porker and Nomentanus.
4. Indicating that he wanted to leave.
5. Mercury was the god of commerce and Trimalchio's patron; Minerva was the goddess of wisdom and the arts.
6. Lictors carred the rods and axes, not men of Trimalchio's inferior position.
7. As on the speaker's rostrum in the forum.
8. Symbolising senatorial rank.
9. Quite incongruous with the gold ring.
10. A satyr.
11. A quotation from Virgil *Aeneid* 2, 44.
12. Famous astronomers.
13. Domitian.

14. i.e. the man in the street.

15. A famous gourmet.

16. The Muses.

17. Lake Azov.

18. Informers.

19. Thyestes' feast consisted of the bodies of his two sons; Phoebus was horrified at this.

20. Geese were fattened on figs to enormous sizes. See Horace *Sat* 2,8,88; Juvenal 5, 114

Chapter 7

1. Galen, *On Anatomical Procedures* 1, 2

2. See also *Ep*. 3, 7.

3. Precautions against informers.

4. Domitian.

5. Lucretius, *De Rerum Natura* 4, 1290.

6. *CIL* 6, 10320.

7. Plutarch, *Sulla 3, 2*

8. Petronius, *Satyricon* 74.

9. Catullus 61

10. Lucretius, 4, 1269–1278; Pliny *NH* 29, 27, 85; 20,99, 263; 25, 54,97; 30, 43,123; 25,18,39.

11. *CIL* 4, 107. *CIL* 4, 4185;

12. Seneca, *Controversies* 1, 2, 22. Martial 11, 78.

13. Manetho, *Forecasts* 4,312.

14. Dioscorides *de Materia Medica* 3, 34; 1, 77, 2; 3, 130; 5, 106, 6.

15. James, (1994), Ancient *Inventions*.

16. Jane E. Brody, *New York Times*, 8 August, 1984

17. Aetius 16, 17.

18. Oribasius 68.

19. Pliny, *NH* 8, 209.

20. Ovid, *Amores* 2, 14, 5–10, 19, 20, 27–28, 35–40; 2, 13

21. *CIL* 6, 9720; 9723.

22. *CIL* 6, 6647.

23. *Thesleff* pp. 123–124

24. Eusebius, *Historia Ecclesiastica* 6, 8.

25. Dio, 80, 16. For Elagabalus's transgender tendencies and transsexuality see Godbout, *Elagabalus. GLBTQ: An Encyclopedia of Gay, Lesbian, Bisexual, Transgender, and Queer Culture.*

26. Martial 2, 45; 7, 30; 7, 35; 7, 82.

27. Lucretius, *De Rerum Natura*, 4, 1030–57; See Brown, *Lucretius on Love and Sex*, pp. 62–63.

28. See Dugan, *Preventing Ciceronianism*, pp. 403–404.

29. See Hanson, *The Restructuring of Female Physiology at Rome*, p. 267; *Priapea* 78 and *CIL* 12, 6721(5), one of the Perusine *glandes*.

30. Martial 7, 82; 9, 27, 11, 75; 14, 215. Juvenal 6, 73, 379.

31. Quintilian *Institutio Oratoria* 11, 3, 19. Aristotle, *History of Animals* 781a, 21–27; Celsus, *On Medicine* 7, 25, 3.

32. See also Galen, *De Simplicium Medicamentorum Temperamentis ac Facultatibus*, Kuhn 12, 232. *Ibid, De locis Affectis*, Kuhn 8, 450–451.

33. Pliny *NH* 30, 2.

34. Propertius 4, 11

Chapter 8

1. Diodorus Siculus 4, 6, 5. Isidore of Seville, *Eytmologiae* 11, 3, 11. Pliny, *NH* 7, 33; 36; 51; 30; 23.
2. Dionysius of Halicarnassus 2, 15
3. Suetonius, *Augustus* 94, 3; Musonius Rufus, *Reliquae* 80f.
4. Soranus, *Gynacology* 2, 10.
5. Philo, *de Specialibus Legibus* 3, 114–115.
6. Livy 27, 37.
7. Suetonius, *Augustus* 94, 3; Musonius Rufus, *Reliquae* 80f.
8. Soranus, *Gynaekia.*

Chapter 9

1. Tacitus, *Annals* 4, 53. Pliny, *NH* 7, 46.
2. *Pleket* 30; *CIL* 6, 33898.
3. *FHG 3, 520ff.* Pornography, of course, is a 19th century term but examples of material of what we would now define as pornographic go back to time immemorial. See Hyde *A History of Pornography.*
4. Martial 10, 35.
5. Musonius Rufus 3, 4, 13a
6. Arrian, *Discourses of Epictetus* fr. 15.
7. Plutarch, *Moralia* 138a-146a.
8. All originally by Cicero: *Orator* 161; *Att.* 7, 2, 21; *Tusculanae Disputationes* 3, 45. See Chrystal, *Investigation* p. 15ff; Ross, *Backgrounds*; Tuplin, Cantores Euphorionis; *idem*, Cantores Euphorionis *Again*; Luck, *Latin Love Elegy* p.49ff; Crowther, *Valerius Cato*; see Lyne *Latin Love Poets* pp. 169–174. For *otium* see Andre, *L'Otium.*
9. On educated women generally, see Best, *Cicero*; Griffin, *op cit* p. 103, and Fau, *op cit* p. 12. Eucharis: *CIL* 1, 1214, see above p.; Cytheris: Cicero, *Fam* 9, 26; *Phil* 2, 69. See also Hallet, *The Role of Women*, and Lyne, *op cit* p. 7.
10. Catullus 10, 4, 17; 33–34; see also his rejection of Flavius' girl 6, 1–2;
11. 32, 1–2.
12. *Ibid* 86, 3–4; see also 43, 4; and 35, 16–17.
13. Cicero, *Pro Caelio* 13, 32.
14. So Rankin, *Clodia II* p.505, 'it would be possible to claim Clodia (Lesbia) as an intellectual on the grounds of poem 36 alone'. Gallus' wife (78, 2) is *lepidissima coniunx*; Laodamia, = Lesbia, is *docta* (68, 80).
15. Propertius 2, 3, 9; 17–21; 1, 2, 27–30; 2, 1, 3–4; 9–10. *Docta* at 1, 7, 11; 2, 11, 6 and 2, 13, 11. Helicon 2, 30, 25–30.
16. Tibullus 1, 5, 25–28; 1, 3, 85–88.
17. *Ibid* 3, 12, 2. For Sulpicia, see Pearcy, *Erasing Cerinthus*; Santirocco, *Sulpicia Reconsidered*; Keith,—*Critical Trends*; Hubbard, *The Invention of Sulpicia*; Holzberg, *Four Poets*; Hallett, *The Eleven Elegies*; Churchill, *Women Writing.*
18. Horace, *Odes* 1, 36, 13–13, 17–20; 2, 11, 22–24; 3, 14, 21–22
19. *Ibid* 2, 12, 17–20; 3, 9, 10; 2, 11, 22; 3, 28, 11; 4, 11, 35–37; 3, 14, 21; 1, 17, 10f.
20. Ovid, *Amores* 2, 4, 9–10; 47–48. See also 2, 10, 5–6. *Ars Amatoria* 3, 311–28; 3, 349–52.
21. Ovid, *Ars Amatoria* 1, 97–98; *ibid* 1, 462; *Amores* 2, 4, 22; *ibid* 3, 8, 5–7; *Ars Amatoria* 2, 107–112.
22. Ovid, *op cit* 281ff.
23. Women reading philosophy: Cicero *Att.* 13, 21a 4–5; 13, 22, 3; Horace *Epod* 8. Epic: Propertius 2, 1, 49–50; Juvenal 6, 434ff. Comedy: Martial, 8, 3, 15–16; 10, 35, 1

24. Statius, *Silvae* 3, 5, 33–36
25. Cicero *Tusc* 1, 5.
26. Pliny, *op cit* 8, 14, 6f
27. Suetonius, *On Grammarians* 3; Quintilian 1, 2

Chapter 10

1. *CIL* 13, 2019.
2. *CIL 2,* 497.
3. *Euporista* 3, 1, 13.
4. Baader, *Spezialarzte* p. 233, fn 62.
5. See *CIL* 4, 207; 171; 913; 3291; 1083; 6610; 3678; 3684; 3527; Savunen, *Women and Elections.* For Tatia see Thonemann, *The Women of Akmoneia*; the translation of the inscription is by Thonemann.
6. *CIL*, 10, 810.
7. *Pleket* 8G.
8. *Pleket* 19G.
9. *CIL* 8, 23888.
10. Women reading philosophy: Cicero *Att.* 13, 21a 4–5; 13, 22, 3; Horace *Epod* 8. Epic: Propertius 2, 1, 49–50; Juvenal 6, 434ff. Comedy: Martial, 8, 3, 15–16; 10, 35, 1. Statius' wife, Claudia, reads his poetry, *Silvae* 3,5, 33–36, as does Pliny's, as we have seen at 6, 7 and 4, 19.

Chapter 11

1. i.e. when winter comes.
2. A river in Apulia.
3. Rather than count it.
4. As did Clytemnestra, daughter of Tyndareus.
5. Examples of prodigality.
6. A eunuch in Maecenas's household.
7. Lucilius refers to this.
8. Porphyrion tells us that Rufus started the craze for eating stork; he lost his campaign for the praetorship. 9. Proverbial since Terence *Phormio* 342: a feast so extravagant that you didn't know which parts to eat.
10. After Plato, *Phaedo* 83D—pain and pleasure are nails which fix the soul to the body.
11. An example of their hospitality.
12. i.e. they get drunk.
13. Ofellus' property was confiscated as were Horace's and Virgil's in 41 BCE and assigned to Umbrenus; see *Sat* 2,133.
14. See Tacitus, *Histories* 4, 42 for the background to this.
15. In the manner of an astrologer.
16. The standard practice in schools of rhetoric was to provide three proofs to an argument.
17. The Lipari islands off Sicily.
18. One of the centaurs.
19. Juvenal is telling us that he's had rhetorical training.
20. A respectable woman disgracing herself by performing in the arena.
21. Crispinus was an Egyptian who rose to equestrian rank under Domitian; Canopus was an Egyptian city.
22. Two informers.
23. A famous actor; Thymele was his leading lady.

24. Lyons; losers at the contest were flogged and thrown into the river.
25. Achilles' charioteer.
26. A professional poisoner.
27. Blackened that is by poison.
28. A small island in the Aegean used for banishment.
29. An amateur poet.
30. The story of the flood.
31. i.e. senatorial rank.
32. One of the noblest old Roman families now fallen on hard times.
33. An affluent freedman of Claudius'
34. A slave of Julius Caesar's freed by Augustus and also very rich.
35. Newly imported slaves had their feet whitened to distinguish them from local slaves.
36. The temple of Concord was littered with birds' nests.
37. Angry because of his greed.
38. A politician attacked by Lucilius.
39. Tigellinus' preferred method of torturing Christians.
40. Burials were prohibited within the city walls of Rome.
41. Plutarch, *Cato the Elder* 17; Cicero *De Re Publica* 4,6; Dionysius of Halicarnassus 20, 3; Livy *Periochae* 14, 39, 4; Plutarch *op. cit* 18; Aulus Gellius, 4, 8; 4, 12; Pliny, *Natural History* 18, 3. Dionysius 20, 3; Livy 7,
42. See, for example, Fantham, *Stuprum: Public Attitudes and Penalties for Sexual Offences in Republican Rome*, p. 121; Richlin, *Not before Homosexuality: The Materiality of the* cinaedus *and the Roman Law against Love between Men*, p. 556. The emperor took the job on during the empire.

Chapter 12

1. Tacitus, *Annals* 12. 54, *Histories* 9; Suetonius, *Claudius* 28.
2. See Suetonius, *Claudius* 37; Tacitus, *Annals* 11, 30–8; 12, 1; 12, 57, 65; 13, 1; Dio Cassius 9, 34.
3. See Phlegon, *Marvels* 10, 28.

Chapter 14

1. Juvenal 6, 103–112.
2. Calpurnius Flaccus, *Declamatians* 52.
3. *Historia Augusta*: Marcus Aurelius 19.
4. Dio 61, 17, 3.
5. Dio, 63, 3, 1.
6. Petronius, *Satyricon*, 45.
7. Dio, 66, 25, 1.
8. Martial, *De Spectaculis* 6; 8.
9. Suetonius, *Domitian* 6, 1. Dio, 67, 8, 4.
10. Statius, *Silvae*, 1, 6, 53.
11. Juvenal 1, 22–23
12. Nicolaus of Damascus, *Athletica* 4, 153.
13. Dio, 66, 26, 7.
14. Dio, 76, 16.
15. *CIL*, 9, 2237.
16. Ovid, *Ars Amatoria*, 1, 156.
17. Ropes were slung across the amphitheatre and from these the various delicacies were showered down on the crowds.
18. Modern Israel
19. i.e., it is all free.

20. Amazons
21. Rag and bone men
22. Flamingoes
23. Pheasants

Chapter 15

1. Augustine *De Civ Dei* 6, 9.
2. See also Catullus, 62
3. Cicero, *de Deorum Natura* 2, 70–72; Virgil, *Georgics* 4, 221ff.
4. Cf, however, Beard, *Rome* pp. 25ff who argues against this view.
5. *Roman Questions* 96, *Moralia* 286–287.
6. Cicero, *De Domo Sua*, 53,136.
7. See also Catullus 63
8. Plutarch, *Numa* 10.
9. Cicero, *Cat* 3, 9.
10. Livy 39, 17; 39, 19–22.
11. *P.Oxy* 11, 1380, 214–216.
12. *CIL* 6, 224.
13. Livy 22, 57, 2.
14. Dionysius 2, 68; *RE* vii A 768–770; Valerius Maximus 8, 1, 5.
15. Suetonius, *Domitian* 8, 3–5; Pliny, *Ep* 4, 11, 6.
16. Valerius Maximus 3, 7, 9; 6, 8, 1.
17. Cicero, *Cat* 3, 9.
18. Dio 777, 16, 1–3; 79, 9.
19. Pliny *NH.*28, 13; Macrobius, *Saturnalia* 3, 13, 11.

Chapter 16

1. Plutarch, *Moralia* 138a-146a; *idem, de Superstitione*. Pliny, *NH* 28, 47 and 104; Plato *Laws* 7, 808d. Translation is by T.J. Saunders.
2. Mormo: Plato, *Crito* 46c; Lucian, *Vera Hist* 139; Empusa: Aristophanes, *Frogs* 285–295; Gello: Sappho *frag* 178; Lamia: Horace, *Ars Poetica* 340 warns poets not to 'draw a living boy from the belly of Lamia that dined with him'. Diodorus Siculus 20, 41.
3. Persius 2,34; Juvenal 10, 289; Dio, 49, 43, 5; 52, 36, 2–3. Livy 8, 18.
4. Terence, *Phormio* 705
5. Cicero, *de Div* 1, 34, 74.
6. Livy 31, 17, 12; 21, 62, 3; 3, 10, 6.
7. See also Suetonius, *Divus Julius* 81; *Caligula* 57.
8. Petronius, *Satyricon* 104; Pliny, *NH* 28, 26–29
9. George Orwell, *Coming Up for Air* pp. 51–52 (Harmondsworth 1962).
10. See Dionysius of Halicarnassus 4, 62, 5–6
11. Cassius Dio, *Roman History* 49, 43, 5; 52, 36,3. Livy 39, 8–19; 39, 41; 40, 43. Suetonius, *Tiberius* 63, 1; *idem, Life of Claudius* 25. Pliny, *op. cit* 30,4. Suetonius, *Augustus* 31.
12. Tacitus, *Annals* 2, 69; 2,74; 3,7.
13. 446–531. See Foster (1972) on how Virgil alludes to this at *Aeneid* 1, 349ff
14. *De Republica* 6; see also *Natura Deorum* 2.30 and *Tusculanae Disputationes* 1,166 for example.
15. *ND* 1.57; *In Vatinium* 14.
16. C244-6, including Ephorus *FGH* 70 F134a.
17. Strabo 5, 4, 5.
18. Varro *Antiquitates Rerum Humanarum et Divinarum* 41.
19. Death, Elysium and Tartarus, *Elegies* I,3; witch I,2, 42–66; *nefanda* I, 5, 39–59; 2, 5: divination

20. Life after death: *Odes* 4,7,16; Augustus' life after death, *ibid* 3,3,11–12; Archytas' ghost *ibid* 1, 28; a glimpse of Hades *ibid* 2,13; *Satires* 1,8,18ff necromancy and witches; Canidia the witch *ibid* 2,1,48 and 2,8,95; Odysseus and Teiresias in the underworld, *ibid* 2,5 *Epodes* 5 Canidia, Sagana, Veia and Folia; *ibid* 17

21. See Barrett A. A. The Topography of the Gnat's Descent. *CJ* 1970 65, 255–257.

22. Cynthia's ghost, death and the underworld 4,7; Propertius' curse and the afterlife he wishes on a prostitute 4,5, 1–18; Gallus' ghost 1, 21

23. Pythagoreanism *Metamorphoses* 15, 75ff; Orpheus' *katabasis, ibid* 10; Medea's witchcraft *ibid* 7.159–351 and *Heroides* 6, 83–94; *Fasti* 2, 572–583: the rites of Tacita; *Amores* 3, 7, 27–36, 73–84: Circean witchcraft; Dipsas the witch ibid 1,8, 1–20, 105–14. Quintilian (10, 1, 98) praises his lost tragedy, *Medea;* see also Tacitus *Dial* 12.

24. For Statius' epic poetry sources on the Theban theme see Vessey (1973)

25. Servius, *ad Aeneid 6, 392* mentions a lost *Orpheus* which may be that written by Lucan, now lost but mentioned by Statius, *Silvae* 2, 7, 57 and Servius *ad Georgics* 4, 492.

26. *Satyricon* 63: witches.

27. *Epistulae* 102 deals with the soul after death. *Medea:* witchcraft. *Hercules Furens* has a description of Hercules crossing the Styx at 775ff; the *Agamemnon* features the trance and possession of Cassandra at 710–778.

28. *Epigrams* 12, 57, 15–17; 9, 29, 9.

29. Tacitus, eg: *Annals* 1, 28; Germanicus 2, 69; see also 2, 27; 12, 52; *Dialogus de Oratoribus* 12.

30. Statius, *Silvae* 5, 3, 266–276. See also *Silvae*, 2, 7, 121 where Statius says that the door to Hades lies open to husbands returning to their brides, after the fashion of Protesilaus.

31. Suetonius, *Nero* 34; *Caligula* 50; *Augustus* 31, *Tiberius* 63; *Vitellius* 14.

32. CIL 6, 20905

33. *ILS* 8751; *IG* 3,3,97, 34–41; *CIL* 10, 8249; *IG*, 3,3, 78; *SEG* 27, 1717

34. *CIL* 8, 12507; *PGM* 36, 283–294; 1, 83–87; 1, 167–168; 32.

35. Hyenas: Pliny, *op cit* 28, 106. Virgil, *Aeneid* 6, 71–74. Dionysius of Halicarnassus, *Roman Antiquities* 4, 62, 5–6. Virgil, *Eclogue* 4, 6, 24, 31.

Glossary of Latin Terms

adulterium: adultery—made illegal by Augustus' *Lex Julia de Adulteriis Coercendis* of 18 BC.

affectio maritalis: the declared intention of a betrothed couple to marry.

cursus honorum: the sequence of public offices held by men of senatorial class.

deliciae: darling, delight.

divinatio: divination.

docta puella: an educated, clever woman.

dos: dowry.

equites: the equestrian order ranked below senators; the equites were often middle-class businessmen and farmers.

familia: the family.

filiafamilias: daughter, under paterfamilias

freedman/woman a slave who had been emancipated; many were tradesmen and women.

gravitas: dignified, serious or solemn conduct.

Hellenism: the culture of classical Greece which percolated into Rome.

incestum: unchastity, particularly in Vestal Virgins; incest.

ius patrium, ius vitae necisque: a father's right to decide whether a newborn lives or dies.

lex: law.

magus: magician.

maiestas: majesty, dignity, greatness; treason

manus: an early form of marriage which consigned the woman to the *potestas* of her husband, or his father.

materfamilias: mother, female head of the family.

matrona: a respectable Roman woman.

medica: female doctor.

meretrix: a prostitute.

mos maiorum: the customs of ancestors

murena: lamprey

obstetrix: midwife.

otium: a lifestyle of ease and commercial, political or military inactivity.

paelex: concubine, mistress.

paterfamilias: father, male head of the family.

patria potestas: the father's power over his household.

patrician: the dominant political class.

pietas: dutifulness—in all aspects of life.

pontifex maximus: chief priest.

pudicitia: chastity, fidelity—one of the badges of a good *matrona*.

pudor: modesty, propriety.

puellae Faustinianae: girls who benefited from a welfare programme set up by Antoninus Pius.

res gestae: political and military achievements.

Romanitas: being a Roman, exhibiting Roman characteristics

scortum: a prostitute.

sponsalia: the engagement party; betrothal.

stola: worn by *matronae* over their tunics.

stuprum: sexual depravity.

tutela: guardianship for women who were without husbands or fathers; guardians administered their legal and financial affairs.

univira: a badge of the good matron—a one-man woman.

Primary Sources Quoted & Translated in the main text

Acta Divi Augusti, Rome (1945) 99, 113–116, 123, 126

Aëtius Amidenus, *Tetrabiblion* 16

Ammianus Marcellinus (325/330—after 391); [L] *History* 29, 1–2

Apicius, The; compiled in the late fourth or early fifth century CE, it is often referred to as the *De Re Coquinaria of Apicius.* 1, 4; 2, 46; 4, 139; 4, 176; 6, 229; 6, 231; 7, 323; 8, 396.

Appian (late first century CE—160 + CE), [Gk] *Bellum Civile* 1, 13

Apuleius, late second century CE [L] *Metamorphoses* 9, 12; 9, 39; 11, 7ff; *De Magia* 25–43

Athenaeus of Naucratis (*fl.* end second century CE), [Gk] *Deipnosophistae*

Augustine of Hippo (354–430 CE), [L] *De Civitate Dei,* 4, 8; *Confessions* 9, 9

Aulus Gellius (*c.* 125–after 180 CE), [L] *Noctes Atticae* 1, 6, 2; 1, 17, 4; 3, 3, 5; 4, 2, 1; 10, 23, 5.

BGU, *Berliner Griechische Urkunden* 380

Boccaccio (1313–1375), *Concerning Famous Women,* p. 188

Caesar, Julius (100 BCE–44 BCE), [L], *De Bello Gallico; Bellum Civile* 3, 53

Catalogue of the Literary Papyri of the British Museum, 253

Cato the Elder, *De Re Floria* in Aulus Gellius frag 57; *On Agriculture* 139–41

Catullus (*c.* 84–54 BCE), [L] *Carmina* 2; 3; 62, 63–70; 63, 4–8;

Celsus, (before 47 BCE) [L] *De Medicina* 7, 25

Cicero (106 BCE–43 BCE), [L] *Ad Atticum* 1, 2, 1; 1, 5, 1; 5, 1, 3–4; 11, 2, 2; 12, 15; 12, 46; 14, 9; 14, 13, 5; *Ad Familiares* 7, 26; 16, 16; *Brutus* 37; 140; 211; 305–16; *De Officiis* 1, 42; *De Oratore* 2, 239; *De Re Publica* 4, 3; *Pro Murena* 34; *Tusculanae Disputationes* 1, 39, 93; *In Verrem* 2, 5, 162; 2, 5, 167; *On Friendship* 20, 74; *Letters to His Brother Quintus* 1, 3, 3; 4, 2, 2

CIL, *Corpus Inscriptionum Latinarum,* [Berlin 1863] 1, 1211; 1, 1214; 1, 1221; 1, 1570; 1, 1604; 1, 1837; 3, 3572; 3, 8267; 4, 64; 4, 113; 4, 138; 4, 206, 4, 294; 4, 434; 4, 336; 4, 353; 4, 373; 4, 490; 4, 960; 4, 497; 4, 677; 4, 710; 4, 743; 4, 826; 4, 864; 4, 1136; 4, 4957; 4, 8149; 4, 7164; 4, 7273; 4, 7473, 4, 6672; 6, 10230; 6, 15258; 6, 1527; 6, 19159; 6, 22355a; 6, 29896; 6, 36467; 6, 37695; 6, 9213; 6, 9222; 6, 9731; 6, 11027; 8, 1641; 8, 1793; 9, 1721; 11, 137; 13, 1983; 14, 2112; 14, 4827; 15, 7914

Columella, (4–*c.* 70 CE) *De Re Rustica* [L] 1, 8; 8

Corpus Glossariorum Latinorum III, pp. 645–7

Dio Cassius (*c.* 155–235 CE), [Gk] *Historia Romanae,* 54, 16, 1–1; 62, 13, 4; 62, 18

Diodorus Siculus (*fl.* between 60 and 30 BCE), [Gk] *Bibliotheca Historica* 5, 38, 1; 23, 18, 4–5

Dionysius of Halicarnassus, (*c.* 60 BCE—after 7 BCE) [Gk], *Roman Antiquities* 2, 15; 2, 25,-7; 2, 26–27; 4, 24, 4–8

Florus, *Epitome of Roman History* 3, 20

Frontinus, *De Aquis* 2, 116–7

Fronto, *Letters to Marcus Aurelius* 415

Galen, (130–200 CE) *De Semine* 1, 16, 30–32; *Introductio sive Medicus* 10, 14, 76, 12–15

Horace (65 BCE—8 BCE), [L] *Satires* 1, 1; 1, 6, 65–92; 2, 2; 2, 6; 2, 8; *Epistles* 2, 1, 70–1; *Ars Poetica* 325–30

IGUR 1176

ILS = *Inscriptiones Latinae Selectae,* ed. H. Dessau. 1046a; 7760; 7802

Julius Obsequens, *Book of Prodigies* 50, 51, 53.

Juvenal (*fl.* early second century CE), [L] *Satires* 1; 3; 4, 1–72; 6, 52ff; 6, 82–103; 6, 184–191; 6, 300; 6, 314–334; 6, 336–342; 6 366–8; 7, 215–7; 219–224; 230–1; 234–243

L'Annee Epigraphique 17 (1904) 21

Lex Cornelia de Sicariis et Veneficis

Livy (59 BCE-17 CE), [L] *Ab Urbe Condita* 1, 26; 1, 57–60; 2, 10; 3, 26–9; 3, 44–58; 10, 40, 1–5, 14; 27, 37; 34, 2, 1—2; 34, 7; 34, 8–11

Longinus, *De Sublimitate* 44, 5

Lucan (39–65 CE), [L] *De Bello Civili* 1, 584f

Lucian (*c.* 125—after 180 CE) *A Feast of Lapithae* 18; *The Dream* 1–4

Lucretius (*c.* 99 BCE—*c.* 55 BCE) *De Rerum Natura* [L] 1, 132ff; 2, 594f; 4, 1269–78

Marcus Aurelius, (161–180 CE) *M. Cornelius Fronto: Epistulae ad M.Aurelium* 4, 6

Martial (*c.* 40–100 CE), [L] *Epigrams* 1, 4; 1, 13; 1, 30; 1, 47; 1, 62; 1, 66; 1, 89; 2, 11; 1, 109; 2, 37; 3, 45; 3, 52; 3, 94; 4, 8; 4, 21; 4, 72; 5, 9; 5, 10; 5, 20; 5, 34; 5, 78; 6, 7; 6, 39; 6, 53; 6, 66; 6, 88; 7, 61; 8, 14, 5–6; 8, 23; 8, 74; 9, 18; 9, 30, 3–6; 9, 68 1–4, 8–12; 10, 35, 1–4, 8–13, 15–6; 9.79; 10, 31; 10, 47; 10, 58; 10, 61; 10, 68; 10, 92; 11, 3; 11, 39; 11, 53; 11, 66; 11, 69; 11, 82; 13, 58; 13, 67; 14, 1, 23, 68, 70, 134 *De Spectaculis* 22; 28.

Matthew

Minucius Felix, *Octavius* 30

Nepos, Cornelius (*c.* 110—*c.* 25 BCE) [L] *Noctes Atticae; De Viris Illustribus praef.* 6

Ovid (43 BCE—17 CE), [L] *Fasti* 4, 905–941; *Tristia,* 1, 6, 26; 3, 7, 1–4, 11–12, 23–4; 4, 10, 69ff; *Metamorphoses* 8, 646–678; 9, 675–679; *Ars Amatoria* 1, 31–34; 1, 135–63; 1, 635–8; *Amores,* 1, 4; 1, 7; 1, 8, 73; 2, 4, 25–31; 2, 6, 1–2, 59–62; 2, 14, 5–10, 19, 20.

Paul (Saul) of Tarsus, (*c.* 5—*c.* 67 CE), *Opinions* 1, 21; 2, 26, 1–8, 10–12, 14–17.

Paulus of Aegina, *De Re Medica Libri Septem* 6, 70

Peek = *Griechische Verse- Inschriften,* Berlin 1955, 1233

P. Bour. = *Les Papyrus Bouriant* 25

Petronius (*c.* 27—66 CE), [L] *Satyricon, Cena Trimalchionis* 26–36; 29; 37, 8; 38, 6–7, 39–41; 97; 126

Philo of Alexandria (*c.* 20 BCE—40 CE) [Gk] *Questions and Answers on Genesis* 3, 47; *De Specialibus Legibus* 3; 114–115; 172–5

Phlegon of Tralles (*fl.* second century CE), [Gk] *Miracles*

Plautus (*c.* 254–184 BCE), [L] *Aulularia* 498–550; 505–22; *Mercator* 823–9; *Captivi* 889; *Poenulus* 32–35, 28–31; *The Boeotian Woman* (Fragment v.21 Goetz); *Asinaria* 3, 3, 103

Pliny the Elder (23–79 CE), [L] *Historia Naturalis* 7, 16; 9, 39, 77; 29, 8, 16–18; 28, 5; 29, 27, 85; 35, 4

Pliny the Younger (*c.* 61—113 CE), [L] *Epistulae* 1, 10; 1, 12; 1, 13; 1, 14; 1, 15, 1–10; 1, 16, 6; 1, 21; 2, 4; 2, 6; 2, 20; 3, 3; 3, 14; 3, 16 3–6; 4, 2, 3; 4, 19; 4, 13, 3–6, 9; 4, 21; 5, 16 1–7; 6, 3; 6, 7; 6, 34; 7, 5; 7, 24; 8, 5; 8, 10; 8, 16; 8, 21; 9, 6; 9, 17, 1; 10, 33; 10, 34; 10, 96; 10, 97

Plutarch, (*c.* 45–125 CE), [Gk] *Romulus* 21, 3–5; 22; *Cato Maior* 20, 2–5; 22–23; *Cicero* 20; 49, 2; *Gaius Gracchus* 19, 1–3; *Moralia* 138–9; 141a; *De Curiositate* 10/*Moralia* 520c; 145a; *Numa* 10, 4–7; *Crassus* 8.

Polybius (*c.* 204–122 BCE), [Gk], *Histories* 2, 56, 7; 6, 53–6; 6, 54,3; 31, 24; 31, 27

P. Oxy = *The Oxyrhynchus Papyrus* 744; 1206; 1895; 6, 903; 95 [*Select Papyri* 1, 32]

Propertius (b. 50–45 BCE—15 BCE), [L] *Elegies* 2, 5, 21–6; 2, 8; 2, 33, 1–22; 4, 11, 45–6

P. Wisc. = *The Wisconsin Papyri* 16, 5

Quintilian (*c.* 35–90 CE), [L], *Institutiones Oratoriae* 1, 1, 4–5; 1, 1, 6–8, 15–17, 20; 1 3, 13–14; 1, 4, 1–4; 6, *praefatio* 3–6; 6–11.

Sallust (*c.* 86–35 BCE), [L], *Bellum Catilinae*25

Sammelbuch 6262

Scriptores Historiae Augustae, The Life of Hadrian, 18, 7–11

Seneca, L. (*c.* 4 BCE-65 CE), [L] *Ad Helviam* 2,4; 19, 1–3; *Ad Marciam*16, 1; *De Beneficiis,* 3, 38, 2; *De Ira,* 2, 21, 1–6; 2, 31, 6; *Moral Letters to Lucilius* 7, 3–5; 19, 4; 41, 3; 47, 1–11; 50, 2; 54, 1–4, 6; 56, 1–2; 70, 19–21, 23; *De Providentia* 2, 5

Seneca, M. (54 BCE—*c.* 39 CE*), Controversiae* [L] 1, 2; 10, 4; *Suasoriae* 3, 6, 7

Sidonius Apollinaris *Poems* 23, 323–424

Soranus (*fl.* 100 CE) [Gk], *Gynaikea* 1, 2, 4; 1, 34, 1; 1, 64, 1–1; 1, 65, 1–7; 4, 9;

Leonidas

St Ambrose, (*c.* 340—397 CE) quoted in *Ductor Dubitantium,* or The *Rule of Conscience* (1660) by Jeremy Taylor 1, 1, 5

St Jerome *Chronicles,* for 41 BCE

Statius (*c.* 45—*c.* 96 CE) [L] *Silvae* 1, 6; 1, 6, 57–65; 2, 4, 1–7; 2, 5, 1–7; 3, 5; 5, 1, 1–9

Strabo (64 BCE—*c.* 24 CE) [Gk], *Geographia* 4, 9; 4 16; 5, 3, 8;

Suetonius (*c.* 69–140 CE) [L], *Augustus* 34; 67; 69; *Claudius* 25, 2; 41–42; *Nero* 12, 1–2; 29; 35, 3; *Tiberius* 2, 2; 71; *On Grammarians* 9; 13; 16; 17.

Tacitus (56–118 CE) [L], *Agricola* 4, 2–4; 6; *Annals* 2, 69; 3, 25; 12, 43, 1; 12, 64; 13, 32; 14, 30; 14, 42–5; 15, 32; 15, 34; 15, 37; *Dialogus de Oratoribus* 28, 6; 34, 1–6; *Histories* 3, 32–4

Tebtunis Papyri 330

Terence (*fl. c.* 170–160 BCE) *Hecyra* 28f.

Tertullian, (third century) *Pallio, On the Cloak* 4, 1; 4, 1–2

The Code of Theodosius 11, 27, 10

Tertullian, *On the Apparel of Women 1, 1, 1–3; 2, 2, 4–6; De Spectaculis* 22–23

Tibullus (*c.* 55 BCE–19 BCE) [L], *Elegies* 1, 10, 51–8; 3, 23–34

I Timothy 2, 11–15

Twelve Tables (450 BCE) 4, 1; 7, 3

Ulpian (*c.* 170–228 CE), [L], *Digest; Regulae* 11, 1, 21, 27, 28.

Valerius Maximus (14–27 CE), [L], *Memorable Deeds and Sayings* 6, 1, 3 and 6; 6, 3, 9; 9, 1, 3

Varro (116 BCE—27 BCE) [L], *De Lingua Latina; On Agriculture* 2, 10, 6

Virgil (70 BCE—19 BCE), [L] *Aeneid* 6, 71–4.

De Viribus Illustribus (first half of fourth century CE) [L], anonymous

Wisconsin Papyrus 16, 4

Xenophon (*fl.* 371 BCE) *Memorabilia* [Gk]; *Life of Crassus* 8

Ziebarth 24, 1–4, pp. 1042ff.

Further reading

Adams, J. N., 'Romanitas and the Latin Language', *Classical Quarterly* 53 (2003) 184–205

Amunsden, D. W., 'The Age of Menarche in Classical Greece and Rome', *Human Biology* 42, (1970), 79–86

—*Medicine and the Birth of Defective Children: Approaches of the Ancient World*, in R. C. McMillan, H. T. Engelhardt, Jr., S. F. Spicker (ed.) *Euthanasia and the Newborn*, (Dordrecht 1987), 3–22.

Andre, J. M., *L'Otium dans la Vie Morale et Intellectuelle Romaine des Origins a la Epoque Augusteenne* (Paris 1966)

Angst, J., 'Bipolarity from Ancient to Modern times: Conception, Birth and Rebirth', *Journal of Affective Disorders* 67, 1–3 (2001) 3–19

Ankerloo, B., *Witchcraft and Magic in Europe Vol 2: Ancient Greece and Rome* (London 1998)

Archer, L. J. (ed.) *Women in Ancient Societies* (London 1994)

Aterman, K., 'Why Did Hephaestus Limp?', *American Journal of Diseases of Children* 109 (1995) 381–392.

Atkins, R., *Poverty in the Ancient World*, Cambridge 2006.

Baird, J., *Ancient Graffiti in Context* (London 2010)

Baker, P. S., 'Incomplete Adults: the Mentally Impaired in Classical Antiquity', *AClass 50* (2007) 171–172

Baldwin, B., Horace on Sex, *AJPh* 91 (1970), 460–465

'Women in Tacitus', *Prudentia* 4 (1972), 83–101

Balsdon, J. P. V. D., *Life and Leisure in Ancient Rome* (London 1969)

Bauman, R. A., *Women and Politics in Ancient Rome* (London 1992)

Crime and Punishment in Ancient Rome (London 1996)

Beard, M., The Sexual Status of the Vestal Virgins, *JRS* 70 (1980), 12–27

Literacy in the Roman World (Ann Arbor 1991)

Re-Reading (Vestal) Virginity in Hawley (1995), 166–177

Religions of Rome: A Sourcebook (Cambridge 1998)

Bertman, S., *The Conflict of Generations in Ancient Greece and Rome* (Amsterdam 1976)

Best, E. E., Cicero, Livy and Educated Roman Women, *CJ* 65 (1970), 199–204

Betz, H. D., *Greek Magical Papyri in Translation 2/e* (Chicago 1997)

Blayney, J., *Theories of Conception in the Ancient Roman World* in Rawson, Family 230–236

Blok, J., (ed.) *Sexual Asymmetry: Studies in Ancient Society* (Amsterdam 1987)

Bloomer, W. M., 'Schooling in Persona: Imagination and Subordination in Roman Education', *Cl. Ant* 16 (1997), 57–78

Boatwright, M. T., Women and Gender in the Forum Romanum, *TAPA* 141 (2011), 107–143

Bodel, J., *Epigraphic Evidence: Ancient History from Inscriptions* (London 2001)

Bogden, R., *Freak Show: Presenting Human Oddities for Amusement and Profit.* (Chicago 1988)

Bonner, S. F., *Education in Ancient Rome: From Cato the Elder to the Younger Pliny* (London 1977)

Bosman, P., (ed.) *Mania: Madness in the Greco-Roman World* (Pretoria 2009)

Bourne, E., The Epitaph of Allia Potestas, *CW* 9, (1916) 14–16

Bouvrie, S., Augustus' Legislation on Morals, *SO* 59 (1984), 93–113

Bowman, A. K., *Life and Letters on the Roman Frontier: Vindolandia and its People* (London 1994)

Boyd, B. W., *The Death of Corinna's Parrot Reconsidered: Poetry and Ovid's 'Amores. Classical Journal.* 82, (1987) 199–207

Bradley, K. R., *Wet Nursing in Rome* in Rawson, *The Family* (1986)
Discovering the Roman Family: Studies in Roman Social History (New York 1991)
The Roman Child in Sickness and in Health in George, *The Roman Family* (2005) 68–92

Brignell, V., 'Disability in the Ancient World', *New Statesman*, 7 April, 2008

Brown, R., 'Livy's Sabine Women and the Ideal of *concordia*', *TAPA* 125, (1995), 291–319

Brunet, S., 'Female and Dwarf Gladiators', *Mouseion* 3. (2004), 145–71
Dwarf Athletes in the Roman Empire. *AHB* 17 (2003), 17–32

Brunt, P. A., *Roman Manpower 225 BC–AD 14* (Oxford 1971)

Bryk, F., *Circumcision in Man and Woman: Its History, Psychology and Ethnology* (Honolulu 2001)

Burriss, E. E., *Taboo, Magic, Spirits: A Study of Primitive Elements in Roman Religion* (Oxford 1931)

Cantarella, E., *Pandora's Daughters: The Role and Status of Women in Greek and Roman Antiquity* (London 1987)

Carcopino, J., *Daily Life in Ancient Rome* (London 1941)

Chalmers, W. A., *Plautus and His Audience* in Dorey, *Roman Drama*, 1965

Chrystal, P., *Differences in Attitude to Women as Reflected in the Work of Catullus, Propertius, the Corpus Tibullianum, Horace and Ovid* (MPhil thesis, University of Southampton, 1982)
Women in Ancient Rome (2013)
Roman Women: The Women Who Influenced Roman History (2015)
In Bed with the Romans: Sex and Sexuality in Ancient Rome (2015)
Wars and Battles of the Roman Republic: The Bloody Road to Empire (2015)
Roman Military Disasters: Dark Days and Lost Legions (2015)
Ancient Greece in 100 Facts (2017)
How to be a Roman (2017)
Women in Ancient Greece: Seclusion, Exclusion, or Illusion? (2017)
In Bed with the Ancient Greeks: Sex & Sexuality in Ancient Greece (2016)
'Deadlier than the Male: Women Warriors', *Minerva* September 2016, 36–40
Women at War in the Classical World (2017)
Roman Record Keeping and Communication (2017)

Churchill, L. J., *Women Writing Latin Vol 1: From Roman Antiquity to Early Modern Europe*, (New York 2002)

Cilliers, L., *Mental Illness in the Greco-Roman Era* in Bosman (2009), 130–140

Clark, A. J., *Divine Qualities: Cult and Community in Republican Rome* (Oxford 2007)

Clark, G., *Women in the Ancient World* (Oxford 1989)

Clarke, J. R., *Looking at Lovemaking: Constructions of Sexuality in Roman Art 100 BC–AD 250* (Berkeley 1998)
Roman Sex 100 BC to AD 250 (London 2003)

Clarke, M. L., *Higher Education in the Roman World* (London 1971)

Cohen, D., *Seclusion, Separation and the Status of Women* in McAuslan, I. *Women in Antiquity* pp. 134–145

Colin, G., *Rome et la Grece de 200 a 146 BC avant JC* (Paris 1905)

Luxe Oriental et Parfums Masculins dans la Rome Alexandrine, *RBPH 33* (1935), 5–19

Colton, R. E., Juvenal and Martial on Women who Ape Greek Ways, *CB* 50 (1973), 42–44

Corbier, M., Child Exposure and Abandonment, in S. Dixon (ed.), Childhood, Class and Kin in the Roman World, (London 2001), 52–73

Corte, M. D., *Loves and Lovers in Ancient Pompeii* (Salerno 1976)

Crook, J. A., *Patria Potestas, CQ* 17 (1967) 113

Croom, A., *Roman Clothing and Fashion* (Stroud 2010)

Cruse, A., *Roman Medicine* (Stroud 2004)

Daehner, J., (ed.) *The Herculaneum Women: History, Context, Identities* (Los Angeles 2007)

D'Ambra, E., The Cult of Virtues and the Funerary Relief of Ulpia Epigone
    Latomus 48 (1989), pp. 392–400
    Roman Women (Cambridge, 2007)
    Women in the Bay of Naples in James, *Companion* (2012), 400–413

D'Ambrosio, A., *Women and Beauty in Pompeii* (New York 2002)

D'Avino, M., *The Women of Pompeii* (Naples 1967)

Dayton, L., 'The Fat, Hairy Women of Pompeii', *New Scientist* 1944, 24 September 1994

Deacy, S., (ed.) *Rape in Antiquity* (London 1997)

del Castillo, A. The Position of Women in the Augustan Age, *LCM* 2 (1977), 167–173

Dersin D., (ed.) *What Life was Like When Rome Ruled the World* (Richmond VA, 1997)

Deslauriers, M., *Women, Education and Philosophy* in James, *Companion* (2012), 343–353

Deutsch, M., The Women of Caesar's Family, *CJ* 13 (1918), 502–514

Dickie, M. W., Magic and Magicians in the Graeco-Roman World (London 2001)

Dickison, S., 'Abortion in Antiquity', *Arethusa* 6 (1973), 158–166

Dixon, S., 'The Family Business: Women and Politics in the Late Republic', *C&M* 34 (1983), 91–112
    'Family Finances: Tullia and Terentia', *Antichthon* 18 (1984), 78–101
    'Polybius on Roman Women and Property', *AJPh* 106 (1985), 147–170
    The Roman Mother (London 1988)
    The Roman Family (Baltimore 1992)
    Reading Roman Women (London 2001)
    Exemplary Housewife or Luxurious Slut: Cultural Representations of Women in the Roman Economy in McHardy, Women's *Influence* (2004)

Dobbins, J. J., (ed.) *The World of Pompeii* (London 2007)
    'A Roman Funerary Relief of a Potter and His Wife', *Arts in Virginia* 25 (1985), 24–33

Dudley, D., *Roman Society* (London 1975)
    (ed.) *Neronians and Flavians: Silver Latin I* (London 1972)

Dupont, F., *Daily Life in Ancient Rome* (Oxford 1992)

Durry, M., 'Le Mariage des Filles Impuberes dans la Rome Antique', *REL* 47 (1970), 17–25

Edwards, C., *The Politics of Immorality in Ancient Rome* (Cambridge 1993)
    Unspeakable Professions: Public Performance and Prostitution in Ancient Rome in Hallett, *Roman Sexualities* (1998), 66–95
    Death in Ancient Rome (London 2007)
    'Putting Agrippina in her Place: Tacitus and Imperial Women', *Omnibus 63* (2012), 22–24

Elia, O., *Pitture Murali e Mosaici nel Musea Nazionale di Napoli* (Rome 1932)

Elliot, A., (ed.) *Roman Food Poems* (Totnes 2003)

Engels, D., The Problem of Female Infanticide in the Greco-Roman World, *CPh* 75 (1980), 112–120

Evans, J. K., *War, Women and Children in Ancient Rome* (London 1991)

Eyben, E., 'Antiquity's View of Puberty', *Latomus* 31 (1972), 677–697
    'Family Planning in Graeco-Roman Antiquity', *Anc.Soc* 11–12 (1980), 5–82

Fantham, E., 'Stuprum: Public Attitudes and Penalties for Sexual Offences in Republican Rome', *EMC 35 (1991)*, 267–291
    Women in the Classical World: Image and Text (New York, 1994)

Amelia Pudentilla or the Wealthy Widow's Choice in Hawley R. *Women in Antiquity* (1995), 220–232

Fau, G., *L'Emancipation Feminine a Rome* (Paris 1978)

Fenton, T., The Late Roman Infant Cemetery Near Lugnano, *Journal of Paleopathology* (1995), 13–42

Ferguson, J., *The Religions of the Roman Empire* (London 1970)

Ferrill, A., Augustus and his Daughter: A Modern Myth, *Latomus* 168 (1980), 332–346

Field, J. A., 'The Purpose of the Lex Iulia et Papia Poppaea', *Classical Journal* 40 (1945), 398–416

Filbee, M., *A Woman's Place* (London 1980)

Fildes, V., *Breasts, Bottles and Babies: A History of Infant Feeding* (Edinburgh 1987)
   Wet Nursing: A History from Antiquity to the Present (Oxford 1998)

Finley, M. I., *Aspects of Antiquity* (Harmondsworth 1972)
   The Etruscans and Early Rome in Finley, *Aspects* pp. 110–123
   The Silent Women of Rome in Finley, *Aspects* pp. 124–137
   Studies in Ancient Society (London 1974)
   Ancient Slavery and Modern Ideology (Harmondsworth 1983)

Flemming, R., '*Quae corpora quaestum facit:* The Sexual Economy of Female Prostitution in the Roman Empire', *JRS* 89 (1999), 38–61
   Medicine and the Making of Roman Women (Oxford 2000)
   'Women, Writing and Medicine in the Classical World', *CQ* 57 (2007), 257–279

Foley, H., (ed.) *Reflections of Women in Antiquity* (London 1981)

Forbes, C. A., 'The Education and Training of Slaves in Antiquity', *TAPA* 86 (1955), 321–360

Frank, R. I., 'Augustus' Legislation on Marriage and Children', *CSCA* 8 (1975), 41–52

Fraschetti, A., (ed.) *Roman Women* (Chicago 2001)

Frederick, D. C., Beyond the Atrium to Ariadne: Erotic Painting and Visual Pleasure in the Roman House, *Cl. Ant* 14 (1995), 266–287
   Reading Broken Skin: Violence in Roman Elegy in Hallett, *Roman Sexualities* (1998), 172–193

French, V., *Midwives and Maternity Care in the Roman World* in Skinner, *Rescuing Creusa* (1987), 69–84

Friedlander, L., *Roman Life and Manners under the Early Empire Vols 1–4* (London) 1965

Furst, L. R., (ed.) *Women Physicians and Healers* (Lexington 1997)

Gage, J., 'Matronalia', *Latomus* 60, 1963

Gager, J., *Curse Tablets and Binding Spells from the Ancient World* (New York 1992)

Galinsky, K., Augustus' Legislation on Morals and Marriage, *Philologus* 125 (1981), 126–144

Gardner, J. F., *The Roman Household: A Sourcebook* (London 1991)
   Women in Roman Law and Society (Bloomington 1995)
   Family and Familia *in Roman Law and Life* (Oxford 1998)

Garland, R., *The Eye of the Beholder: Deformity and Disability in the Graeco-Roman World* (Bristol 2010)

Garlick, B., (ed.) *Stereotypes of Women in Power* (New York 1992)

Garnsey, P., *Food and Society in Classical Antiquity*, Cambridge 1999

George, M., (ed.) *The Roman Family in the Empire: Rome, Italy, and Beyond* (Oxford 2005)
   Family Imagery and Family Values in Roman Italy in George, *The Roman Family* 37–66

Gevaert, G., What's in a Monster? Pliny the Elder, Teratology and Bodily Disability, in Laes, (2013) 211–230.

Golden, M., 'Did the Ancients Care When their Children Died?' *G&R* 35, 1988, 152–163
   Sex and Difference in Ancient Greece and Rome (Edinburgh 2008)

Gowers, E., *The Loaded Table: Representations of Food in Roman Literature* (Oxford 1993)

Graf, F., *Magic in the Ancient World* (Harvard 1999)

Grant, M., *Roman Cookery* (London 2008)

Graumann, L. A., 'Monstrous Births and Retrospective Diagnosis: the Case of Hermaphrodites in Antiquity', in Laes, (2013) 181–209.

Green, M. H., *Making Women's Medicine Masculine: The Rise of Male Authority in Pre-Modern Gynaecology* (Oxford 2008)

Griffin, J., Augustan Poetry and the Life of Luxury. *JRS* 66 (1976), 87–105

Grimal, P., *Love in Ancient Rome* (Norman, OK 1986)

Grmek, M., *Les Maladies a l'Aube de la Civilisation Occidentale* (Paris 1983)
Diseases in the Ancient Greek World (Baltimore 1989)

Grubbs, J. E., *Women and the Law in the Roman Empire: A Sourcebook on Marriage, Divorce and Widowhood* (London 2002)
Parent-Child Conflict in the Roman Family in George, *The Roman Family* (2005) 93–128

Gruen, E. S., *Culture and National Identity in Republican Rome* (New York 1992)

Gwynn, A., *Roman Education from Cicero to Quintilian* (Oxford 1926)

Haj, F., *Disability in Antiquity* (New York, 1970)

Hallet, J. P., 'The Role of Women in Roman Elegy: Cross-Cultural Feminism', *Arethusa* 6 (1973), 103–124
Fathers and Daughters in Roman Society: Women and the Elite Family (Princeton 1984)
'Martial's Sulpicia and Propertius' Cynthia', *CW* 86 (1992), 99–123
Matriot Games? Cornelia and the the Forging of Family-oriented Political Values in McHardy, *Women's Influence* (2004) 26–39
Women in Augustan Rome in James, *Companion* (2012), 372–384

Hamilton, E., *The Roman Way*, New York (1932)

Hamilton, G., Society Women Before Christ, *North American Review* 151 (1896)

Hands, A. R., *Charities and Social Aid in Greece and Rome* (London 1968)

Hanson, A. E., 'The Eight Months' Child and the Etiquette of Birth: *obsit omen!*', *BHM* 61 (1987), 589–602

Harkness, A. G., Age at Marriage and at Death in the Roman Empire, *TAPhA* 27 (1896) 35–72

Harris, W. V., The Theoretical Possibility of Extensive Female Infanticide in the Graeco-Roman World, *CQ* 32 (1982), 114–116
Ancient Literacy (Cambridge Mass 1989)

Hawley R., (ed.) *Women in Antiquity: New Assessments* (London 1995)

Hemelrijk, E., Matrona Docta: *Educated Women in the Roman Elite from Cornelia to Julia Domna* (London 1999)
Public Roles for Women in the Cities of the Latin West in James, *Companion* (2012), 478–490

Hermann, C., '*Le Role Judicaire et Politique des Femmes sous la Republique Romain*', *Latomus* 67 (1964)

Hersch, K. K., *The Roman Wedding: Ritual and Meaning in Antiquity* (Cambridge 2010)

Hexter, R., (ed.) *Innovations in Antiquity* (London 1992)

Heyob, S. K., *The Cult of Isis Among Women of the Graeco-Roman World* (Leiden 1975)

Hill, T. B., Ambitiosa Mors: *Suicide and the Self in Roman Thought and Literature* (London 1997)

Hillard, T., 'Republican Politics, Women and the Other Evidence', *Helios* 16 (1989), 65–182
'Family Violence: Punishment and Abuse in the Late Roman Household'

Hoffsten R., *Roman Women of Rank in the Early Empire As Portrayed by Dio, Paterculus, Suetonius and Tacitus* (Philadelphia 1939)

Holland, L. L., *Women and Roman Religion* in Companion to Women (2012), 204–214

Hope, V., (ed.) *Death and Disease in the Ancient City* (London 2000)

Hopkins, K., The Age of Roman Girls at Marriage, *Population Studies* 18 (1965), 309–327
Contraception in the Roman Empire, *Comparative Studies in Society & History* 8 (1965), 124–151
Elite Mobility in the Roman Empire in Finley, *Ancient Society* (1974), 103–120
Conquerors and Slaves (Cambridge 1978)

Horsfall, N., 'Allia Potestas and Murdia: Two Roman Women', *Ancient Society* 12 (1982), 27–33

Horstmanshoff, M., Disability and Rehabilitation in the Graeco-Roman World, in Breitwieser (2012) 1–9.

Hus, A., *Doctus* et les Adjectifs de Sens Voisin en Latin Classique, *RPh* 46 (1972), 238–245

Jackson, R., *Doctors and Diseases in the Roman Empire* (London 1988)

James, S. L., *Learned Girls and Male Persuasion: Gender and Reading in Roman Love Elegy* (Berkeley 2003)

Companion to Women in the Ancient World (Chichester 2012)

Janowitz, N., *Magic in the Roman World* (London 2001)

Johns, C., *Sex or Symbol: Erotic Images of Greece and Rome* (London 1981)

Johnson, M., *Sexuality in Greek and Roman Society and Literature: A Sourcebook* (London 2005)

Johnson, W. A., (ed.) *Ancient Literacies: The Culture of Reading in Greece and Rome* (New York 2007)

Johnson W. H., 'The Sister-in-law of Cicero', *CJ* 1913, 160–165

Jones, C. P., Stigma: Tattoing and Branding in Graeco-Roman Antiquity, *JRS* 7 (1987), 139–155

Joshel, S. R., *Work, Identity and Legal Status at Rome: A Study of the Occupational Inscriptions* (Norman OK 1992)

The Body Female and the Body Politic: Livy's Lucretia and Verginia in Richlin, *Pornography* (1992), 112–130

Women and Slaves in Graeco-Roman Culture (London 1998)

Kagan, D., *Problems in Ancient History Vol 2: The Roman World 2/e* (New York 1975)

Kajanto, I., 'On Divorce among the Common People of Rome', *REL* 47 1969, 97–113

Kapparis, K. A., *Abortion in Antiquity* (London 2002)

Keith, A., '*Corpus Eroticum*: Elegiac Poets and Elegiac *Puellae* in Ovid's *Amores*', *CW* 88 (1994), 27–40

Kenyon, F. G., *Books and Readers in Ancient Greece and Rome* (Oxford 1932)

Kiefer, O., *Sexual Life in Ancient Rome* (London 1934)

King, H., *Once upon a Text: Hysteria from Hippocrates* in Gilman, S. *Hysteria*

Self-help, Self-knowledge: in Search of the Patient in Hippocratic Gynaecology in Hawley, *Women in Antiquity* (1995), 135–148

Hippocrates' Woman: Reading the Female Body in Ancient Greece (London 1998)

Greek and Roman Medicine (London 2003)

The Disease of Virgins: Green Sickness, Chlorosis and the Problems of Puberty (New York 2004)

Healthy, Wealthy and—Dead ? *Ad Familiares* 33 (2007), 3–4

Knapp, R. K., *Invisible Romans: Prostitutes, Outlaws, Slaves, Gladiators, Ordinary Men and Women* (London 2013)

Knight, M., 'Curing Cut or Ritual Mutilation?: Some Remarks on the Practice of Female and Male Circumcision in Graeco-Roman Egypt', *Isis*, 92 2001, 317–338.

Kraemer, R. S., *Women's Religions in the Greco-Roman World: A Sourcebook* (New York, 2004)

Kudlien, F., *Medical Education in Classical Antiquity* in O'Malley, *The History of Medical Education* (1970), 3–37

Laes, C., *Children in the Roman Empire: Outsiders Within* (Cambridge 2009)

(ed.) Disabilities in Roman Antiquity: Disparate Bodies A Capite ad Calcem Silent Witnesses. Deaf-mutes in Greco-Roman Antiquity, Classical World 104, (2011) 451–473.

Drunkeness, Alcoholism, and Ancient History', in Laes, Goodey, Rose (2013) 73–75.

'Silent History? Speech Impairment in Roman Antiquity, in Goodey, Laes, Rose' (2013) 145–180.

'Approaching Disabilities *a Capite ad Calcem*: Hidden Themes in Roman Antiquity, in Laes, Goodey, Rose' (2013) 1–15

La Follette, L., *The Costume of the Roman Bride* in Sebesta 54–64

Laidlaw, W. A., '*Otium*', *G&R* 15 (1968), 42–52

Langlands, R., *Sexual Morality in Ancient Rome* (Cambridge 2006)

Larson, J., *Greek and Roman Sexualities: A Sourcebook* (London 2012)

Larsson, L. L., (ed.) *Aspects of Women in Antiquity* (1997)

'*Lanam fecit*': Woolmaking and Female Virtue in Larsson, *Aspects of Women in Antiquity* (1997), 85–95

Laurence, R., *Roman Passions* (London 2009)

Lazenby, F. D., 'Greek and Roman Household Pets', *Classical Journal* 44 (5): (1949) 299–307.

Lefkowitz, M. R., *Heroines and Hysterics* (London 1981)

   Women's Life in Greece & Rome 3rd Ed. (London 2005)

Lewis, N., (Ed) *Roman Civilization Vol I Selected Readings The Republic 3rd Ed* (New York 1990)

   Roman Civilization Vol II Selected Readings The Empire 3rd Ed (New York 1990)

Lilja, S., *The Roman Elegists' Attitude to Women* (Helsinki, 1965)

Liveley, G., 'Who's that Girl? The Case of Ovid's Corinna', *Omnibus* 54 (2007), 1–3

Lloyd, G. E. R., (ed.) *Hippocratic Writings* (Harmondsworth 1978)

   Magic, Reason and Experience (Cambridge 1979)

Longrigg, J., *Greek Rational Medicine* (London 1993)

   Greek Medicine: From the Heroic to the Hellenistic Age A Source Book (London 1998)

Loven, L. L., (ed.) *The Family in the Imperial and Late Antique Roman World* (New York 2011)

Lowe, J. E., *Magic in Greek and Latin Literature* (Oxford 1929)

Luck, G., Arcana Mundi: *Magic and the Occult in the Greek and Roman Worlds* (Baltimore 1985)

   Latin Love Elegy 2/e (London 1969)

Lyne, R. O. A. M., *The Latin Love Poets from Catullus to Ovid* (Oxford 1980)

Macmullen, R., Women in Public in the Roman Empire, *Historia* 29 (1980), 208–218

   Women's Power in the Principate, *Klio* 68 (1986), 434–443

Mantle, I., *Violentissimae et Singulares Mortes*, CA News 39 (2008), 1–2

   'Women of the Bardo', *Omnibus* 65, January 2013, 4–6

Marshall, A. J., 'Roman Women and the Provinces', *Anc Soc* 6 (1975), 109–129

   'Tacitus and the Governor's Lady, A Note on *Annals* 3, 33–34', *G&R* 22 (1975), 11–18

   'Library Resources and Creative Writing at Rome', *Phoenix* 30 (1976), 252–264

Martin, M., *Magie et Magiciens dans le Monde Gréco-romain* (Paris 2005)

   Sois maudit!: Malédictions et Envoûtements dans l'Antiquité (Paris 2010)

   La Magie dans l'Antiquité (Paris 2012)

Massey, M., *Women in Ancient Greece and Rome* (Cambridge 1988)

Matz, D., *Voices of Ancient Greece and Rome: Contemporary Accounts of DailyLife* (New York 2012)

McAuslan, I., (ed.) *Women in Antiquity* (Oxford 1996)

McGinn, T. A., *Prostitution, Sexuality and the Law in Ancient Rome* (New York 1998)

   The Economy of Prostitution in the Roman World (Ann Arbor 2004)

McHardy, F., (ed.) *Women's Influence on Classical Civilisation* (London 2004)

Melchior, A., 'Caesar in Vietnam: Did Roman Soldiers Suffer from Post-Trauma Disorder', *G&R* 58 (2011) 209–223.

Miles, G. B., *The First Roman Marriage and the The Theft of the Sabine Women* in Hexter (1992), 161–196

Minozzi, S., 'Ill-Treatment of Women in Ancient Rome: Contribution of Paleopathology to the Reconstruction of Violence', *Journal of Biological Research* 85, 2012, 250–1

Mohler, S. L., 'Feminism in the *CIL*'. *CW* 25 (1932) 113–116

   'Slave Education in the Roman Empire', *TAPA* 71 (1940), 262–280

Montesquieu, C., *Considerations on the Causes of the Greatness of the Romans and Their Decline*, (ed.) David Lownthal (Hackett Publishing, 1999)

Moore, T. J., 'Morality, History and Livy's Wronged Women', *Eranos* 91 (1993), 38–46

   The Theater of Plautus: Playing to the Audience (Austin 1998)

Moreau, P., '*Incestus et prohibitae nuptiae*': *L'inceste à Rome* (Paris 2002)

Morel, W., Fragmenta Poetarum Latinorum (Leipzig 1927)

Morgan, T., *Literate Education in the Hellenistic and Roman Worlds* (Cambridge 1998)

Motto, A. L., Seneca on Women's Liberation, *CW* 65 (1972), 155–157

Mustakallio, K., *Hoping for Continuity: Childhood Education and Death in Antiquity* (Helsinki 2005)

Nadeau, Y., (1984). Catullus' Sparrow, Martial, Juvenal and Ovid. *Latomus*. 43: 861–868.

Neils, J., *Women in the Ancient World* (London 2011)

Nikolaidis, A. G. Plutarch on Women and Marriage, *WS* 110 (1997), 27–88

Noy, D., Wicked Stepmothers in Roman Society and Imagination, *Jnl of Family History* 16 (1991), 345–361

Nutton, V., 'The Drug Trade in Antiquity', *Jnl of the Royal Society of Medicine* 78 (1985), 138–145
   Murders and Miracles: Lay Attitudes to Medicine in Antiquity (1985) in Porter: *Patients and Practitioners* 25–53
   Ancient Medicine 2/e (London 2013)

Ogden, D., *Magic, Witchcraft and Ghosts in the Greek and Roman Worlds* (Oxford 2002)
   Greek and Roman Necromancy (Princeton 2004)
   Night's Black Agents: Witches, Wizards and the Dead in the Ancient World (London 2008)

Ogilvie, R. M., *The Romans and their Gods in the Age of Augustus* (London 1974)
   Roman Literature and Society (Harmondsworth 1980)

Oliensis, E., Canidia, Canicula and the Decorum of Horace's *Epodes*, *Arethusa* 24

Olsen, K., *Dress and the Roman Woman: Self-Presentation and Society* (London 2008)

O'Malley, C. D., (ed.) *The History of Medical Education* (Berkeley 1970)

Pantel, P. S., *A History of Women from Ancient Goddesses to Christian Saints* (Cambridge MA 1992)

Paoli, U. E., *Rome: Its People, Life and Customs* (Bristol 1990)

Parker, H. N., 'Why Were the Vestal Virgins?' *AJP* 125 (2004), 563–601
   Women and Medicine in James, *Companion* (2012), 107–124

Parkin, T. G., *Old Age in the Roman World* (Baltimore 2003)

Peachin, M., *Handbook of Social Relations in the Roman World* (Oxford 2011)

Pellison, N., *Women and Marriage During Roman Times* (New York 2008)

Petrocelli, C., *Cornelia the Matron* in Fraschetti, *Roman Women* (1993), 34–65

Phang, S. E., *The Marriage of Roman Soldiers (13 B.C.–A.D. 235): Law and Family in the Imperial Army* (Leiden 2001)

Phillips, E. D., Doctor and Patient in Classical Greece, *G&R* (1953), 70–81

Phillips, J. E., Roman Mothers and the Lives of their Adult Daughters, *Helios* 6 (1978), 69–80

Pitcher, R. A., *Martial and Roman Sexuality* in Hillard, *Ancient History* (1998) 309–315

Plant, I. M., *Women Writers of Ancient Greece and Rome* (Norman 2004)

Pollard, E. A., 'Witch-Crafting in Roman Literature and Art: New Thoughts on an Old Image', *Magic, Ritual, and Witchcraft* 3 (2008)

Pomeroy, S. B., 'Selected Bibliography on Women in Antiquity', *Arethusa* 6 (1973) 125–157
   'The Relationship of the Married Woman to Her Blood Relatives in Rome', *Ant. Soc.* 7 (1976), 215–227
   Women in Roman Egypt: A Preliminary Study Based on Papyri in Foley, pp. 301–322
   (ed.) *Women's History and Ancient History* (Chapel Hill, 1991)
   Goddesses, Whores, Wives and Slaves (New York 1995)
   The Murder of Regilla: A Case of Domestic Violence in Antiquity (Harvard 2007)

Purcell, N., 'Livia and the Motherhood at Rome', *PCPhS* 212 (1986), 78–105

Putnam, E. J., 'The Roman Lady', *Atlantic Monthly* 105 (1910)

Raia, A., *Women's Roles in Plautine Comedy* (paper delivered October 1983)
   www.vroma.org/~araia/plautinewomen
   (ed.) *Marriage, Divorce and Children in Ancient Rome* (Oxford 1986)
   Villains, Wives and Slaves in the Comedies of Plautus in Joshel, *Women* (1998), 92–108

Rapsaet-Charlier, M., 'Th. Ordre Senatorial et Divorce sous le Haut Empire', *ACD* (1981) 17–18, 161–173

Rawson, B., 'Family Life Among the Lower Classes at Rome in the First Two Centuries of the Empire', *CP* 61 (1966), 71–83
   'Roman Concubinage and Other de facto Marriages', *TAPhA* 104 (1974), 279–305
   Intellectual Life in the Late Roman Republic (London 1985)
   Marriage, Divorce and Children in Ancient Rome (Oxford 1991)
   Children and Childhood in Roman Italy (Oxford 2005)
   (ed.) *A Companion to Families in the Greek and Roman Worlds* (Chichester 2010)

Reinhold, M., *The Generation Gap in Antiquity* in Bertman, pp. 15–54

Reiss, W., Rari Exempla Femina: *Female Virtues on Roman Funerary Inscriptions* in James, *Companion* (2012), 491–501

Richlin, A., *Sexuality in the Roman Empire* in D. S. Potter (ed.): *A Companion to the Roman Empire* (Oxford 2006)

   Approaches to the Sources on Adultery at Rome in Foley, *Reflections* (1981) 379–404

   'Invective Against Women in Roman Satire', *Arethusa* 17 (1984), 67–80

   Carrying Water in a Sieve: Class and the Body in Roman Women's Religion in King, *Women and Goddess Traditions* (1997), 330–374

   (ed.) *Pornography and Representation in Greece and Rome* (Oxford 1992)

   The Garden of Priapus: Sexuality and Aggression in Roman Humour 2nd Ed (Oxford 1992)

Rose, M., 'Ashkelon's Dead Babies', *Archaeology* 50 (1997)

   www.archaeology.org/9703/newsbriefs/ashkelon

Rouselle, A., *Body Politics in Ancient Rome* in Pantel (1992), 296–336

   Porneia: *On Desire and the Body In Antiquity* (Oxford 1993)

Rudd, N., Romantic Love in Classical Times? *Ramus* 10 (1981), 140–158

Russell, D. A., Arts and Sciences in Ancient Education, *G&R* 36 (1989), 210–224

Ryberg, I. S., Rites of the State Religion in Roman Art, *Memoirs of the American Academy in Rome* 22 (1955); p. 41

Salazar, C. F., *The Treatment of War Wounds in Graeco-Roman Antiquity* (Leyden 2000)

Sallares, R., *Malaria and Rome: A History of Malaria in Ancient Italy* (Oxford 2002)

Saller, R. P., *Familia, Domus* and the Roman Conception of the Family, *Phoenix* 3 (1984), 336–355

   Patria Potestas and the Stereotype of the Roman Family, *Continuity & Change* 1 (1986), 7–22

   Men's Age at Marriage and Its Consequences in the Roman Family, *CP* 82 (1987), 21–34

   Patriarchy, Property and Death in the Roman Family (Cambridge 1994)

   Symbols of Gender and Status Hierarchies in the Roman Household in Joshel, *Women* (1998), 85–91

Santoro L'Hoir, F. S., Tacitus and Women's Usurpation of Power, *CW* 88 (1994), 5–25

Savunem, L., *Women and Elections in Pompeii* in Hawley, *Women* (1995), 194–206

Scafuro, A., (ed.) *Studies on Roman Women Part 2, Helios* 16 (1989)

   Livy's Comic Narrative of the Bacchanalia in Scafuro (1989), 119–142

Scarborough, J., *Roman Medicine* (London 1969)

Schaps, D. M., 'The Women Least Mentioned: Etiquette and Women's Names', *CQ* 27 (1977), 323–330

Scheid, J., *The Religious Roles of Roman Women* in Pantel (1992), 377–408

Scheidel, W., The Most Silent Women of Greece and Rome: Rural Labour and Women's Life, *G&R* 42 and 43 (1995–1996), 202–17, 1–10

   Libitina's Bitter Gains: Seasonal Mortality and Endemic Disease, *Ancient Society* 25 (1994), 151–175

   The Cambridge Economic History of the Greco-Roman World (Cambridge 2007)

   Demography in Scheidel (ed.), *The Cambridge Economic History* (2007), 38–86

Schulz, C. E., *Women's Religious Activity in the Roman Republic* (Chapel Hill NC 2006)

Scobie, A., 'Slums, Sanitation and Mortality in the Roman World', *Klio* 68 (1986), 399–433

Scott, E., 'Unpicking a Myth: the Infanticide of Female and Disabled Children in Antiquity', in G. Davies et al. (ed.), *Proceedings of the Tenth Annual Theoretical Roman Archaeology Conference*, (London 2000, Oxford 2000), 143–151.

Scurlock, J. A., 'Baby-snatching Demons, Restless Souls and the Dangers of Childbirth', *Incognita* 2 (1991), 135–183

Seller, R., *The Family and Society* in Bodel (2001), 95–117

Sharrock, A R., 'Womanufacture', *JRS* 81 (1991), 36–49

Shaw, B. D., 'Age of Roman Girls at Marriage: Some Reconsiderations', *JRS* 77 (1987), 30–46

Shelton, J-A., 'Pliny the Younger and the Ideal Wife', *C&M* 61 (1990), 163–186

   As the Romans Did 2nd Ed (New York 1998)

Skinner, M. B., (ed.) 'Rescuing Creusa', *Helios* 13 (1987)

(ed.) *Sexuality in Graeco-Roman Culture* (Oxford 2005)

Slater, W. J., (ed.) *Dining in a Classical Context* (Ann Arbor 1991)
   Roman Theatre and Society (Ann Arbor 1996)

Smith, P., 'Identification of Infanticide in Archaeological Sites', *Jnl of Archaeological Science* 19 (1992), 667–675

Smith, W. S., (ed.) *Satiric Advice on Women and Marriage: From Plautus to Chaucer* (Ann Arbor 2005)

Snyder, J. M., 'Lucretius and the Status of Women', *CB* 53, (1976), 17–20
   The Woman and the Lyre: Women Writers in Classical Greece and Rome (Carbondale, Ill 1989)

Soren, D., 'What Killed the Babies of Lugnano?' *Archaeology* 48/5 (1995), 43–48
   Excavations of a Roman Villa and a Late Roman Infant Cemetery Near Lugnano (Rome 1999)

Staden, H. von, 'Women, Dirt and Exotica in the *Hippocratic Corpus*', *Helios* 19 (1992), 7–30

Stahl, J., 'Physically Deformed and Disabled People' in M. Peachin (ed.), *The Oxford Handbook of Social Relations in the Roman World*, (Oxford 2011), 715–733.

Stanton, D. C., (ed.) *Discourses of Sexuality: From Aristotle to Aids* (Ann Arbor 1992)

Staples, A., *From Good Goddess to Vestal Virgins: Sex and Category in Roman Religion* (London 1998)

Stehle, E., *Venus, Cybele and the Sabine Women: The Roman Construction of Female Sexuality in Scafuro* (1989), 43–64

Stevenson, J., *Women Latin Poets: Language, Gender, and Authority from Antiquity to the Eighteenth Century* (Oxford 2008)

Stromberg, A., *The Family in the Graeco-Roman World* (New York 2011)

Sullivan, J. P., Martial's Sexual Attitudes, *Philologus* 123 (1979), 288–302

Summerton, N., *Medicine and Healthcare in Roman Britain* (Princes Risborough 2007)

Syme, R., Princesses and Others in Tacitus, *G&R* 28 (1981), 40–52

Tacaks, S., *Vestal Virgins, Sibyls, and Matrons* (Austin 2008)

Temkin, O., *Soranus'* Gynecology (Baltimore 1956), 21–23

Thomas, Y., *The Division of the Sexes in Roman Law* in Pantel (1992), 83–138

Thonemann, P., The Women of Akmoneia, *JRS* 100 (2010) 163–178

Todman, D., 'Childbirth in Ancient Rome: From Traditional Folklore to Obstetrics' (2007), *Australian & New Zealand Journal of Obstetrics and Gynecology.*

Toner, J., *Popular Culture in Ancient Rome* (Cambridge 2009)

Too, Y. L., (ed.) *Education in Greek and Roman Antiquity* (Leiden 2002)

Townend, G., *The Augustan Poets and the Permissive Society* (Abingdon 1972)

Toynbee, J. M. C., *Animals in Roman Life and Art* (Barnsley 2013)

Tracy, V. A., The Poet-Lover in Augustan Elegy, *Latomus* 35 (1976), 571–581

Treggiari, S., Libertine Ladies, *CW* 64 (1971), 196–198
   'Domestic Staff at Rome During the Julio-Claudian Period', *Histoire Sociale* 6 (1973), 241–255
   Concubinae, Papers of the British School at Rome 49 (1981), 59–81
   Roman Marriage (Oxford 1991)
   Putting the Family Across: Cicero on Natural Affection in George, *The Roman Family* (2005) 9–36
   Roman Social History (London 2002)
   Terentia, Tullia and Publilia: The Women of Cicero's Family (New York 2007)

Trentin, L., Deformity in the Roman Imperial Court, *G&R* 58 (2011)
   Exploring Visual Impairment in Roman Antiquity, in Laes (2013) 89–114

Veyne, P., (ed.) *A History of Private Life Vol I* (Cambridge, Mass 1987)

Viden, G., *Women in Roman Literature: Attitudes of Authors under the Early Empire* (Goteborg 1993)

Villers, R., 'Le Statut de la Femme a Rome jusqu'a la Fin de la Republique'. *Recueils de la Societe Jean Bodin II* (1958), 177–189

Watson, P. A., Ancient Stepmothers, *Mnemosyne* 143 (1995)

Watts, W. J., 'Ovid, the Law and Roman Society on Abortion', *AC* 16 (1973), 89–101

Welsford, E., *The Fool: His Social and Literary History.* (New York 1961)

Wenham, L. P., *The Roman-British Cemetery at Trentholme Drive, York* (York 1968)

Wiedemann, T. E. J., *Slavery* (Oxford 1987)

Wildfang, R. I., *Divination and Portents in the Roman World* (Odense 2000)
  Rome's Vestal Virgins (London 2006)

Wilkinson, B. M., Family Life among the Lower Classes in Rome in the First Two Centuries of the Empire, *CP* 61 (1966), 71–83

Will, E. L., Women in Pompeii, *Archaeology* 32 (1979), 34–43

Williams, G., Some Aspects of Roman Marriage Ceremonies and Ideals, *JRS* 48 (1958), 16–29

Wiseman, T. P., *Cinna the Poet* (Leicester 1974)
  Summoning Jupiter: Magic in the Roman Republic in Wiseman *Unwritten Rome*
  Unwritten Rome (Exeter 2008)

Woodhull, M. L., *Matronly Patrons in the Early Roman Empire: the Case of Salvia Postuma* in McHardy, F., (ed.) *Women's Influence* (2004), 75–91

Woolf, G., *Becoming Roman: The Origins of Provincial Civilization in Gaul* (2000)

Worsfold, T. C., *The History of the Vestal Virgins of Rome* (London 1934)

Wyke, M., Written Women: Propertius' *scripta puella*, *JRS* 77, (1987), 47–61
  The Elegiac Woman at Rome, *PCPhS* 213 (ns 330) (1987), 153–178
  Mistress and Metaphor in Augustan Elegy, *Helios* 16 (1989), 25–47
  Augustan Cleopatras: Female Power and Poetic Authority in Powell, *Women in the Mirror: The Rhetoric of Adornment in the Roman World*
  The Roman Mistress (Oxford 2002)

Yardley, J. H., *The Symposium in Roman Elegy* in Slater, *Dining in a Classical Context* 149–155

Younger, J. G., *Sex in the Ancient World from A–Z* (London 2005)

Index